Exam 70-561: Microsoft .NET Framework 3.5—ADO.NET Application Development

OBJECTIVE	LOCATION IN BOOK
CONNECTING TO DATA SOURCES	
Managing connection strings.	Chapter 1, Lesson 1
Manage connection objects.	Chapter 1, Lesson 1
Work with data providers.	Chapter 1, Lesson 2
Connect to data source by using a generic data access interface.	Chapter 1, Lesson 2
Handle and diagnose database connection exceptions.	Chapter 1, Lessons 1 and 2
SELECTING AND QUERYING DATA	
Build command objects.	Chapter 2, Lesson 1
Query data from data sources.	Chapter 2, Lesson 1
Retrieve data source data by using the DataReader.	Chapter 2, Lesson 2
Manage data by using the DataAdapter or the TableAdapter.	Chapter 2, Lesson 2 Chapter 3, Lesson 1 Chapter 4, Lesson 1
Execute an asynchronous query.	Chapter 2, Lesson 2
Handle special data types.	Chapter 2, Lesson 2 Chapter 7, Lessons 1 and 2
Query data sources by using LINQ.	Chapter 6, Lessons 1 and 2 Chapter 8, Lesson 1
Manage exceptions when selecting data.	Chapter 2, Lessons 1 and 2
MODIFYING DATA	
Manage transactions.	Chapter 4, Lesson 2
Manage data integrity.	Chapter 4, Lesson 2
Update data.	Chapter 4, Lesson 1
Manage exceptions when modifying data.	Chapter 4, Lesson 2
Transform data by using LINQ.	Chapter 6, Lessons 1 and 2
SYNCHRONIZING DATA	
Monitor event notifications.	Chapter 5
Cache data.	Chapter 5, Lesson 1
Manage update conflicts between online data and offline data.	Chapter 5, Lesson 2
Partition data for synchronization.	Chapter 5, Lesson 2
Implement Synchronization Services.	Chapter 5, Lesson 2

OBJECTIVE	LOCATION IN BOOK
WORKING WITH DISCONNECTED DATA	
Manage occasionally connected data.	Chapter 3, Lessons 1 and 2
Programmatically create data objects.	Chapter 3, Lesson 1
Work with untyped DataSets and DataTables.	Chapter 3, Lesson 1
Expose a DataTableReader from a DataTable or from a DataSet.	Chapter 3, Lesson 1
Work with strongly typed DataSets and DataTables.	Chapter 3, Lesson 2
OBJECT RELATIONAL MAPPING BY USING THE ENTITY FRAMEWORK	
Define and implement an Entity Data Model.	Chapter 9, Lesson 1
Query data by using Object Services.	Chapter 9, Lesson 1
Map data by using the Entity SQL Language.	Chapter 9, Lesson 1
Access entity data by using the EntityClient Provider.	Chapter 9, Lesson 1

Exam objectives   The exam objectives listed here are current as of this book's publication date. Exam objectives are subject to change at any time without prior notice and at Microsoft's sole discretion. Please visit the Microsoft Learning Web site for the most current listing of exam objectives: *http://www.microsoft.com/learning/mcp/*.

Microsoft®

MCTS Self-Paced Training Kit (Exam 70-561): Microsoft® .NET Framework 3.5—ADO.NET Application Development

Training Kit

Shawn Wildermuth
Mark Blomsma
Jim Wrightman

PUBLISHED BY
Microsoft Press
A Division of Microsoft Corporation
One Microsoft Way
Redmond, Washington 98052-6399
Library of Congress Control Number: 2009920790

Printed and bound in the United States of America.

1 2 3 4 5 6 7 8 9   QWT   4 3 2 1 0 9

Distributed in Canada by H.B. Fenn and Company Ltd.

A CIP catalogue record for this book is available from the British Library.

Microsoft Press books are available through booksellers and distributors worldwide. For further infor¬mation about
international editions, contact your local Microsoft Corporation office or contact Microsoft Press International directly at
fax (425) 936-7329. Visit our Web site at www.microsoft.com/mspress. Send comments to tkinput@microsoft.com.

Acquisitions Editor: Ken Jones
Developmental Editor: Laura Sackerman
Project Editor: Maureen Zimmerman
Editorial Production: Christian Holdener, S4Carlisle Publishing Services
Technical Reviewer: Matt Stoecker; Technical Review services provided by Content Master, a member of CM Group, Ltd.
Cover: Tom Draper Design

Body Part No. X15-41556

To Tricia:
"See it wasn't that bad..."
—SHAWN WILDERMUTH

To Marcel de Vries:
Thanks!
—MARK BLOMSMA

To Eleanor:
"You are #1, everyone else is #2 or lower."
—JAMES WIGHTMAN

Contents at a Glance

Contents

What do you think of this book? We want to hear from you!

Microsoft is interested in hearing your feedback so we can continually improve our
books and learning resources for you. To participate in a brief online survey, please visit:

www.microsoft.com/learning/booksurvey/

Chapter 7 XML 323

Chapter 8   LINQ to SQL   361

Acknowledgments

The authors' names appear on the cover of this book, but the authors are only part of a much larger team. Thank you to all of those who patiently contributed to the editing and production of this title including Kristy Saunders who graciously contributed to the writing of the Practice Test Questions that can be found on the companion CD that accompanies this title.

In addition, each author would like to acknowledge the following:

Shawn Wildermuth

I would like to thank everyone involved with this book, including my co-authors, Mark and Jim. For their help making sure that right story is told about ADO.NET Data Services, I want to thank Pablo Castro and Mike Flasko. And finally, for answering every odd LINQ question (and not blocking me on Instant Messenger), I want to thank Jim Wooley.

Mark Blomsma

I'd like to thank my friends and family for supporting me during the writing of this book. Many late nights and weekends went into creating it, and sacrifices were made, plans cancelled last minute, and schedules rearranged. A special thank-you to my parents, who are always there for me, and also a special word of thanks to my fellow MVPs, Marcel de Vries and Maurice de Beijer, who never turn me away when I need help. Lastly, to my co-authors: thanks for the experience, sharing your insights, and the fun we had creating this book!

James Wightman

Without this sounding too much like an acceptance speech at the Oscars, I would like to thank my co-authors, Shawn and Mark, with whom it has been an honor to work, and everyone at Microsoft Press, including Ken Jones, Laura Sackerman, Maureen Zimmerman, and Ben Ryan. For support, I cannot forget to thank Gareth Beynon, and for forgiving my absence from Xbox Live for most of 2008, my closest friend (and boss) Neil Cant. For the most enjoyable and productive working environment I've ever had, I need to thank everyone at British Telecom, including Dave Baker, Glenn Mantle, Peter Scott, Martin Neath, Lee Ingram, Jude Mahoney, and the simply excellent Paul Prior. And finally, on behalf of every developer out there, I want to thank William H. Gates III for giving us the opportunity to write code for a living.

Introduction

This training kit is designed for developers who plan to take Microsoft Certified Technical Specialist (MCTS) exam 70-561, as well as for developers who need to know how to create data-driven applications using the ADO.NET and Microsoft .NET Framework 3.5. We assume that before you begin using this kit, you have a working knowledge of the .NET Framework, databases, and Microsoft Visual Basic or C#.

By using this training kit, you learn how to do the following:

- Connect to a variety of data sources
- Query data
- UseLanguage Integrated Query (LINQ)
- Change data and use transactions
- Work with the Entity Framework and LINQ to SQL for object-relational mapping
- Synchronize data across disparate devices and tiers
- Work with ADO.NET Data Services for Internet applications

Hardware Requirements

The following hardware is required to complete the practice exercises:

- A computer with a 600 MHz or faster processor
- A minimum of 192 MB of RAM
- 2 GB of available hard disk space
- A CD-ROM drive
- A display with a minimum of 256 colors and 1,024 x 768 resolution
- A keyboard and a Microsoft mouse or compatible pointing device

Software Requirements

The following software is required to complete the practice exercises:

- One of the following operating systems:
  - Microsoft Windows 2000 SP4
  - Windows XP SP 2
  - Windows XP Professional x64 edition (WOW)

- Windows Server 2003 SP 1
- Windows Server 2003, x64 edition (WOW)
- Windows Server 2003 R2
- Windows Server 2003 R2, x64 edition (WOW)
- Windows Vista

■ Microsoft Visual Studio 2008 SP1

NOTE **EVALUATION EDITION OF VISUAL STUDIO**

A 90-day evaluation edition of Visual Studio 2008 Professional edition is included on a DVD with this training kit.

■ Microsoft SQL Server Express (normally installed with Visual Studio 2008).

Using the CD

A companion CD is included with this training kit. The companion CD contains the following:

■ **Practice Tests** You can reinforce your understanding of how to create ADO.NET 3.5 applications by using electronic practice tests that you customize to meet your needs from the pool of "Lesson Review" questions in this book. Alternatively, you can practice for the 70-561 certification exam by using tests created from a pool of 200 realistic exam questions, which is enough to give you many different practice exams to ensure that you're prepared.

■ **Code** Most chapters in this book include sample files associated with the lab exercises at the end of every lesson. For some exercises, you are instructed to open a project prior to starting the exercise. For other exercises, you create a project on your own and need to reference a completed project on the CD if you experience a problem following the exercise.

■ **An eBook** An electronic version (eBook) of this book is included for times when you don't want to carry the printed book with you. The eBook is in Portable Document Format (PDF), and you can view it by using Adobe Acrobat or Adobe Reader.

Digital Content for Digital Book Readers: If you bought a digital-only edition of this book, you can enjoy select content from the print edition's companion CD.
Visit **http://go.microsoft.com/fwlink/?LinkId=142363** to get your downloadable content. This content is always up-to-date and available to all readers.

How to Install the Practice Tests

To install the practice test software from the companion CD to your hard disk, perform the following steps:

1. Insert the companion CD into your CD drive and accept the license agreement. A CD menu appears.

> **NOTE** **IF THE CD MENU DOESN'T APPEAR**
>
> If the CD menu or the license agreement doesn't appear, AutoRun might be disabled on your computer. Refer to the Readme.txt file on the CD for alternate installation instructions.

2. Click the Practice Tests item and follow the instructions on the screen.

How to Use the Practice Tests

To start the practice test software, follow these steps:

1. Click Start, All Programs, Microsoft Press Training Kit Exam Prep. A window appears that shows all the Microsoft Press training kit exam prep suites installed on your computer.

2. Double-click the lesson review or practice test that you want to use.

> **NOTE** **LESSON REVIEWS VS. PRACTICE TESTS**
>
> Select the (70-561) Microsoft .NET Framework 3.5, ADO.NET Application Development to use the questions from the "Lesson Review" sections of this book. Select the (70-561) Microsoft .NET Framework 3.5, ADO.NET Application Development to use a pool of 200 practice test questions similar to those on the 70-561 certification exam.

Lesson Review Options

When you start a lesson review, the Custom Mode dialog box appears so that you can configure your test. You can click OK to accept the defaults, or you can customize the number of questions you want, how the practice test software works, which exam objectives you want the questions to relate to, and whether you want your lesson review to be timed. If you're retaking a test, you can select whether you want to see all the questions again or only those questions you missed or didn't answer.

After you click OK, your lesson review starts.

- To take the test, answer the questions and use the Next, Previous, and Go To buttons to move from question to question.

- After you answer an individual question, if you want to see which answers are correct—along with an explanation of each correct answer—click Explanation.
- If you'd rather wait until the end of the test to see how you did, answer all the questions and then click Score Test. You see a summary of the exam objectives you chose and the percentage of questions you got right, both overall and per objective. You can print a copy of your test, review your answers, or retake the test.

Practice Test Options

When you start a practice test, you choose whether to take the test in Certification Mode, Study Mode, or Custom Mode, as follows:

- **Certification Mode**   Closely resembles the experience of taking a certification exam. The test has a set number of questions, it's timed, and you can't pause and restart the timer.
- **Study Mode**   Creates an untimed test in which you can review the correct answers and the explanations after you answer each question.
- **Custom Mode**   Gives you full control over the test options so that you can customize them as you like.

In all modes, the user interface you see when taking the test is basically the same, but with different options enabled or disabled, depending on the mode. The main options are discussed in the section entitled "Lesson Review Options," earlier in this Introduction.

When you review your answer to an individual practice test question, a "References" section is provided that lists the location in the training kit where you can find the information that relates to that question and also provides links to other sources of information. After you click Test Results to score your entire practice test, you can click the Learning Plan tab to see a list of references for every objective.

How to Uninstall the Practice Tests

To uninstall the practice test software for a training kit, use the Add Or Remove Programs option in Control Panel in Windows (in Vista this is called Programs and Features).

Microsoft Certified Professional Program

The Microsoft certifications provide the best method of demonstrating your command of current Microsoft products and technologies. The exams and corresponding certifications are developed to validate your mastery of critical competencies as you design and develop, or implement and support, solutions with Microsoft products and technologies. Computer professionals who become Microsoft-certified are recognized as experts and are sought after industry-wide. Certification brings a variety of benefits to the individual and to employers and organizations.

> **MORE INFO** **ALL THE MICROSOFT CERTIFICATIONS**
>
> For a full list of Microsoft certifications, go to *http://www.microsoft.com/learning/mcp/ default.asp.*

Technical Support

Every effort has been made to ensure the accuracy of this book and the contents of the companion CD. If you have comments, questions, or ideas regarding this book or the companion CD, please send them to Microsoft Press by using either of the following methods:

E-mail:
tkinput@microsoft.com

Postal Mail:
Microsoft Press
Attn: MCTS Self-Paced Training Kit (Exam 70-561): Microsoft .NET Framework 3.5—ADO.NET Application Development Editor
One Microsoft Way
Redmond, WA 98052–6399

For additional support information regarding this book and the CD-ROM (including answers to commonly asked questions about installation and use), visit the Microsoft Press Technical Support Web site at *http://www.microsoft.com/learning/support/books/*. To connect directly to the Microsoft Knowledge Base and enter a query, visit *http://support.microsoft.com/search/*. For support information regarding Microsoft software, please connect to *http://support.microsoft.com*.

Evaluation Edition Software Support

The 90-day evaluation edition provided with this training kit is not the full retail product and is provided only for the purposes of training and evaluation. Microsoft and Microsoft Technical Support do not support this evaluation edition.

Information about any issues relating to the use of this evaluation edition with this training kit is posted to the Support section of the Microsoft Press Web site (*http://www.microsoft.com/ learning/support/books/*). For information about ordering the full version of any Microsoft software, please call Microsoft Sales at (800) 426-9400 or visit *http://www.microsoft.com*.

Creating Database Connections

Using ADO.NET to consume a data source must begin with creating a connection. One of the fundamental pillars of ADO.NET is the *Connection* object, which provides a highly configurable conduit through which a data source may be consumed and manipulated.

The ADO.NET *Connection* object exposes a number of simple properties and methods, encapsulating a complex and incredibly flexible connection framework. *Connection* objects are inherited from a common set of base classes allowing specific data providers to be used, which takes direct advantage of each data source type. Data provider properties are configured through the *Connection* object instance, allowing access to security credentials, encryption, and other properties.

This chapter provides an introduction to the available methods of connecting to a data source. Lesson 1, "Connecting to a Data Source," covers the basic connection, connecting to a native SQL Server source. Lesson 2, "Using Data Providers and More Complex Connection Scenarios," explores database connections in more detail and also examines connecting to other kinds of data sources. Lesson 3, "Working with Multiple Active Result Sets," looks at how to use Multiple Active Result Sets.

Exam objectives in this chapter:

- Manage connection strings.
- Manage connection objects.
- Work with data providers.
- Connect to a data source by using a generic data access interface.
- Handle and diagnose database connection exceptions.

Lessons in this chapter:

Before You Begin

To complete the lessons in this chapter, you must have:

- A computer that meets or exceeds the minimum hardware requirements listed in the "Introduction" section at the beginning of the book

- Microsoft Visual Studio 2008 Professional edition installed on your computer, along with the Microsoft .NET Framework version 3.5

- An understanding of Microsoft Visual Basic or C# syntax and familiarity with the .NET Framework version 3.5 SP1

- A relational database, such as a recent version of Microsoft SQL Server

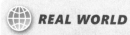

REAL WORLD

James Wightman

To fully appreciate the power and performance of ADO.NET 3.5, one must recall its more humble beginnings—from Data Access Objects (DAOs), Remote Data Objects (RDOs), ActiveX Data Objects (ADOs), and the earlier versions of ADO.NET that shipped with previous editions of the .NET Framework. Since 1996, Microsoft has been building on their Data Access technology—previously known as Microsoft Data Access Components (MDAC)—rapidly evolving capability and performance with each release.

Setting up the database connection has always been the first step when developing a Microsoft Windows–based software solution. Generally speaking, the majority of the decisions about how to connect to a data source revolve around the target database technology and the type of security being used. From project to project, many of the configurable options stay the same—for example, the use of connection pooling, the type of data provider, timeout thresholds, and other connection properties.

The reality is that while you are typically using identical code in each project to connect to your desired data source—except for modifying the connection string slightly, that is—it is incredibly useful to appreciate the nuances and subtleties of the *Connection* object for those times where a project veers from the well-trodden path. Many developers I know have created a set of classes—helpers, if you will—that contain the code necessary to connect to a data source and can be reused in different projects. I personally take the time to review my database helper classes regularly so I can use the latest and most appropriate features of ADO.NET. Aside from these occasional updates, I can reuse my database helper classes each time I need to consume a data source, which means I can concentrate on implementing business rules instead of worrying about how I'm consuming the data.

Lesson 1: Connecting to a Data Source

Having a connection to a data source is fundamental to working with your data. Although conceptually simple, the way in which a database connection is made and maintained colors the subsequent data access experience. Any good database access technology retains this fundamental simplicity, and ADO.NET is no different. It provides a fully featured, highly configurable object model with which to connect to your data source. In this lesson, you learn how to use the object model and connect to a native SQL Server database using available security options and the most-used configuration options.

After this lesson, you will be able to:

- Describe the ADO.NET *Connection* object
- Identify the most frequently configured properties of a database connection
- Connect to a native SQL Server data source

Estimated lesson time: 60 minutes

Connection Object Overview

The *Connection* object is effectively the topmost layer through which all data access requests pass. Configuration is performed through exposed properties. The *Connection* object is used with other objects in the ADO.NET object model to perform operations on a target data source.

Figure 1-1 shows a simple overview of the four pillars of the ADO.NET object model. This chapter concentrates on the *Connection* object, whereas Chapter 2, "Selecting and Querying Data," looks at querying data using the DataReader and DataAdapter.

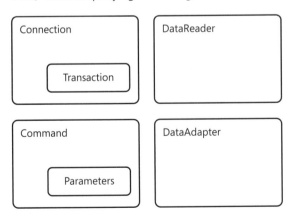

FIGURE 1-1 The ADO.NET object model

In its simplest form, a database connection can be opened using only a few lines, as follows:

```vb
' VB
Imports System.Data.SqlClient

Module Module1

    Sub Main()

        ' configure and open the database connection here
        Dim theConnection As New SqlConnection()

        theConnection.ConnectionString = "Data Source=jim-pc;Initial
            Catalog=VideoGameStoreDB;Integrated Security=SSPI;"

        theConnection.Open()

        If (theConnection.State = System.Data.ConnectionState.Open) Then
            Console.WriteLine("Database Connection is Open")
        End If

    End Sub

End Module
```

```csharp
// C#
using System;
using System.Data.SqlClient;

namespace TK70561
{
    class Program
    {
        static void Main(string[] args)
        {
            // configure and open the database connection here
            SqlConnection theConnection = new SqlConnection();

            theConnection.ConnectionString = "Data Source=jim-pc;Initial
                Catalog=VideoGameStoreDB;Integrated Security=SSPI;";

            theConnection.Open();
```

```
            if (theConnection.State == System.Data.ConnectionState.Open)
                Console.WriteLine("Database Connection is Open");


        }
    }
}
```

As a precursor to discussing the concepts found in the previous code listing, it is useful to identify exactly what is happening. A new instance of a native (SQL Server only) *Connection* object is created first, and then it is primed with a connection string. Given that a SQL Server instance is running on a server called jim-pc, which hosts a database called *VideoGameStoreDB* and is using Integrated Security, a valid connection string can be supplied to a *Connection* object. In this example, the minimum properties possible have been supplied to get the *Connection* object talking to the database because again, this is only the simplest of examples.

Inside the connection string, the *Data Source* property holds the name of the server to which one wishes to connect, *Initial Catalog* is the name of the database, and the *Integrated Security* property refers to the type of security to use. Once the connection string is assigned to the *Connection* object using the object's *ConnectionString* property, the code can go ahead and call the *Open()* method. Finally, checks should be made to see if the connection is open by querying the *State* property of the *Connection* object and checking for a value of *ConnectionState.Open*.

The *Connection* object has a number of interesting properties and methods, as described in Tables 1-1 and 1-2.

TABLE 1-1 *Connection* Object Methods

METHOD NAME	DESCRIPTION
BeginTransaction	Begins a database transaction.
ChangeDatabase	Changes the current database for an open *SqlConnection*.
ChangePassword	Changes the SQL Server password for the user indicated in the connection string to the supplied new password.
ClearAllPools	Empties the connection pool.
ClearPool	Empties the connection pool associated with the specified connection.
Close	Closes the connection to the database. This is the preferred method of closing any open connection.
CreateCommand	Creates and returns a *SqlCommand* object associated with the *SqlConnection*.
CreateDbCommand	Creates and returns a *DbCommand* object associated with the current connection.

TABLE 1-1 *Connection* Object Methods

METHOD NAME	DESCRIPTION
EnlistDistributed Transaction	Enlists in the specified *System.EnterpriseServices.ITransaction* as a distributed transaction.
EnlistTransaction	Enlists in the specified *System.Transactions.Transaction* as a distributed transaction. This method is preferable to *EnlistDistributedTransaction* since it leverages features of the *System.Transactions* namespace.
GetSchema	Overloaded. Returns schema information for the data source of this *SqlConnection*.
GetService	Returns an object that represents a service provided by the component or by its container.
OnStateChange	Raises the *StateChange* event.
Open	Opens a database connection with the property settings specified by the *ConnectionString*.
ResetStatistics	If statistics gathering is enabled, all values are reset to zero.
RetrieveStatistics	Returns a name-value pair collection of statistics at the point in time the method is called.

TABLE 1-2 *Connection* Object Properties

PROPERTY NAME	DESCRIPTION
CanRaiseEvents	Gets a value indicating whether the component can raise an event.
ConnectionString	Gets or sets the string used to open a SQL Server database.
ConnectionTimeout	Gets the time to wait while trying to establish a connection before terminating the attempt and generating an error.
Container	Gets the *IContainer* that contains the component.
Database	Gets the name of the current database or the database to be used after a connection is opened.
DataSource	Gets the name of the instance of SQL Server to which to connect.
DbProviderFactory	Gets the *DbProviderFactory* for this *DbConnection*.
Events	Gets the list of event handlers that are attached to this component.
FireInfoMessageEvent OnUserErrors	Gets or sets the *FireInfoMessageEventOnUserErrors* property.

TABLE 1-2 *Connection* Object Properties

PROPERTY NAME	DESCRIPTION
PacketSize	Gets the size (in bytes) of network packets used to communicate with an instance of SQL Server.
ServerVersion	Gets a string that contains the version of the instance of SQL Server to which the client is connected.
Site	Gets or sets the *ISite* of the component.
State	Indicates the state of the *SqlConnection*.
StatisticsEnabled	When set to True, enables statistics gathering for the current connection.
WorkstationId	Gets a string that identifies the database client.

Obviously, some of these properties need to be configured more often than others, though one in particular—the connection string—requires configuration that is specific to the server, SQL Server instance, and hosted database in use.

Connection Strings

You can see from the example above that the connection string plays a major part in connecting to a data source. Depending on the data provider used—in this case, the native SQLClient provider—many different configurable properties are available, as shown in Table 1-3.

TABLE 1-3 Complete List of Properties Available for Configuration Through the SQLClient Provider

PROPERTY	DEFAULT	DESCRIPTION
Application Name	N/A	The name of the application.
Async	False	When set in the affirmative (True or Yes), this enables asynchronous operation support. Negative values are False or No.
AttachDBFilename or *Initial File Name*	N/A	This property is for the specification of a primary database file. The value should include the full path and should point to an attachable database file that has an .mdf file extension. The database file must not be read-only, or the attachment fails.
		The *database* keyword (or one of the aliases) can be used to specify the database name, though again an exception is thrown if you use the *database* keyword and a log file exists in the same directory as the data file. Simply delete the log file in this case; a new one is generated upon attachment.

PROPERTY	DEFAULT	DESCRIPTION
		The *DataDirectory* substitution string can be used to supply absolute or relative paths, though the database file must exist within a subdirectory of the directory pointed to by the substitution string.
		Remote server, Hypertext Transfer Protocol (HTTP), and Universal Naming Convention (UNC) path names are not supported.
Connect Timeout or *Connection Timeout*	15	The length of time in seconds to wait for a successful connection to the database server before giving up and throwing an exception.
Context Connection	False	If an in-process connection to SQL Server should be made, set this to True.
Current Language	N/A	The SQL Server Language record name.
Data Source or *Server* or *Address* or *Addr* or *Network Address*	N/A	The name or network address of the instance of SQL Server to which to connect. In addition, a port number can be specified after the server name as follows: `server=tcp:servername, portnumber` The value of (local) should be used to specify a local instance. To force a protocol, add one of the following prefixes: `np:(local), tcp:(local), lpc:(local)`
Encrypt	False	When set to True, SQL Server uses Secure Sockets Layer (SSL) encryption for all data sent between the client and server if the server has a certificate installed. Recognized values are True, False, Yes, and No.
Enlist	False	True indicates that the SQL Server connection pooler automatically enlists the connection in the creation thread's current transaction context.
Failover Partner	N/A	The name of the failover partner server where database mirroring is configured.
Initial Catalog or *Database*	N/A	The name of the database.

TABLE 1-3 Complete List of Properties Available for Configuration Through the SQLClient Provider

PROPERTY	DEFAULT	DESCRIPTION
Integrated Security or Trusted_Connection	False	When False, User ID, and Password must be specified in the connection string. When True, the current Windows account credentials are used for authentication.
		Recognized values are True, False, Yes, No, and SSPI. Specifying SSPI is equivalent to specifying True. The use of SSPI or True is highly recommended for reasons of leveraging a more robust security model.
MultipleActive ResultSets	False	If Multiple Active Result Sets (MARS) need to be used, this value should be set to True. An application must otherwise process or cancel any active result sets from a batch before any further result sets can be open on the connection.
Network Library or Net	dbmssocn	This property is used to specify a particular network library which will be used to connect to a SQL Server instance. Possible values include: <ul><li>dbnmpntw (Named Pipes)</li><li>dbmsrpcn (Multiprotocol)</li><li>dbmsadsn (Apple Talk)</li><li>dbmsgnet (VIA)</li><li>dbmslpcn (Shared Memory)</li><li>dbmsspxn (IPX/SPX)</li><li>dbmssocn (TCP/IP)</li></ul> The corresponding dynamic link library (DLL) must be installed on the system to which you connect. If no library is specified and the connection is to a local server, shared memory is used.
Packet Size	8192	Size in bytes of the network packets used to communicate with a SQL Server instance.
Password or Pwd	N/A	The password for the SQL Server–security account logging on. Naturally, sending a password of clear text to SQL Server isn't the best idea—consider using the Integrated Security or Trusted_Connection keywords instead.

TABLE 1-3 Complete List of Properties Available for Configuration Through the SQLClient Provider

PROPERTY	DEFAULT	DESCRIPTION
Persist Security Info	False	This property specifies whether sensitive security information, such as a password, gets returned as a part of the connection if it is or has been open. Use False or No to disable and True or Yes to enable. Leaving this setting disabled is recommended.
Replication	False	True if replication is supported on the connection.
Transaction Binding	Implicit Unbind	This property specifies how a *System.Transactions* transaction interacts with the SQL Server connection. Possible values are: ■ Transaction Binding=Implicit Unbind. ■ Transaction Binding=Explicit Unbind. ■ The Implicit Unbind setting causes the connection to detach from the transaction when it ends. Once detached, further requests on the connection are performed in autocommit mode. In addition, the *System.Transactions.Transaction .Current* property is not checked when executing requests while the transaction is active. After the transaction has ended, additional requests are performed in autocommit mode. A value of Explicit Unbind causes the connection to remain attached to the transaction until the connection is closed or an explicit *SqlConnection.TransactionEnlist(null)* is called. An *InvalidOperationException* is thrown if *Transaction.Current* is not the enlisted transaction or if the enlisted transaction is not active.
TrustServerCertificate	False	When this value is set to True, SSL is used to encrypt the channel when bypassing walking the certificate chain to validate trust. If *TrustServerCertificate* is set to True and *Encrypt* is set to False, the channel is not encrypted.
Type System Version	N/A	A string value that indicates the type system the application expects. Possible values are: ■ Type System Version=SQL Server 2000 ■ Type System Version=SQL Server 2005 ■ Type System Version=SQL Server 2008 ■ Type System Version=Latest

TABLE 1-3 Complete List of Properties Available for Configuration Through the SQLClient Provider

PROPERTY	DEFAULT	DESCRIPTION
		If the Type System is set to SQL Server 2000, the SQL Server 2000 type system is used. Conversions are performed when connecting to a SQL Server 2005 instance.
		When set to SQL Server 2005, the SQL Server 2005 type system is used. No conversions are made.
		When set to Latest, the latest version that this client-server pair can make use of is implemented. This automatically moves forward as the client and server components are upgraded.
User ID	N/A	This property relates to the SQL Server-security user account. As with the *Password* property, it is easy to see that passing this information over clear text isn't the most secure option. Consider using integrated security by using the *Integrated Security* or *Trusted_Connection* keywords instead.
User Instance	False	Setting this value means that a connection will be made to a running user-instance of SQL Server rather than the default.
Workstation ID	The local computer name	The name of the workstation connecting to SQL Server.

As can be seen from Table 1-3, *Connection String* properties exist as name-value pairs. These can easily be set as part of the connection string as follows:

```vb
' VB
Imports System.Data.SqlClient

Module Module1

    Sub Main()

        ' configure and open the database connection here
        Dim theConnection As New SqlConnection()

        theConnection.ConnectionString = "Data Source=jim-pc;Initial
            Catalog=VideoGame StoreDB;Integrated Security=SSPI;Workstation
            ID=Odin;Network
            Library=dbmssocn;Connect Timeout=5"

        theConnection.Open()
```

```
        If (theConnection.State = System.Data.ConnectionState.Open) Then
            Console.WriteLine("Database Connection is Open")
        End If

    End Sub

End Module

// C#
using System;
using System.Data.SqlClient;

namespace Sample1_2
{
    class Program
    {
        static void Main(string[] args)
        {
            // configure and open the database connection here
            SqlConnection theConnection = new SqlConnection();

            theConnection.ConnectionString = "Data Source=jim-pc;Initial
                Catalog=VideoGameStoreDB;Integrated Security=SSPI;Workstation
                ID=Odin;Network Library=dbmssocn;Connect Timeout=5";

            theConnection.Open();

            if (theConnection.State == System.Data.ConnectionState.Open)
                Console.WriteLine("Database Connection is Open");
        }
    }
}
```

The previous code listing illustrates how additional properties can easily be added to a connection string. Before moving on to looking at an easy way to access these properties, it is worth noting a subtly different method of specifying a connection string and opening a database connection:

```
' VB
Imports System.Data.SqlClient

Module Module1

    Sub Main()

        ' configure and open the database connection here
```

```vbnet
        Dim theConnectionString As String = "Data Source=jim-pc;Initial
            Catalog=VideoGameStoreDB;Integrated Security=SSPI;Workstation
            ID=Odin;Network Library=dbmssocn;Connect Timeout=5"

        Dim theConnection As New SqlConnection(theConnectionString)

        theConnection.Open()

        If (theConnection.State = System.Data.ConnectionState.Open) Then
            Console.WriteLine("Database Connection is Open")
        End If

    End Sub

End Module
```

```csharp
// C#
using System;
using System.Data.SqlClient;

namespace CS_Sample1_3
{
    class Program
    {
        static void Main(string[] args)
        {

            string theConnectionString = "Data Source=jim-pc;Initial
                Catalog=VideoGameStoreDB;Integrated Security=SSPI;Workstation
                ID=Odin;Network Library=dbmssocn;Connect Timeout=5";

            SqlConnection theConnection = new SqlConnection(theConnectionString);

            theConnection.Open();

            if (theConnection.State == System.Data.ConnectionState.Open)
                Console.WriteLine("Database Connection is Open");

        }
    }
}
```

> **NOTE   USING CONNECTION STRING CODE**
>
> The connection string is first assigned to a string before being passed as a parameter into the code, which creates a *Connection* object instance. This code has the same net result—the database connection is open—but it is a useful alternative and can make for more compact code.

ConnectionStringBuilder

The SqlClient data provider offers another alternative way of building a connection string: the *SqlConnectionStringBuilder* object. Because an ADO.NET data provider explicitly exposes configurable *Connection* properties through the *ConnectionStringBuilder*, you can also address them explicitly instead of using a connection string to do so.

Figure 1-2 shows the properties and methods contained in the *SqlConnectionStringBuilder* object. Table 1-4 describes these properties in detail, though you probably recognize that a large number of them match the same name-value pair properties shown in Table 1-1. Refer back to Table 1-1 for more detailed descriptions of the properties.

FIGURE 1-2 *SqlConnectionStringBuilder* class diagram

TABLE 1-4 *SqlConnectionStringBuilder* Properties

NAME	DESCRIPTION
ApplicationName	Gets or sets the name of the application associated with the connection string.
AsynchronousProcessing	Gets or sets a Boolean value that indicates whether asynchronous processing is allowed by the connection.
AttachDBFilename	Gets or sets a string that contains the name of the primary data file (.mdf files only). This includes the full path name of an attachable database.
BrowsableConnectionString	Gets or sets a value indicatomg whether the *ConnectionString* property is visible in Visual Studio designers.
ConnectionReset	Gets or sets a Boolean value that indicates whether the connection is reset when drawn from the connection pool. This property is now obsolete.
ConnectionString	Gets or sets the connection string associated with the *DbConnectionStringBuilder*.
ConnectTimeout	Gets or sets the connection timeout.
ContextConnection	Gets or sets a value that indicates whether a client/server or in-process connection to SQL Server should be made.
Count	Returns the number of name-value pairs specified within the *ConnectionString* property.
CurrentLanguage	Gets or sets the SQL Server language.
DataSource	Gets or sets the name or network address of the instance of SQL Server to which to connect.
Encrypt	Gets or sets a Boolean value that indicates whether SQL Server uses SSL encryption for all data sent between the client and server—if the server has a certificate installed.
Enlist	Gets or sets a Boolean value that indicates whether the SQL Server connection pooler automatically enlists the connection in the creation thread's current transaction context.
FailoverPartner	Gets or sets the name or address of the partner server to connect to if the primary server is down. This property can prove very useful indeed.
InitialCatalog	Gets or sets the name of the database associated with the connection.

TABLE 1-4 *SqlConnectionStringBuilder* Properties

NAME	DESCRIPTION
IntegratedSecurity	Gets or sets a Boolean value that indicates whether User ID and Password are specified in the connection string (when False) or whether the current Windows account credentials are used for authentication (when True). For a more secure connection, this property should be used liberally.
IsFixedSize	Returns a value specifying whether the *SqlConnectionStringBuilder* has a fixed size.
IsReadOnly	Gets a value that indicates whether the *DbConnectionStringBuilder* is read-only.
Item	Gets or sets the value associated with the specified key. In C#, this property is the indexer.
Keys	Gets an *ICollection* that contains the keys in the *SqlConnectionStringBuilder*.
LoadBalanceTimeout	Gets or sets the minimum time, in seconds, for the connection to live in the connection pool before being destroyed.
MaxPoolSize	Gets or sets the maximum number of connections allowed in the connection pool for this specific connection string.
MinPoolSize	Gets or sets the minimum number of connections allowed in the connection pool for this specific connection string.
MultipleActiveResultSets	Gets or sets a Boolean value that indicates whether MARS will be used with the connection.
NetworkLibrary	Gets or sets a string that contains the name of the network library used to establish a connection to the SQL Server.
PacketSize	Gets or sets the size in bytes of the network packets used to communicate with a SQL Server instance.
Password	Gets or sets the password for the SQL Server account. Again, this isn't recommended in the majority of cases since the security details can easily be harvested.
PersistSecurityInfo	Gets or sets a Boolean value that indicates if security-sensitive information such as user name and password is returned as part of the connection—if the connection is open or has ever been in an open state.
Pooling	Gets or sets a Boolean value that indicates whether the connection is pooled or explicitly opened every time that the connection is requested.

TABLE 1-4 *SqlConnectionStringBuilder* Properties

NAME	DESCRIPTION
Replication	Gets or sets a Boolean value that indicates whether this connection supports replication.
TransactionBinding	Gets or sets a string value that indicates how the connection maintains its association with an enlisted *System.Transactions* transaction.
TrustServerCertificate	Gets or sets a value that indicates whether the channel is encrypted while bypassing walking the certificate chain to validate trust.
TypeSystemVersion	Gets or sets a string value that indicates the type system the application expects.
UserID	Gets or sets the user ID to be used when connecting to SQL Server. This practice isn't recommended because the security details can be intercepted easily.
UserInstance	Gets or sets a value that indicates whether to redirect the connection from the default SQL Server instance to a named user instance.
Values	Returns an *ICollection* that contains the values in the *SqlConnectionStringBuilder*.
WorkstationID	Gets or sets the name of the workstation connecting to SQL Server.

Another advantage to using the *SqlConnectionStringBuilder* is that it throws an exception when an invalid connection string is entered. Usually, invalid connection strings that are assigned directly to the *Connection* object are found to be invalid only when an exception is raised on the *Open()* call.

Now that you have a valid connection string, where should it be stored? As a value stored inside the compiled code? No, because if it needed to be changed, this would require recompilation. What about in an external file? That's a possibility—but rather than using a bespoke user-generated file to store the value, the .NET Framework offers the use of an Extensible Markup Language (XML) config file as part of a project that has a section specifically reserved for connection strings. If you are developing a Windows application, this file is called an App.config file. For Web projects, connection strings can be stored in a Web.config file.

An App.config file can be added to your Visual Studio project using a number of different methods. With a solution open, you can choose to right-click a particular project and select Add, New Item... then choose the relevant config file type. You can also select File, New, New File from the menu bar, and choose the config file type from the window shown in Figure 1-3.

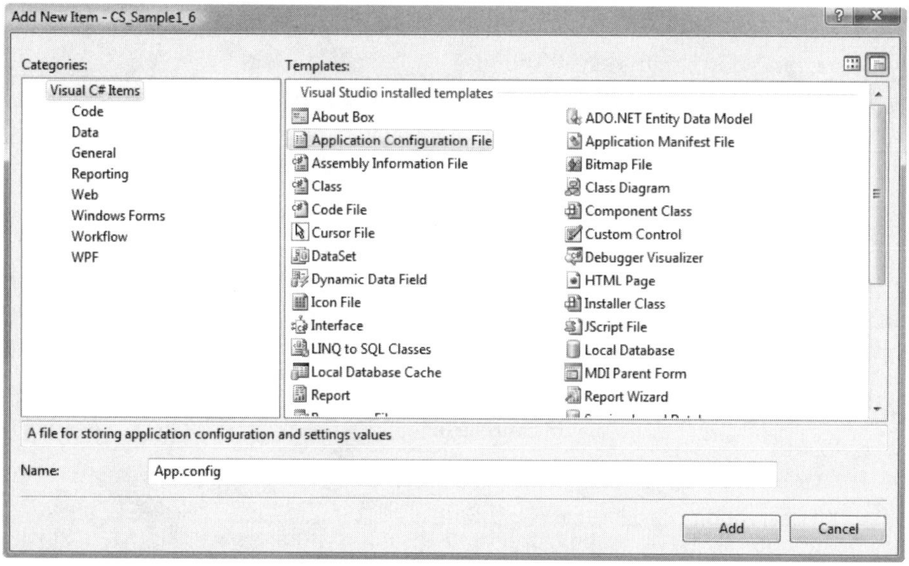

FIGURE 1-3 Adding an Application.config file to a Windows application

In code, the *System.Configuration* namespace is used to access the configurable items stored in the application configuration file. The following code shows an example of how a connection string stored in an App.config file can be retrieved and used to connect to a data source:

```vb
' VB
Dim theConnectionString As String

theConnectionString = _
    ConfigurationManager.ConnectionStrings("MainConnection").ToString()

Dim theConnection As New SqlConnection(theConnectionString)
theConnection.Open()

If (theConnection.State = System.Data.ConnectionState.Open) Then
        Console.WriteLine("Database Connection is Open")
End If
```

```csharp
// C#
string theConnectionString =
    ConfigurationManager.ConnectionStrings["MainConnection"].ToString();

SqlConnection theConnection = new SqlConnection(theConnectionString);
theConnection.Open();

    if (theConnection.State == System.Data.ConnectionState.Open)
            Console.WriteLine("Database Connection is Open");
```

Protecting the Connection String with Protected Configuration

Whether your connection string contains sensitive information, such as a user name and password, or you simply wish to prevent anyone gaining knowledge of a data source location, it can be useful to encrypt the connection information. The method used for encryption is relatively new and was introduced particularly for use with ASP.NET Web.config files, though it is equally useful for application configuration files.

If a configuration section is encrypted, at run time the section is decrypted automatically and transparently so the values contained within can be used. For the purposes of demonstration, refer to the following two samples—the first sample uses *RsaProtectedConfigurationProvider* to encrypt Web.config sections, and the other uses *DataProtectionConfigurationProvider*. Both methods are fully capable of encrypting sections of the configuration file but each have reasons for why you would use one over the other.

RSAPROTECTEDCONFIGURATIONPROVIDER

Encryption and decryption is performed using RSA public-key encryption. This type of encryption allows the export and import of keys, which is useful when the solution is deployed in a distributed fashion, such as in a Web farm.

The first code section encrypts the configuration section programmatically using *RsaProtectedConfigurationProvider*:

```vb
' VB
Imports System.Web.Configuration
Imports System.Configuration

Partial Class _Default
    Inherits System.Web.UI.Page

    Protected Sub Page_Load(ByVal sender As Object, ByVal e As System.EventArgs)
        Handles Me.Load

        Dim theConfiguration As Configuration = _
            WebConfigurationManager.OpenWebConfiguration("~")

        Dim connectionStringConfigSection As ConfigurationSection = _
            theConfiguration.GetSection("connectionStrings")

        If (Not (IsDBNull(connectionStringConfigSection)) _
            And Not (connectionStringConfigSection.IsReadOnly()) _
            And Not (connectionStringConfigSection.SectionInformation.IsProtected) _
            And Not (connectionStringConfigSection.SectionInformation.IsLocked)) Then

            connectionStringConfigSection.SectionInformation.ProtectSection _
                ("DataProtectionConfigurationProvider")
            connectionStringConfigSection.SectionInformation.ForceSave = True
            theConfiguration.Save(ConfigurationSaveMode.Full)
```

```
        Else

            connectionStringConfigSection.SectionInformation.UnprotectSection()
            connectionStringConfigSection.SectionInformation.ForceSave = True
            theConfiguration.Save(ConfigurationSaveMode.Full)
        End If

    End Sub
End Class


// C#
using System;
using System.Configuration;
using System.Web;
using System.Web.Configuration;
using System.Web.UI;
using System.Web.UI.WebControls;

public partial class _Default : System.Web.UI.Page
{
    protected void Page_Load(object sender, EventArgs e)
    {
        Configuration theConfiguration =
            WebConfigurationManager.OpenWebConfiguration("~");

        ConfigurationSection connectionStringConfigSection =
            theConfiguration.GetSection("connectionStrings");

        if (connectionStringConfigSection != null
            && !connectionStringConfigSection.IsReadOnly()
            && !connectionStringConfigSection.SectionInformation.IsProtected
            && !connectionStringConfigSection.SectionInformation.IsLocked)
        {
            connectionStringConfigSection.SectionInformation.ProtectSection
                ("RsaProtectedConfigurationProvider");
            connectionStringConfigSection.SectionInformation.ForceSave = true;
            theConfiguration.Save(ConfigurationSaveMode.Full);
        }
        else
        {
            connectionStringConfigSection.SectionInformation.UnprotectSection();
            connectionStringConfigSection.SectionInformation.ForceSave = true;
            theConfiguration.Save(ConfigurationSaveMode.Full);
        }
    }
}
```

Using the previous code listing, look at how the configuration values appear before and after encryption. The following snippet shows a Web.config file before the protection takes place:

```
<connectionStrings>
        <add name="MainConnection" connectionString="Data Source=jim-pc;Initial
            Catalog=VideoGameStoreDB;Integrated Security=SSPI;"/>
</connectionStrings>
```

This snippet shows how the same section looks once it is protected:

```
<connectionStrings configProtectionProvider="RsaProtectedConfigurationProvider">
  <EncryptedData Type="http://www.w3.org/2001/04/xmlenc#Element"
  xmlns="http://www.w3.org/2001/04/xmlenc#">
  <EncryptionMethod Algorithm="http://www.w3.org/2001/04/xmlenc#tripledes-cbc" />
  <KeyInfo xmlns="http://www.w3.org/2000/09/xmldsig#">
   <EncryptedKey xmlns="http://www.w3.org/2001/04/xmlenc#">
    <EncryptionMethod Algorithm="http://www.w3.org/2001/04/xmlenc#rsa-1_5" />
    <KeyInfo xmlns="http://www.w3.org/2000/09/xmldsig#">
     <KeyName>Rsa Key</KeyName>
    </KeyInfo>
    <CipherData>
     <CipherValue>fmPApWnxxXROYUX95ae3mlNSCagMUKkDXstuOxp1IqWvnh5YW/TbNE8FWXqaxQ8uAM7U
         2jicHG9HniBFyV29iKJnhqefl7HumOnEtzyb6wpHs7iwaUsso3yt+6kMS9weIxsqkX+
         1n7h8ox2aAdATMQzItMhJXtdHcZri2Uoj49Y=</CipherValue>
    </CipherData>
   </EncryptedKey>
  </KeyInfo>
  <CipherData>
   <CipherValue>gjbKsoFWiTjxb75LJtL5owvIidzjq5cw6yCP2Y41R7Fpnlwv0ul2VHHP4hjohNNAjgk
       mi/bfuCoswgWXVdpoHtM61LGStpvERsMdRger2ZvPOOJB5gIXcZ2nNgUShpLrVgVhi3FmXdylOerN2r
       nvfCsiC4LLypo90Seg571ZHTMm3VK9EJYoG8MA7gRhWMOWf75yq+Ea9K5a2l9sbftaORjzMGjzU7L
       FkX6r4/EbWEFS+bzd2y2KSZ8UzOKivOKA1QLRUjO1MpLZTTGlQAc6bePlVVd7Ce81iBm
       ITEMyqDwl283TxQTG7MeQ7vExZhhX81timWOnFgAyblAmnPJkf3pwVH3AHS3cfgwKiVLfEP9Q4
       Ays92izcvg4i3aPpq4x4Olv+b9YeyF/vUNur20jLyqfzYtc8aQih+C2UBr4F+
       pLflg19UUcjgCHbTRl7WCmOUYrEyzSyTRXNdOpDYGDegp6+UvJ9IBjxJhDmstXUIXOuPP7
       gUjyalLwFs93/yNCB15QN475UX6yriQQf9aYeFQSDSC5xOqytIHZ6j
       VIBEBISySWWIClTQ==</CipherValue>
  </CipherData>
  </EncryptedData>
</connectionStrings>
```

DATAPROTECTIONCONFIGURATIONPROVIDER

Encryption and decryption is performed using the Windows Data Protection API (DPAPI). Because DPAPI does not allow the exporting of keys, this provider should be used in situations where the deployed solution is limited to a single server.

The code when using the *DataProtectionConfigurationProvider* is similar to using the *RsaProtectedConfigurationProvider*:

```vb
' VB
Imports System.Web.Configuration
Imports System.Configuration

Partial Class _Default
    Inherits System.Web.UI.Page

    Protected Sub Page_Load(ByVal sender As Object, ByVal e As System.EventArgs)
        Handles Me.Load

        Dim theConfiguration As Configuration = _   .
            WebConfigurationManager.OpenWebConfiguration("~")

        Dim connectionStringConfigSection As ConfigurationSection = _
            theConfiguration.GetSection("connectionStrings")

        If (Not (IsDBNull(connectionStringConfigSection)) _
            And Not (connectionStringConfigSection.IsReadOnly()) _
            And Not (connectionStringConfigSection.SectionInformation.IsProtected) _
            And Not (connectionStringConfigSection.SectionInformation.IsLocked)) Then

            connectionStringConfigSection.SectionInformation.ProtectSection
                ("DataProtectionConfigurationProvider")
            connectionStringConfigSection.SectionInformation.ForceSave = True
            theConfiguration.Save(ConfigurationSaveMode.Full)

        Else

            connectionStringConfigSection.SectionInformation.UnprotectSection()
            connectionStringConfigSection.SectionInformation.ForceSave = True
            theConfiguration.Save(ConfigurationSaveMode.Full)
        End If

    End Sub

End Class
```

```csharp
// C#
using System;
using System.Configuration;
using System.Web;
using System.Web.Configuration;
using System.Web.UI;
using System.Web.UI.WebControls;

public partial class _Default : System.Web.UI.Page
{
    protected void Page_Load(object sender, EventArgs e)
    {
        Configuration theConfiguration =
            WebConfigurationManager.OpenWebConfiguration("~");

        ConfigurationSection connectionStringConfigSection =
            theConfiguration.GetSection("connectionStrings");

        if (connectionStringConfigSection != null
            && !connectionStringConfigSection.IsReadOnly()
            && !connectionStringConfigSection.SectionInformation.IsProtected
            && !connectionStringConfigSection.SectionInformation.IsLocked)
        {
            connectionStringConfigSection.SectionInformation.ProtectSection
                ("DataProtectionConfigurationProvider");
            connectionStringConfigSection.SectionInformation.ForceSave = true;
            theConfiguration.Save(ConfigurationSaveMode.Full);
        }
        else
        {
            connectionStringConfigSection.SectionInformation.UnprotectSection();
            connectionStringConfigSection.SectionInformation.ForceSave = true;
            theConfiguration.Save(ConfigurationSaveMode.Full);
        }
    }
}
```

For example, before encryption, a connection string stored in a config file might look like the following code:

```xml
<connectionStrings>
        <add name="MainConnection" connectionString="Data Source=jim-pc;Initial
            Catalog=VideoGameStoreDB;Integrated Security=SSPI;"/>
</connectionStrings>
```

Observe the multiple changes that are made to the same section once it is encrypted:

```
<connectionStrings configProtectionProvider="DataProtectionConfigurationProvider">
  <EncryptedData>
   <CipherData>
    <CipherValue>AQAAANCMnd8BFdERjHoAwE/Cl+sBAAAAKfQYgIcvuU29lPu8SZPkhAQAAAACAAAAAAADZgA
    AqAAAABAAAAAABx/rCqGB3mzVDj/EkLxp2AAAAAASAAACgAAAAEAAAAErJW6QrtV1zc6ePqQBnKBO4AwA
    AbAv2EJj7vMjvE6IyLvbuFy8pRahugiDPY6BelrN2iy0Z3rvyS4+GbSVswwDGdEN1B8iFSImXyDbD5LgKMo5
    Z3KMfCns9i08/zFqhd9cxXtc5XLlg9wVbO9UP+dxmpi0cgYCKcnDvUaj8JXTxjGdoKVVfdBLBrvkt4HoRA+A
    e5iEnjP1ZNuoh8UTTVP1rRVT8gR7nEzXpu9CMlglgRkyMDdQCrc8bejDiSEom1j5Za+YFjJDaL1gkJTWlk23
    1hQiea1zIe9AjDjaJZnbbnRQjYkkT9YygefXi3q+Q/JU6QUEpZ7UpFv+8sREpV5+5Pamxg+9YkUkZhcVtJb4
    31d8mzVu2g3TwOFK9jB7qBwfhA9NmALFoiC4IsXBMIdrbyvLjKZx1QXqXNj06oMBcuEL4OcUphCUoaUoH4
    NLmrILdqmhUKlrgzZCc1H7tFpp754goWJiEqY1V7KHgsnA2JyFPOoltHQ1H+0N3UVXqmMSGBSu4ySaOiizV2
    n5MartqzcOXuvd/MXYu72YAbX99Y4SMt7CoXJ5jRIQXIcJN9Eue8VJ0qn07eafi/07sPqCeAafKDdcFqm
    tcUxOy/kpjVwVH4bA68LebTVyHWO+KycYmvo8JZ/3yMS/eepW/WB4BsAyZssP7AOsHXujI+60bug2eYCmRJ/
    LLgN7xUS1a/cuXkpnqJXUNvGnEBuXDesaRKZW+k9qmI30Z9P5ziCyfuTMhmo0Sx1FN0BLd4jnC8cSdzfMN0e
    EI/F08fMOkG5gxVCZVcXjRo76vyf/WfxsSadiwV35GBGmyAU4DbHP/PSjG08J9IOVEvu2i/RWf7Heipjy
    Bw8INfJ1MQg4bp849/FMwg7C0dUWTYs9m38hghNcSjtKhFieOKk1kkALN9Z5MQeTJJKRdjuWhbDKOc+8QHsO
    AQQVNnguza4faEHnwd+NofeOJ1MhNX/B1FPOXHBNs6PsifoKc/IXau+agD/HsV6qVGTP8dq3AHAL8i85/
    XCquAGUp2OpcuGkZOTzSgfdnJ5THRgoNhHgV/m0BfpuLXM2D7iXmVqW5TkHkaa92Znqw/6vKgWHs/Kjp2O
    Dtdn5HDLFJPdW96PjTIyOUAAAA1sEedgyyvV4uafu9GfiOOg6b+Es=</CipherValue>
   </CipherData>
  </EncryptedData>
</connectionStrings>
```

It is possible (if not actually preferable) to encrypt sections of the configuration file in a non-programmatic fashion. Doing this means that the configuration section can be encrypted before use and then, as suggested earlier, it is decrypted transparently at run time only for use by the server. This can all be achieved at the command prompt using the Aspnet_regiis utility. Note that the sections parameter is case-sensitive.

The following listings demonstrate the use of the Aspnet_regiis utility to encrypt and decrypt configuration sections using the two standard providers. This code is used with *DataProtectionConfigurationProvider*:

```
aspnet_regiis -pe "connectionStrings" -app "/website" -prov
    "DataProtectionConfigurationProvider"
```

A similar command can be issued to specify the use of *RSAProtectedConfigurationProvider*:

```
aspnet_regiis -pe "connectionStrings" -app "/website" -prov
    "RSAProtectedConfigurationProvider"
```

Figure 1-4 shows that an alternative syntax can be used instead. Using the *–pef* and *–pdf* options instead specifies that the application path argument is a filesystem path rather than an HTTP location. Notice also how when decrypting a configuration section, a provider does not need to be specified as an argument.

FIGURE 1-4 Encrypting a configuration section

The command to decrypt a configuration section using the default *DataProtection-ConfigurationProvider* might look as follows:

```
aspnet_regiis -pd "connectionStrings" -app "/website"
```

The output from the command is shown in Figure 1-5.

FIGURE 1-5 Decrypting the configuration section

For completeness, the command to perform decryption using *RSAProtectedConfiguration-Provider* follows:

```
aspnet_regiis -pd "connectionStrings" -app "/website" -prov
    "RSAProtectedConfigurationProvider"
```

Again, the alternative syntax of *–pef* and *–pdf* can be used instead.

Encrypting configuration sections is not limited to the Web.config file. Most types of configuration files can be protected in a similar way, including the Machine.config file and the App.config file that is shipped with an application.

It should be noted that the encryption of configuration sections can cause problems. If the section is encrypted using *DataProtectionConfigurationProvider* and the config file is moved to a different machine, this new location cannot decrypt the value. With *RSAProtectedConfigurationProvider,* however, the key can be exported to a different machine along with the configuration file; this means decryption can take place using the same exported key.

Visual Studio—New Data Source

The final method of creating a new database connection is to use the Data, Add New Data Source… option from the menu in Visual Studio. Figure 1-6 shows the location of the menu item.

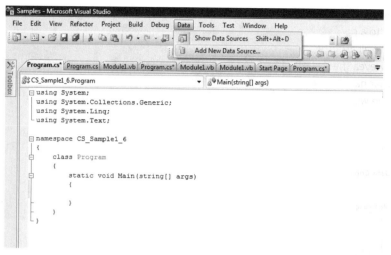

FIGURE 1-6 Adding a new data source using Visual Studio: the most GUI-friendly way of creating a data source connection

It makes good sense to use the Data Source Configuration Wizard at least until you are more comfortable building your own connection strings. The wizard does a great job of gently guiding the developer through connecting to a data source and provides a valid and usable connection string for use with the *Connection* object. Figure 1-7 shows the first screen you see.

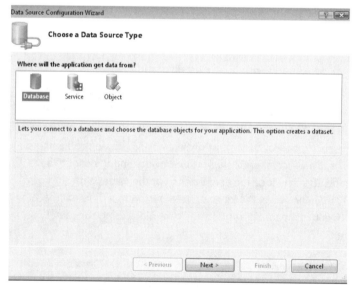

FIGURE 1-7 Introducing the Data Source Configuration Wizard: a simple and familiar wizard for creating a data source connection

Notice how you are given a choice of Database, Service, and Object at this point. Choosing the Service option allows you to locate and select a Web Service or Windows Communication Foundation (WCF) service from which you can consume data. The Object source type assists in the location of an assembly with which data-bound controls can be used.

The remaining choice is the Database source type, which guides you through the steps necessary to connect to a data source and to configure it as necessary. This is great because it is possible to configure all aspects of the connection by browsing properties and altering their values. Ultimately however, the settings presented are all configurable inside the connection string using the familiar name-value pairs, as discussed earlier in Table 1-4. Figure 1-8 shows the second page of the wizard, which contains a textual representation of the connection string as it is being built.

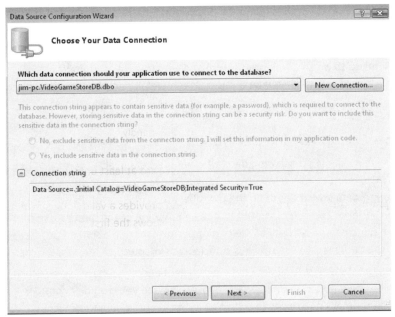

FIGURE 1-8 The second page of the wizard, which changes the connection string as you specify connection properties

Another advantage to using the wizard is that it is impossible to create a syntactically incorrect connection string; however, this doesn't mean that you can't create a connection string that doesn't connect to the data source because of security problems or other incompatibilities. It does help to troubleshoot these problems in a friendlier manner than previous methods.

✔ **Quick Check**
- What are the available methods for specifying the properties to connect to a data source?

Quick Check Answer
- Specifying the connection string on the *Connection* object's *ConnectionString* property, passing the connection string in the *Connection* object constructor, and using the Visual Studio Data Source Wizard.

Attaching a Database File

Whichever method you use to create the connection to your data source, you have an opportunity through the exposed SqlClient data provider properties to attach a database file rather than connect to a database already attached to a database server. This is useful in situations where, for example, a higher level of security is required and the database file is attached at the start of a database operation. Once the connection is closed, the database can be detached from the server.

However, there are some problems, including the requirement to be an administrator, and therefore have access to the attached database, or to have an administrator available who can create a valid user and for you to access the attached database.

The problem of needing to be an administrator is solved with the use of user instances, which are discussed in a section entitled "Database Instances—Default and User Instances," later in this lesson.

Data Protection—Encryption and Decryption

A number of options are available for securing data, whether it is held in SQL Server, an Oracle database, or a Comma-Separated Variable (CSV) file. The reality is that the most effective way of securing data is by minimizing the potential attack surface of the whole system. Real-world experience has demonstrated that the encryption of the data held in a database has a minimal increase in security at the cost of performance. In a suitably secure server environment, the data held on the server is sufficiently protected.

Consider, however, the transmission of data between a client and a database server. Much like the communications between a Web server and a Web browser, you wouldn't consider entering your credit card details onto a site that didn't fully protect the data transmission. Financial institutions and other companies requiring secure transactions employ SSL to provide encryption of any transmitted data. In these circumstances, a certificate is required to be installed on the Web server.

In a similar fashion, if the computer running SQL Server has a certificate installed, it is possible to set the proper property on the connection string that uses secure SSL communications between the client and the computer running SQL Server. After ensuring the SQL Server server is correctly configured with a valid certificate, the *Encrypt* property can be set to True on the connection string, as shown in the following code:

```
' VB
Imports System.Data.SqlClient


Module Module1

    Sub Main()

        ' configure and open the database connection here
```

```
        Dim theConnectionString As String = "Data Source=jim-pc;Initial
            Catalog=VideoGameStoreDB;Integrated Security=SSPI;Workstation
            ID=Odin;Network Library=dbmssocn;Connect Timeout=5;Encrypt=true"

        Dim theConnection As New SqlConnection(theConnectionString)

        theConnection.Open()

        If (theConnection.State = System.Data.ConnectionState.Open) Then
            Console.WriteLine("Database Connection is Open")
        End If

    End Sub

End Module

// C#
using System;
using System.Data.SqlClient;

namespace CS_Sample1_6
{
    class Program
    {
        static void Main(string[] args)
        {

            string theConnectionString = "Data Source=jim-pc;Initial
                Catalog=VideoGameStoreDB;Integrated Security=SSPI;Workstation
                ID=Odin;Network Library=dbmssocn;Connect Timeout=5;Encrypt=true;";

            SqlConnection theConnection = new SqlConnection(theConnectionString);

            theConnection.Open();

            if (theConnection.State == System.Data.ConnectionState.Open)
                Console.WriteLine("Database Connection is Open");

        }
    }
}
```

> **WARNING OPEN() METHOD EXCEPTION**
>
> If the server or SQL Server is incorrectly configured and cannot accept an encrypted
> connection, you will receive an exception when calling the *Open()* method of the
> *Connection* object. Figure 1-9 shows the error in detail.

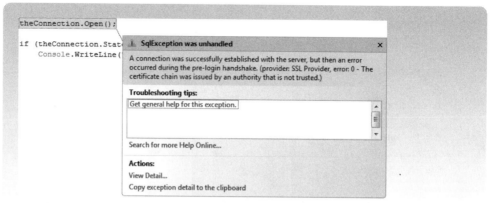

FIGURE 1-9 A *SqlException* thrown by an incorrectly installed certificate

Depending on the combination of connection string properties specified and their values, different results occur. Table 1-5 shows each of the possible variations and the resulting situation.

TABLE 1-5 Encryption Scenarios

FORCE PROTOCOL ENCRYPTION	TRUST SERVER CERTIFICATE	ENCRYPT/USE ENCRYPTION FOR DATA	TRUST SERVER CERTIFICATE	RESULT
CLIENT SETTING	CLIENT SETTING	CONNECTION STRING/ ATTRIBUTE	CONNECTION STRING/ ATTRIBUTE	
No	N/A	No (default)	Ignored	No encryption occurs.
No	N/A	Yes	No (default)	Encryption occurs only if there is a verifiable server certificate; otherwise, the connection attempt fails.
No	N/A	Yes	Yes	Encryption occurs only if there is a verifiable server certificate; otherwise, the connection attempt fails.
Yes	No	Ignored	Ignored	Encryption occurs only if there is a verifiable server certificate; otherwise, the connection attempt fails.
Yes	Yes	No (default)	Ignored	Encryption occurs only if there is a verifiable server certificate; otherwise, the connection attempt fails.

TABLE 1-5 Encryption Scenarios

FORCE PROTOCOL ENCRYPTION	TRUST SERVER CERTIFICATE	ENCRYPT/USE ENCRYPTION FOR DATA	TRUST SERVER CERTIFICATE	RESULT
CLIENT SETTING	CLIENT SETTING	CONNECTION STRING/ ATTRIBUTE	CONNECTION STRING/ ATTRIBUTE	
Yes	Yes	Yes	No (default)	Encryption occurs only if there is a verifiable server certificate; otherwise, the connection attempt fails.
Yes	Yes	Yes	Yes	Encryption occurs only if there is a verifiable server certificate; otherwise, the connection attempt fails.

Database Instances—Default and User Instances

Generally speaking, when a database connection is made, it is made to the default running instance of SQL Server. There are, however, situations where it is desirable to create and connect to a user instance of a database. Luckily, SQL Server offers this facility, access to which is made available through two more connection string properties. The concept of user instances in SQL Server is centered around engineering a tight integration with Visual Studio and its file-based approach of solutions development. In deployment terms, this means that a project can distribute all executable and support files in one package, attaching the database file in a user instance when necessary.

It is important to remember that user instances must first be enabled on the target server running SQL Server. They can be enabled during the initial installation of SQL Server or by modifying configuration settings later.

Security

Two types of authentication are available when connecting to data sources. With SQL Server particularly, depending on the configuration, it is possible to use either Windows Authentication or SQL Server Authentication. In the majority of cases, Windows Authentication is the method to use because it doesn't expose user credentials in an open format, though of course there are times where SQL Server authentication is required.

Windows Authentication uses Security Support Provider Interface (SSPI). SSPI is actually an application programming interface (API) exposed and used by Windows to provide authentication and other security-related functions. The use of SSPI in SQL Server is to provide authentication based upon Windows user credentials. This means that the Windows user must be configured in the server running SQL Server, but authentication from the user account to the server running SQL Server is relatively transparent.

The connection string yields a number of properties to choose from, which dictate the type of security we want to use. If Integrated Security is set (Integrated Security=SSPI), Windows Authentication is used; otherwise, *User ID* and *Password* should be set for SQL Server Authentication. The following code listings show the use of these properties in the connection string.

To use Windows Authentication, the connection string should contain the *Integrated Security* property, as follows:

```
' VB
Imports System.Data.SqlClient

Module Module1

    Sub Main()

        Dim theConnectionString As String = "Data Source=jim-pc;Initial
            Catalog=VideoGameStoreDB;Integrated Security=SSPI;"

        Dim theConnection As New SqlConnection(theConnectionString)

        theConnection.Open()

        If (theConnection.State = System.Data.ConnectionState.Open) Then
            Console.WriteLine("Database Connection is Open")
        End If

    End Sub

End Module
```

```
// C#
using System;
using System.Data.SqlClient;

namespace CS_Sample1_7
{
    class Program
    {
        static void Main(string[] args)
        {

            string theConnectionString = "Data Source=jim-pc;Initial
                Catalog=VideoGameStoreDB;Integrated Security=SSPI;";

            SqlConnection theConnection = new SqlConnection(theConnectionString);
```

```
            theConnection.Open();

            if (theConnection.State == System.Data.ConnectionState.Open)
                Console.WriteLine("Database Connection is Open");

        }
    }
}
```

To use SQL Server authentication, the *User ID* and *Password* properties should be specified, as follows:

' VB
```vb
Imports System.Data.SqlClient

Module Module1

    Sub Main()

        Dim theConnectionString As String = "Data Source=jim-pc;Initial
            Catalog=VideoGameStoreDB;User ID=jim;Password=mypassword;"

        Dim theConnection As New SqlConnection(theConnectionString)

        theConnection.Open()

        If (theConnection.State = System.Data.ConnectionState.Open) Then
            Console.WriteLine("Database Connection is Open")
        End If

    End Sub

End Module
```

// C#
```csharp
using System;
using System.Data.SqlClient;

namespace CS_Sample1_8
{
    class Program
    {
        static void Main(string[] args)
        {

            string theConnectionString = "Data Source=jim-pc;Initial
                Catalog=VideoGameStoreDB;User ID=jim;Password=mypassword;";
```

```
SqlConnection theConnection = new SqlConnection(theConnectionString);

theConnection.Open();

if (theConnection.State == System.Data.ConnectionState.Open)
    Console.WriteLine("Database Connection is Open");

        }
    }
}
```

Connection Lifetime

The lifetime of a connection is defined from the point the *Connection* object's *Open()* method is called to the point where the *Close()* method is called, assuming the *Connection* object instance remains in scope. It could be argued that if connection pooling is enabled, the connection lifetime in reality is extended for as long as the connection lives on in the pool.

Connection Pooling

In terms of processing and Inter-Process Communication (IPC), it is quite expensive to create a connection to a data source. You can see this if you step through any code that creates an initial data source connection—there is a significant delay while the network channel is opened, handshaking with the server occurs, a connection to the SQL Server is made, and user credentials are authenticated. This process is true even with the most simple connection—more complex connections that include transactions or the attaching of database files take even longer.

Inside an application, it would be unusual to find that a different type of connection or data source location is required for each database operation. Perhaps, then, it would make sense if, instead of the connection being destroyed after each operation, it could be reused to save the expense of opening a new connection? *Connection pooling* performs this connection optimization.

If the connection string values match between connection requests and an existing connection exists in the connection pool, ADO.NET reuses the existing connection instead of creating a new connection. Different connection pools are created based upon differing connection string values, transactions, and Integrated Security identity. It is good practice— and strongly recommended—that you close the *Connection* object after each operation so it can be returned to the connection pool.

The good news is that connection pooling is enabled by default and in most cases does not require any configuration to suit your requirements. There are, however, a number of connection string properties that provide configuration options. These are shown in Table 1-6.

TABLE 1-6 *Connection Pooling* Properties

NAME	DEFAULT	DESCRIPTION
Connection Lifetime	0	When a connection is returned to the pool, its creation time is compared with the current time, and the connection is destroyed if that time span (in seconds) exceeds the value specified by *Connection Lifetime*. This is useful in clustered configurations to force load balancing between a running server and a server just brought online. A value of zero (0) causes pooled connections to have the maximum connection timeout.
Connection Reset	True	Determines whether the database connection is reset when being drawn from the pool. For SQL Server version 7.0, setting to False avoids making an additional server round-trip when obtaining a connection, but you must realize that the connection state, such as database context, is not being reset. The connection pooler is not influenced by the *ChangeDatabase* method so long as you do not set *Connection Reset* to False. As the connection comes out of the pool, the connection is reset, with the server moving back to the login time database. No new connections or reauthentications are created. If you set *Connection Reset* to False, connections in the pool to different databases might result.
Enlist	True	When True, the pooler automatically enlists the connection in the creation thread's current transaction context. Recognized values are True, False, Yes, and No.
Load Balance Timeout	0	The minimum time, in seconds, for the connection to be in the connection pool before being destroyed.
Max Pool Size	100	The maximum number of connections allowed in the pool.
Min Pool Size	0	The minimum number of connections allowed in the pool. By default, any connections in the pool are closed after a period of inactivity. If the value is greater than zero, however, the connections are not closed until the *AppDomain* is unloaded.
Pooling	True	When True, the *SQLConnection* object is drawn from the appropriate pool, or if it is required, is created and added to the appropriate pool. Recognized values are True, False, Yes, and No.

Persistent Connections

A persistent connection is one which, once opened, remains available for use until it is closed explicitly after performing all required database operations. To do this, connection pooling must be disabled. This is configured by setting *Pooling=false* in the connection string, as in the following code:

```vb
' VB
Imports System.Data.SqlClient

Module Module1

    Sub Main()

        Dim theConnectionString As String = "Data Source=jim-pc;Initial
            Catalog=VideoGameStoreDB;Integrated Security=SSPI;Pooling=false;"

        Try

            Dim theConnection As New SqlConnection(theConnectionString)

            theConnection.Open()

            If (theConnection.State = System.Data.ConnectionState.Open) Then
                Console.WriteLine("Database Connection is Open")
            End If
        Catch sqlexception As SqlException
            Console.WriteLine(sqlexception.Message)
        Catch exception As Exception
            Console.WriteLine(exception.Message)
        End Try

    End Sub

End Module
```

```csharp
// C#
using System;
using System.Data.SqlClient;

namespace CS_Sample1_11
{
    class Program
    {
        static void Main(string[] args)
        {
            string theConnectionString = "Data Source=jim-pc;Initial
                Catalog=VideoGameStoreDB;Integrated Security=SSPI;Pooling=false;";
```

```
        try
        {
            SqlConnection theConnection = new SqlConnection(theConnectionString);

            theConnection.Open();

            if (theConnection.State == System.Data.ConnectionState.Open)
                Console.WriteLine("Database Connection is Open");
        }
        catch (SqlException sqlexception)
        {
            Console.WriteLine(sqlexception.Message);
        }
        catch (Exception exception)
        {
            Console.WriteLine(exception.Message);
        }
    }
  }
}
```

With connection pooling disabled, you must ensure that the *Connection* object does not go out of scope—and thus be garbage-collected—and also that the *Close()* method of the *Connection* object is not called until all operations are complete.

Connection Exceptions

It would be unreasonable and unrealistic to assume that the act of connecting to a data source will go perfectly every time. Therefore, it is a good idea to trap and handle any problems as they happen. Fortunately C# and VB.NET both offer a simple yet effective way of handling exceptions in code with the use of *try/catch* blocks.

A *try/catch* block typically has three elements, and they are all fairly self-explanatory. These are *try, catch,* and *finally.* When used together, these keywords provide a powerful means of handling exceptions.

TRY

A *try* block should contain code that could possibly cause an exception. It can contain as little or as much code as you like, but you don't need to include *all* your code within a *try/catch* block, just code that could throw an exception.

CATCH

A *catch* block should be used to handle specific exceptions thrown by the code inside the *try* block. It is possible to employ multiple blocks to trap a number of different, individual exceptions. *Catch* blocks give the coder an opportunity to handle the thrown exception gracefully and either rectify the problem, report or log the error, or throw the exception a level farther up the call stack.

FINALLY

The *finally* block is entirely optional, but any code contained within is executed regardless of whether an exception has been thrown (and handled) or otherwise. This means it is useful for closing object references or running other cleanup code as the final act in a block of logic.

The rest of this section looks at handling connection exceptions using *try/catch* blocks, but the information is pertinent to any code that is capable of throwing an exception. This starts with the following code snippet, which shows a basic example of how to trap connection errors using *try/catch:*

```vb
' VB
Imports System.Data.SqlClient

Module Module1

    Sub Main()

        Dim theConnectionString As String = "Data Source=jim-pc;Initial
            Catalog=VideoGameStoreDB;User ID=jim;Password=mypassword;"

        Try

            Dim theConnection As New SqlConnection(theConnectionString)

            theConnection.Open()

            If (theConnection.State = System.Data.ConnectionState.Open) Then
                Console.WriteLine("Database Connection is Open")
            End If
        Catch sqlexception As SqlException
            Console.WriteLine(sqlexception.Message)
        Catch exception As Exception
            Console.WriteLine(exception.Message)
        End Try

    End Sub

End Module
```

```csharp
// C#
using System;
using System.Data.SqlClient;

namespace CS_Sample1_9
{
    class Program
    {
        static void Main(string[] args)
```

```
        {
            string theConnectionString = "Data Source=jim-pc;Initial
                Catalog=VideoGameStoreDB;User ID=jim;Password=mypassword;";

            try
            {
                SqlConnection theConnection = new SqlConnection(theConnectionString);

                theConnection.Open();

                if (theConnection.State == System.Data.ConnectionState.Open)
                    Console.WriteLine("Database Connection is Open");
            }
            catch (SqlException sqlexception)
            {
                Console.WriteLine(sqlexception.Message);
            }
            catch (Exception exception)
            {
                Console.WriteLine(exception.Message);
            }
        }
    }
}
```

Now that a problem has been identified by catching the connection exception (and the error has been output to the console), troubleshooting can begin to find a solution. For problems like the one illustrated previously, it should be pretty easy to resolve. In this case, the user jim does not exist, and in fact, the SQL Server instance is set to use Windows Authentication only so that the attempted connection would never work. If *Integrated Security = SSPI* is set in the connection string, then the code works. The login failed exception message, when output, looks like Figure 1-10. Login fails when the *Open()* method is called.

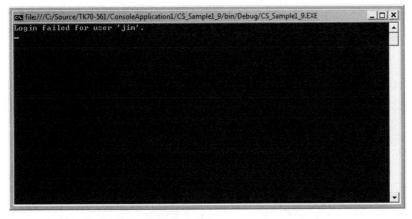

FIGURE 1-10 Displaying the caught exception

A more problematic exception is raised by the following code listing:

```vb
' VB
Imports System.Data.SqlClient

Module Module1

    Sub Main()

        Dim theConnectionString As String = "DataSource=jim-pc;Initial
            Catalog=VideoGameStoreDB;User ID=jim;Password=mypassword;"

        Try

            Dim theConnection As New SqlConnection(theConnectionString)

            theConnection.Open()

            If (theConnection.State = System.Data.ConnectionState.Open) Then
                Console.WriteLine("Database Connection is Open")
            End If
        Catch sqlexception As SqlException
            Console.WriteLine(sqlexception.Message)
        Catch exception As Exception
            Console.WriteLine(exception.Message)
        End Try

    End Sub

End Module
```

```csharp
// C#
using System;
using System.Data.SqlClient;

namespace CS_Sample1_10
{
    class Program
    {
        static void Main(string[] args)
        {
            string theConnectionString = "DataSource=jim-pc;Initial
                Catalog=VideoGameStoreDB;User ID=jim;Password=mypassword;";

            try
            {
                SqlConnection theConnection = new SqlConnection(theConnectionString);
```

```
            theConnection.Open();

            if (theConnection.State == System.Data.ConnectionState.Open)
                Console.WriteLine("Database Connection is Open");
        }
        catch (SqlException sqlexception)
        {
            Console.WriteLine(sqlexception.Message);
        }
        catch (Exception exception)
        {
            Console.WriteLine(exception.Message);
        }
    }
  }
}
```

The output from executing this code will be the following:

```
Keyword not supported: 'datasource'.
```

This time, we get a *System.Exception* instead of a *SqlClient.SqlException*.

The message returned here is actually very useful because it points towards an invalid exception in the connection string. Checking the code in the listing shows that the data source keyword is incorrect: it does not include a space between the words. If this is fixed, the code runs correctly.

Notice how the code includes a *try/catch* block for both the *SqlException* and *Exception* types. The previous example demonstrates why this is necessary. Because an invalid value was included in the connection string, the *Connection* object could not open a connection, and therefore, a *System.Exception* is thrown. In the previous example, where the *Connection* object could not log into the database with the supplied credentials, a *SqlException* was thrown. This occurs because the exception is coming from the server running SQL Server, not the client code.

It's worth making a few notes at this point about some of the best practices when it comes to implementing exception handling. These best practices apply to general coding activities too, not just when working with ADO.NET. This is an interesting and wide-reaching topic, and I would encourage you to read beyond this book and consider the best exception handling implementations for your needs.

MORE INFO   EXCEPTION HANDLING BEST PRACTICES

An interesting and useful article on this topic can be found at *http://msdn.microsoft.com/ en-us/library/seyhszts.aspx*.

Some of the considerations that should be made when implementing exception handling are:

- Don't use exception handling when you can perform a programmatic check instead. Remember that an exception should be an *exceptional* event.

- Introduce *catch* blocks beginning with traps for specific exceptions. Once specific exceptions are covered, create *catch* blocks for more general exceptions.

- Only handle exceptions that are relevant and understandable to the particular method. Otherwise, throw the exception so it can be handled by code that *is* relevant.

- When reporting or recording an error, use *Exception.ToString()* so that all the error information is listed; this includes the error number, message, and stack trace.

Database Transactions

Database transactions are relatively simple to use in ADO.NET. Transactions offer the ability to ensure the consistency and integrity of your database by allowing operations to be committed to the database if the operations work correctly or rolled back (cancelled) if there are errors.

The *BeginTransaction* method of the *Connection* object returns a *Transaction* object. This *Transaction* object then needs to be passed to each command that is to take part in the overall transaction.

Transaction objects have capabilities exposed through methods and properties. A good place to start is by taking a look at the *SQLTransaction* class. Table 1-7 lists some of the more interesting methods of the class, whereas Table 1-8 looks at the properties.

TABLE 1-7 Important *Transaction* Methods

NAME	DESCRIPTION
Commit	Commits the database transaction.
Rollback	Rolls back a transaction from a pending state.
Save	Creates a save point in the transaction that can be used to roll back a part of the transaction and specifies the save point name.

TABLE 1-8 Important *Transaction* Properties

NAME	DESCRIPTION
Connection	Gets the *SqlConnection* object associated with the transaction, or a null reference (*Nothing* in Visual Basic) if the transaction is no longer valid.
DbConnection	Specifies the *DbConnection* object associated with the transaction.
IsolationLevel	Specifies the *IsolationLevel* for this transaction.

But what is the point of using transactions? What benefit does using them offer? The answer can be described with four letters: ACID, which stands for *atomicity, consistency, isolation*, and *durability*.

ATOMICITY

A transaction describes an atomic unit of work which is a set of indivisible operations. The operations contained in a transaction, specified by the user, generally share a common purpose. All operations in a transaction should complete successfully or the whole transaction should be cancelled. Atomicity helps avoid data inconsistencies by ensuring that the data is always in an expected state.

CONSISTENCY

As alluded to previously, transactions help maintain consistency by ensuring that all operations succeed, taking data from a beginning state to an end state. Consistency exists at the beginning of the transaction because data is in an expected state, and it exists after the transaction has completed (whether committed or rolled back) because the data has either all operations performed on it successfully or none, and so it is in its original state.

ISOLATION

Isolation specifies that each transaction should appear to be the only transaction manipulating the data store at any point, even though other concurrent transactions might exist. Transactions have the highest level of isolation when they can be serialized because the results of all concurrent transactions, when completed, yield the same results as executing each transaction in series. Isolation comes at the cost of throughput—increased isolation means less concurrent transactions—which in turn means that applications often sacrifice a high level of isolation for increased throughput.

DURABILITY

A transaction is durable because the instant it is committed, the operations contained within it are written to the database and persist from that moment on.

A very simple example of a transaction can be found in the following code sample. This sample code updates a single column in a table and inserts a new row but encapsulates the operation in a *Transaction*. This way, both the update and the insert operation must complete successfully for the changes to be committed to the database.

```vb
' VB
Imports System.Data.SqlClient

Module Module1

    Sub Main()

        Dim theConnectionString As String = "Data Source=jim-pc;Initial
            Catalog=VideoGameStoreDB;Integrated Security=SSPI;"
        Dim theConnection As New SqlConnection()
        Dim theTransaction As SqlTransaction

        Try

            theConnection.ConnectionString = theConnectionString
            theConnection.Open()
```

```vb
            If (theConnection.State = System.Data.ConnectionState.Open) Then
                Console.WriteLine("Database Connection is Open")
            End If

            theTransaction = theConnection.BeginTransaction("myFirstTransaction")

            Dim theCommand As SqlCommand = New SqlCommand()
            theCommand.CommandText = "SELECT top 10 * FROM game"
            theCommand.CommandType = CommandType.Text
            theCommand.Transaction = theTransaction
            theCommand.Connection = theConnection
            theCommand.ExecuteNonQuery()

            Console.WriteLine("First command executed successfully.")

            Dim theSecondCommand As SqlCommand = New SqlCommand()
            theSecondCommand.CommandText = "SELECT top 10 * FROM accessory"
            theSecondCommand.CommandType = CommandType.Text
            theSecondCommand.Transaction = theTransaction
            theSecondCommand.Connection = theConnection
            theSecondCommand.ExecuteNonQuery()

            Console.WriteLine("Second command executed successfully.")

            theTransaction.Commit()

            Console.WriteLine("Transaction committed.")

        Catch sqlexception As SqlException
            Console.WriteLine(sqlexception)
            theTransaction.Rollback()
            Console.WriteLine("Transaction rolled back due to sql error.")
        Catch exception As Exception
            Console.WriteLine(exception)
            theTransaction.Rollback()
            Console.WriteLine("Transaction rolled back due to general error.")
        Finally
            If (theConnection.State = ConnectionState.Open) Then
                theConnection.Close()
            End If
            Console.WriteLine("Database Connection closed.")
        End Try

    End Sub

End Module
```

```csharp
// C#
using System;
using System.Data.SqlClient;

namespace CS_Sample1_17
{
    class Program
    {
        static void Main(string[] args)
        {
            string theConnectionString = "Data Source=jim-pc;Initial
                Catalog=VideoGameStoreDB;Integrated Security=
                SSPI;MultipleActiveResultSets=true;";

            SqlTransaction theTransaction = null;
            SqlConnection theConnection = new SqlConnection();

            try
            {
                theConnection.ConnectionString = theConnectionString;
                theConnection.Open();

                if (theConnection.State == System.Data.ConnectionState.Open)
                    Console.WriteLine("Database Connection is Open");

                theTransaction = theConnection.BeginTransaction("myFirstTransaction");

                SqlCommand theCommand = new SqlCommand();
                theCommand.CommandText = "UPDATE product SET listprice = 59.99
                    WHERE productid = 2020";
                theCommand.CommandType = System.Data.CommandType.Text;
                theCommand.Connection = theConnection;
                theCommand.Transaction = theTransaction;
                theCommand.ExecuteNonQuery();

                Console.WriteLine("First command executed successfully.");

                SqlCommand theSecondCommand = new SqlCommand();
                theSecondCommand.CommandText =
                    "INSERT INTO product (ProductName, ProductDescription, ListPrice,
                        ProductTypeID, ReleaseDate, ListPriceCurrency) " +
                    "VALUES ('Super Fight 2', 'The sequel to the #1 XBox 360 game
                        that never was', 59.99, 1, '2008-11-01', 'USD')";
                theSecondCommand.CommandType = System.Data.CommandType.Text;
                theSecondCommand.Connection = theConnection;
                theSecondCommand.Transaction = theTransaction;
                theSecondCommand.ExecuteNonQuery();
```

```
            Console.WriteLine("Second command executed successfully.");

            theTransaction.Commit();

            Console.WriteLine("Transaction committed.");

        }
        catch (SqlException sqlexception)
        {
            Console.WriteLine(sqlexception);
            theTransaction.Rollback();
            Console.WriteLine("Transaction rolled back due to sql error.");
        }
        catch (Exception exception)
        {
            Console.WriteLine(exception.Message);
            theTransaction.Rollback();
            Console.WriteLine("Transaction rolled back due to general error.");
        }
        finally
        {
            if (theConnection.State == System.Data.ConnectionState.Open)
                theConnection.Close();

            Console.WriteLine("Database Connection closed.");
        }
    }
  }
}
```

When this code is executed, the *Transaction* completes successfully (because there is no reason for it to fail) and commits the operatons to the database. Figure 1-11 shows the output. No errors are encountered as the two operations in the transaction are completed.

FIGURE 1-11 *Transactions* in action

Looking in the database in this case, it can be seen that both the update and insert queries have worked as expected. If there had been a problem, then the database would not have been updated.

 Quick Check

- Which name-value pair should be used in a connection string to specify the use of Windows Security?

Quick Check Answer

- The *Integrated Security=SSPI;* code tells the data provider to use Windows Security when connecting to the data source.

`LAB`   **Connecting to a Database**

In this lab, you create a class library to connect to a data source. You also create a unit test to see if the code in the class library performs as expected. You need to have the *VideoGameStoreDB* database installed to perform these exercises. Each exercise builds on the previous one. You can install the files for this lab, including the complete solution containing the code for all the exercises, from the Code folder on the companion CD.

EXERCISE 1   Connecting to a Data Source

In this exercise, you define connection properties and connect to a data source—just about the most basic, though nonetheless essential, database operation possible.

1. Start a new Class Library project named DataAccessLayer.

2. Add a connection string to the project settings named *VideoGameStoreDB* and have it contain a valid connection string to the *VideoGameStore* database. The connection string should contain valid values for the *Data Source, Initial Catalog,* and *Integrated Security* properties.

   Hint: Use the Settings tab in the Project Properties dialog box to accomplish this.

3. Add an assembly reference to System.Configuration.dll.

4. Add a class named *DataAccessComponent*.

5. Add a method named *ConnectToDatabase* by performing the following steps:

   a. Get a reference to the connection string from the application configuration.

   b. Create a SQL connection.

   c. Open the database connection.

   d. Close the connection.

   e. Implement exception handling.

   f. Return the status of the connection (or any error condition).

Your code should look like this:

```vb
' VB
Public Function ConnectToDatabase() As String

    Dim returnMessage As String = String.Empty
    Try
        Dim theConnectionString As ConnectionStringSettings
        theConnectionString = ConfigurationManager.ConnectionStrings _
            ("VideoGameStoreDB")

        Dim theConnection As SqlConnection
        theConnection = New SqlConnection(theConnectionString.ConnectionString)
        theConnection.Open()

        If (theConnection.State = System.Data.ConnectionState.Open) Then
            returnMessage = "Database Connection is Open"
        End If

    Catch aSqlException As SqlException
        returnMessage = aSqlException.Message
    Catch anException As Exception
        returnMessage = anException.Message
    End Try

    Return returnMessage

End Function
```

```csharp
// C#
public string ConnectToDatabase()
{
string returnMessage = String.Empty;

  try
  {
ConnectionStringSettings theConnectionString =
    ConfigurationManager.ConnectionStrings["VideoGameStoreDB"];

SqlConnection theConnection =
    new SqlConnection(theConnectionString.ConnectionString);

theConnection.Open();

        if (theConnection.State == System.Data.ConnectionState.Open)
        returnMessage = "Database Connection is Open";
}
```

```
catch (SqlException sqlexception)
{
        returnMessage = sqlexception.Message;
}
catch (Exception exception)
{
        returnMessage = exception.Message;
}


return returnMessage;
}
```

6. Create a unit test by right-clicking the *ConnectToDatabase* method and then selecting CreateUnitTests from the context menu.

7. Implement the unit test by using the *ConnectToDatabase* method and check the return value.

   Your code should look like this:

   ' VB
   ```
   <TestMethod()> _
   Public Sub ConnectToDatabaseTest()
     Dim target As DataAccessComponent = New DataAccessComponent
     Dim expected As String = "Database Connection is Open"
     Dim actual As String
     actual = target.ConnectToDatabase
     Assert.AreEqual(expected, actual)
   End Sub
   ```

   // C#
   ```
   [TestMethod()]
   public void ConnectToDatabaseTest()
   {
     DataAccessComponent target = new DataAccessComponent();
     string expected = "Database Connection is Open";
     string actual;
     actual = target.ConnectToDatabase();
     Assert.AreEqual(expected, actual);
   }
   ```

8. Run the unit test.

EXERCISE 2 Connecting to a Data Source with an Encrypted Connection String

In this exercise, you encrypt the section of the configuration file containing the connection string and then use the value to connect to the data source.

Continue by using the DataAccessLayer project created in Exercise 1 or by using the code that you installed from the enclosed CD.

1. From the Start menu, open a command prompt.

2. Navigate to the folder containing the AspNet_RegIIS.exe application. You will find this in the Microsoft.Net\Framework\V2.0.50727 directory under your Windows installation folder (for example, C:\Windows\ Microsoft.Net\Framework\V2.0.50727).

3. Issue the Aspnet_regiis.exe command with the correct parameters to encrypt the *connectionStrings* section using the Data Protection Configuration Provider.

   Your command prompt session should contain a command and output like this:

```
C:\Windows\Microsoft.NET\Framework\v2.0.50727>aspnet_regiis.exe -pef
    "connectionStrings" "C:\Source\TK70-561\Labs\E1\CS_DataAccessComponent "
    -prov "DataProtectionConfigurationProvider"
Encrypting configuration section...
Succeeded!
```

4. Check the configuration file to ensure that the configuration section has indeed been encrypted.

5. Using the same code as previously, run the unit test.

   Notice how, even though the configuration section is encrypted, no extra code is required to decrypt the configuration string value for use.

Lesson Summary

- Basic data source connections can be created with very little effort.
- A data source connection can be configured with great flexibility using key-value pairs.
- *ConnectionStringBuilder* can be used to provide an even more simple method of creating a connection string and connecting to a data source.
- Connection pooling is enabled by default in ADO.NET, which optimizes multiple database connections.

Lesson Review

You can use the following questions to test your knowledge of the information in Lesson 1, "Connecting to a Data Source." The questions also are available on the companion CD of this book if you prefer to review them in electronic form.

> **NOTE ANSWERS**
>
> Answers to these questions and explanations of why each answer choice is correct or incorrect are located in the "Answers" section at the end of the book.

1. Which of the following snippets is a valid way to connect to a SQL Server database using the SqlClient provider?

A.

```
' VB
Dim theConnectionString As String = "Data Source=jim-pc;Initial
    Catalog=VideoGameStoreDB;User ID=jim;Password=mypassword;"

Dim theConnection As New SqlConnection(theConnectionString)

theConnection.Open()

If (theConnection.State = System.Data.ConnectionState.Open) Then
    Console.WriteLine("Database Connection is Open")
End If
```

```
// C#
static void Main(string[] args)
{
string theConnectionString = "Data Source=jim-pc;Initial
    Catalog=VideoGameStoreDB;User ID=jim;Password=mypassword;";

SqlConnection theConnection = new SqlConnection(theConnectionString);

theConnection.Open();

if (theConnection.State == System.Data.ConnectionState.Open)
    Console.WriteLine("Database Connection is Open");
}
```

B.

```
' VB
Dim theConnectionString As String = "Data Source=jim-pc;Initial
Catalog=VideoGameStoreDB;Integrated Security=SSPI;"

Dim theConnection As New SqlConnection(theConnectionString)

theConnection.Open()

If (theConnection.State = System.Data.ConnectionState.Open) Then
    Console.WriteLine("Database Connection is Open")
End If
```

```
// C#
static void Main(string[] args)
{
string theConnectionString = "Data Source=jim-pc;Initial
    Catalog=VideoGameStoreDB;Integrated Security=SSPI;";
```

```
SqlConnection theConnection = new SqlConnection(theConnectionString);

theConnection.Open();

if (theConnection.State == System.Data.ConnectionState.Open)
    Console.WriteLine("Database Connection is Open");

}
```

C.

```
' VB
Dim theConnectionString As String = "Initial
    Catalog=VideoGameStoreDB;Integrated Security=SSPI;"

Dim theConnection As New SqlConnection(theConnectionString)

theConnection.Open()

If (theConnection.State = System.Data.ConnectionState.Open) Then
    Console.WriteLine("Database Connection is Open")
End If
```

```
// C#
static void Main(string[] args)
{
string theConnectionString = "Initial
    Catalog=VideoGameStoreDB;Integrated Security=SSPI;";

SqlConnection theConnection = new SqlConnection(theConnectionString);

theConnection.Open();

if (theConnection.State == System.Data.ConnectionState.Open)
    Console.WriteLine("Database Connection is Open");

}
```

D.

```
' VB
Dim theConnectionString As String = "Data Source=jim-pc;Initial
    Catalog=VideoGameStoreDB;User ID=jim;Password=mypassword;"

Dim theConnection As New DbConnection(theConnectionString)

theConnection.Open()
```

```
If (theConnection.State = System.Data.ConnectionState.Open) Then
    Console.WriteLine("Database Connection is Open")
End If
```

```
// C#
static void Main(string[] args)
{
string theConnectionString = "Data Source=jim-pc;Initial
    Catalog=VideoGameStoreDB;Integrated Security=SSPI;";

DbConnection theConnection = new DbConnection(theConnectionString);

theConnection.Open();

if (theConnection.State == System.Data.ConnectionState.Open)
    Console.WriteLine("Database Connection is Open");
}
```

2. What is the best way of implementing exception handling when dealing with a database connection?

   A. Implement a *try/catch* block that catches *System.Exceptions*.

   B. Allow the exception to be thrown by the connection attempt (an unhandled exception) and then check the *Errors* object.

   C. Implement a *try/catch* block that catches individual exception types, such as *SQLException*.

   D. Display a message to the user indicating that an error has occurred.

Lesson 2: Using Data Providers and More Complex Connection Scenarios

ADO.NET is incredibly flexible, not least because of its implementation of a modular architecture. This is a smart move—Microsoft supplies a number of different data providers, including the native provider for SQL Server, but third parties can supply their own (for example, when using the Oracle Relational Database Management Server (RDBMS)) or a custom data provider can be written by any competent developer.

> **After this lesson, you will be able to:**
> - Identify the most suitable data provider in any circumstances
> - Explain the advantages and disadvantages to using particular data providers
> - Build a generic data provider
>
> **Estimated lesson time: 30 minutes**

Data Providers

By default, relatively few data providers are available as a part of the *System.Data* namespace. These are *System.Data.SqlClient, System.Data.OleDb,* and *System.Data.Odbc.* Database-specific data providers are also available, such as *System.Data.OracleClient,* which yields a set of objects for use specifically with the Oracle relational database server.

The most efficient and effective method by which to access a data source is to use a native data provider—a data provider that is built specifically for the type of data source you are connecting to. The SqlClient data provider is by far the best way to connect to SQL Server; it takes advantage of the facets and features of the target database technology. The same is true of the Oracle data provider, which again is built to make the most of the various features of the Oracle database platform.

You might be under the impression at this point that the implementation of data providers in the ADO.NET Connection model is without drawbacks. This isn't quite true, though—as with most things, there are advantages and disadvantages to their use.

Unless you have built and are using your own generic data provider, coding against a specific data provider (for example, *System.Data.SqlClient*) ties you in to the data platform the data provider was written for. Should you need to change the data platform at any point during a project, a much bigger set of changes is required to remove the existing data provider code and replace it with an alternative. This is offset of course by the fact that individual data providers written for specific database technologies can take advantage of technology features and are generally capable of higher performance.

If you are a fan of Microsoft Data Access technologies, you may remember when Open Database Connectivity (ODBC) was "the next big thing" and when Object Linking and

Embedding Database (OLE DB) was introduced. Both had the aim of decoupling the data access layer from the data source by using an intermediate data-source-specific driver. The drawback of using these data access technologies is that they are relatively slow, especially compared to a native .NET provider.

Table 1-9 shows how each data provider has an equivalent set of functions.

TABLE 1-9 Data Provider Example Classes for Comparison

SQLCLIENT CLASS IMPLEMENTATION	*ODBC.NET* CLASS IMPLEMENTATION	*OLE DB* CLASS IMPLEMENTATION	DESCRIPTION
SqlConnection	OdbcConnection	OledbConnection	Represents a connection to the database.
SqlDataAdapter	OdbcDataAdapter	OleDbDataAdapter	Represents a set of command-related properties that are used to work with a *DataSet*.
SqlCommand	OdbcCommand	OleDbCommand	Represents a SQL statement (or command) to be executed against a data source.
SqlParameter	OdbcParameter	OleDbParameter	Represents a parameter to the *Command* object.
SqlDataReader	OdbcDataReader	OleDbDataReader	Represents one or more result sets which can be accessed in read-only, forward-only manner.
SqlTransaction	OdbcTransaction	OleDbTransaction	Represents a transaction to be performed against a data source.

There are situations where it is desirable to be able to use any number of data source types using a single data provider without being locked into a specific implementation. Once again, ADO.NET solves this problem by exposing classes in the *System.Data.Common* namespace.

> **MORE INFO** **OBJECT-ORIENTED PROGRAMMING**
>
> Understanding how to use the *System.Data.Common* namespace requires a sound understanding of object-oriented programming (OOP) principles such as interfaces and abstract classes and a working knowledge of design patterns such as the Abstract Factory Pattern—topics that are beyond the scope of this book.

Consider reading the classic design patterns book (which is conveniently sitting on my desk right now) *Design Patterns: Elements of Reusable Object-Oriented Software* by Erich Gamma, Richard Helm, Ralph Johnson, and John Vlissides (Addison-Wesley, 1994). One might hear of these four authors referred to as the "Gang of Four." In addition, the "Microsoft Patterns and Practices" articles on the MSDN Web site are superb—find them at *http://msdn.microsoft.com/en-us/practices/default.aspx.*

The *System.Data.Common* namespace uses the Abstract Factory Pattern so that exposed methods can return objects of the required type to the caller. The overall aim is to encapsulate the data source interaction code from the client. This client code is written against the interface and not the concrete implementation, which means it is decoupled from the specific provider implementation.

Figure 1-12 shows the *Factory Class* hierarchy. Notice how specific implementations such as *System.Data.SqlClient* inherit from the abstract *Db...* base classes, which in turn implement the *IDb...* interfaces.

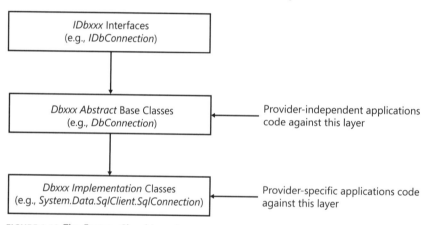

Factory Class Hierarchy

FIGURE 1-12 The *Factory Class* hierarchy

Because the *Db...* layer contains abstract classes, an implementation of them must be created that exposes provider-independent methods and properties. For the purposes of creating an independent provider, it would not make much sense to code against the implementation classes, such as *System.Data.SqlClient,* because they are tied into a specific data source's capabilities; of course, extending data provider capabilities is also possible in this situation.

For example, it is useful to take another quick look at the *System.Data.SqlClient SqlConnection* method. Figure 1-13 shows a diagram that is very similar in nature to Figure 1-12—you can see the interface, the abstract class, and the implementation for a *SqlConnection.*

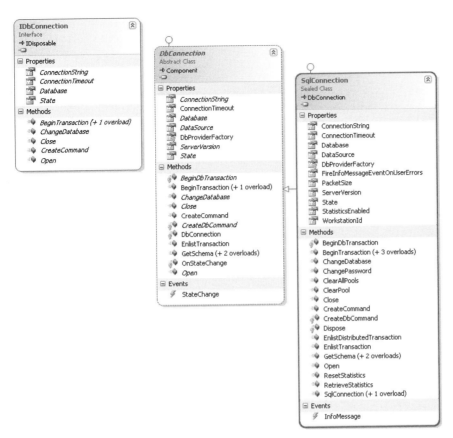

FIGURE 1-13 The *class* hierarchy

You can see the three layers from Figure 1-13: the *IDbConnection* interface; the abstract *DbConnection* class, which implements the interface; and the *SqlConnection* class, which derives from the abstract *DBConnection,* providing a concrete implementation of the *IDbConnection* interface.

One of the methods of the *DbProviderFactories* class is *GetFactory.* Take a look at how you can use that method right now. When using the *System.Data.Common* namespace, you create a *DbProviderFactory* instance, supplying configuration parameters at run time to get a strongly typed *Connection* object returned, ready for use. This means that, for example, a data provider can be specified in an application configuration file and used in the code using a reference generated by the factory classes. Take a look at the following code, which demonstrates how to get hold of this reference:

```
' VB
Imports System.Data.Common

Module Module1
```

```vb
    Sub Main()

        Dim theFactory As DbProviderFactory = DbProviderFactories.GetFactory
            ("System.Data.SqlClient")

        Dim theConnection As DbConnection = theFactory.CreateConnection()

        theConnection.ConnectionString = "Data Source=jim-pc;Initial
            Catalog=VideoGameStoreDB;Integrated Security=SSPI;"

        theConnection.Open()

        If (theConnection.State = System.Data.ConnectionState.Open) Then

            Console.WriteLine("Database connection is open")

            theConnection.Close()

            If (theConnection.State = System.Data.ConnectionState.Closed) Then
                Console.WriteLine("Database connection is open")
            End If
        End If

    End Sub

End Module

// C#
using System;
using System.Text;
using System.Collections.Generic;
using System.Data.Common;

namespace CS_Sample1_19
{
    class Program
    {
        static void Main(string[] args)
        {

            DbProviderFactory theFactory = DbProviderFactories.GetFactory
                ("System.Data.SqlClient");

            DbConnection theConnection = theFactory.CreateConnection();

            theConnection.ConnectionString = "Data Source=jim-pc;Initial
                Catalog=VideoGameStoreDB;Integrated Security=SSPI;";
```

```
            theConnection.Open();

            if (theConnection.State == System.Data.ConnectionState.Open)
            {
                Console.WriteLine("Database connection is open");

                theConnection.Close();

                if (theConnection.State == System.Data.ConnectionState.Closed)
                    Console.WriteLine("Database connection is open");
            }
        }
    }
}
```

Take a look at the previous code listing. The *DBProviderFactories.GetFactory* method supplies a reference to the specified data provider. The *GetFactory* method requires a parameter that indicates the data provider type to use. Any data provider can be used, so long as it is correctly installed. The value for this parameter can be derived from the installed provider, specifically from its invariant name. So where do you get this invariant name from?

Well, aside from being registered in the Global Assembly Cache (GAC), an entry needs to be made into the Machine.config file, under the *DbProviderFactories* section. Each registered data provider must have an entry, and if you look in the file, you should see content similar to that in Figure 1-14. Each registered data provider has an entry under the *DbProviderFactories* section.

```
<system.data>
  <DbProviderFactories>
    <add name="Odbc Data Provider" invariant="System.Data.Odbc" description=".Net Framework Data Provider fo
    <add name="OleDb Data Provider" invariant="System.Data.OleDb" description=".Net Framework Data Provider
    <add name="OracleClient Data Provider" invariant="System.Data.OracleClient" description=".Net Framework
    <add name="SqlClient Data Provider" invariant="System.Data.SqlClient" description=".Net Framework Data Pr
    <add name="Microsoft SQL Server Compact Data Provider" invariant="System.Data.SqlServerCe.3.5" descripti
  </DbProviderFactories>
</system.data>
<system.web>
```

FIGURE 1-14 Sample Machine.config section

We can get at the details contained in the *DbProviderFactories* section of the Machine.config file programmatically using the *DbProviderFactories.GetFactoryClasses* method. The following code shows how to use this functionality:

```
' VB
Imports System.Data.Common

Module Module1

    Sub Main()

        Dim theProviders As DataTable = DbProviderFactories.GetFactoryClasses()
```

```
        Console.ForegroundColor = ConsoleColor.Green
        Console.WriteLine("Provider Name                    Invariant Name")
        Console.ForegroundColor = ConsoleColor.White

        For Each aProvider As DataRow In theProviders.Rows
            Console.ForegroundColor = ConsoleColor.Gray
            Console.Write(aProvider(0).ToString().PadRight(30))
            Console.ForegroundColor = ConsoleColor.White
            Console.Write(aProvider(2).ToString().PadRight(30) + vbCrLf)
        Next

    End Sub

End Module

// C#
using System;
using System.Data;
using System.Data.Common;

namespace CS_Sample1_14
{
    class Program
    {
        static void Main(string[] args)
        {

            DataTable theProviders = DbProviderFactories.GetFactoryClasses();

            Console.ForegroundColor = ConsoleColor.Green;
            Console.WriteLine("Provider Name                    Invariant Name");
            Console.ForegroundColor = ConsoleColor.White;

            string outputLine = String.Empty;

            foreach (DataRow aProvider in theProviders.Rows)
            {
                Console.ForegroundColor = ConsoleColor.Gray;
                Console.Write( aProvider[0].ToString().PadRight(30) );
                Console.ForegroundColor = ConsoleColor.White;
                Console.Write( aProvider[2].ToString().PadRight(30) + "\n");
            }
        }
    }
}
```

And here, presented as Figure 1-15, are the results of running the code. This output shows only two of the four columns that are retrieved using the method.

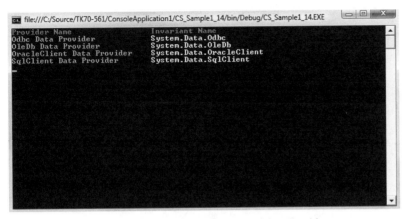

FIGURE 1-15 The result of requesting a list of registered data providers

There are four attributes associated with each provider. These are shown and explained in Table 1-10.

TABLE 1-10 Provider Attributes

COLUMN ORDINAL	COLUMN NAME	EXAMPLE OUTPUT	DESCRIPTION
0	Name	SqlClient data provider	Readable name for the data provider.
1	Description	.NET Framework data provider for SqlServer	Readable description of the data provider.
2	InvariantName	System.Data.SqlClient	Name that can be used programmatically to refer to the data provider.
3	AssemblyQualifiedName	System.Data.SqlClient. SqlClientFactory, System. Data, Version=2.0.0.0, Culture=neutral, PublicKey Token=b77a5c561934e089	Fully qualified name of the factory class, which contains enough information to instantiate the object.

Given this new information about the *DbProviderFactories* installed on a machine, other members of the chosen *DbProviderFactory* can be used by using the other generic classes for transactions, commands, and the other features you would expect. Table 1-11 looks at the methods and Table 1-12 the properties exposed by the *DbProviderFactory* class.

TABLE 1-11 *DbProviderFactory* Methods

NAME	DESCRIPTION
CreateCommand	Returns a new instance of the provider's class that implements the *DbCommand* class.
CreateCommandBuilder	Returns a new instance of the provider's class that implements the *DbCommandBuilder* class.
CreateConnection	Returns a new instance of the provider's class that implements the *DbConnection* class.
CreateConnectionStringBuilder	Returns a new instance of the provider's class that implements the *DbConnectionStringBuilder* class.
CreateDataAdapter	Returns a new instance of the provider's class that implements the *DbDataAdapter* class.
CreateDataSourceEnumerator	Returns a new instance of the provider's class that implements the *DbDataSourceEnumerator* class.
CreateParameter	Returns a new instance of the provider's class that implements the *DbParameter* class.
CreatePermission	Returns a new instance of the provider's class that implements the provider's version of the *CodeAccessPermission* class.

TABLE 1-12 *DbProviderFactory* Properties

NAME	DESCRIPTION
CanCreateDataSourceEnumerator	Specifies whether the specific *DbProviderFactory* supports the *DbDataSourceEnumerator* class.

LAB **Using Data Providers**

In this lab, you create a class library that again connects to a data source. This time, however, you use the OLE DB provider instead of the SqlClient provider (because it isn't always possible or desirable to use the native SqlClient provider).

A unit test is constructed to provide feedback about whether the class library works as expected. As with the previous exercises, you need to have *VideoGameStoreDB* installed. You can install the files for this lab, including the complete solution containing the code for all the exercises, from the Code folder on the companion CD.

EXERCISE 1   Using the OLE DB Provider to Connect to a Data Source

In this exercise, you define connection properties and connect to a data source using the OLE DB provider.

1. Start a new Class Library project named OLEDBDataAccessLayer.

2. Add a connection string to the project settings named *VideoGameStoreDB* and have it contain a valid connection string to the *VideoGameStore* database. The connection string should contain valid values for the *Provider, Server, Database,* and *Trusted_Connection* properties.

3. Add an assembly reference to System.Configuration.dll.

4. Add a class named *DataAccessComponent*.

5. Add a method named *ConnectToDatabase* by performing the following steps:

   a. Get a reference to the connection string from the application configuration.

   b. Create an OLE DB connection.

   c. Open the database connection.

   d. Close the connection.

   e. Implement exception handling.

   f. Return the status of the connection (or any error condition).

   Your code should look like this:

```vb
' VB
Public Function ConnectToDatabase() As String
      Dim returnMessage As String = String.Empty
      Try
          Dim theConnectionString As ConnectionStringSettings =
              ConfigurationManager.ConnectionStrings("VideoGameStoreDB")

          Dim theConnection As OleDbConnection = New OleDbConnection
              (theConnectionString.ConnectionString)

          theConnection.Open()

          If (theConnection.State = System.Data.ConnectionState.Open) Then
              returnMessage = "Database Connection is Open"
          End If

      Catch aOleDbException As OleDbException

          returnMessage = aOleDbException.Message

      Catch anException As Exception
```

```
            returnMessage = anException.Message

        End Try

        Return returnMessage

End Function

// C#
public class DataAccessComponent
{
public string ConnectToDatabase()
{
        string returnMessage = String.Empty;

        try
        {
            ConnectionStringSettings theConnectionString =
                ConfigurationManager.ConnectionStrings["VideoGameStoreDB"];

            OleDbConnection theConnection = new OleDbConnection
                (theConnectionString.ConnectionString);

            theConnection.Open();

            if (theConnection.State == System.Data.ConnectionState.Open)
                returnMessage = "Database Connection is Open";
        }
        catch (OleDbException oledbexception)
        {
            returnMessage = oledbexception.Message;
        }
        catch (Exception exception)
        {
            returnMessage = exception.Message;
        }

        return returnMessage;
    }
}
```

6. Create a unit test by right-clicking the *ConnectToDatabase* method and selecting Create Unit Tests from the context menu.

7. Implement the unit test by using the *ConnectToDatabase* method and check the return value.

Your code should look like this:

```vb
' VB
<TestMethod()> _
Public Sub ConnectToDatabaseTest()
   Dim target As OLEDBDataAccessComponent = New OLEDBDataAccessComponent
   Dim expected As String = "Database Connection is Open"
   Dim actual As String
   actual = target.ConnectToDatabase
   Assert.AreEqual(expected, actual)
End Sub
```

```csharp
// C#
[TestMethod()]
public void ConnectToDatabaseTest()
{
OLEDBDataAccessComponent target = new OLEDBDataAccessComponent();
   string expected = "Database Connection is Open";
   string actual;
   actual = target.ConnectToDatabase();
   Assert.AreEqual(expected, actual);
}
```

8. Run the unit test.

EXERCISE 2 Creating a Generic Database Access Connection

In this exercise, you use *DbProviderFactory* to create a generic database connection that reads a specific provider implementation from a configuration file.

1. Start a new Class Library project named GenericDatabaseConnection.

2. Add a connection string to the project settings named *SqlClientVideoGameStoreDB* and have it contain a valid SqlClient specific connection string to the *VideoGameStore* database. The connection string should contain valid values for the *Data Source, Initial Catalog,* and *Integrated Security* properties.

3. Add an assembly reference to System.Configuration.dll.

4. Add a class named *GenericDataAccessComponent*.

5. Add a method named *ConnectToDatabase* by performing the following steps:

   a. Get a reference to the connection string from the application configuration.

   b. Use the *DbProviderFactories.GetFactory* method to get a reference to the System.Data.SqlClient provider.

   c. Use the *CreateConnection* method on the *DbProviderFactory* to create a connection.

   d. Open the connection.

   e. Close the connection.

f. Implement exception handling.

g. Return the status of the connection (or any error condition).

Your code should look like this:

```vb
' VB
Public Function ConnectToDatabase() As String

Dim returnMessage As String = String.Empty

Try
Dim theFactory As DbProviderFactory
theFactory = DbProviderFactories.GetFactory("System.Data.SqlClient")

    Dim theConnectionString As ConnectionStringSettings
    theConnectionString = ConfigurationManager.ConnectionStrings
        ("SqlClientVideoGameStoreDB");

    Dim theConnection As DbConnection
    theConnection = theFactory.CreateConnection()

    theConnection.Open()

    If (theConnection.State = System.Data.ConnectionState.Open) Then
            returnMessage = "Database Connection is Open"
    End If

    Catch aDbException As DbException
        returnMessage = aDbException.Message

    Catch anException As Exception
        returnMessage = anException.Message
    End Try

    Return returnMessage
End Function
```

```csharp
// C#
public string ConnectToDatabase()
{
string returnMessage = String.Empty;
try
{
DbProviderFactory theFactory = DbProviderFactories.GetFactory
    ("System.Data.SqlClient");

ConnectionStringSettings theConnectionString =
    ConfigurationManager.ConnectionStrings["SqlClientVideoGameStoreDB"];
```

```
        DbConnection theConnection = theFactory.CreateConnection();

        theConnection.Open();

        if (theConnection.State == System.Data.ConnectionState.Open)
                returnMessage = "Database Connection is Open";
    }
    catch (DbException dbexception)
    {
            returnMessage = dbexception.Message;
    }
    catch (Exception exception)
    {
            returnMessage = exception.Message;
    }
    return returnMessage;
    }
```

6. Create a unit test by right-clicking the *ConnectToDatabase* method and selecting Create Unit Tests from the context menu.

7. Implement the unit test by using the *ConnectToDatabase* method and check the return value.

Your code should look like this:

```
' VB
<TestMethod()> _
Public Sub ConnectToDatabaseTest()
    Dim target As GenericDataAccessComponent = New GenericDataAccessComponent
    Dim expected As String = "Database Connection is Open"
    Dim actual As String
    actual = target.ConnectToDatabase
    Assert.AreEqual(expected, actual)
End Sub


// C#
[TestMethod()]
public void ConnectToDatabaseTest()
{
GenericDataAccessComponent target = new GenericDataAccessComponent();
    string expected = "Database Connection is Open";
    string actual;
    actual = target.ConnectToDatabase();
    Assert.AreEqual(expected, actual);
}
```

8. Run the unit test.

Lesson Summary

- It is important to select the most suitable data provider for the task.
- Each data provider has a different set of name-value pairs for configuration purposes.
- The *System.Data.Common* namespace contains features for implementing generic data access components.

Lesson Review

You can use the following questions to test your knowledge of the information in Lesson 2, "Data Providers and More Complex Connection Scenarios." The questions also are available on the companion CD of this book if you prefer to review them in electronic form.

> **NOTE ANSWERS**
>
> Answers to these questions and explanations of why each answer choice is correct or incorrect are located in the "Answers" section at the end of the book.

1. Which data provider should be used to get the maximum performance from a connection to SQL Server?

    A. The OLE DB data provider.

    B. The ODBC data provider.

    C. The SqlClient data provider.

    D. The Oracle data provider.

2. Which of the following snippets is a valid way to use the *System.Data.Common* namespace?

    A.

```vb
' VB
Dim theFactory As DbProviderFactory
theFactory = DbProviderFactories.CreateFactory("System.Data.OracleClient")
Dim theConnectionString As ConnectionStringSettings
theConnectionString = ConfigurationManager.ConnectionStrings
    ("OracleClientVideoGameStoreDB");
Dim theConnection As DbConnection
theConnection = theFactory.CreateConnection()
theConnection.Open()
```

```csharp
// C#
DbProviderFactory theFactory = DbProviderFactories.CreateFactory
    ("System.Data.OracleClient");
ConnectionStringSettings theConnectionString =
    ConfigurationManager.ConnectionStrings["OracleClientVideoGameStoreDB"];
DbConnection theConnection = theFactory.CreateConnection();
theConnection.Open();
```

B.

```vb
Dim theFactory As DbProviderFactory
theFactory = DbProviderFactories.GetFactory("System.Data.OracleClient")
Dim theConnectionString As ConnectionStringSettings
theConnectionString = ConfigurationManager.ConnectionStrings
    ("OracleClientVideoGameStoreDB");
Dim theConnection As DbConnection
theConnection = theFactory.CreateConnection()
theConnection.Open()
```

// C#

```csharp
DbProviderFactory theFactory = DbProviderFactories.GetFactory
    ("System.Data.OracleClient");
ConnectionStringSettings theConnectionString =
    ConfigurationManager.ConnectionStrings["OracleClientVideoGameStoreDB"];
DbConnection theConnection = theFactory.CreateConnection();
theConnection.Open();
```

C.

' VB

```vb
Dim theFactory As DbProviderFactory
theFactory = new System.Data.OracleClient();
Dim theConnectionString As ConnectionStringSettings
theConnectionString = ConfigurationManager.ConnectionStrings
    ("OracleClientVideoGameStoreDB");
Dim theConnection As DbConnection
theConnection = theFactory.CreateConnection()
theConnection.Open()
```

// C#

```csharp
DbProviderFactory theFactory = new System.Data.OracleClient();
ConnectionStringSettings theConnectionString =
    ConfigurationManager.ConnectionStrings["OracleClientVideoGameStoreDB"];
DbConnection theConnection = theFactory.CreateConnection();
theConnection.Open();
```

D.

```vb
' VB
Dim theConnectionString As ConnectionStringSettings
theConnectionString = ConfigurationManager.ConnectionStrings("VideoGameStoreDB");
Dim theConnection As DbConnection
theConnection = DbConnection.CreateConnection()
theConnection.Open()
```

```csharp
// C#
ConnectionStringSettings theConnectionString =
    ConfigurationManager.ConnectionStrings["VideoGameStoreDB"];
DbConnection theConnection = DbConnection.CreateConnection();
theConnection.Open();
```

Lesson 3: Working with Multiple Active Result Sets

Multiple Active Result Sets (MARS) is a relatively new—and very welcome—addition to ADO.NET. Although it shouldn't necessarily be used in every situation (as with many development disciplines, it can be easy to use product features because of poor software design rather than to best take advantage of features), it is a powerful and useful tool for working with and consuming data.

> **After this lesson, you will be able to:**
> - Identify when to use MARS
> - Explain the advantages and disadvantages of using MARS
> - Identify the situations in which MARS can be used
>
> **Estimated lesson time: 30 minutes**

MARS

On a standard connection—that is, one that doesn't use MARS—it is possible to have only a single open result set at any moment during the lifetime of the connection. This means that should multiple operations be required, the connection must be closed and reopened each time, which can be an expensive process.

The following code shows what happens if you try to open two result sets with the same connection:

```vb
' VB
Imports System.Data.SqlClient

Module Module1

    Sub Main()

        Dim theConnectionString As String = "Data Source=jim-pc;Initial
            Catalog=VideoGameStoreDB;Integrated Security=SSPI;"

        Try

            Dim theConnection As New SqlConnection(theConnectionString)

            theConnection.Open()

            If (theConnection.State = System.Data.ConnectionState.Open) Then
                Console.WriteLine("Database Connection is Open")
            End If
```

```
            Dim theCommand As SqlCommand = New SqlCommand()
            theCommand.CommandText = "SELECT top 10 * FROM game"
            theCommand.Connection = theConnection
            Dim theResult As SqlDataReader = theCommand.ExecuteReader()

            Console.WriteLine("First DataReader is Open")

            Dim theSecondCommand As SqlCommand = New SqlCommand()
            theSecondCommand.CommandText = "SELECT top 10 * FROM accessory"
            theSecondCommand.Connection = theConnection
            Dim theSecondResult As SqlDataReader = theSecondCommand.ExecuteReader()

            Console.WriteLine("Second DataReader is Open")

        Catch sqlexception As SqlException
            Console.WriteLine(sqlexception.Message)
        Catch exception As Exception
            Console.WriteLine(exception.Message)
        End Try

    End Sub

End Module

// C#
using System;
using System.Data.SqlClient;

namespace CS_Sample1_12
{
    class Program
    {
        static void Main(string[] args)
        {

            string theConnectionString = "Data Source=jim-pc;Initial
                Catalog=VideoGameStoreDB;Integrated Security=SSPI;";

            try
            {
                SqlConnection theConnection = new SqlConnection(theConnectionString);

                theConnection.Open();

                if (theConnection.State == System.Data.ConnectionState.Open)
                    Console.WriteLine("Database Connection is Open");
```

```
            SqlCommand theCommand = new SqlCommand();
            theCommand.CommandText = "SELECT top 10 * FROM game";
            theCommand.Connection = theConnection;
            SqlDataReader theResult = theCommand.ExecuteReader();

            Console.WriteLine("First DataReader is Open");

            SqlCommand theSecondCommand = new SqlCommand();
            theSecondCommand.CommandText = "SELECT top 10 * FROM accessory";
            theSecondCommand.Connection = theConnection;
            SqlDataReader theSecondResult = theSecondCommand.ExecuteReader();

            Console.WriteLine("Second DataReader is Open");
        }
        catch (SqlException sqlexception)
        {
            Console.WriteLine(sqlexception.Message);
        }
        catch (Exception exception)
        {
            Console.WriteLine(exception.Message);
        }
    }
}
}
```

The result of running this code is shown in Figure 1-16. There are two result sets on one connection, which causes an exception to be thrown because there is already a result set open.

FIGURE 1-16 Two result sets on one connection

If MARS is enabled, however, depending upon the type of operation required, multiple result sets can be opened on the same connection entirely transparently.

To use MARS, a simple modification to the connection string is required, namely, another name-value pair called *MultipleActiveResultSets=true*. Look at what happens with this setting enabled, as shown in the following code:

```vb
' VB
Imports System.Data.SqlClient

Module VB_Sample1_13

    Sub Main()

        Dim theConnectionString As String = "Data Source=jim-pc;Initial _
            Catalog=VideoGameStoreDB;Integrated _
            Security=SSPI;MultipleActiveResultSets=true;"

        Try

            Dim theConnection As New SqlConnection(theConnectionString)

            theConnection.Open()

            If (theConnection.State = System.Data.ConnectionState.Open) Then
                Console.WriteLine("Database Connection is Open")
            End If

            Dim theCommand As SqlCommand = New SqlCommand()
            theCommand.CommandText = "SELECT top 10 * FROM game"
            theCommand.Connection = theConnection
            Dim theResult As SqlDataReader = theCommand.ExecuteReader()

            Console.WriteLine("First DataReader is Open")

            Dim theSecondCommand As SqlCommand = New SqlCommand()
            theSecondCommand.CommandText = "SELECT top 10 * FROM accessory"
            theSecondCommand.Connection = theConnection
            Dim theSecondResult As SqlDataReader = _
                    theSecondCommand.ExecuteReader()

            Console.WriteLine("Second DataReader is Open")

        Catch sqlexception As SqlException
            Console.WriteLine(sqlexception.Message)
        Catch exception As Exception
            Console.WriteLine(exception.Message)
        End Try
```

```
        End Sub

End Module

// C#
using System;
using System.Data.SqlClient;

namespace CS_Sample1_13
{
    class Program
    {
        static void Main(string[] args)
        {

            string theConnectionString = "Data Source=jim-pc;Initial
              Catalog=VideoGameStoreDB;Integrated
              Security=SSPI;MultipleActiveResultSets=true;";

            try
            {
                SqlConnection theConnection = new SqlConnection(theConnectionString);

                theConnection.Open();

                if (theConnection.State == System.Data.ConnectionState.Open)
                    Console.WriteLine("Database Connection is Open");

                SqlCommand theCommand = new SqlCommand();
                theCommand.CommandText = "SELECT top 10 * FROM game";
                theCommand.Connection = theConnection;
                SqlDataReader theResult = theCommand.ExecuteReader();

                Console.WriteLine("First DataReader is Open");

                SqlCommand theSecondCommand = new SqlCommand();
                theSecondCommand.CommandText = "SELECT top 10 * FROM accessory";
                theSecondCommand.Connection = theConnection;
                SqlDataReader theSecondResult =
                    theSecondCommand.ExecuteReader();

                Console.WriteLine("Second DataReader is Open");
            }
```

```
            catch (SqlException sqlexception)
            {
                Console.WriteLine(sqlexception.Message);
            }
            catch (Exception exception)
            {
                Console.WriteLine(exception.Message);
            }
        }
    }
}
```

You can see with this small change how it is now possible to have two active result sets open, as Figure 1-17 shows.

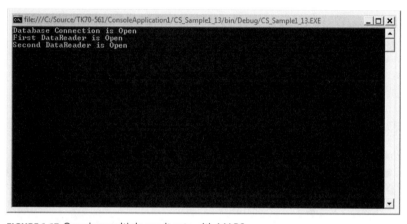

FIGURE 1-17 Opening multiple result sets with MARS

Of course, as useful as MARS is, its use is not possible in all circumstances; and naturally, there is a cost for using it. Take a look at some of its limitations. The SQL statement types that can take advantage of MARS are shown in the following list:

- **SELECT**   The standard *SELECT* statement can take advantage of MARS.

- **FETCH**   The *FETCH* statement can be used with MARS for populating a cursor or cursors.

- **RECEIVE**   The *RECEIVE* statement can be used if *SET XACT ABORT ON* is specified for the batch and if data is arriving. If the *RECEIVE* is in the waiting state it cannot be part of a MARS situation.

- **READTEXT**   Used to read text, ntext, or image values from a text, ntext, or image column, this statement is compatible for use with MARS.

- **BULK INSERT**   The *BULK INSERT* statement can be used if *SET XACT ABORT ON* is specified for the batch and if execute triggers on the table have been disabled.

- **Asynchronous CURSOR population**   Asynchronous CURSOR population is employed to increase the performance of a set of cursors. This approach is compatible with MARS.

Taking a common example scenario, the effects of using MARS can be examined with different SQL statement types. Take a situation where a MARS-enabled *Connection* object is opened and a large *INSERT* operation is instigated. Should a *SELECT* statement be executed on the same connection, the *INSERT* operation must finish before the *SELECT* statement executes. This is because the *INSERT* cannot take advantage of MARS. In a similar situation, when a *SELECT* statement is being executed, if an *UPDATE* request is made on the same connection, the *SELECT* is paused until the *UPDATE* execution has finished, and then it resumes.

On a final note, transactions are affected by a MARS environment in a number of subtle ways. Using MARS removes the ability to use transaction savepoints, rollbacks, or commits when there are multiple running operations. In practice, these limitations are fairly easy to design and code around; using a single transaction for all operations while avoiding the use of save points is a recommended way to go.

LAB   Using MARS

In this lab, you create a class library that connects to a data source configured to use MARS. A unit test is constructed to provide feedback about whether the class library works as expected. As with the previous exercises, you need to have *VideoGameStoreDB* installed. You can install the files for this lab, including the complete solution containing the code for all the exercises, from the Code folder on the companion CD.

EXERCISE 1   Enabling MARS on a Database Connection

In this exercise, you define connection properties, including enabling MARS, and connect to a data source.

1. Start a new Class Library project named MARSDataAccessLayer.

2. Add a connection string to the project settings named *VideoGameStoreDB* and have it contain a valid connection string to the *VideoGameStore* database. The connection string should contain valid values for the *Data Source, Initial Catalog,* and *Integrated Security* properties.

3. Add an assembly reference to System.Configuration.dll.

4. Add a class named *MARSDataAccessComponent.*

5. Add a method named *ConnectToDatabase* by performing the following steps:

   a. Get a reference to the connection string from the application configuration.

   b. Create a SqlClient connection.

   c. Open the database connection.

   d. Close the connection.

   e. Implement exception handling.

   f. Return the status of the connection (or any error condition).

Your code should look like this:

```vb
' VB
Public Function ConnectToDatabase() As String

  Dim returnMessage As String = String.Empty
  Try
          Dim theConnectionString As ConnectionStringSettings
          theConnectionString = ConfigurationManager.ConnectionStrings
              ("VideoGameStoreDB")

          Dim theConnection As SqlConnection
          theConnection = New SqlConnection(theConnectionString.ConnectionString)
          theConnection.Open()

           If (theConnection.State = System.Data.ConnectionState.Open) Then
              returnMessage = "Database Connection is Open"
           End If

      Catch aSqlException As SqlException
          returnMessage = aSqlException.Message
      Catch anException As Exception
          returnMessage = anException.Message
      End Try

      Return returnMessage

End Function
```

```csharp
// C#
public string ConnectToDatabase()
{
    string returnMessage = String.Empty;

    try
    {
      ConnectionStringSettings theConnectionString =
          ConfigurationManager.ConnectionStrings["VideoGameStoreDB"];

      SqlConnection theConnection =
          new SqlConnection(theConnectionString.ConnectionString);

      theConnection.Open();

      if (theConnection.State == System.Data.ConnectionState.Open)
              returnMessage = "Database Connection is Open";
```

```
        }
        catch (SqlException sqlexception)
        {
                returnMessage = sqlexception.Message;
        }
        catch (Exception exception)
        {
                returnMessage = exception.Message;
        }

        return returnMessage;
    }
```

6. Create a unit test by right-clicking the *ConnectToDatabase* method and selecting Create Unit Tests from the context menu.

7. Implement the unit test by using the *ConnectToDatabase* method and check the return value.

Your code should look like this:

' VB
```
<TestMethod()> _
Public Sub ConnectToDatabaseTest()
    Dim target As MARSDataAccessComponent = New MARSDataAccessComponent
    Dim expected As String = "Database Connection is Open"
    Dim actual As String
    actual = target.ConnectToDatabase
    Assert.AreEqual(expected, actual)
End Sub
```

// C#
```
[TestMethod()]
public void ConnectToDatabaseTest()
{
MARSDataAccessComponent target = new MARSDataAccessComponent();
    string expected = "Database Connection is Open";
    string actual;
    actual = target.ConnectToDatabase();
    Assert.AreEqual(expected, actual);
}
```

8. Run the unit test.

Lesson Summary

- Using MARS can be worthwhile and necessary; it can also be used to rescue poor application design.
- If you want to have multiple result sets open on a connection, use MARS.

Lesson Review

You can use the following questions to test your knowledge of the information in Lesson 3, "Using Multiple Active Result Sets." The questions also are available on the companion CD of this book if you prefer to review them in electronic form.

> **NOTE ANSWERS**
>
> Answers to these questions and explanations of why each answer choice is correct or incorrect are located in the "Answers" section at the end of the book.

1. Which of the following data providers support the use of MARS? (Choose all that apply.)

   A. The OLE DB data provider

   B. The ODBC data provider

   C. The SqlClient data provider

   D. The DbConnection provider

2. Which syntax for enabling MARS on the connection is correct?

   A. `MultipleResultSets=true`

   B. `MultipleActiveResultSet=true`

   C. `MARS=true`

   D. `MultipleActiveResultSets=true`

Chapter Review

To practice and reinforce the skills you learned in this chapter further, you can do any or all of the following:

- Review the chapter summary.
- Review the list of key terms introduced in this chapter.
- Complete the case scenarios. These scenarios set up real-world situations involving the topics of this chapter and ask you to create a solution.
- Complete the suggested practices.
- Take a practice test.

Chapter Summary

- ADO.NET uses data providers to connect to a data source. This gives complete flexibility in the type of data source that can be used, from an RDBMS to a Microsoft Office Excel spreadsheet to a text file.
- The database connection string controls the many ways in which a connection is made to a database using key-name pairs.
- ADO.NET offers the ability to have multiple result sets open on a single connection using MARS.
- Sensitive connection string information can be encrypted and then decrypted transparently at run time.
- Network traffic between the client and the data source can be encrypted using an SSL certificate.
- Custom data providers can be written to consume any type of data source should one not already exist.

Key Terms

Do you know what these key terms mean? You can check your answers by looking up the terms in the glossary at the end of the book.

- Connection pooling
- Multiple Active Result Sets (MARS)

Case Scenario

In the following case scenario, you apply what you've learned about how to use a variety of methods to retrieve data from a database. You can find answers to the questions posed in this scenario in the "Answers" section at the end of this book.

Case Scenario: Connecting to a Sensitive Data Source

You are brought in to consult for a company looking to produce a new .NET application. The application itself is fairly straightforward in nature and uses a single relational database as the data store. Not only is the data of a sensitive nature, but the application also is supposed to be used from uncontrolled computers in various locations around the country. Your task is to advise about the best methods of connecting to the data store given the circumstances.

In interviews, these people have said the following:

IT MANAGER

"I feel uneasy about leaving database connection information on the client PC. This is a major security hole."

CTO

"Data security is our number one priority."

QUESTION

Answer the following question for your manager:

- What can we do to ensure the security of the data being transmitted over the network?

Suggested Practice

To help you master the exam objectives presented in this chapter, complete the following task.

- **Practice 1** Create a reusable class library that can be used to connect programmatically to a data source. It should include passing parameters on a *Connection* method so that the connection string parameters are encapsulated by friendlier method parameters—for example, you might have a Boolean *useSSPI* parameter, which inserts the correct key-value pair into the connection string.

Take a Practice Test

The practice tests on this book's companion CD offer many options. For example, you can test yourself on just the content covered in this chapter, or you can test yourself on the entire 70-561 certification exam content. You can set up the test so that it closely simulates the experience of taking a certification exam, or you can set it up in study mode, which allows you to look at the correct answers and explanations after you answer each question.

> **MORE INFO** **PRACTICE TESTS**
>
> For details about all the available practice test options, see the section entitled "How to Use the Practice Tests," in the Introduction of this book.

Selecting and Querying Data

After you are connected to a data source, the possibilities are endless for what you can or might want to do with your data. To facilitate this, you can use another of the features of the ADO.NET object model—the *Command* object.

The *Command* object can be used to utilize data source features and to execute Structured Query Language (SQL) statements that can perform operations on the data source, including the execution of stored procedures or the manipulation of database objects.

This chapter provides an introduction to the available methods of selecting and querying data from a connected data source. It builds upon the knowledge gained in Chapter 1, "Creating Database Connections," and features two lessons. Lesson 1, "Building *Command* Objects," covers using the *Command* object to query data. Lesson 2, "Consuming Data Before You Begin," looks at ways to manage data using objects such as the *DataAdapter* and *DataReader*.

Exam objectives in this chapter:

- Build command objects.
- Query data from data sources.
- Retrieve data source data by using the *DataReader*.
- Manage data by using the *DataAdapter* or the *TableAdapter*.
- Execute an asynchronous query.
- Handle special data types.
- Manage exceptions when selecting data.

Lessons in this chapter:

To complete the lessons in this chapter, you must have:

- A computer that meets or exceeds the minimum hardware requirements listed in the "Introduction" section at the beginning of the book

- Microsoft Visual Studio 2008 Professional edition installed on your computer along with Microsoft .NET Framework 3.5

- An understanding of Microsoft Visual Basic or C# syntax and familiarity with .NET Framework 3.5

- A relational database, such as a recent version of Microsoft SQL Server

 REAL WORLD

James Wightman

While working onsite at a large client in the U.K., I was debugging the data access layer code and struggling to understand why a particular method that used a pretty simple *Command* object wasn't working as expected. I noticed the developer had left a comment in the code suggesting the method had worked fine before being "optimized," which gave me a clue as to the problem. On closer examination, the *CommandType* property of one of the *Command* objects was not being set in the code. Once I had specified the *CommandType* as *StoredProcedure*, the method worked again. The moral of the story, for me at least, is to ensure each time I use a *Command* object, I populate all of the necessary properties each and every time.

Lesson 1: Building *Command* Objects

One of the greatest achievements of the .NET Framework is the ability to provide code that performs any kind of task in any number of different ways. This can also cause a programmer to feel somewhat overwhelmed at the functionality that is available, but this is a symptom of the inherent encapsulated complexity of dealing with an operating system such as Microsoft Windows. The same is true of ADO.NET, where, on the surface at least, there appears to be any number of methods to perform similar tasks. The first thing to say is that generally, the subtle differences between methods is there for a good reason. It is rare to find one part of the .NET Framework that can be directly replaced with another to achieve the same results. The second thing to remember is that dealing with data and data stores in a simple and consistent manner can easily become a nightmare if the methods of access are poorly designed and implemented.

ADO.NET, although incredibly powerful, offers a flexible and wonderfully natural view of the data and the data sources you might wish to consume. Although the hundreds of classes supported by thousands of properties and methods may seem like overkill, the intelligent way that ADO.NET was designed caused data access to become as rewarding to implement as it is today.

After this lesson, you will be able to:

- Describe the ADO.NET *Command* object
- Identify the most frequently used methods and properties of the *Command* object
- Query a data source using the most appropriate methods

Estimated lesson time: 60 minutes

Command Object Overview

The *Command* object works with the *Connection* object to execute queries against a data source. A *Command* object instance offers a number of configuration options and methods to best suit data consumption requirements.

Chapter 1 describes the mechanisms by which it is possible to connect to a data source. Taking this further, it is quite easy to build on the connection and execute a simple command, like calling a stored procedure, as shown in Listing 2-1.

LISTING 2-1 Executing a Simple Command

```
' VB
Dim theConnection As SqlConnection
theConnection = New SqlConnection(theConnectionString)
theConnection.Open()

If (theConnection.State = System.Data.ConnectionState.Open) Then
    Console.WriteLine("Database Connection is Open\n\n")
End If
```

```vbnet
Dim theCommand As SqlCommand = New SqlCommand()
theCommand.Connection = theConnection

theCommand.CommandText = "GetProductsByName"
theCommand.CommandType = CommandType.StoredProcedure

theCommand.Parameters.Add(New SqlParameter("productName", "king"))

Dim theResult As SqlDataReader = theCommand.ExecuteReader()

If (theResult.HasRows) Then
   Console.WriteLine("Data has been successfully retrieved\n")
End If
```

```csharp
// C#
SqlConnection theConnection = new SqlConnection(theConnectionString);

theConnection.Open();

if (theConnection.State == System.Data.ConnectionState.Open)
   Console.WriteLine("Database Connection is Open\n\n");

SqlCommand theCommand = new SqlCommand();
theCommand.Connection = theConnection;

theCommand.CommandText = "GetProductsByName";
   theCommand.CommandType = CommandType.StoredProcedure;

   theCommand.Parameters.Add(new SqlParameter("productName", "king"));

SqlDataReader theResult = theCommand.ExecuteReader();

if (theResult.HasRows)
{
   Console.WriteLine("Data has been successfully retrieved\n");
}
```

After the connection is open, the code creates an instance of the *SqlCommand* class and populates a few of the more basic properties—for example, setting the name of the stored procedure in the *CommandText* property and setting the *CommandType* to *CommandType.StoredProcedure*. In addition, a new parameter is added to the *Command* because the stored procedure expects it. Finally, the *ExecuteReader* method is called on the *Command,* and the result is assigned to a *SqlDataReader*. The different classes, such as *DataReader*, *DataAdapter*, and *DataSet*, which are used to hold the result of queries executed on the *Command* object, are discussed in more detail later in this section. In addition, Chapter 3, *"DataSets,"* examines these classes and their uses at much greater length.

In the same way as specific *Data Provider Connection Object* implementations derive from *DbConnection*, found in the *System.Data.Common* namespace, all data provider implementations of the *Command* object derive from the *DbCommand* class. For example, the *SqlClient* data provider has the *SqlCommand* class, the *OleDb* provider has the *OleDbCommand* class, and all are individual implementations of the *Command* object derived from *DbCommand*. The abstract class *DbCommand* implements the *IDbCommand* interface, which defines a base set of methods and properties.

An introduction to the *DbCommand* class's members (methods and properties) is shown in Tables 2-1 and 2-2. Only the most pertinent information is included.

TABLE 2-1 *DbCommand* Object Methods

METHOD	DESCRIPTION
Cancel	An attempt is made to cancel the execution of *DbCommand*.
CreateDbParameter	Used to create a new instance of a *DbParameter* object.
CreateParameter	Used to create a new instance of a *DbParameter* object.
ExecuteDbDataReader	This method is used to execute the *DbCommand* using the contents of the populated *CommandText* property against the *Connection*.
ExecuteNonQuery	Used to execute a SQL statement against a *Connection* object. As the name suggests, this method is used when the statement returns no rows, such as an *INSERT*, *DELETE* or *UPDATE* query.
ExecuteReader	Executes the *CommandText* against the *Connection* and returns a *DbDataReader*. This method is used when the *Command* is expected to return a set of data. *DbDataReader*s are discussed in more detail later in this lesson.
ExecuteScalar	Used to execute a query and return the first column of the first row in the result set returned by the query. All other column/row information is discarded.
Prepare	This method creates a compiled version of the command on the data source.

Table 2-2 describes the *DbCommand* properties. Again, only the most pertinent properties are listed:

TABLE 2-2 *DbCommand* Properties

PROPERTY	DESCRIPTION
CommandText	A value representing the text command to execute against the data source.
CommandTimeout	Refers to the time to wait before terminating an execution attempt and generating an error.

TABLE 2-2 *DbCommand* Properties

PROPERTY	DESCRIPTION
CommandType	This property specifies how the *CommandText* property is interpreted. Values are found in the *System.Data.CommandType* enumeration, which include *StoredProcedure, TableDirect,* and *Text*.
Connection	Supplies a reference to the *DbConnection* used by this *DbCommand*.
DbConnection	Supplies a reference to the *DbConnection* used by this *DbCommand*.
DbParameterCollection	Returns a collection of *DbParameter* objects.
DbTransaction	This property provides a mechanism to set or get the *DbTransaction* within which this *DbCommand* executes.
Parameters	Returns a collection of *DbParameter* objects.
Transaction	This property provides a mechanism to set or get the *DbTransaction* within which this *DbCommand* executes.
UpdatedRowSource	Specifies how command results are applied to the *DataRow* when used by the *DbAdapter Update* method.

As mentioned earlier, specific data providers contain different implementations of the *DbCommand* abstract class. As you understand by now from the object-oriented design of the .NET Framework, classes that implement or inherit from base classes (such as the *SqlCommand* class, the *SqlClient* derivation of *DbCommand*) can also have methods and properties in addition to those in the base class.

One such method available on the *System.Data.SqlClient.SqlCommand* class is the *ExecuteXmlReader* method. This method provides a way (in addition to *ExecuteNonQuery, ExecuteReader,* and *ExecuteScalar,* that is) in which to return data from a SQL Server data source, though this time in the format of an *XmlReader* object.

Further examination of the *SqlCommand* class shows additional methods such as *BeginExecuteNonQuery* and *EndExecuteNonQuery,* which provide the ability to execute queries asynchronously.

An important property on the *DbCommand* class is *CommandType*. This property is used to advise the class as to the type of command being executed. It uses a simple enumerator, the values for which are presented in the following list:

- **CommandType.StoredProcedure** Used to inform the *Command* object that the value in the *CommandText* property is a stored procedure
- **CommandType.Text** Tells the *Command* object that the *CommandText* value contains a SQL query
- **CommandType.TableDirect** Used to tell the *Command* object that the *CommandText* property contains the name of a table to open

With the properties on the *Command* object now properly populated, one of the available *Execute* methods can be called to retrieve data from the data source. The decision on which method to use depends upon the type of command being executed and the format of the expected results. The following list describes how to choose the appropriate *Execute* method:

- **ExecuteNonQuery** This method should be chosen if the *CommandText* contains a Transact-SQL (T-SQL) statement that doesn't return a set of results. Instead, the method returns the number of rows affected as an *Integer* value.

- **ExecuteReader** This method should be used when the *CommandText* value is to return a set of results. The returned values build a *SqlDataReader* ready for use.

- **ExecuteScalar** Use this method to execute the query and return the first column of the first row of the result set only.

- **ExecuteXmlReader** This method should be used when the *CommandText* value is to return a set of results in an *XmlReader*.

The *ExecuteReadewr* method is overloaded and can be called with or without a *CommandBehavior* parameter. This parameter is used to provide a description of the query results and its effect on the data source. Table 2-3 describes the *CommandBehavior* enumeration values:

TABLE 2-3 *CommandBehavior* Values

NAME	DESCRIPTION
CloseConnection	Specifies that the *Connection* object should be closed once the *DataReader* object is closed.
Default	Specifies that the query may return multiple result sets, and that execution may affect the database state. Equivalent to calling *ExecuteReader()*.
KeyInfo	Specifies that the query returns column and primary key information.
SchemaOnly	Specifies that the query returns only column information. When using this value, the *SqlClient* data provider precedes the statement being executed with SET FMTONLY ON.
SequentialAccess	This value provides a way for the *DataReader* to handle rows that contain columns with large binary values. Instead of loading the entire row, *SequentialAccess* enables the *DataReader* to load data as a stream. The *GetBytes* or *GetChars* method can be employed to specify a byte location to start the read operation, and a buffer size for the data being returned.
SingleResult	Specifies that the query returns a single result set.
SingleRow	Specifies that the query is expected to return a single row and that query execution may affect the database state. If the SQL statement is expected to return only a single row, specifying this value can improve application performance. Note this value can still be used with multiple result sets but in that case each result set has a single row.

In a similar way to how *DbConnectionStringBuilder* is available to help build *Connection* strings, *DbCommandBuilder* can be used to build a *Command*. The *SqlClient* implementation of the *DbCommandBuilder* abstract class is the *SqlCommandBuilder* class. In the appropriate situation—and in limited circumstances—using *SqlCommandBuilder* can save time and effort.

Based on a supplied *SqlDataAdapter* and a *SELECT* statement, the *SqlCommandBuilder* can generate the other statement types—*INSERT, UPDATE,* and *DELETE.* Listing 2-2 demonstrates how *SqlCommandBuilder* can be used to save coding effort.

LISTING 2-2 Using *SqlCommandBuilder*

```vb
' VB
Dim theConnectionString As String = "Data Source=jim-pc;Initial
    Catalog=VideoGameStoreDB;Integrated Security=SSPI;"

Dim theConnection As SqlConnection = New SqlConnection(theConnectionString)

theConnection.Open()

If (theConnection.State = System.Data.ConnectionState.Open) Then
    Console.WriteLine("Database Connection is Open" & vbCrLf & vbCrLf)
End If

Dim theCommand As SqlCommand = New SqlCommand()

theCommand.Connection = theConnection

theCommand.CommandText = "SELECT * FROM product"

theCommand.CommandType = CommandType.Text

Dim theAdapter As SqlDataAdapter = New SqlDataAdapter(theCommand)

Dim theBuilder As SqlCommandBuilder = New SqlCommandBuilder(theAdapter)

Console.WriteLine(theBuilder.GetInsertCommand().CommandText & vbCrLf & vbCrLf)

Console.WriteLine(theBuilder.GetUpdateCommand().CommandText & vbCrLf & vbCrLf)

Console.WriteLine(theBuilder.GetDeleteCommand().CommandText & vbCrLf & vbCrLf)
```

```csharp
// C#
string theConnectionString = "Data Source=jim-pc;Initial
    Catalog=VideoGameStoreDB;Integrated Security=SSPI;";

SqlConnection theConnection = new SqlConnection(theConnectionString);
```

```
theConnection.Open();

if (theConnection.State == System.Data.ConnectionState.Open)
    Console.WriteLine("Database Connection is Open\n\n");

SqlCommand theCommand = new SqlCommand();

theCommand.Connection = theConnection;

theCommand.CommandText = "SELECT * FROM product";

theCommand.CommandType = CommandType.Text;

SqlDataAdapter theAdapter = new SqlDataAdapter(theCommand);

SqlCommandBuilder theBuilder = new SqlCommandBuilder(theAdapter);

Console.WriteLine(theBuilder.GetInsertCommand().CommandText + "\n\n");

Console.WriteLine(theBuilder.GetUpdateCommand().CommandText + "\n\n");

Console.WriteLine(theBuilder.GetDeleteCommand().CommandText + "\n\n");
```

Figure 2-1 shows the output from running the previous code.

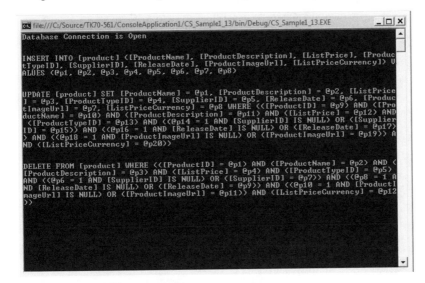

FIGURE 2-1 Using *SqlCommandBuilder*

Notice how *SqlCommandBuilder* automatically generates the *INSERT, UPDATE,* and *DELETE* statements based upon the original *SELECT CommandText.* This can be very useful when only basic CRUD (*CREATE, READ, UPDATE, DELETE*) operations are required or even as a starting point for more complex functionality. This functionality might include the execution of stored procedures using supplied parameters. The available methods for creating and accessing *Command* object parameters are discussed in the next section.

DbParameters Object

As demonstrated in the previous section, it is relatively easy to supply all the information necessary to execute a command against a data source. One of the more involved requirements—and one of the easiest to get wrong—centers around the *DbParameters* property of the *Command* object.

As with everything in the .NET Framework, a number of different methods of adding parameters to a *Command* object exist. This lesson concentrates specifically on the methods available through the *SqlClient.SqlCommand* class, although all the different data provider class implementations feature similar if not identical methods. The *SqlCommand* class uses a collection of *SqlParameter* objects, where *SqlParameter* is the implementation of the *DbParameter* abstract class.

As an introduction to using parameters, the following code concentrates on the declaration of a new *SqlParameter* and the assignment of datatype, value, direction, and size:

```vb
' VB
Dim theCommand as SqlCommand = new SqlCommand()
theCommand.Connection = theConnection

theCommand.CommandText = "SelectProductByName"
theCommand.CommandType = CommandType.StoredProcedure

Dim nameParameter as SqlParameter = new SqlParameter()

nameParameter.ParameterName = "productName"
nameParameter.DbType = DbType.String
nameParameter.Direction = ParameterDirection.Input
nameParameter.Size = 50
nameParameter.Value = "Gears of War 3"

theCommand.Parameters.Add(nameParameter)
```

```csharp
// C#
SqlCommand theCommand = new SqlCommand();
theCommand.Connection = theConnection;

theCommand.CommandText = "SelectProductByName";
theCommand.CommandType = CommandType.StoredProcedure;
```

```
SqlParameter nameParameter = new SqlParameter();

nameParameter.ParameterName = "productName";
nameParameter.DbType = DbType.String;
nameParameter.Direction = ParameterDirection.Input;
nameParameter.Size = 50;
nameParameter.Value = "Gears of War 3";

theCommand.Parameters.Add(nameParameter);
```

The *DbParameters* class exposes a number of interesting methods and properties, as shown in Tables 2-4 and 2-5.

TABLE 2-4 *DbParameters* Methods

METHOD	DESCRIPTION
ResetDbType	Resets the *DbType* property to its original settings.

TABLE 2-5 *DbParameter* Properties

PROPERTY	DESCRIPTION
DbType	Refers to the *DbType* of the parameter. (A list of possible *DbTypes* is presented later in this lesson in Table 2-6.)
Direction	Used to set or retrieve the parameter direction—Input-only, Output-only, Bidirectional, or stored procedure Return Value parameter.
IsNullable	A Boolean value that indicates whether the parameter accepts null values.
ParameterName	The name of the *DbParameter*.
Size	Used to get or set the maximum size in bytes of the data in the data column.
SourceColumn	Used to get or set the name of the source column, mapped to the *DataSet*, and used for loading/returning the value.
SourceColumnNullMapping	Refers to a value which indicates whether the source column is nullable. This property is used to allow the *DbCommandBuilder* to generate *UPDATE* statements for nullable columns.
SourceVersion	Gets or sets the *DataRowVersion* to use when you populate the *Value* property.
Value	Gets or sets the parameter value.

The *SqlParameter* class has a number of useful constructors that can be used in an inline fashion to initialize *SqlParameter* for use with a *SqlCommand*. The use of a suitable constructor can cut down on the amount of code required, as shown in the following list:

- **SqlParameter()**   The most simple constructor, it initializes a new instance of the *SqlParameter* class.

- **SqlParameter(String, SqlDbType, Int32, ParameterDirection, Boolean, Byte, Byte, String, DataRowVersion, Object)**   Initializes a new instance of the *SqlParameter* class using *Name, Type, Size, Direction, Precision, Scale, Source Column, DataRowVersion*, and *Value*.

- **SqlParameter(String, SqlDbType, Int32, ParameterDirection, Byte, Byte, String, DataRowVersion, Boolean, Object, String, String, String)**   Initializes a new instance of the *SqlParameter* class using *Name, Type, Size, Direction, Precision, Scale, Source Column, DataRowVersion, Source Column* mapping, *Value, Database* name where the XML schema collection is located, the owning relational schema where the schema collection for this XML instance is located, and the name of the schema collection for this parameter.

- **SqlParameter(String, SqlDbType)**   Initializes a new instance of the *SqlParameter* class using the *SqlDbType*.

- **SqlParameter(String, Object)**   Initializes a new instance of the *SqlParameter* class using a *Parameter* name and a *Value*.

- **SqlParameter(String, SqlDbType, Int32)**   Initializes a new instance of the *SqlParameter* class using using a *Parameter* name, the datatype, and the *Parameter* size.

- **SqlParameter(String, SqlDbType, Int32, String)**   Initializes a new instance of the *SqlParameter* class using a *Parameter* name, the datatype, the *Parameter* size, and the source column name.

After a parameter is created, it must be added to the *Command* parameters collection before the *Command* is executed. This is achieved simply using code similar to this:

```
theCommand.Parameters.Add(aSqlParameter);
```

An alternative way of adding a parameter is to use the *AddWithValue* method:

```
' VB
theCommand.Parameters.AddWithValue("parameterName", parameterValue)
```

```
// C#
theCommand.Parameters.AddWithValue("parameterName",
    parameterValue);
```

Multiple parameters can be specified to create a parameters collection, as in the following code:

```
' VB
theCommand.CommandText = "SelectProductByNameAndDate"
```

```
theCommand.CommandType = CommandType.StoredProcedure

Dim nameParameter As SqlParameter = New SqlParameter()

Dim dateParameter As SqlParameter = New SqlParameter()

nameParameter.ParameterName = "productName"

nameParameter.DbType = DbType.String

nameParameter.Direction = ParameterDirection.Input

nameParameter.Size = 50

nameParameter.Value = "Halo"

dateParameter.ParameterName = "releaseDate"

dateParameter.DbType = DbType.Date

dateParameter.Direction = ParameterDirection.Input

dateParameter.Size = 10

nameParameter.Value = "01 January 2008"

theCommand.Parameters.Add(nameParameter)

theCommand.Parameters.Add(dateParameter)

// C#
theCommand.CommandText = "SelectProductByNameAndDate";

theCommand.CommandType = CommandType.StoredProcedure;

SqlParameter nameParameter = new SqlParameter();

SqlParameter dateParameter = new SqlParameter();

nameParameter.ParameterName = "productName";

nameParameter.DbType = DbType.String;

nameParameter.Direction = ParameterDirection.Input;
```

```
nameParameter.Size = 50;

nameParameter.Value = "Halo";

dateParameter.ParameterName = "releaseDate";

dateParameter.DbType = DbType.Date;

dateParameter.Direction = ParameterDirection.Input;

dateParameter.Size = 10;

nameParameter.Value = "01 January 2008";

theCommand.Parameters.Add(nameParameter);

theCommand.Parameters.Add(dateParameter);
```

After a *Parameter* has been added to the *Command* object, it can then be accessed either by index or by name. The following code demonstrates this:

```
' VB
Console.WriteLine(theCommand.Parameters("productName").Value)
Console.WriteLine(theCommand.Parameters(0).Value)
```

```
// C#
Console.WriteLine(theCommand.Parameters["productName"].Value);
Console.WriteLine(theCommand.Parameters[1].Value);
```

In addition, the *SqlCommand* object has an overloaded *Add* method, which can be used to add parameters with and without a direct reference to a *SqlParameter*, as shown in the following list:

- **Add(SqlParameter)**   As in the previous code sample, this overload adds the provided *SqlParameter* object to the *SqlParameterCollection*.
- **Add(String, SqlDbType)**   Adds a *SqlParameter* to the *SqlParameterCollection* using a *Parameter* name and the datatype.
- **Add(String, SqlDbType, Int32)**   Adds a *SqlParameter* to the *SqlParameterCollection* using a *Parameter* name, datatype, and *Parameter* size.
- **Add(String, SqlDbType, Int32, String)**   Adds a *SqlParameter* to the *SqlParameterCollection* using a *Parameter* name, datatype, column length, and source column name.

It's time to address some of the other properties of the *Parameters* object. As it is incredibly important to specify the correct datatype for the entities in a database, the *System.Common.DbType* enumeration is used to match datatypes between the data provider and the database. Table 2-6 lists the enumerator values:

TABLE 2-6 *DbType* Values

MEMBER	DESCRIPTION
AnsiString	A variable-length stream of between 1 and 8,000 non-Unicode characters.
Binary	A variable-length stream of between 1 and 8,000 bytes of binary data.
Byte	An 8-bit unsigned integer (values between 0 and 255).
Boolean	True or False.
Currency	A currency value ranging from +/–2^{63} with accuracy to a ten-thousandth of a currency unit.
Date	A date value.
DateTime	A date and time value.
DateTime2	More date/time data. Date values range from January 1,1 AD to December 31, 9999 AD. The time range is 00:00:00 through 23:59:59.9999999 with an accuracy of within 100 nanoseconds.
DateTimeOffset	Represents date/time data with time zone awareness. Date values range from January 1,1 AD through December 31, 9999 AD. Time values range from 00:00:00 through 23:59:59.9999999 with an accuracy of within 100 nanoseconds. The time zone value range is –14:00 through +14:00.
Decimal	Represents values from 1.0×10^{-28} to around 7.9×10^{28} with 28-29 significant digits.
Double	A floating point type ranging from around 5.0×10^{-324} to 1.7×10^{308} with a precision of 15–16 digits.
Guid	A globally unique identifier (GUID).
Int16	Represents a signed 16-bit integer ranging from –32768 to 32767.
Int32	Represents a signed 32-bit integer with values between –2147483648 and 2147483647.
Int64	Represents a signed 64-bit integer with values between –9223372036854775808 and 9223372036854775807.
Object	This is a generic type which represents any reference or value type not explicitly represented by another DbType value.
SByte	A type which represents a signed 8-bit integer (values between –128 and 127).
Single	A floating point type which represents values from approximately 1.5×10^{-45} to 3.4×10^{38}—with a precision of 7 digits.
String	A type which represents Unicode character strings.

TABLE 2-6 *DbType* Values

MEMBER	DESCRIPTION
Time	Used to represent time values.
UInt16	Represents an unsigned 16-bit integer with values between 0 and 65535.
UInt32	This represents an unsigned 32-bit integer with values between 0 and 4294967295.
UInt64	Represents an unsigned 64-bit integer with values between 0 and 18446744073709551615.
VarNumeric	A variable-length numeric value.
AnsiStringFixedLength	A fixed-length non-Unicode stream of characters.
StringFixedLength	A fixed-length string of Unicode characters.
Xml	Represents a parsed Extensible Markup Document (XML) document or fragment.

In addition to the *DbType* values shown in Table 2-6, there are specific native types for use directly with SQL Server. SQL Server datatypes are transparently converted to *SqlTypes* and then to *SqlDbTypes* to provide a safer and faster mechanism of using types. These are shown in Table 2-7.

TABLE 2-7 *System.Data.SqlTypes*

NATIVE SQL SERVER	.NET FRAMEWORK *SQLTYPES*	.NET FRAMEWORK *SQLDBTYPE*
binary	*SqlBinary*	*Binary*
Bigint	*SqlInt64*	*BigInt*
Char	*SqlString*	*Char*
datetime	*SqlDateTime*	*DateTime*
decimal	*SqlDecimal*	*Decimal*
Float	*SqlDouble*	*Float*
image	*SqlBinary*	*Image*
Int	*SqlInt32*	*Int*
Money	*SqlMoney*	*Money*
nchar	*SqlString*	*NChar*
Ntext	*SqlString*	*NText*
nvarchar	*SqlString*	*NVarChar*
Numeric	*SqlDecimal*	*Numeric*
Real	*SqlSingle*	*Real*
smalldatetime	*SqlDateTime*	*SmallDateTime*

TABLE 2-7 *System.Data.SqlTypes*

NATIVE SQL SERVER	.NET FRAMEWORK *SQLTYPES*	.NET FRAMEWORK *SQLDBTYPE*
smallint	SqlInt16	SmallInt
smallmoney	SqlMoney	SmallMoney
sql_variant	Object	Variant
sysname	SqlString	VarChar
text	SqlString	Text
timestamp	SqlBinary	TimeStamp
tinyint	SqlByte	TinyInt
varbinary	SqlBinary	VarBinary
varchar	SqlString	VarChar
uniqueidentifier	SqlGuid	UniqueId

One of the important and often-used properties of the *SqlParameter* class is the *Direction* property. This property specifies the direction of the parameter, whether it is an input parameter, output parameter, bi-directional, or a return value. *Direction* is used to identify to the executing command how the parameter should be treated. A standard input parameter is used to pass a value to the subject of the command (for example a stored procedure), whereas an output parameter is used to retrieve values from the subject of the command. In a stored procedure, an output parameter can be assigned to and queried after the *Command* has been executed in the client code. A bidirectional *InputOutput* direction can be specified to be used as both an *Input* and *Output* parameter. Finally, a *ReturnValue Direction* parameter allows the subject of the *Command* to return a value specifying, for example, a status value signifying the success or failure of the *Command* operation.

LAB   Building *Command* Objects

In this lab, you create a class library that connects to a data source and retrieves a set of data using a *Command* object and a *DataReader*.

You construct a unit test to provide feedback of whether the class library works as expected. As with the exercises in Chapter 1, you need to have the *VideoGameStoreDB* installed. You can install the files for this lab, including the complete solution containing the code for all the exercises, from the Code folder on the companion CD.

EXERCISE 1   Building a *Command* Object

In this exercise, you define connection properties, connect to a data source, and execute a *DataReader* to retrieve a set of data.

1. Start a new Class Library project named DataAccessLayerWithDataReaders.

2. Add a connection string to the project settings named *VideoGameStoreDB* and have it contain a valid connection string to the *VideoGameStore* database.

3. Add an assembly reference to System.Configuration.dll.

4. Add a class named *DataAccessComponent*.

5. Add a method named *GetAllProducts* by performing the following steps:

   a. Get a reference to the connection string from the application configuration.

   b. Create a *SqlClient* connection.

   c. Open the database connection.

   d. Create a *SqlCommand* object, populating the *CommandText* property to select the first three columns from the Product table.

   e. Loop through the retrieved data.

   f. Close the connection.

   g. Implement exception handling.

   h. Return the number of rows iterated through.

   Your code should look like this:

```vb
' VB
Public Function GetAllProducts() As Integer

    Dim rowCount As Integer = 0

    Try
        Dim theConnectionString As ConnectionStringSettings = _
            ConfigurationManager.ConnectionStrings( _
            "TK70561.My.MySettings.VideoGameStoreDB")

        Dim theConnection As SqlConnection = New _
            SqlConnection(theConnectionString.ConnectionString)

        theConnection.Open()

        Dim theCommand As SqlCommand = New SqlCommand()
        theCommand.Connection = theConnection
        theCommand.CommandText = "SELECT productId, productName, " & _
            "productDescription FROM product"
        theCommand.CommandType = System.Data.CommandType.Text

        Dim theReader As SqlDataReader = theCommand.ExecuteReader()

        While (theReader.Read())
            rowCount = rowCount + 1
        End While

        theReader.Close()
        theConnection.Close()
```

```
      Catch aSqlException As SqlException
         Throw New ApplicationException("Exception Occured")
      Catch anException As Exception
         Throw New ApplicationException("Exception Occured")
      End Try


      Return rowCount


   End Function

// C#
public int GetAllProducts()
{
   int rowCount = 0;

   try
   {

      ConnectionStringSettings theConnectionString =
         ConfigurationManager.ConnectionStrings
         ["TK70561.Properties.Settings.VideoGameStoreDB"];

      SqlConnection theConnection = new
         SqlConnection(theConnectionString.ConnectionString);

      theConnection.Open();

      SqlCommand theCommand = new SqlCommand();
      theCommand.Connection = theConnection;
      theCommand.CommandText = "SELECT productId, productName, productDescription
         FROM product";

      theCommand.CommandType = System.Data.CommandType.Text;

      SqlDataReader theReader = theCommand.ExecuteReader();

      while (theReader.Read())
      {
         rowCount++;
      }

   theReader.Close();
   theConnection.Close();

   }
```

```
        catch (SqlException sqlexception)
        {
            throw;
        }
        catch (Exception exception)
        {
            throw;
        }

        return rowCount;
    }
```

6. Create a unit test by right-clicking the *GetAllProducts* method.

7. Implement the unit test by using the *GetAllProducts* method and check the return value. Your code should look like this:

```vb
' VB

<TestMethod()> _
Public Sub ConnectToDatabaseTest()
    Dim target As DataAccessComponent = New DataAccessComponent
    Dim expected As Integer = 864
    Dim actual As Integer
    actual = target.GetAllProducts()
    Assert.AreEqual(expected, actual)
```

```csharp
// C#
[TestMethod()]
public void ConnectToDatabaseTest()
{
    DataAccessComponent target = new DataAccessComponent();
    int expected = 864;
    int actual;
    actual = target.GetAllProducts();
    Assert.AreEqual(expected, actual);
}
```

8. Run the unit test.

Lesson Summary

- The *Command* object is at the core of all data retrieval operations in ADO.NET.
- A *Command* object has a *Parameters* collection, which is manipulated to supply a correctly typed *Parameters* data source.

Lesson Review

You can use the following questions to test your knowledge of the information in Lesson 1, "Building *Command* Objects." The questions also are available on the companion CD of this book if you prefer to review them in electronic form.

> **NOTE** **ANSWERS**
>
> Answers to these questions and explanations of why each answer choice is correct or incorrect are located in the "Answers" section at the end of the book.

1. Which *CommandType* value is incorrect?

   A. *StoredProcedure*

   B. *TableDirect*

   C. *TableSchema*

   D. *Text*

2. Which of the following SQL statements is syntactically correct?

   A.

   ```
   SELECT pt.ProductTypeName as ProductType, SUM(p.listPrice) as CostByProductType
   FROM product p LEFT INNER JOIN productType pt on pt.ProductTypeID =
        p.ProductTypeID

   GROUP BY pt.ProductTypeName
   ```

   B.

   ```
   SELECT pt.ProductTypeName as ProductType, SUM(p.listPrice) as CostByProductType
   FROM product p INNER JOIN productType on pt.ProductTypeID = p.ProductTypeID
   GROUP BY pt.ProductTypeName
   ```

   C.

   ```
   SELECT pt.ProductTypeName as ProductType, SUM(p.listPrice) as CostByProductType
   FROM product p LEFT INNER JOIN productType pt on pt.ProductTypeID = p.ProductTypeID
   ORDER BY pt.ProductTypeName
   ```

   D.

   ```
   SELECT pt.ProductTypeName as ProductType, SUM(p.listPrice) as CostByProductType
   FROM product p LEFT OUTER productType pt on pt.ProductTypeID = p.ProductTypeID
   GROUP BY pt.ProductTypeName
   ```

Lesson 2: Consuming Data Before You Begin

Up until this point in the book, the discussion has concentrated on connecting to a data source and retrieving data. But this is only one side of the story—the other side is how data is consumed on the client.

Generally speaking, the priority when consuming data is around the rapid retrieval and use of data on the client. To achieve this, care must be taken to retrieve only pertinent data and to use a suitable construct on the client to provide a performant and easily manipulated data consumption experience.

This lesson addresses the best methods of data retrieval and the variety of containers available to consume the retrieved results.

> **After this lesson, you will be able to:**
> - Work with data and consume it on the client
> - Use the *DataAdapter* and *TableAdapter* classes
> - Execute queries asynchronously
> - Use Language Integrated Query (LINQ) to query a data source
>
> **Estimated lesson time: 90 minutes**

Writing Queries

To query any data source, regardless of its type and whether the query itself is exposed and viewable, SQL is used. SQL is a simple and logically constructed language which provides access to the entities in a data source in a straightforward fashion using a limited (yet refined) set of keywords.

In its most basic form, data can be retrieved from a data source using a very simple SQL query, which consists of the *SELECT* and *FROM* keywords. The *SELECT* statement tells the query what columns are required, and the FROM clause identifies the table or view from which the data should be selected. Here's a sample of such a query:

```
SELECT * FROM tablename
```

This simple query forms the basis for most other SQL operations that require the selection of data. The first thing to note is that for the purposes of efficiency, using the *SELECT* * syntax is probably not the best option unless all fields will be consumed as a result of running the query. The better option is to explicitly name the parameters as required in the *SELECT* part of the query, as follows:

```
SELECT productId, productName, listPrice FROM product
```

The next part of the query to address is how to filter the data during the *SELECT* process—again to retrieve only the set of values required for consumption. This is achieved using another keyword, *WHERE,* as follows:

```
SELECT productId, productName, listPrice FROM product
WHERE productName LIKE '%gears%'
```

As might be expected when running the previous query against the *VideoGameStoreDb*, a set of data containing only products where the *productName* column value matches the value in the WHERE clause is retrieved. The results are shown in Figure 2-2.

	productId	productName	listPrice
1	2019	Gears of War®	39.99
2	2020	Gears of War® 2	59.99

FIGURE 2-2 *SELECT* query results

So far, the query contains much of the information needed to run the majority of queries against a data source. The exception is probably situations where data needs to be selected from more than one table, which requires the use of table joins. Using joins makes the query only slightly more complex:

```
SELECT p.productId, p.productName, p.listPrice, g.Genre
FROM product p INNER JOIN Game g on g.ProductID = p.ProductID
WHERE p.productName LIKE '%gears%'
```

Here the product table is joined to the game table based upon matching ProductID columns. This example introduces the SQL join syntax INNER JOIN, which essentially means that only those rows for which the specified column values match get returned in the query results. Another type of SQL join is an OUTER JOIN:

```
SELECT p.productId, p.productName, p.listPrice, g.Genre
FROM product p LEFT OUTER JOIN Game g on g.ProductID = p.ProductID
WHERE p.productName LIKE '%gears%'
```

This time, instead of the query returning only rows where the columns specified in the JOIN clause match, records are returned as before (where column values match) but also where the left table (the table on the left side of the join, in this case, Product) has a record but the right side (in this case, the Game table) does not have a matching record. In those circumstances, any columns that are from the non-matching table are retrieved as NULL values. In the previous example, this might look like the results in Figure 2-3.

	productId	productName	listPrice	Genre
1	2019	Gears of War®	39.99	NULL
2	2020	Gears of War® 2	59.99	NULL

FIGURE 2-3 Using LEFT OUTER JOIN

The alternative to LEFT OUTER JOIN is to use RIGHT OUTER JOIN. As the syntax suggests, records from the right side of the join are retrieved regardless of whether the join condition matches values on the left side of the join.

The sorting of data is achieved using another clause as part of the query. This is the ORDER BY clause. ORDER BY takes one or more parameters which, in conjunction with ASC (ascending) or DESC (descending), specifies the order in which data should be returned:

```
SELECT p.productId, p.productName, p.listPrice, g.Genre as Genre
FROM product p inner join Game g on g.ProductID = p.ProductID
WHERE p.productName like '%gears%'
ORDER BY p.ProductName ASC, p.ListPrice DESC
```

The previous query orders the data first by the values in the ProductName column (in ascending order), then by values in the ListPrice column (in descending order).

Finally, another useful feature of SQL is the ability to aggregate data. A simple example of an aggregating function might be the following:

```
SELECT SUM(p.listPrice) as TotalPrice
FROM product p
WHERE p.productName like '%g%'
```

This query adds all the values in the product.listPrice column for records where *productName* matches the WHERE clause. For more complex situations, for example where one might want to get totals based on some changing criteria, the GROUP BY clause can be introduced:

```
SELECT pt.ProductTypeName as ProductType, SUM(p.listPrice) as
CostByProductType
FROM product p INNER JOIN productType pt on pt.ProductTypeID =
    p.ProductTypeID
GROUP BY pt.ProductTypeName
```

The GROUP BY clause groups the data by matching the specified column value, so an aggregated value is produced for each group of data. In the previous query, this produces the output shown in Figure 2-4.

	ProductType	CostByProductType
1	Accessory	25
2	Console	399.99
3	Game	134327.590000001

FIGURE 2-4 Using GROUP BY to show total cost by Product Type

Other aggregation functions are available in SQL such as *COUNT, AVG* (Average), *MAX* (Maximum Value), and *MIN* (Minimum Value).

Whatever the format of the query, whether executed directly as a SQL statement or through the execution of a stored procedure, the handling of data in terms of quantity returned to the client demands some important decisions. Does the client need all of the data at once? Could it instead be returned in smaller batches to increase client performance? Check out the Lab at the end of this lesson to look at one of the options available for providing data paging which retrieves the data rows in batches. Also, ADO.NET Data Services provide an effective method of data paging which is described in Chapter 10.

Once the query has been written to retrieve the data from the data source, it must be consumed on the client using one of the classes provided. This is achieved through classes such as *DataReader*, which is discussed in detail in the following section.

Using *DataReader*

DataReader is used to retrieve a read-only, forward-only set of data from a data source. *DataReader* retrieves data as the query is executed rather than waiting for the query to finish, which can be beneficial to application performance. Only a single row of data is stored in memory at any time. *DataReader* is a good class to use when data needs to be processed sequentially and performance and memory considerations are important.

DataReader is assigned by using the *ExecuteReader* method of the *Command* object. Once assigned, the *Read* method of the *DataReader* is used to retrieve further rows of data:

```
' VB
Dim theDataReader As SqlDataReader
theDataReader = _
    theCommand.ExecuteReader(CommandBehavior.CloseConnection)

Dim outputRow As String = String.Empty

If (theDataReader.HasRows) Then
    Console.WriteLine("ExecuteReader results...\n\n")
    While (theDataReader.Read())
        outputRow = theDataReader.GetString(0).PadRight(50) & vbTab & _
            theDataReader.GetString(1) & vbCrLf
        Console.WriteLine(outputRow)
    End While
End If
```

```
// C#
SqlDataReader theDataReader =
    theCommand.ExecuteReader(CommandBehavior.CloseConnection);

string outputRow = String.Empty;
```

```
        if (theDataReader.HasRows)
        {
            while (theDataReader.Read())
            {
                outputRow =
                    theDataReader.GetString[0].PadRight(50) + "\t" +
                        theDataReader.GetString[1] + "\n";

                Console.WriteLine(outputRow);
            }
        }
```

After *DataReader* has been used and no more data is available, it is important to call the *Close* method. Until *DataReader* is closed, any output parameters or return values are unavailable. In addition, while the *DataReader* is open, the active *Connection* is used exclusively by that *DataReader* and no other *Commands* can be executed until the original *DataReader* is closed.

The *SqlClient* implementation of *DbDataReader* and *SqlDataReader*, has a number of useful methods that give access to the returned columns. For best performance, several methods are exposed, giving access to the column values in their native datatypes. These include *GetBoolean()*, *GetInt32()*, and *GetString()*, where the parameter to supply refers to the ordinal position of the column. Obviously, prior knowledge of the selected column datatypes is required to use these methods.

In a similar fashion, column values can be retrieved in their *SqlTypes* form using another series of exposed methods such as *GetSqlBoolean()*, *GetSqlInt32()*, and *GetSqlString()*.

Alternatively, the individual columns can be accessed using the *Item* property of *DataReader*, which is overloaded to allow a parameter of column index or column name.

DataReader also provides support for multiple result sets. If multiple result sets are returned, the *NextResult* method of *DataReader* should be used, which iterates through each returned result set in order. Taking the previous code snippet as an example, if multiple result sets were returned by the executed query, the code would look similar to this:

```
' VB
Dim theDataReader As SqlDataReader
theDataReader = _
    theCommand.ExecuteReader(CommandBehavior.CloseConnection)

Dim outputRow As String = String.Empty
Dim hasMoreResults as Boolean = True

If (theDataReader.HasRows) Then
    Console.WriteLine("ExecuteReader results...\n\n")
    While (hasMoreResults)
        While (theDataReader.Read())
            outputRow = theDataReader.GetString(0).PadRight(50) & vbTab & _
                theDataReader.GetString(1) & vbCrLf
```

```
            Console.WriteLine(outputRow)
        End While
        hasMoreResults = theDataReader.NextResult()
    End While
End If
```

```csharp
// C#
SqlDataReader theDataReader =
    theCommand.ExecuteReader(CommandBehavior.CloseConnection);

string outputRow = String.Empty;

if (theDataReader.HasRows)
{
    bool hasMoreResults = true;
    while (hasMoreResults)
    {
        while (theDataReader.Read())
        {
            outputRow =
                theDataReader.GetString[0].PadRight(50) + "\t" +
                theDataReader.GetString[1] + "\n";

            Console.WriteLine(outputRow);
        }
        hasMoreResults = theDataReader.NextResult();
    }
}
```

For situations where something more than a sequential, read-only, forward-only set of results is required, there are alternatives. These include *DataAdapter* and *TableAdapter*, which are discussed in the following section.

Using *DbDataAdapter* and *DbTableAdapter*

DataAdapter is a conduit between a client *DataSet* and the data source. It provides easy methods to retrieve, insert, update, or delete data. Depending upon the direction of the data, either the *Fill* method or the *Update* method is employed, which causes *DataAdapter* to change the data in the *DataSet* to match the data source (in the case of the *Fill* method) or to change the data in the data source to match that in the *DataSet* (with the *Update* method).

A simple example of using the *SqlDataAdapter* is presented in the following code snippet:

```vbnet
' VB
Dim theDataAdapter As SqlDataAdapter
theDataAdapter = New SqlDataAdapter(theCommand)

Dim theDataset As DataSet = New DataSet()
theDataAdapter.Fill(theDataset)
```

```
// C#
SqlDataAdapter theDataAdapter = new SqlDataAdapter(theCommand);
DataSet theDataset = new DataSet();
theDataAdapter.Fill(theDataset);
```

The *Fill* method is overloaded and can take a number of different parameters to suit requirements. Because this is an important method, the overloads are listed in Table 2-8.

TABLE 2-8 The *Fill* Method Overloads

NAME	DESCRIPTION
Fill(DataSet)	Adds or refreshes *DataSet* rows.
Fill(DataTable)	Adds or refreshes *DataSet* rows in a specified range so as to match those in the data source using the *DataTable* name.
Fill(DataTable, IDataReader)	Adds or refreshes *DataTable* rows in the to match those in the data source using the *DataTable* name and the provided *IDataReader*.
Fill(DataSet, String)	Adds or refreshes *DataSet* rows to match those in the data source using the *DataSet* and *DataTable* names.
Fill(DataTable, IDbCommand, CommandBehavior)	Adds or refreshes *DataTable* rows to match those in the data source using the specified *DataTable*, *IDbCommand*, and *CommandBehavior*.
Fill(Int32, Int32, array<DataTable>[]()[])	Adds or refreshes *DataTable* rows in a to match those in the data source. The *Fill* starts at the specified record and retrieves up to the specified maximum number of records.
Fill(array<DataTable>[]()[], IDataReader, Int32, Int32)	Adds or refreshes *DataTable* rows in a specified range to match those in the data source.
Fill(DataSet, Int32, Int32, String)	Adds or refreshes *DataSet* rows in a specified range to match those in the data source using the *DataSet* and *DataTable* names.
Fill(DataSet, String, IDataReader, Int32, Int32)	Adds or refreshes *DataSet* rows in a specified range to match those in the data source using the *DataSet* and *DataTable* names.
Fill(array<DataTable>[]()[], Int32, Int32, IDbCommand, CommandBehavior)	Adds or refreshes *DataSet* rows in a specified range to match those in the data source using the *DataSet* and *DataTable* names.
Fill(DataSet, Int32, Int32, String, IDbCommand, CommandBehavior)	Adds or refreshes *DataSet* rows in a specified range to match those in the data source using the *DataSet* and source table names, command string, and command behavior.

The slightly more complex (and indeed ingenious) side of *SqlDataAdapter* relates to the updating of data. When a *SqlDataAdapter* is instantiated, as the previous code snippet shows, it is possible to provide a *Command* to the constructor. This *Command*, by default, is used to populate the *SelectCommand* property of the *DataAdapter*. When the *Fill* method is called on the *DataAdapter*, the retrieval of data is performed using the contents of the *SelectCommand* property. Alongside this property are others that cover deleting, inserting, and updating—the *DeleteCommand, InsertCommand,* and *UpdateCommand* properties. Each property contains a reference to a *Command* object used to perform the individual operations.

As was demonstrated previously in Listing 2-2, to populate the action query properties automatically, a *SqlCommandBuilder* must be used and primed with a populated *SELECT Command* object where the *SELECT* statement is a simple, single table query. This is fine unless you need to use queries with JOINs, but for operations, such as calling a stored procedure, a manual approach to assigning the property values is required.

This is as simple as constructing a new *Command* object for each of the types of action query required (which could be a *CommandType.Text* query or a call to a stored procedure) and assigning them to the relevant *DataAdapter* property. After any desired operation has taken place within the *DataSet,* the *Update* method can be called on the *DataAdapter,* which puts the data back into the proper format for the data store and executes the action query.

An alternative to *DataAdapter* is *TableAdapter.* Though conceptually quite similar, *TableAdapter* is an evolutionary step from *DataAdapter* in terms of simplicity and functionality, such as the ability to contain multiple queries. *TableAdapter* also has a built-in *Connection* object.

TableAdapters are created using the DataSet Designer in Visual Studio. The toolbox contains objects that can be used to create a *DataSet,* including *TableAdapter.* Dragging the icon onto the design surface opens a TableAdapter wizard, which allows easy configuration, including the ability to specify the properties of the *Connection* and how and whether to autogenerate the action queries (if the *SELECT* statement is single-table in nature). Figure 2-5 shows the wizard in action.

After the *TableAdapter* has been created by completing the wizard, a representation of it appears on the design surface of the DataSet Designer, as in Figure 2-6.

Observe how the bottom part of *TableAdapter,* under the *ProductTableAdapter* heading, has the name of the two methods configured during the wizard process: *Fill* and *GetData.*

By right-clicking the mouse in this area, a context menu appears which offers the option to add a query. By specifying a query to use and entering a method name, additional *TableAdapter* queries can be created and called as necessary.

As with *DataAdapter, TableAdapter* uses the *DeleteCommand, InsertCommand, SelectCommand,* and *UpdateCommand* properties to hold the individual commands required for CRUD operations. These commands can all be specified in the DataSet Designer using the properties window. The *Update* method of *TableAdapter* is used to perform the action queries.

As an alternative, the created *TableAdapter* can be referenced and configured within code.

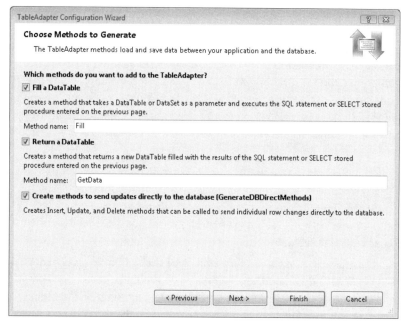

FIGURE 2-5 Choosing which methods to generate for *TableAdapter*

FIGURE 2-6 The visual representation of *TableAdapter*

Asynchronous Queries

For long-running queries, or simply to provide a more responsive user experience, one option is to consider executing queries against a data source asynchronously. Although the idea might sound complex, it is actually quite easy to implement asynchronous processing through methods provided by the various methods on the *DataReader* class. In situations where asynchronous processing isn't offered natively through the object model (for example when using *DbAdapter*), slightly more knowledge of the .NET Framework is required to create a method delegate and to handle the processing of additional threads.

With regards to the *DataReader* class, the following code demonstrates how asynchronous processing can be achieved. A more detailed examination follows the code block.

```vb
' VB
Sub Main()

    Dim theConnectionString As String

    theConnectionString = "Data Source=jim-pc;Initial " & _
        "Catalog=VideoGameStoreDB;Integrated Security=SSPI;Asynchronous " & _
        "Processing=true;"

    Dim theConnection As SqlConnection = New _
        SqlConnection(theConnectionString)

    Dim theCommand As SqlCommand

    theCommand = New SqlCommand("SELECT * FROM PRODUCT", theConnection)

    theConnection.Open()

    Console.WriteLine("Connection Open and asynchronous processing starting.")

    theCommand.BeginExecuteReader(New AsyncCallback(AddressOf DataReady), theCommand)

    Console.ReadKey()

End Sub

Private Sub DataReady(ByVal asyncResult As IAsyncResult)

    Dim theCommand As SqlCommand = asyncResult.AsyncState

    theCommand.EndExecuteReader(asyncResult)

    theCommand.Connection.Close()

    Console.WriteLine("Data Ready for use.")

End Sub
```

```csharp
// C#
static void Main(string[] args)
{
    string theConnectionString =
        "Data Source=jim-pc;Initial Catalog=VideoGameStoreDB;Integrated
        Security=SSPI;";
```

```
SqlConnection theConnection = new SqlConnection(theConnectionString);
SqlCommand theCommand = new SqlCommand("SELECT * FROM PRODUCT",
    theConnection);

theConnection.Open();

Console.WriteLine("Connection Open and asynchronous processing
    started.");

theCommand.BeginExecuteReader(new AsyncCallback(DataReady), theCommand);

Console.ReadKey();
}

private static void DataReady(IAsyncResult asyncResult)
{
    SqlCommand theCommand = (SqlCommand) asyncResult.AsyncState;

    theCommand.EndExecuteReader(asyncResult)

    theCommand.Connection.Close();

    Console.WriteLine("Data Ready for use.");
}
```

This code, instead of calling the *ExecuteReader* method directly, calls the *BeginExecuteReader* method, which is its asynchronous counterpart. By providing what is referred to as a callback (a separate method) and passing a reference to it to the *BeginExecuteReader* method, the callback method is executed as soon as the *DataReader* has retrieved data.

After the callback method is called, within it a reference to the running *SqlCommand* is retrieved and the *EndExecuteReader* method should be called before closing the *Connection*.

As mentioned previously, implementing asynchronous processing when using other classes such as *DataAdapter* is not offered natively through the *DataAdapter* class. This must be implemented through more traditional asynchronous processing methods using the *System. Threading* namespace. Although this topic is beyond the scope of this chapter, it is worth identifying that the principles behind providing asynchronicity are very similar to the previous example. A callback method is still used (but implemented through what are called *Delegates*) but a new *System.Threading.Thread* is created and executed to perform the processing while the main thread continues and awaits an event signifying that data processing has completed.

> **MORE INFO** **SYSTEM.THREADING NAMESPACE AND ASYNCHRONOUS PROGRAMMING**
>
> Information about the *System.Threading* namespace and Asynchronous programming using the .NET Framework can be found on the Microsoft MSDN website at
> *http://msdn.microsoft.com/en-us/library/2e08f6yc.aspx.*

Special Datatypes

There are a handful of datatypes that can be considered as special cases when dealing with command execution, because they must be treated in a particular way. Some are new to SQL Server 2008 and ADO.NET 3.5 SP1.

Using BLOBs

The acronym BLOB stands for Binary Large Object, such as an MP3 file or a video file. An advantage of using BLOBs in a database is that they can be read directly from the database rather than containing a reference to a filesystem location. Because BLOBs can be large—certainly more than the few bytes in size that most other datatypes are—their use in code in terms of retrieving, inserting, and updating BLOB values requires special handling. Depending upon the type of BLOB, they can be stored using the *nvarchar(max)*, *varbinary(max)*, or *varchar(max)* datatypes.

The *GetBytes* method of the *SqlDataReader* can be employed to retrieve a *varbinary(max)* value as a byte array, whereas the *GetString* method can be used to retrieve the *nvarchar(max)* or *varchar(max)* value as a string.

SqlDataAdapter automatically converts a *varbinary(max)* value to a byte array and the *nvarchar(max)* and *varchar(max)* values to strings. This makes consuming and writing BLOBs incredibly easy.

In addition, the *GetSqlBytes* method can be used to retrieve *varbinary(max)* values as *SqlBytes* objects, and the *GetSqlString* and *GetSqlChars* methods to retrieve *nvarchar(max)* and *varchar(max)* values as *SqlString* or *SqlChars* objects.

FileStream

The *FileStream* datatype can be used as an alternative to using BLOBs. The *FileStream* storage attribute is used in conjunction with the *varbinary(max)* datatype to store binary data on the filesystem, yet make it accessible and manageable through the usual querying methods.

The BLOB data is stored in the filesystem in special FILESTREAM filegroups, which are referred to as *containers*. These containers contain the filesystem directories, not the files themselves. The files cannot be opened from the filesystem directly; instead, they must be accessed through SQL Server. One big advantage is that the storage size is not limited by SQL Server—the BLOB can be as large as the filesystem volume.

The following code snippet demonstrates how the standard *SqlCommand* and *SqlDataReader* can be employed to read and write to a column specified with the *FILESTREAM* storage attribute:

```
' VB
Dim theConnectionString As String

theConnectionString = "Data Source=jim-pc;Initial " & _
"Catalog=VideoGameStoreDB;Integrated Security=SSPI;"
```

```
Dim theConnection As SqlConnection
theConnection = New SqlConnection(theConnectionString)

theConnection.Open()

If (theConnection.State = System.Data.ConnectionState.Open) Then
   Console.WriteLine("Database Connection is Open\n\n")
End If


Dim theCommand As SqlCommand = New SqlCommand()
theCommand.Connection = theConnection

theCommand.CommandText = "select Top(1) SupplierName, " & _
   GET_FILESTREAM_TRANSACTION_CONTEXT () FROM product"

Dim theReader As SqlDataReader = theCommand.ExecuteReader()

While (theReader.Read())

   Dim filePath = theReader.GetString(0)

   Dim transactionContext As Byte() = theReader.GetSqlBytes(1).Buffer

   Dim fileStream As SqlFileStream = New SqlFileStream(filePath, _
      theReader.GetValue(1), _
      FileAccess.ReadWrite, _
      FileOptions.SequentialScan, 0)


   fileStream.Seek(0, SeekOrigin.End)

   ' Append a single byte
   fileStream.WriteByte(1)
   fileStream.Close()

End While

// C#
SqlConnection theConnection = new SqlConnection(theConnectionString);

theConnection.Open();

if (theConnection.State == System.Data.ConnectionState.Open)
   Console.WriteLine("Database Connection is Open\n\n");
```

```
SqlCommand theCommand = new SqlCommand();
theCommand.Connection = theConnection;

theCommand.CommandText = "select Top(1) SupplierName,
    GET_FILESTREAM_TRANSACTION_CONTEXT () FROM product";

using (SqlDataReader reader = theCommand.ExecuteReader())
{
    while (reader.Read())
    {
        // Get the pointer for file
        string path = reader.GetString(0);
        byte[] transactionContext = reader.GetSqlBytes(1).Buffer;

        SqlFileStream fileStream = new SqlFileStream(path,
            (byte[])reader.GetValue(1),
            FileAccess.ReadWrite,
            FileOptions.SequentialScan, 0);

        fileStream.Seek(0, SeekOrigin.End);
        fileStream.WriteByte(0x01);
        fileStream.Close();
    }
}
```

Using Spatial Datatypes

SQL Server 2008 features two new datatypes for handling spatial data. The geometry datatype
supports planar (Euclidean) data. The *geometry* datatype conforms to the Open Geospatial
Consortium (OGC) Simple Features for SQL Specification. In addition, support is included for the
geography datatype, which can store ellipsoidal data such as global positioning system (GPS)
latitude and longitude coordinates.

The *geometry* and *geography* datatypes support 11 spatial data objects (or instance types),
only 7 of which can be instantiated. They derive properties from their parent datatypes,
distinguishing them as *Points, LineStrings, Polygons,* or a *GeometryCollection* containing
multiple *geometry* or *geography* instances.

Although the concepts and specifications behind the structure and usage of geographical
data are beyond the scope of this book, it is worth looking at an brief example in code that
demonstrates how to access and manipulate these new datatypes:

```
' VB
Dim theCommand As SqlCommand = New SqlCommand()
theCommand.Connection = theConnection

Dim spatialValue As SqlGeometry = New SqlGeometry()
```

```
Dim theGeoBuilder As SqlGeometryBuilder = New SqlGeometryBuilder()

theGeoBuilder.AddLine(10.0, 20.0)

spatialValue = theGeoBuilder.ConstructedGeometry

theCommand.CommandText = "AddGeometry"
theCommand.CommandType = CommandType.StoredProcedure

theCommand.Parameters.Add("reviews", SqlDbType.Udt)
theCommand.Parameters("location").UdtTypeName = "GEOMETRY"
theCommand.Parameters("location").SourceVersion = DataRowVersion.Current
theCommand.Parameters("location").Value = spatialValue

theCommand.ExecuteNonQuery()

// C#
SqlCommand theCommand = new SqlCommand();
theCommand.Connection = theConnection;

SqlGeometry spatialValue = new SqlGeometry();
SqlGeometryBuilder theGeoBuilder = new SqlGeometryBuilder();

theGeoBuilder.AddLine(10.0, 20.0);

spatialValue = theGeoBuilder.ConstructedGeometry;

theCommand.CommandText = "AddGeometry";
theCommand.CommandType = CommandType.StoredProcedure;

theCommand.Parameters.Add("reviews", SqlDbType.Udt);
theCommand.Parameters["location"].UdtTypeName = "GEOMETRY";
theCommand.Parameters["location"].SourceVersion =
    DataRowVersion.Current;

theCommand.Parameters["location"].Value = spatialValue;

theCommand.ExecuteNonQuery();
```

> **MORE INFO** **SPATIAL DATA**
>
> A more detailed discussion around the use of Spatial Data with the .NET Framework and SQL Server 2008, including the data standards involved, can be found at *http://msdn.microsoft.com/en-us/library/bb933876.aspx.*

Table Value Parameters

Table Value Parameters are new to T-SQL in SQL Server 2008. This allows the use of a *TABLE* value instance of a parameter so it can be passed to a stored procedure. Essentially, this makes it much easier to pass a set of values to a stored procedure without making multiple round trips. The following code demonstrates how this new feature can be used:

```vb
' VB
Dim theCommand As SqlCommand = New SqlCommand()
theCommand.Connection = theConnection

' a TVP can be a DataTable, IEnumerable<SqlDataRecord> or DbDataReader.
Dim theDataTable As DataTable = New DataTable()
theDataTable.Columns.Add("productid", Type.GetType("System.Int32"))
theDataTable.Columns.Add("score", Type.GetType("System.Int32"))

' use productid 2020 for 'Gears Of War 2'
theDataTable.Rows.Add(New Object() {2020, 10})

' and another score for GoW2
theDataTable.Rows.Add(New Object() {2020, 9})

theCommand.CommandText = "AddReview"
theCommand.CommandType = CommandType.StoredProcedure

theCommand.Parameters.Add("reviews", SqlDbType.Structured)
theCommand.Parameters("reviews").Value = theDataTable
theCommand.ExecuteNonQuery()

Console.WriteLine("Data Added to ReviewScores table via TVP:\n\n")
```

```csharp
// C#
SqlCommand theCommand = new SqlCommand();
theCommand.Connection = theConnection;

// a TVP can be a DataTable, IEnumerable<SqlDataRecord> or DbDataReader.
DataTable theDataTable = new DataTable();
theDataTable.Columns.Add("productid", Type.GetType("System.Int32"));
theDataTable.Columns.Add("score", Type.GetType("System.Int32"));
// use productid 2020 for 'Gears Of War 2'
theDataTable.Rows.Add(new object[] {2020, 10});
// and another score for GoW2
theDataTable.Rows.Add(new object[] { 2020, 9});

theCommand.CommandText = "AddReview";
theCommand.CommandType = CommandType.StoredProcedure;
```

```
theCommand.Parameters.Add("reviews", SqlDbType.Structured);
theCommand.Parameters["reviews"].Value = theDataTable;

theCommand.ExecuteNonQuery();
```

Using LINQ

Language Integrated Query (LINQ) is a very useful technology that can be used to query a variety of objects from within the C# or VB.NET language in syntax not dissimilar to SQL. LINQ to SQL is a particular implementation of LINQ that is used to provide a layer of abstraction away from the database. The manipulation of objects instead of the data source directly negates the need to issue database commands.

Chapter 6, "Introducing LINQ," examines LINQ in much more detail.

LAB   Consuming Data

In this lab, you create a console application which connects to a data source using the *SqlClient* provider and retrieve data. Using *DataReader,* you implement a simple example of data paging.

As with the previous exercises, you need to have the *VideoGameStoreDB* installed. You can install the files for this lab, including the complete solution containing the code for all the exercises, from the Code folder on the companion CD.

EXERCISE 1   Implementing Data Paging Using *DataReader*

In this exercise, you connect to a SQL Server database using the *SqlClient* data provider and, using *SqlDataReader,* implement data paging to allow forward and backward navigation through the data.

1. Start a new Console project named *SqlClientDataPaging.*

2. Add a connection string to the project settings named *VideoGameStoreDB* and have it contain a valid connection string to the *VideoGameStore* database.

3. Add an assembly reference to System.Configuration.dll.

4. Add a class named *PagingDataAccessComponent.*

5. Add a method named *PageThroughProductTable* by performing the following steps:

    a. Get a reference to the connection string from the application configuration.

    b. Create a *SqlClient* connection.

    c. Open the database connection.

    d. Create a *SqlDataReader* and a *DataSet* and use the proper *Fill* method overload to read data in chunks of 10 rows.

    e. Check key presses for Next Page and Previous Page, handle the population of the paged data, and wait for user input. Create a loop which uses the *Fill* method, as in step d, to populate the *DataSet* with records beginning at the correct offset.

f. Close the connection.

g. Implement exception handling.

h. Make sure the *Main()* method of the *Program* class instantiates the *PagingDataAccessComponent* and calls the *PageThroughProductTable* method.

Your code should look like this:

```vb
' VB
Public Function PageThroughProductTable() As Boolean

    Dim returnMessage As String = String.Empty
    Dim anError As Boolean = False


    Try

        Dim theConnectionString As ConnectionStringSettings = _
            ConfigurationManager.ConnectionStrings _
            ("TK70561.Properties.Settings.VideoGameStoreDB")

        Dim theConnection As SqlConnection = New _
            SqlConnection(theConnectionString.ConnectionString)

        theConnection.Open()

        Dim theCommand As SqlCommand = New SqlCommand()
        theCommand.Connection = theConnection

        theCommand.CommandText = "SELECT * FROM product"
        theCommand.CommandType = CommandType.Text

        ' DataSet
        Dim theDataAdapter As SqlDataAdapter = New SqlDataAdapter(theCommand)

        Dim startPosition As Integer = 1
        Dim recordsToRetrieve As Integer = 10
        Dim pageNumber As Integer = 1
        Dim readData As Boolean = True
        Dim theKey As ConsoleKeyInfo
        Dim localDataSet As DataSet

        While (readData)

            Try
                localDataSet = GetPagedData(theDataAdapter, "productsbyname", _
                    startPosition, recordsToRetrieve)
```

```vbnet
            If (localDataSet.Tables("productsbyname").Rows.Count > 0) Then
                Console.WriteLine(vbCrLf & vbCrLf)
                Console.WriteLine("------ Page " & pageNumber.ToString() & _
                    "".PadRight(30, "-"))
                Console.WriteLine(vbCrLf & vbCrLf)

                For Each theRow As DataRow In _
                    localDataSet.Tables("productsbyname").Rows

                Console.WriteLine(theRow("ProductName").ToString() & vbTab & _
                    theRow("ReleaseDate").ToString() & vbCrLf)
                Next

                Console.WriteLine(vbCrLf & vbCrLf & " Press F to page data " & _
                    Forwards or B for backwards (or Q to exit)")

                theKey = Console.ReadKey(True)

                If (theKey.Key = ConsoleKey.F) Then
                    If (localDataSet.Tables("productsbyname").Rows.Count = _
                        recordsToRetrieve) Then
                        startPosition += recordsToRetrieve
                        pageNumber = pageNumber + 1
                    Else
                        Console.WriteLine("Already at end of data")
                    End If
                ElseIf (theKey.Key = ConsoleKey.Q) Then
                    Exit While
                ElseIf (theKey.Key = ConsoleKey.B) Then
                    If (pageNumber > 1) Then
                        startPosition = startPosition - recordsToRetrieve
                            pageNumber = pageNumber - 1
                    Else
                        Console.WriteLine("Already at start of data")
                    End If
                End If
            Else
                readData = False
            End If

        Catch
            anError = True
            readData = False
        End Try
    End While
```

```
        theConnection.Close()

    Catch
        anError = True
    End Try


    Return anError

End Function

Private Function GetPagedData(ByVal theDataAdapter As SqlDataAdapter, _
    ByVal tableName As String, ByVal startPosition As Integer, _
    ByVal recordCount As Integer) As DataSet

    Dim theDataSet As DataSet = New DataSet()

    Try
        theDataAdapter.Fill(theDataSet, startPosition, recordCount, tableName)

    Catch
        Throw New ApplicationException("Exception Occured")
    End Try

    Return theDataSet

End Function

// C#
public bool PageThroughProductTable()
{
    string returnMessage = String.Empty;
    bool anError = false;

    try
    {
        ConnectionStringSettings theConnectionString =
        ConfigurationManager.ConnectionStrings
        ["TK70561.Properties.Settings.VideoGameStoreDB"];

        SqlConnection theConnection = new
            SqlConnection(theConnectionString.ConnectionString);

        theConnection.Open();
```

```
SqlCommand theCommand = new SqlCommand();
theCommand.Connection = theConnection;

theCommand.CommandText = "SELECT * FROM product";
theCommand.CommandType = CommandType.Text;

// DataSet
SqlDataAdapter theDataAdapter = new SqlDataAdapter(theCommand);

int startPosition = 1;
int recordsToRetrieve = 10;
int pageNumber = 1;
bool readData = true;
ConsoleKeyInfo theKey;
DataSet localDataSet;

do
{
   try
   {
      localDataSet = GetPagedData(theDataAdapter, "productsbyname",
         startPosition, recordsToRetrieve);

   if (localDataSet.Tables["productsbyname"].Rows.Count > 0)
   {
      Console.WriteLine("\n\n");
      Console.WriteLine("------ Page " + pageNumber.ToString() +
         "".PadRight(30, '-'));
      Console.WriteLine("\n\n");

         foreach (DataRow theRow in localDataSet.Tables["productsbyname"].Rows)
         {
            Console.WriteLine(theRow["ProductName"].ToString() + "\t" +
               theRow["ReleaseDate"].ToString() + "\n");
         }
      Console.WriteLine("\n\n Press F to page data forwards or B for
         backwards (or Q to exit)");
      theKey = Console.ReadKey(true);
      if (theKey.Key == ConsoleKey.F)
      {
         if (localDataSet.Tables["productsbyname"].Rows.Count ==
            recordsToRetrieve)
         {
            startPosition += recordsToRetrieve;
            pageNumber++;
         }
```

```
            else
            {
                Console.WriteLine("Already at end of data");
            }
        }
        else if (theKey.Key == ConsoleKey.Q)
        {
            break;
        }
        else if (theKey.Key == ConsoleKey.B)
        {
            if (pageNumber > 1)
            {
            startPosition -= recordsToRetrieve;
            pageNumber--;
            }
            else
                Console.WriteLine("Already at start of data");
            }
        }
        else
        {
            readData = false;
        }
    }
    catch (Exception ex)
    {
        anError = true;
        readData = false;
    }
    } while (readData);

    theConnection.Close();
  }
  catch (Exception exception)
  {
    anError = true;
  }
  return anError;
}

private static DataSet GetPagedData(SqlDataAdapter theDataAdapter,
  string tableName, int startPosition, int recordCount)
  {
  DataSet theDataSet = new DataSet();
```

```
        try
        {
            theDataAdapter.Fill(theDataSet, startPosition, recordCount, tableName);
        }
        catch (Exception ex)
        {
            Console.WriteLine(ex.ToString());
        }

        return theDataSet;
    }
```

EXERCISE 2   Using the *CommandBuilder* and the *DataAdapter*

In this exercise, you use the *CommandBuilder* class to select data from a database and change the value of one of the columns.

1. Start a new Class Library project named DataAccessLayer.

2. Add a connection string to the project settings named *SqlClientVideoGameStoreDB* and have it contain a valid *SqlClient*-specific connection string to the *VideoGameStore* database.

3. Add an assembly reference to System.Configuration.dll.

4. Add a class named *DataAccessComponent*.

5. Add a method named *UpdateProductTable* by performing the following steps:

   a. Get a reference to the connection string from the application configuration.

   b. Create a *SqlClient* connection.

   c. Open the database connection.

   d. Open the connection.

   e. Define a *SqlCommand* object to select a row from the Product table where the product name is "Gears of War."

   f. Use *SqlCommandBuilder* to configure a *SqlDataAdapter* and autogenerate the *Insert, Update,* and *Delete* methods.

   g. Use *SqlDataAdapter* to update the ListPrice column to 89.99.

   h. Close the connection.

   i. Implement exception handling.

   j. Return the number of rows affected.

   Your code should look like this:

   ' VB
```
Public Function UpdateProductTable() As Integer

    Dim rowsAffected As Integer = 0
```

```
    Try

        Dim theConnectionString As ConnectionStringSettings
        theConnectionString = _
            ConfigurationManager.ConnectionStrings _
            ("TK70561.My.MySettings.VideoGameStoreDB")

        Dim theConnection As SqlConnection = New _
            SqlConnection(theConnectionString.ConnectionString)

        theConnection.Open()

        Dim theCommand As SqlCommand = New SqlCommand()
        theCommand.Connection = theConnection
        theCommand.CommandText = "SELECT productId, listPrice FROM product " & _
            "WHERE productName = 'Gears of War®'"
        theCommand.CommandType = System.Data.CommandType.Text

        Dim theDataAdapter As SqlDataAdapter
        theDataAdapter = New SqlDataAdapter(theCommand)

        Dim theBuilder As SqlCommandBuilder
        theBuilder = New SqlCommandBuilder(theDataAdapter)

        Dim theDataset As DataSet = New DataSet()

        theDataAdapter.Fill(theDataset)

        ' update the value
        theDataset.Tables(0).Rows(0)("listPrice") = 89.99

        rowsAffected = theDataAdapter.Update(theDataset)

        theConnection.Close()

    Catch anException As Exception

        Throw New ApplicationException("Exception Occured")

    End Try

    Return rowsAffected

End Function
```

```csharp
//  C#
public int UpdateProductTable()
{
   int rowsAffected = 0;

   try
   {

      ConnectionStringSettings theConnectionString =
         ConfigurationManager.ConnectionStrings
         ["TK70561.Properties.Settings.VideoGameStoreDB"];

      SqlConnection theConnection = new
         SqlConnection(theConnectionString.ConnectionString);

      theConnection.Open();

      SqlCommand theCommand = new SqlCommand();
      theCommand.Connection = theConnection;
      theCommand.CommandText = "SELECT productId, listPrice FROM product
         WHERE productName = 'Gears of War®'";
      theCommand.CommandType = System.Data.CommandType.Text;

      SqlDataAdapter theDataAdapter = new SqlDataAdapter(theCommand);
      theDataAdapter.MissingSchemaAction = MissingSchemaAction.AddWithKey;

      SqlCommandBuilder theBuilder = new SqlCommandBuilder(theDataAdapter);

      DataSet theDataset = new DataSet();
      theDataAdapter.Fill(theDataset, "product");

      // modify the value
      theDataset.Tables[0].Rows[0]["listPrice"] = 89.99;

      rowsAffected = theDataAdapter.Update(theDataset, "product");

      theConnection.Close();

   }
   catch (Exception exception)
   {
      throw;
   }

   return rowsAffected;
}
```

6. Create a unit test by right-clicking the *UpdateProductTable* method.

7. Implement the unit test by using the *UpdateProductTable* method and check the return value.

   Your code should look like this:

   ```vb
   ' VB
   <TestMethod()> _
   Public Sub ConnectToDatabaseTest()
       Dim target As DataAccessComponent = New DataAccessComponent
       Dim expected As Integer = 1
       Dim actual As Integer
       actual = target.UpdateProductTable()
       Assert.AreEqual(expected, actual)
   End Sub
   ```

   ```csharp
   // C#
   [TestMethod()]
   public void ConnectToDatabaseTest()
   {
       DataAccessComponent target = new DataAccessComponent();
       int expected = 1;
       int actual;
       actual = target.UpdateProductTable();
       Assert.AreEqual(expected, actual);
   }
   ```

8. Run the unit test.

Lesson Summary

- The consumption of data is performed using a *DataReader*, a *DataAdapter*, a *TableAdapter*, or LINQ.
- *DataReader* consumes data sequentially and in an unbuffered fashion.
- *TableAdapter* can have multiple result sets by implementing any number of methods to retrieve data.

Lesson Review

You can use the following questions to test your knowledge of the information in Lesson 2, "Consuming Data Before You Begin." The questions also are available on the companion CD of this book if you prefer to review them in electronic form.

1. Which *SqlCommand* execution method is the most efficient way to retrieve the value of the first column of the first row from a table of data?

   A. The *ExecuteNonQuery* method

   B. The *ExecuteReader* method

   C. The *ExecuteXmlReader* method

   D. The *ExecuteScalar* method

2. Which of the following "special" datatypes can be used to pass a set of data to a stored procedure?

   A. The *Spatial* datatype

   B. The *VarChar* datatype

   C. Table Value Parameters

   D. The *varbinary(max)* datatype

Chapter Review

To practice and reinforce the skills you learned in this chapter further, you can do any or all of the following:

- Review the chapter summary.
- Review the list of key terms introduced in this chapter.
- Complete the case scenario. This scenario sets up a real-world situation involving the topics of this chapter and asks you to create a solution.
- Complete the suggested practices.
- Take a practice test.

Chapter Summary

- ADO.NET uses *Command* objects, *DataReaders*, *DataAdapters*, *TableAdapters*, and LINQ to retrieve data from a data source.
- Application performance can be improved when querying data using asynchronous processing.
- Using the *FILESTREAM* attribute on a *varbinary(max)* column allows BLOBs to be stored and accessed from within the database, limited only by filesystem storage space.
- *TableAdapter* is created and administered through the DataSet Designer.
- The LINQ implementation for use with SQL is called LINQ to SQL.
- It is preferable to select only the data that is required by using column names in a SQL query rather than the *SELECT* * construct.

Key Terms

Do you know what these key terms mean? You can check your answers by looking up the terms in the glossary at the end of the book.

- *Command* object
- *DataAdapter*
- *DataReader*
- *TableAdapter*

Case Scenario

In the following case scenario, you apply what you've learned about *Command* objects and how to consume data on the client. You can find answers to the questions posed in this scenario in the "Answers" section at the end of this book.

Case Scenario: Improving Application Performance

A coworker leaves your company and you inherit an important Windows Forms application. Your line manager has been receiving complaints from users that the application seems to freeze when retrieving large amounts of data from a SQL Server database. You are asked to investigate the problem and provide a solution as soon as possible. Previous investigation has revealed that the application uses a synchronous *DataReader* to retrieve the data.

QUESTION

Answer the following question for your manager:

- What can we do in the short term to improve the responsiveness of the application when data is being retrieved?

Suggested Practice

To help you master the exam objectives presented in this chapter, complete the following task.

- **Practice 1**   Create a reusable class library that can connect to a data source and consume data using all the different methods available—*DataReader*, *DataAdapter*, *TableAdapter*, and LINQ. Compare the performance of each method and try to discern why there is a performance differential and exactly where the differences lie.

Take a Practice Test

The practice tests on this book's companion CD offer many options. For example, you can test yourself on just the content covered in this chapter, or you can test yourself on the entire 70-561 certification exam content. You can set up the test so that it closely simulates the experience of taking a certification exam, or you can set it up in study mode, which allows you to look at the correct answers and explanations after you answer each question.

> **MORE INFO   PRACTICE TESTS**
>
> For details about all the available practice test options, see the section entitled "How to Use the Practice Tests," in the Introduction to this book.

CHAPTER 3

DataSets

*D*ataSets are the Microsoft .NET Framework solution for representing relational data in an in-memory structure. The in-memory structure can be a reflection of the tables in your database or a custom relational structure. Like a relational database, a *DataSet* can contain one or more tables, and tables consist of columns and rows. Tables within a *DataSet* can be related to each other and it is possible to implement constraints on them.

This chapter introduces you to the fundamentals of building applications using *DataSets* and reading data into *DataSets*. Lesson 1, "Introduction to *DataSets*," covers the basics: structure, reading data, and row validation. Lesson 2, "Working with *Typed DataSets*," explores the use of *Typed DataSets,* which are a feature of Microsoft Visual Studio that helps developers work with *DataSets* in a more efficient manner.

> **MORE INFO**   **UPDATING DATA**
>
> Updating data in the database based upon changes in your *DataSet* is covered in Chapter 4, "Updating Data."

Exam objectives in this chapter:

- Manage data by using the *DataAdapter* or the *TableAdapter*.
- Manage occasionally connected data.
- Programmatically create data objects.
- Work with untyped *DataSets* and *DataTables*.
- Expose a *DataTableReader* from a *DataTable* or from a *DataSet*.
- Work with strongly *Typed DataSets* and *DataTables*.

Lessons in this chapter:

Before You Begin

To complete the lessons in this chapter, you must have *Customer*:

- A computer that meets or exceeds the minimum hardware requirements listed in the "Introduction" section at the beginning of the book
- Visual Studio 2008 Professional Edition installed on your computer
- An understanding of Microsoft Visual Basic or C# syntax and familiarity with the .NET Framework version 3.5
- An understanding of relational data

 REAL WORLD

Mark Blomsma

When developing line of business applications, one of the first choices to make in terms of application architecture is how to deal with data. It all boils down to two choices: use some form of object relational mapping or use *DataSets*. When using object relational mapping, the data is read from a database and projected onto objects. The objects are used within your application. For instance, a customer is stored as a row in the database, it is read from the database, and then it is projected onto a customer class to create an in-memory object. The object is used to program your application or business logic.

DataSets take a different approach. A *DataSet* replicates the data from the database to memory in the format that the database produces it. This can be a mapping of tables in the database to *DataTables* in the *DataSet* or from views in the database to *DataTables* in the *DataSet* or from stored procedures to *DataTables* in the *DataSet*. Rows in the database are represented as *DataRows* in memory. The advantage is that no projection is needed and therefore no performance loss, which may be significant when dealing for instance with batch-oriented system. Another area where *DataTables* are strong is when dealing with views. A form or Web page which displays a listing of items based on a view or query really only needs to retrieve data from the database and bind it to a grid control. Little or no additional processing is needed. I've found *DataSets* to be very efficient for this purpose.

Lesson 1: Introduction to *DataSets*

DataSets comprise an extensive object model allowing you to represent data in a relational manner. In this lesson, you become familiar with the classes in the DataSet object model and also see how *DataSets* are database-independent by default yet can still deal with database-specific features when needed. You learn how *DataSets* can be serialized to Extensible Markup Language (XML) or binary format, making them powerful tools in a service-oriented environment.

After this lesson, you will be able to:

- Describe the objects in the *DataSet* object model
- Create a *DataSet* with tables, relationships, rows, and constraints
- Serialize a *DataSet* to XML and binary format
- Assign a custom type to a column in a *DataTable*
- Load data from a database into a *DataSet*
- Manipulate disconnected data
- Create a *DataTableReader*

Estimated lesson time: 30 minutes

DataSet Class Hierarchy

The *DataSet* object is central to supporting disconnected, distributed data scenarios with ADO.NET. A *DataSet* is a memory-resident representation of data that provides a consistent relational programming model regardless of the data source. It can be used with multiple and differing data sources, with XML data, or to manage data local to the application. *DataSet* represents a complete set of data, including related tables, constraints, and relationships among the tables. Figure 3-1 shows the *DataSet* object model.

The code in Listing 3-1 demonstrates how the *DataSet, DataTable,* and *DataRow* work together to create a *DataSet* which contains one table, named "Product". We'll use the table to store computer game–related products. There is a primary key constraint on the table and a unique constraint on the name of the country.

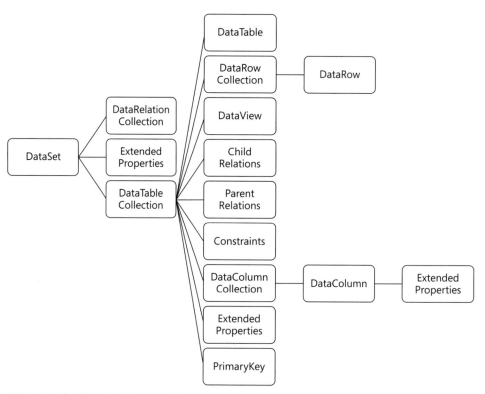

FIGURE 3-1 The *DataSet* object model

LISTING 3-1 Building a Dataset

```vb
' VB
Function BuildDataSet() As DataSet

    Dim ds As New DataSet
    Dim dt As New DataTable("Product")

    Dim dcProductID As New DataColumn("ProductID", GetType(Integer))

    Dim dcProductName As New DataColumn("ProductName", GetType(String))
    dcProductName.MaxLength = 100

    Dim dcReleaseDate As New DataColumn("ReleaseDate", GetType(DateTime))

    dt.Columns.Add(dcProductID)
    dt.Columns.Add(dcProductName)
    dt.Columns.Add(dcReleaseDate)

    Dim key() As DataColumn = { dcProductID }
    dt.PrimaryKey = key
```

```
    Dim unique As New UniqueConstraint(dcProductName)
    dt.Constraints.Add(unique)

    dt.Rows.Add(New Object() {1, "4x4 EVO 2", DateTime.Now})
    dt.Rows.Add(New Object() {2, "Halo 3", DateTime.Now})
    dt.Rows.Add(New Object() {3, "Paperboy", DateTime.Now})

    ds.Tables.Add(dt)

    Return ds
End Function

// C#
private static DataSet BuildDataSet()
{
    DataSet ds = new DataSet();
    DataTable dt = new DataTable( "Product" );

    DataColumn dcProductID = new DataColumn( "ProductID", typeof( int ) );

    DataColumn dcProductName =
                new DataColumn( "ProductName", typeof( String ) );
    dcProductName.MaxLength = 100;

DataColumn dcReleaseDate =
    new DataColumn( "ReleaseDate", typeof( DateTime ) );

    dt.Columns.Add( dcProductID );
    dt.Columns.Add( dcProductName );
    dt.Columns.Add( dcReleaseDate );

    dt.PrimaryKey = new DataColumn[] { dcProductID };
    dt.Constraints.Add( new UniqueConstraint( dcProductName) );

    dt.Rows.Add( new object[] { 1, "4x4 EVO 2", DateTime.Now } );
    dt.Rows.Add( new object[] { 2, "Halo 3", DateTime.Now } );
    dt.Rows.Add( new object[] { 3, "Paperboy", DateTime.Now } );

    ds.Tables.Add( dt );
    return ds;
}
```

The next section takes a closer look at the objects in the *DataSet* object model.

DataSet

The *DataSet* is the root object for the object tree containing tables and relationships between the tables, representing an in-memory cache of data. A list of commonly used properties is listed in Table 3-1 and a list of the most commonly used methods is listed in Table 3-2.

TABLE 3-1 Commonly Used Properties on the *DataSet* Class

PROPERTY	DESCRIPTION
DataSetName	Name of the *DataSet*.
EnforceConstraints	Boolean value indicating whether constraint rules are applied when updating any data in the *DataSet*.
HasErrors	Boolean value indicating whether any of the *DataTables* in the *DataSet* have errors.
RemotingFormat	*SerializationFormat* value indicating how the *DataSet* should be serialized during remoting. Possible values are *Xml* and *Binary*. Note that for backward compatability with .NET Framework 1.x the default is set to Xml.
SchemaSerializationMode	How a *DataSet* serializes its schema and instance data by default in Web services and remoting scenarios. Possible values: *IncludeSchema* and *ExcludeSchema*. Note that *ExcludeSchema* should be used only in cases where the schema information of the underlying typed *DataTables*, *DataRelations*, and *Constraints* has not been modified.

TABLE 3-2 Commonly Used Methods on the *DataSet* Class

PROPERTY	DESCRIPTION
AcceptChanges	*DataSets*, tables, and *DataRows* track all the changes that are made to the data. Calling *AcceptChanges* commits all the changes made to the *DataSet* since it was loaded or since the last time *AcceptChanges* was called.
Clear	Remove all data in all the *DataTables*.
HasChanges	Returns a boolean value indicating whether any changes, inserts, or deletions have been made to the data in the *DataSet*.
Merge	The *Merge* method is used to merge two *DataSet* objects that have largely similar schemas.
ReadXml	Reads the *XML* schema and data into the *DataSet*. Often used to load XML from a file.
RejectChanges	Rolls back all the changes to the data in the *DataSet*, similar to a rollback at database level except this is done to the in-memory data.
WriteXml	Write XML data, and optionally the schema, from the *DataSet*. Often used to write the contents of a *DataSet* to a file easily.

Tracking changes in data is a core piece of functionality offered by the *DataSet* object model. Running the code in Listing 3-1 and inspecting the state of the *DataSet* at various levels will show that at *DataSet-*, *DataTable-*, and *DataRow*-level changes are being tracked automatically. Printing this information to the *Console* using the extension methods listed in Listing 3-2 results in the printout shown in Figure 3-2.

LISTING 3-2 Printing a *DataSet* to the Console

```vb
' VB
Imports System.Runtime.CompilerServices

Module DataSetExtensions

    <Extension()> _
    Public Sub PrintToConsole(ByVal ds As DataSet)
        Dim old As ConsoleColor = Console.ForegroundColor
        Console.ForegroundColor = ConsoleColor.Green
        Console.WriteLine("DataSetName: {0}.", ds.DataSetName)
        Console.WriteLine("Has Changes: {0}.", ds.HasChanges)
        Console.ForegroundColor = old
        Console.WriteLine("-".PadRight(79, "-"))
        For Each dt As DataTable In ds.Tables
            dt.PrintToConsole()
        Next
        Console.ForegroundColor = old
    End Sub

    <Extension()> _
    Public Sub PrintToConsole(ByVal dt As DataTable)
        Console.ForegroundColor = ConsoleColor.Yellow
        Console.WriteLine("DataTable: {0}.", dt.TableName)
        Console.WriteLine("Has Changes: {0}.", dt.GetChanges().Rows.Count)
        Console.WriteLine("-".PadRight(79, "-"))
        Dim colHeader As String = String.Empty
        For Each dc As DataColumn In dt.Columns
            colHeader += dc.ColumnName.PadRight(dc.FiveOrLength())
        Next
        colHeader += " RowState"
        Console.WriteLine(colHeader)
        Console.WriteLine("-".PadRight(79, "-"))
        For Each dr As DataRow In dt.Rows
            dr.PrintToConsole()
        Next
    End Sub

    <Extension()> _
    Public Function FiveOrLength(ByVal dc As DataColumn) As Integer
        If dc.DataType Is GetType(DateTime) Then
            Return 20
        End If
        If dc.MaxLength < 5 Then
            Return 5
```

```vbnet
            Else
                Return dc.MaxLength
            End If
        End Function


        <Extension()> _
        Public Sub PrintToConsole(ByVal dr As DataRow)
            Console.ForegroundColor = ConsoleColor.White
            Dim row As String = String.Empty
            For Each dc As DataColumn In dr.Table.Columns
                row += dr(dc).ToString().PadRight(dc.FiveOrLength())
            Next
            row += " " + dr.RowState.ToString()
            Console.WriteLine(row)
        End Sub
End Module
```

```csharp
// C#
public static class DataSetExtensions
{
    public static void PrintToConsole( this DataSet ds )
    {
        ConsoleColor old = Console.ForegroundColor;
        Console.ForegroundColor = ConsoleColor.Green;
        Console.WriteLine( "DataSetName: {0}.", ds.DataSetName );
        Console.WriteLine( "Has Changes: {0}.", ds.HasChanges() );
        Console.ForegroundColor = old;
        Console.WriteLine( "-".PadRight( 79, '-' ) );
        foreach ( DataTable dt in ds.Tables )
        {
            dt.PrintToConsole();
        }
        Console.ForegroundColor = old;
    }


    public static void PrintToConsole( this DataTable dt )
    {
        Console.ForegroundColor = ConsoleColor.Yellow;
        Console.WriteLine( "DataTable: {0}.", dt.TableName );
        Console.WriteLine( "Has Changes: {0}.", (dt.GetChanges().Rows.Count > 0) );
        Console.WriteLine( "-".PadRight( 79, '-' ) );
        Console.ForegroundColor = ConsoleColor.Cyan;
        string colHeader = String.Empty;
        foreach ( DataColumn dc in dt.Columns )
        {
            colHeader += dc.ColumnName.PadRight( dc.FiveOrLength() );
        }
```

```
        colHeader += " RowState";
        Console.WriteLine( colHeader );
        Console.WriteLine( "-".PadRight( 79, '-' ) );
        foreach ( DataRow dr in dt.Rows )
        {
            dr.PrintToConsole();
        }
        Console.WriteLine();
    }

    public static int FiveOrLength( this DataColumn dc )
    {
        if ( dc.DataType == typeof( DateTime ) )
            return 20;
        if ( dc.MaxLength < 5 )
            return 5;
        else
            return dc.MaxLength;
    }

    public static void PrintToConsole( this DataRow dr )
    {
        Console.ForegroundColor = ConsoleColor.White;
        string row = String.Empty;
        foreach ( DataColumn dc in dr.Table.Columns )
        {
            row += dr[dc].ToString().PadRight( dc.FiveOrLength() );
        }
        row += " " + dr.RowState.ToString();
        Console.WriteLine( row );
    }
}
```

FIGURE 3-2 A printout of the contents of the *DataSet* created in Listing 3-1

Figure 3-2 shows the output of *PrintToConsole* if it would be called on the *DataSet* created in Listing 3-1. Should the *AcceptChanges* method on the *DataSet* be called before printing the *DataSet,* then the changes are commited and the output is as shown in Figure 3-3.

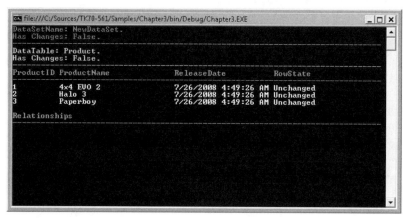

FIGURE 3-3 A printout of the *DataSet* after *AcceptChanges()* has been called

DataTable

A *DataTable* represents one table of in-memory data. If you are creating a *DataTable* programmatically, you must first define its schema by adding *DataColumn* objects to the *DataColumnCollection* (accessed through the *Columns* property). To add rows to a *DataTable,* you must first use the *NewRow* method to return a new *DataRow* object. The *NewRow* method returns a row with the schema of the *DataTable,* as it is defined by the table's *DataColumnCollection*. Alternatively, you can call the *Add* method on the *DataRowCollection* and pass an array of objects, but note that the order of the objects needs to match the order of the columns. The *DataTable* also contains a collection of *Constraint* objects that can be used to ensure the integrity of the data.

Table 3-3 shows the commonly used properties of a *DataTable* and Table 3-4 the commonly used methods of a *DataTable*.

TABLE 3-3 Commonly Used Properties on the *DataTable* Class

PROPERTY	DESCRIPTION
Columns	A *DataColumnCollection* value returning the columns that belong to this table.
Constraints	A *ConstraintCollection* value returning the constraints maintained by this table. An example of a constraint is the *UniqueConstraint*.
PrimaryKey	An array of *DataColumn* values with the columns that make up the primary key of the table.
RemotingFormat	A *SerializationFormat* value indicating how the table should be serialized during remoting. Possible values are *Xml* and *Binary*.
TableName	A *String* value with the name of the table.

TABLE 3-4 Commonly Used Methods on the *DataTable* Class

PROPERTY	DESCRIPTION
AcceptChanges	Commits all the changes made to this table since the last time *AcceptChanges* was called.
Clear	Clears the table of all data.
Clone	Clones the structure of the table, including all schema information and constraints, but without the data.
Copy	Copies both the structure and the data in the table.
GetChanges	Gets a copy of the table containing all changes made to it since it was last loaded, or since *AcceptChanges* was called.
Load	Fills the table with values from a data source using the supplied *IDataReader*.
Merge	Merge the data from two *DataTables* into one. If the schema definition of the two tables does not match, this method tries to resolve the differences if you want.
NewRow	Create a new *DataRow* with the schema of the table.
RejectChanges	Rolls back all the changes to the data in the *DataSet*, similar to a rollback at database level except this is done to the in-memory data.
Select	Perform a query on the table to select a set of *DataRow* objects.
WriteXml	Writes the current contents of the table as XML.

DataRow and *DataColumn*

Rows and columns are central to storing the data in a *DataTable*. The *DataRow* object provides a dictionary-style access to a selection of columns, allowing the values of the row to be stored. The row can contain data retrieved from a database and can be used to insert, update, and delete values in the *DataTable*.

A new *DataRow* can be created using the *NewRow* method of the *DataTable* object. The new row can be populated with values after which the *Add* method can be used to add the new row to the *DataRowCollection*. A *DataRow* can be deleted from the *DataRowCollection* by calling the *Remove* method of the *DataRowCollection* or by calling the *Delete* method of the *DataRow* object. The *Remove* method removes the row from the collection. In contrast, *Delete* marks the *DataRow* for removal. The actual removal occurs when you call the *AcceptChanges* method. By calling *Delete*, you can programmatically check which rows are marked for removal before actually deleting them.

DataColumns define the fields available in each *DataRow*. Each *DataColumn* has a *DataType* property that determines the kind of data the *DataColumn* contains. Properties such as *AllowDBNull*, *Unique*, and *ReadOnly* put restrictions on the entry and updating of data, thereby helping to guarantee data integrity. You can also use the *AutoIncrement*, *AutoIncrementSeed*, and *AutoIncrementStep* properties to control automatic value generation.

You can use the *Expression* property of the *DataColumn* object to calculate the values in a column, or create an aggregate column.

Listing 3-1, earlier in this lesson, showed how to create rows by passing an array of objects to the *DataRowCollection.Add* method. The following code shows the three ways of setting the values in a *DataRow* using the *DataRow* object, using the name of the column, the column index, or the column reference, respectively:

```vb
' VB
' Construct the DataTable with columns
Dim dt As New DataTable("Product")

Dim dcCode As New DataColumn("ProductID", GetType(Integer))
Dim dcName As New DataColumn("ProductName", GetType(String))

dt.Columns.Add(dcCode)
dt.Columns.Add(dcName)

' Add rows to the table
Dim row1 As DataRow = dt.NewRow()
row1("Code") = 1
row1("Name") = "4x4 EVO 2"
dt.Rows.Add(row1)

Dim row2 As DataRow = dt.NewRow()
row2(0) = 2
row2(1) = "Halo 3"
dt.Rows.Add(row2)

Dim row3 As DataRow = dt.NewRow()
row3(dcCode) = 3
row3(dcName) = "Paperboy"
dt.Rows.Add(row3)
```

```csharp
// C#
// Construct the DataTable with columns
DataTable dt = new DataTable( "Product" );

DataColumn dcCode = new DataColumn( "ProductID", typeof( int ) );
DataColumn dcName = new DataColumn( "ProductName", typeof( String ) );

dt.Columns.Add( dcCode );
dt.Columns.Add( dcName );

// Add rows to the table
DataRow row1 = dt.NewRow();
```

```
row1["Code"] = 1;
row1["Name"] = "4x4 EVO 2";
dt.Rows.Add( row1 );

DataRow row2 = dt.NewRow();
row2[0] = 2;
row2[1] = "Halo 3";
dt.Rows.Add( row2 );

DataRow row3 = dt.NewRow();
row3[dcCode] = 3;
row3[dcName] = "Paperboy";
dt.Rows.Add( row3 );
```

DataRelation

Relationships in *DataSets* are created using the *DataRelation* class. The *DataRelation* instance usually represents a one-to-many relationship. The parent table is on the "one" side of the relationship, and the child table is on the "many" side of the relationship. The relationship is created by specifying a column in the parent table, the contents of which needs to match with the contents of the corresponding column in the child table. To define a relationship, the *DataType* of the parent and child columns needs to be identical.

The following code shows how to create a relationship between two tables. The foreign key constraint is enabled, so only existing values for the *ContactType* field are allowed:

```
' VB
Public Function BuildDataSetWithRelation() As DataSet
    Dim ds As New DataSet
    Dim dtSupplier = BuildSupplierTable()
    Dim dtProduct = BuildProductTable()

    ds.Tables.Add(dtSupplier)
    ds.Tables.Add(dtProduct)

    Dim parent = dtSupplier.Columns("SupplierID")
    Dim child = dtProduct.Columns("SupplierID")

    Dim dr = New DataRelation("FK_Supplier2Product", _
                          parent, child, True)
    ds.Relations.Add(dr)

    ' will fail because of FK constraint
    dtProduct.Rows.Add(New Object() {1, "Bill", "Malone", 1})

    ' succeeds because supplier exists
    dtSupplier.Rows.Add(New Object() {1, "Support/Helpdesk"})
```

```vb
        dtProduct.Rows.Add(New Object() {1, "Bill", "Malone", 1})

        Return ds

End Function


Public Function BuildSupplierTable() As DataTable
    Dim dt As New DataTable("Supplier")
    Dim key As DataColumn = dt.Columns.Add("SupplierID", GetType(Integer))
    dt.Columns.Add("SupplierName", GetType(String))
    Dim keys() As DataColumn = New DataColumn() {key}
    dt.PrimaryKey = keys
    Return dt
End Function


Public Function BuildProductTable() As DataTable
    Dim dt As New DataTable("Product")
    Dim key As DataColumn = dt.Columns.Add("ProductId", GetType(Integer))
    dt.Columns.Add("ProductName", GetType(String))
    dt.Columns.Add("SupplierID", GetType(Integer))
    Dim keys() As DataColumn = New DataColumn() {key}
    dt.PrimaryKey = keys
    Return dt
End Function


// C#
private static DataSet BuildDataSetWithRelation()
{
    DataSet ds = new DataSet();
    DataTable dtProduct = BuildProductTable();
    DataTable dtSupplier = BuildSupplierTable();

    ds.Tables.Add(dtProduct);
    ds.Tables.Add(dtSupplier);

    DataColumn parent = dtSupplier.Columns["SupplierID"];
    DataColumn child = dtProduct.Columns["SupplierID"];

DataRelation dr =
    new DataRelation( "FK_Supplier2Product", parent, child, true );
    ds.Relations.Add( dr );

    // next statement will fail at runtime because of FK constraint
    dtProduct.Rows.Add(new object[] { 1, "Halo 3", 1 });

    // next two statements succeed because supplier now exists
    dtSupplier.Rows.Add(new object[] { 1, "Microsoft" });
```

```
        dtProduct.Rows.Add(new object[] { 1, "Halo 3", 1 });
        return ds;
}


private static DataTable BuildSupplierTable()
{
    DataTable dt = new DataTable ( "Supplier" );
    DataColumn key = dt.Columns.Add ( "SupplierID", typeof ( int ) );
    dt.Columns.Add ( "SupplierName", typeof ( string ) );
    dt.PrimaryKey = new DataColumn[] { key };  // Set the PK
    return dt;
}


private static DataTable BuildProductTable()
{
    DataTable dt = new DataTable ( "Product" );
    DataColumn key =
        dt.Columns.Add ( "ProductID", typeof ( int ) );
    dt.Columns.Add ( "ProductName", typeof ( string ) );
    dt.Columns.Add ( "SupplierID", typeof ( int ) );
    dt.PrimaryKey = new DataColumn[] { key };
    return dt;
}
```

In the previous code, the *BuildDataSetWithRelation* method creates two tables, adds them to the *DataSet,* and then proceeds to build a *DataRelation* between the two tables, from the *ContactType* field in *Contact* to the primary key in the *ContactTypes* table. By enabling constraints when creating the relationship, the foreign key constraint is automatically implemented. Adding data that holds a reference to a non-existing entry in the *ContactTypes* table will cause an exception to be thrown. Adding the *ContactTypes* entry before adding the Contact works fine.

DataView

Just as in the database, the *DataView* creates a view on a *DataTable,* allowing data presented in the view to be a subset of the data in the *DataTable,* to have a different sorting, or both.

> **NOTE DATAVIEW**
>
> A *DataView* creates a view on a *DataTable* that is not on the *DataSet.* It is not possible to create a join between two *DataTables* using a *DataView.*

DataColumn

A *DataColumn* can be more than a container for values. It can also provide a computed value using an expression. To do this, set the *Expression* property of the *DataColumn.* Using the *Child* keyword in the expression allows you to traverse relationships within the *DataSet.*

For example, the following code sets the expression for the *OrderLinesCount* column of the *Orders* table:

```
' VB
Tables("Suppliers").Columns("ProductCount").Expression =  "Count(Child(Product))"
```

```
// C#
Tables["Suppliers "].Columns["Product Count"].Expression = "Count(Child(Product))";
```

When you create an expression, use the *ColumnName* property to refer to columns. For example, if the *ColumnName* for one column is *UnitPrice* and another is *Quantity,* the expression would be as follows:

```
"UnitPrice * Quantity"
```

> **BEST PRACTICES**   **VERIFYING THE *EXPRESSION* PROPERTY**
>
> The *Expression* property is of type *String;* therefore, it is prone to errors because neither the C# nor the VB .NET compiler checks for errors in the string. It is a recommended practice to make sure that one or more unit tests are created to check the correctness of the *Expression* property.

Expressions are formulated as mathematical equations where columns are used as variables. A number of aggregation functions such as *Count, Average,* and *Sum* are also supported.

Validation and Errors

You've seen a number of ways to validate data as it gets inserted into the *DataRow*. Most likely, you also want to build custom validations to match business rules in your organization. For instance, a business rule for your application might specify that the expected delivery date for an order cannot be a date in the past. If a date does not match the rule, the *DataTable* has properties that can be used to specify that there is an error and the location of the error. The *DataTable* can contain a message aimed at the user that specifies what's wrong. The *DataRow.RowError* property and *DataRow.SetColumnError* method can be used to add error information to the *DataRow.*

Aside from storing the error information, you need to implement the validation. There are two approaches to implement such a validation. The first is to implement a method that validates a single *DataRow*. The second is to validate data as it is entered, based on an event. The first approach might look as follows:

```
' VB
Private Sub ValidateProductRow(ByVal row As DataRow)
    Dim productID As Integer = row.Field(Of Integer)("ProductID")
    Dim dcReleaseDate As DataColumn = row.Table.Columns("ReleaseDate")
    Dim releaseDate As DateTime? = row.Field(Of DateTime?)(dcReleaseDate)
```

```vb
    If releaseDate.HasValue And releaseDate.Value > DateTime.Today Then
        row.SetColumnError(dcReleaseDate, _
                            "Release data cannot be in the future.")
        row.RowError = _
            String.Format("Product {0} is invalid.", productID)
    End If
End Sub
```

```csharp
// C#
private void ValidateProductRow( DataRow row )
{
    int productID = row.Field<int>( "ProductId" );
    DataColumn dcReleaseDate = row.Table.Columns["ReleaseDate"];
    DateTime? releaseDate = row.Field<DateTime?>( dcReleaseDate );

    if (releaseDate.HasValue &&
        releaseDate.Value > DateTime.Today
      )
    {
        // datetime is in the past
        row.SetColumnError(dcReleaseDate,
                            "Release date cannot be in the future." );
        row.RowError =
            String.Format( "Product {0} is invalid.", productID);
    }
}
```

For the second approach, you need to look at the events fired by the *DataSet* object model. All tracking through events is done at the *DataTable* level. There are numerous events to which you can be attached to track changes, like *ColumnChanged*, *RowChanged*, *RowDeleted*, *TableCleared,* and *TableNewRow.* The following code illustrates this second approach:

```vb
' VB
Dim dt As DataTable = BuildProductTable()
AddHandler dt.ColumnChanged, AddressOf dt_ColumnChanged

Sub dt_ColumnChanged(ByVal sender As Object, ByVal e As DataColumnChangeEventArgs)
    If e.Column.ColumnName = "ReleaseData" Then
        Dim releaseDate As DateTime? = _
            e.Row.Field(Of DateTime?)(e.Column)
        Dim productId As Integer = _
            e.Row.Field(Of Integer)("ProductId")

        If releaseDate.HasValue And releaseDate.Value > DateTime.Today Then
            e.Row.SetColumnError(e.Column, _
                            "Release date can not be in the future.")
```

```
                e.Row.RowError = _
                    String.Format("Product {0} is invalid.", productId)

            End If
        End If
    End Sub


// C#
DataTable dt = BuildProductsTable();
dt.ColumnChanged += new DataColumnChangeEventHandler( dt_ColumnChanged );

void dt_ColumnChanged( object sender, DataColumnChangeEventArgs e )
{

    if ( e.Column.ColumnName == "ReleaseDate" )
    {
        DateTime? releaseDate = e.Row.Field<DateTime?>( e.Column );
        int productId = e.Row.Field<int>( "ProductId" );

        if ( releaseDate.HasValue &&
             releaseDate.Value > DateTime.Today
           )
        {
            // datetime is in the future
            e.Row.SetColumnError( e.Column,
                            "Release date cannot be in the future." );
            e.Row.RowError = String.Format( "Product {0} is invalid.",
                                    productID );
        }
    }
}
```

A big advantage to using the fields in the *DataRow* to store error information is that controls such as the *DataGridView* automatically display the error information per row and field.

Serialization and RemotingFormat

DataSet and *DataTable* objects can both be serialized. However, *DataRow* objects cannot. This means that when building a Windows Communication Foundation (WCF) service, you can use *DataSet* and *DataTable* as the return type or parameter type. It is important to note that the method of serialization used by WCF is based completely on the configuration of the WCF service. The *RemotingFormat* property is *not* used by WCF. The *RemotingFormat* is used only by applications using .NET Remoting and .NET Framework 2.0 or higher.

XML

Chapter 7, "XML," covers ADO.NET and XML in detail, but we will discuss these topics in relation to *DataSets* now. It is important to know that *DataSets* fully support the transformation of relational data to XML because they are able to be written to and read from XML. The following sample writes both the schema and contents of a *DataSet* to file and then reads the schema and data back into memory. Overloads of these methods include writing the data not just to a file but also any *Stream* or *XmlReader:*

```vb
' VB
Dim dsSource As DataSet = BuildDataSet()
' write schema to file
dsSource.WriteXmlSchema("c:\dataset_schema.xml")
' write data to file
dsSource.WriteXml("c:\dataset.xml")

Dim dsDest As New DataSet
' read schema before loading data
dsDest.ReadXmlSchema("c:\dataset_schema.xml")
' read data
dsDest.ReadXml("c:\dataset.xml")
```

```csharp
// C#
DataSet dsSource = BuildDataSet();
// write schema to xml file
dsSource.WriteXmlSchema( @"c:\dataset_schema.xml" );
// write dataset to xml file
dsSource.WriteXml( @"c:\dataset.xml" );

DataSet dsDest = new DataSet();
// read schema before reading data
dsDest.ReadXmlSchema( @"c:\dataset_schema.xml" );
// read data
dsDest.ReadXml( @"c:\dataset.xml" );
```

Reading Data from a Database

The *DataAdapter* class is used to retrieve data from the database and populate the *DataSet* and *DataTables*. The *DataAdapter* uses the database connection and database commands discussed in Chapter 2, "Querying Data," to create a *DataReader* that efficiently reads the data from the database and inserts it into a table in the *DataSet*. By default, the schema information of the *DataTable,* which is available from the database, is not updated when performing a fill. The *FillSchema* method needs to be called to enrich the *DataTable* with schema information:

```vb
' VB
Function ReadFromDatabase() As DataSet
```

```
        Dim ds As New DataSet
        Using conn = New SqlConnection("Data Source=.;Initial" _
                + "Catalog=GameVideoStoreDB;Integrated Security=True")
            Using cmdSelect = New SqlCommand("select * from Supplier", conn)
                Using adapter = New SqlDataAdapter(cmdSelect)
                    adapter.Fill(ds, "Supplier")
                    adapter.FillSchema(ds, SchemaType.Source, "Supplier")
                    Return ds
                End Using
            End Using
        End Using

End Function

// C#
private DataSet ReadFromDatabase()
{
    DataSet ds = new DataSet();
    using ( SqlConnection conn =
    new SqlConnection( @"Data Source=.;Initial
    Catalog=GameVideoStoreDB;Integrated Security=True" ) )
    {
        using ( SqlCommand cmdSelect =
 new SqlCommand( "select * from Supplier",
    conn ) )
        {
            using ( SqlDataAdapter adapter =
    new SqlDataAdapter( cmdSelect ) )
            {
                adapter.Fill( ds, "Supplier" );
                adapter.FillSchema( ds, SchemaType.Source,
                                    "Supplier" );
                return ds;
            }
        }
    }
}
```

The *DataAdapter* can also be used to write changes in the *DataSet* and *DataTable* back to the database. Updating data is covered in Chapter 4.

DataSet Datatypes

The *DataSet* and the *DataSet* object model reside in the *System.Data* namespace and are completely database agnostic. Once the data is loaded into the *DataSet*, the source of data becomes immaterial and cannot be deduced by looking at the *DataSet*. By default, the *DataAdapter* converts any datatype that it encounters in a .NET Framework common type. There might, however, be times when you want to have the *DataSet* contain database provider–specific types instead. For instance, instead of having a field be of type *System.String* you want access to the original *System.Data.SqlClient.SqlXml* because you want to create an *XmlReader* to read the data rather than cast the full XML to a string.ID.

> **NOTE FILLSCHEMA**
>
> **FillSchema does not work when setting *ReturnProviderSpecificTypes* to True.**

SQL Server User-Defined Types

Microsoft SQL Server 2005 and SQL Server 2008 allow you to create a user-defined type using any .NET Framework language. The *DataSet* object model fully supports this and automatically changes the datatype of the column to the custom type. The project needs to know the type, so the project defining the custom database type needs to be referenced from the current project.

 Quick Check

- What is the difference between a *DataSet* containing two *DataTables* (for instance, *Order* and *OrderDetails*) and having two separate *DataTables*, one with *Orders* and one with *OrderDetails*?

Quick Check Answer

- Both can contain the same data, but a *DataSet* is able to track relationships between *DataTables* and maintain referential integrity.

Sample: *Order* and *OrderDetails*

Listing 3-3 combines what you've learned so far into a working sample that uses the *AdventureWorks* database to load data from the database into a *DataSet* and then defines the relationship between *Order* and *Orderdetails* so that it allows the *DataSet* to maintain referential integrity, delete an order, and add an order.

LISTING 3-3 *Order and OrderDetails*

```vb
' VB
Public Class OrderDB

Const cConnectionString As String = _
"Data Source=.;Initial Catalog=AdventureWorks;Integrated Security=True"

Sub Main()
    Dim ds As DataSet

    ' 1. Read orders and details for customer 77
    ds = ReadOrdersAndOrderDetails(77)
```

```
        ' 2. Add foreign key relationship to datasetd
        AddForeignKey(ds)

        ' 3. Inspect the dataset
        ds.PrintToConsole()
        Console.ReadLine()
        Console.Clear()

        ' 4. Delete order 46965
        DeleteOrder(ds, 46965)

        ' 5. Add an order
        AddOrder(ds)

        ' 6. Inspect changes
        ds.GetChanges().PrintToConsole()
        Console.ReadLine()
    End Sub

    Sub AddOrder(ByVal ds As DataSet)

        Dim drOrder = ds.Tables("Orders").NewRow()

        drOrder("SalesOrderID") = 99001
        drOrder("SalesOrderNumber") = "SO99001"
        drOrder("Status") = 1
        ds.Tables("Orders").Rows.Add(drOrder)

        Dim drOrderDetail = ds.Tables("OrderDetails").NewRow()
        drOrderDetail("SalesOrderID") = 99001   'FK
        drOrderDetail("ProductID") = 888
        drOrderDetail("OrderQty") = 8
        drOrderDetail("LineTotal") = 19.99

        ds.Tables("OrderDetails").Rows.Add(drOrderDetail)
    End Sub

    Sub DeleteOrder(ByVal ds As DataSet, ByVal orderId As Integer)
        Dim dv = New DataView(ds.Tables("Orders"))
        dv.RowFilter = "SalesOrderID = " + orderId.ToString()
        For Each dr As DataRowView In dv ' Should be exactly one match
            dr.Row.Delete()
        Next
    End Sub
```

```vb
Sub AddForeignKey(ByVal ds As DataSet)
    Dim parent = ds.Tables("Orders").Columns("SalesOrderID")
    Dim child = ds.Tables("OrderDetails").Columns("SalesOrderID")
    Dim relation = New DataRelation("FK_Orders2OrderDetails", parent, child, True)
    ds.Relations.Add(relation)
End Sub

Function ReadOrdersAndOrderDetails(ByVal customerId As Int16) As DataSet
    Dim ds As New DataSet

    Using conn As SqlConnection = New SqlConnection(cConnectionString)
        Using cmd As SqlCommand = New SqlCommand
            cmd.Connection = conn
            cmd.CommandType = CommandType.Text
            cmd.CommandText = "select SalesOrderID, SalesOrderNumber, " & _
                            "Status from Sales.SalesOrderHeader Orders " & _
                            "where CustomerID = @customerId order by SalesOrderID"
            cmd.Parameters.Add(New SqlParameter("@customerId", customerId))
            Using adapter As SqlDataAdapter = New SqlDataAdapter(cmd)
                adapter.Fill(ds, "Orders")
                adapter.FillSchema(ds, SchemaType.Source, "Orders")
            End Using

            cmd.CommandText = "select OrderDetails.SalesOrderID, " & _
        "OrderDetails.ProductID, OrderDetails.OrderQty , " & _
        "OrderDetails.LineTotal from Sales.SalesOrderHeader Orders, " & _
        "Sales.SalesOrderDetail OrderDetails where Orders.CustomerID = " & _
        "@customerId and OrderDetails.SalesOrderID = Orders.SalesOrderID" & _
        "order by OrderDetails.SalesOrderID, OrderDetails.ProductID"
            Using adapter As SqlDataAdapter = New SqlDataAdapter(cmd)
                adapter.Fill(ds, "OrderDetails")
                adapter.FillSchema(ds, SchemaType.Source, "OrderDetails")
            End Using
        End Using
    End Using
    Return ds
End Function

End Class

// C#
public class OrderDB {

const string cConnectionString =
    "Data Source=.;Initial Catalog=AdventureWorks;Integrated Security=True";
```

```csharp
static void Main( string[] args )
{
    // 1. Read orders and details for customer 77
    DataSet ds = ReadOrdersAndOrderDetails( 77 );

    // 2. Add foreign key relationship to dataset
    AddForeignKey( ds );

    // 3. Inspect dataset
    ds.PrintToConsole();
    Console.ReadLine();
    Console.Clear();

    // 4. Delete order 46965
    DeleteOrder( ds, 46965);

    // 5. Add an order
    AddOrder( ds );

    // 6. Inspect changes
    ds.GetChanges().PrintToConsole();
    Console.ReadLine();
}

static void AddOrder( DataSet ds )
{
    DataRow drOrder = ds.Tables["Orders"].NewRow();
    drOrder["SalesOrderID"] = 99001;
    drOrder["SalesOrderNumber"] = "SO99001";
    drOrder["Status"] = 1;
    ds.Tables["Orders"].Rows.Add( drOrder );

    DataRow drOrderDetail = ds.Tables["OrderDetails"].NewRow();
    drOrderDetail["SalesOrderID"] = 99001;   //FK
    drOrderDetail["ProductID"] = 888;
    drOrderDetail["OrderQty"] = 8;
    drOrderDetail["LineTotal"] = 19.99;
    ds.Tables["OrderDetails"].Rows.Add( drOrderDetail );
}

static void DeleteOrder( DataSet ds, int orderId )
{
    DataView dv = new DataView( ds.Tables["Orders"] );
    dv.RowFilter = "SalesOrderID = " + orderId.ToString();
    foreach(DataRowView dr in dv)
    {
        dr.Row.Delete();
    }
```

```
    //DataRow[] rows = ds.Tables["Orders"].Select( "SalesOrderID = " + orderId.ToString() );
    //if ( rows != null && rows.Length > 0 )
    //{
    //    rows[0].Delete();
    //}
}


static void AddForeignKey( DataSet ds )
{
    DataColumn parent = ds.Tables["Orders"].Columns["SalesOrderID"];
    DataColumn child = ds.Tables["OrderDetails"].Columns["SalesOrderID"];
    DataRelation relation = new DataRelation( "FK_Orders2OrderDetails", parent, child,
        true );
    ds.Relations.Add( relation );
}


static DataSet ReadOrdersAndOrderDetails( int customerId )
{
    DataSet ds = new DataSet();
    using ( SqlConnection conn = new SqlConnection( cConnectionString ) )
    {
        using ( SqlCommand cmd = new SqlCommand() )
        {
            cmd.Connection = conn;
            cmd.CommandType = CommandType.Text;
            cmd.CommandText = "select SalesOrderID, SalesOrderNumber, Status " +
                            "from Sales.SalesOrderHeader Orders " +
                            "where CustomerID = @customerId order by SalesOrderID";
            cmd.Parameters.Add( new SqlParameter( "@customerId", customerId ) );
            using ( SqlDataAdapter adapter = new SqlDataAdapter( cmd ) )
            {
                adapter.Fill( ds, "Orders" );
                adapter.FillSchema( ds, SchemaType.Source, "Orders" );
            }

            cmd.CommandText = "select OrderDetails.SalesOrderID, " +
                            "OrderDetails.ProductID, OrderDetails.OrderQty, " +
                            "OrderDetails.LineTotal " +
                            "from Sales.SalesOrderHeader Orders, " +
                            "Sales.SalesOrderDetail OrderDetails " +
                            "where Orders.CustomerID = @customerId and " +
                            "OrderDetails.SalesOrderID = Orders.SalesOrderID " +
                            "order by OrderDetails.SalesOrderID, " +
                            "OrderDetails.ProductID";
            using ( SqlDataAdapter adapter = new SqlDataAdapter( cmd ) )
            {
                adapter.Fill( ds, "OrderDetails" );
```

```
                    adapter.FillSchema( ds, SchemaType.Source, "OrderDetails" );
                }
            }
        }
        return ds;
    }
}
```

Next, you look at the six steps in the *Main* method of this console application. The *Main* method is the entry point for the Console application.

ReadOrderAndOrderDetails

The *ReadOrderAndOrderDetails* method builds up a connection, command, and data adapter, and then reuses the command to perform consecutive selects. The first selects all the orders of customer 77, and the second selects all the details for the orders of customer 77. Both results are stored in the same *DataSet*.

Notice how employing the *using* keyword ensures that the the *Dispose()* method is called, releasing valuable resources as soon as possible.

Add Foreign Key to the *DataSet*

By using the *FillSchema* when reading the data, the sample ensures that the table schemas are complete. The *FillSchema* method, however, do not take care of the relationship between tables, this needs to be done manually. The *AddForeignKey* method looks up the parent and child columns in the *Order* and *OrderDetails* tables and binds them into a *DataRelation*. The fourth parameter is set to True to enforce the validation of foreign key constraints and enable cascaded deletions.

Inspect the *DataSet*

Dumping the contents of the *DataSet* to the *Console* (using the extension method from Listing 3-2) allows a view of the contents of the *DataSet,* shown in Figure 3-4.

DeleteOrder

The *DeleteOrder* method uses a *DataView* to find a specific order in the table. It then deletes the order. Note that instead of using a *DataView,* you could also have used the *Select* method, which takes a filter as a parameter and returns an array of *DataRows*.

AddOrder

The *AddOrder* method uses *DataTable.NewRow* and *DataRowCollection.Add* to add a row to both the *Order* and *OrderDetails* table. Note that if the *SalesOrderID* of the *drOrderDetails DataRow* does not exist in the *Order* table the *DataSet* object model will throw a *ForeignKeyViolationException*.

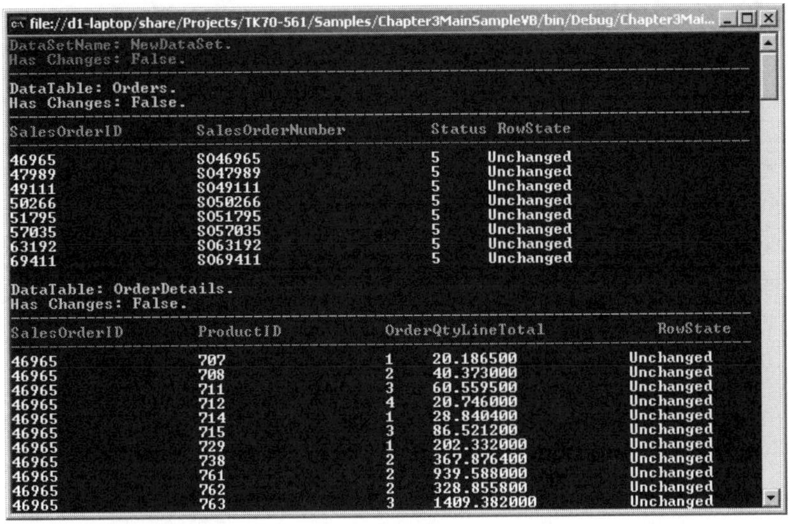

FIGURE 3-4 The orders and order details in the *DataSet*

Inspect Changes

After deleting and adding some data, the changes in the database need to be printed to the *Console*. Figure 3-5 shows that the order has been deleted and all the *OrderDetails* have also been deleted.

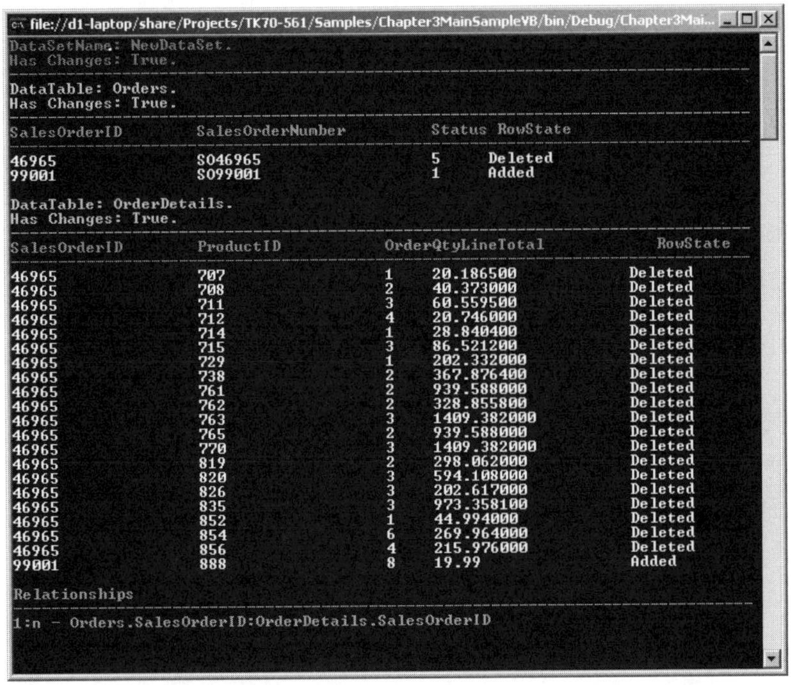

FIGURE 3-5 Viewing the changes in the *DataSet*

Using a *DataTableReader*

A *DataTableReader* can be used to read data from a *DataTable* or *DataSet*. It performs the same functions as a *SqlDataReader,* except it takes its data from a *DataTable* or *DataSet* rather than the database. This means that a *DataTableReader* does not require an open connection to the database to iterate over a *DataSet* or *DataTable*. A *DataTableReader* comes in handy when streaming data, such as when a Web service returns a huge amount of data.

The following code shows how to create a *DataTableReader:*

```
' VB
Dim dtr As New DataTableReader(ds.Tables("Products"))
While dtr.NextResult() = True
    Console.WriteLine(dtr("ProductID"))
    Console.WriteLine(dtr("ProductName"))
End While
```

```
// C#
DataTableReader dtr = new DataTableReader ( ds.Tables["Products"] );
while ( dtr.NextResult () == true )
{
    Console.WriteLine ( dtr["ProductID"] );
    Console.WriteLine ( dtr["ProductName"] );
}
```

LAB Using *DataSets* to Build an Application

In this lab, you create a class library to read data into a *DataSet*, perform data manipulation, and expose a datatable as a service. You need to have the *VideoGameStoreDB* database installed to perform these exercises, as described in Chapter 1, "Database Connections." Each exercise builds on the previous one. You can install the complete solution containing the code for all the exercises from the Code folder on the companion CD.

EXERCISE 1 Create a *DataSet* with a Customer and Purchase Details Table

In this exercise, you create a class library project which implements a data access layer for customers.

1. Start a new Class Library project named DataAccess.
2. Add a class named *CustomerDB*.
3. Implement a new method named *GetCustomersDataSet*, which returns a *DataSet*. Within the method, perform the following steps:
   a. Create a new *DataSet*.
   b. Create a new datatable named *Customer* with a column ID of type *Integer* and a *Name* of type *String*. Set *ID* to be the primary key.

c. Create a new datatable named *Purchases* with a column ID of type *Int32*, a *CustomerID* of type *Int32*, a *Details* of type *String* and *PurchaseDate* of type *DateTime*. Set *ID* to be the primary key.

d. Add the tables to the *DataSet*.

e. Add a foreign key named *FK_Customer2Purchases*.

f. Return the *DataSet*.

Your code should look like this:

```vb
' VB
Public Function GetCustomersDataSet() As DataSet
    Dim ds As New DataSet

    Dim tblCustomer As New DataTable("Customer")
    Dim customerKey = tblCustomer.Columns.Add("ID", GetType(Integer))
    tblCustomer.Columns.Add("Name", GetType(String))
    Dim primaryCustomerKey(1) As DataColumn
    primaryCustomerKey(0) = customerKey
    tblCustomer.PrimaryKey = primaryCustomerKey

    Dim tblPurchase As New DataTable("Purchase")
    Dim purchaseKey = tblPurchase.Columns.Add("ID", GetType(Integer))
    tblPurchase.Columns.Add("CustomerID", GetType(Integer))
    tblPurchase.Columns.Add("PurchaseDate", GetType(DateTime))
    tblPurchase.Columns.Add("Details", GetType(String))
    Dim primaryPurchaseKey(1) As DataColumn
    primaryPurchaseKey(0) = purchaseKey
    tblPurchase.PrimaryKey = primaryPurchaseKey

    ds.Tables.Add(tblCustomer)
    ds.Tables.Add(tblPurchase)

    Dim dr = New DataRelation("FK_Customer2Purchase", _
                        customerKey, purchaseKey)

    ds.Relations.Add(dr)

    Return ds
End Function
```

```csharp
// C#
public DataSet GetCustomerDataSet()
{
    DataSet ds = new DataSet ();
    DataTable tblCustomer = new DataTable ( "Customer" );
    DataColumn customerKey = tblCustomer.Columns.Add ( "ID", typeof ( int ) );
```

```
tblCustomer.Columns.Add ( "Name", typeof ( string ) );
tblCustomer.PrimaryKey = new DataColumn[] { customerKey };

DataTable tblPurchase = new DataTable ( "Purchase" );
DataColumn purchaseKey = tblPurchase.Columns.Add ( "ID", typeof ( int ) );
tblPurchase.Columns.Add ( "CustomerID", typeof ( int ) );
tblPurchase.Columns.Add ( "PurchaseDate", typeof ( DateTime ) );
tblPurchase.Columns.Add ( "Details", typeof ( string ) );
tblPurchase.PrimaryKey = new DataColumn[] { purchaseKey };

ds.Tables.Add ( tblCustomer );
ds.Tables.Add ( tblPurchase );

DataRelation dr = new DataRelation( "FK_Customer2Purchase", customerKey, purchaseKey
);
ds.Relations.Add ( dr );

return ds;
}
```

EXERCISE 2   Read Data into a *DataSet*

Continue with the solution from Exercise 1 or use the code for Exercise 1 from the Code folder on the companion CD. In this exercise, you add code to the solution that reads data into a *DataSet*.

1. Add a new method named *GetCustomers*, which returns a *DataSet*. Within the method, perform the following steps:

   a. Create a connection to the *VideoGameStoreDB*.

   b. Create a sql data adapter which uses the connection.

   c. Create an new *DataSet* using *GetCustomerDataSet*.

   d. Use the *TableAdapter* to load data from both the *Customer* and *Purchase* tables into the *DataSet*.

   Your code should look like this:

```
' VB
Public Function GetCustomers() As DataSet
    Dim ds As DataSet = GetCustomersDataSet()

    Using conn = New SqlConnection("")
        Using adapter = New SqlDataAdapter()
            Using cmd = New SqlCommand("select * from customer", conn)
                adapter.SelectCommand = cmd
                adapter.Fill(ds, "Customer")
            End Using
```

```
            Using cmd = New SqlCommand("select * from purchase", conn)
                adapter.SelectCommand = cmd
                adapter.Fill(ds, "Purchase")
            End Using
        End Using
    End Using


    Return ds
End Function


// C#
public DataSet GetCustomers()
{
    DataSet ds  = GetCustomerDataSet ();

    using ( SqlConnection conn =
        new SqlConnection (
        "Data Source=.;Initial Catalog=VideoGameStoreDB;Integrated Security=True" ) )
    {
        using ( SqlDataAdapter da = new SqlDataAdapter () )
        {
            using ( SqlCommand cmd =
              new SqlCommand (
                "select CustomerID as ID, CustomerName as Name from Customer", conn ) )
            {
                da.SelectCommand = cmd;
                da.Fill ( ds.Tables["Customer"] );
            }
            using ( SqlCommand cmd =
              new SqlCommand (
                  "select PurchaseID as ID, CustomerID, PurchaseDate, Details " +
                  "from Purchase", conn ) )
            {
                da.SelectCommand = cmd;
                da.Fill ( ds.Tables["Purchase"] );
            }
        }
    }

    return ds;
}
```

EXERCISE 3 Delete Data from the *Order* Table

Continue with the solution from Exercise 2 or use the code for Exercise 2 from the Code
folder on the companion CD. Taking things a step further, in this exercise, you implement
code that deletes data from a *DataTable*.

1. Add a new method named *DeleteCustomer,* which takes one parameter of type *Integer* named *ID.* Within the method, perform the following steps:

   a. Create an new *DataSet* using *GetCustomers.*

   b. From the *DataSet,* select from the *Customer* table the customer with the ID of 2.

   c. Delete that customer.

   d. Accept the changes on the *DataSet.*

2. Create a unit test to debug the created code. Look at the number of rows in the *Purchases* table. Notice that the foreign key relationship deletes the purchases for customer 2 as well as deleting the customer itself.

Your code should look like this:

```vb
' VB
Public Sub DeleteCustomer(ByVal id As Integer)
    Dim ds As DataSet = GetCustomers()
    Dim results() = ds.Tables("Customer").Select("ID = " + id.ToString())
    If results.Length > 0 Then
        results(0).Delete()
    End If
    ds.AcceptChanges()
End Sub
```

```csharp
// C#
public void DeleteCustomer( int id )
{
    DataSet ds = GetCustomers ();
    DataRow[] results = ds.Tables["Customer"].Select ( "ID = " + id.ToString () );
    if ( results.Length > 0 )
    {
        results[0].Delete ();
    }
    ds.AcceptChanges ();
}
```

EXERCISE 4 Return a *DataTable* from a WCF Service

Continue with the solution from Exercise 3 or use the code for Exercise 3 from the Code folder on the companion CD. In this exercise you use what you've learned to build a WCF service and implement a method that returns a *DataTable.*

1. Add a new project of type *WCF* service named *CustomerService.*

2. Add a project reference to the *DataAccess* project.

3. Add a new service named *CustomerService.*

4. Implement a service operation named *GetCustomers.*

5. Use the *CustomerDB* class to return the *DataSet* of customers.

6. Modify the Web.config to enable the WCF service.

Your code should look like this:

```vb
' VB
<ServiceContract()> _
Public Class CustomerService

    Public Sub New()
    End Sub

    <OperationContract()> _
    Public Function GetCustomers() As DataSet
        Dim cdb As New CustomerDB()
        Return cdb.GetCustomers()
    End Function
End Class
```

```csharp
// C#
[ServiceContract]
public class CustomerService
{
    [OperationContract]
        public DataSet GetCustomers()
        {
            CustomerDB cdb = new CustomerDB ();
            return cdb.GetCustomers ();
        }
}
```

Inspect the Web Service Definition Language (WSDL) of the service. Notice that the WSDL contains only generic information about the *DataSet* structure and no specific information about the *Customer* or *Purchases* table.

Lesson Summary

- *DataSets* are an object model for dealing with relational data. The key classes are *DataSet*, *DataTable*, *DataColum*, *DataRow*, and *DataAdapter*.
- *DataSets* can manage relationships between *DataTables*.
- *DataTables* can have a schema to allow for field validation.
- *DataTable* schemas can be inferred from a database query.
- A *DataRow* can contain error information about the row and field in the row.
- *DataSets* and *DataTables* can serialize to be used in (Web) services.

- *DataSets* and *DataTables* offer full support for user-defined types, allowing a custom type to be read from the database and the type to be used as the datatype for that column.
- By default, datatypes in the *DataTable* are database-agnostic, but it is possible to override this behavior and use data provider–specific datatypes.

Lesson Review

You can use the following questions to test your knowledge of the information in Lesson 1, "Introduction to *DataSets*." The questions also are available on the companion CD of this book if you prefer to review them in electronic form.

> **NOTE ANSWERS**
>
> Answers to these questions and explanations of why each answer choice is correct or incorrect are located in the "Answers" section at the end of the book.

1. Which of the following snippets sets an error?

    A.

    ```
    ' VB
    dataRow.SetRowError("This order is invalid.")
    ```

    ```
    // C#
    dataRow.SetRowError("This order is invalid.");
    ```

    B.

    ```
    ' VB
    dataRow.RowError = "This order is invalid"
    ```

    ```
    // C#
    dataRow.RowError = "This order is invalid";
    ```

    C.

    ```
    ' VB
    dataTable.SetColumnError(0, "This field is invalid")
    ```

    ```
    // C#
    dataTable.SetColumnError(0, "This field is invalid");
    ```

    D. None of the above.

2. Which of the following snippets loads a schema of the *Orders DataTable?*

    A.

    ```
    ' VB
    Dim ds as New DataSet
    dataAdapter.Fill(ds, SchemaType.Source)
    ```

```
// C#
DataSet ds = new DataSet();
dataAdapter.Fill(ds, SchemaType.Source);
```

B.

```
' VB
Dim ds as New DataSet
sqlCommand.FillSchema(ds, SchemaType.Source, "Orders")
```

```
// C#
DataSet ds = new DataSet();
sqlCommand.FillSchema(ds, SchemaType.Source, "Orders");
```

C.

```
' VB
Dim ds as New DataSet
dataAdapter.FillSchema(ds)
```

```
// C#
DataSet ds = new DataSet();
dataAdapter.FillSchema(ds);
```

D.

```
' VB
Dim ds as New DataSet
dataAdapter.FillSchema(ds, SchemaType.Source, "Orders")
```

```
// C#
DataSet ds = new DataSet();
dataAdapter.FillSchema(ds, SchemaType.Source ,"Orders")
```

Lesson 2: Working with *Typed DataSets*

In Lesson 1, you looked at using *DataSets*, *DataTables*, and *DataRows*. In this lesson, you look at how Visual Studio offers functionality around these framework classes to allow you to develop software in a more strongly typed manner.

> **After this lesson, you will be able to:**
> - Create and use a *Typed DataSet*
> - Create and use a *TableAdapter*
>
> **Estimated lesson time: 30 minutes**

Using *Typed DataSets*

It's important to know that *Typed DataSets* are not part of the .NET Framework. Rather, they are a feature of Visual Studio that allows you to generate code to map tables and relationships onto *DataSets* and *DataTables* easily and use them in a strongly typed manner in your code. Additionally, the *Typed DataSets* allows Visual Studio to help you be more productive by providing Intellisense on *DataSets* and *DataTables*.

Strongly Typing Values

In Lesson 1, you saw that when using a *DataRow* object, you need to use either an ordinal or a column name to access a specific field in a row. Not only that, but to retrieve the right type, you need to cast the value to the correct type. This looked like the following code:

```vb
' VB
Dim dt As DataTable = BuildProductTable()
Dim dr As DataRow = dt.NewRow()
dr("ProductID") = 1

Dim productID As Integer
productID = CType(dr("ProductID"), Integer)
```

```csharp
// C#
DataTable dt = BuildProductTable();
DataRow dr = dt.NewRow();
dr["ProductID"] = 1;

int productID = (int) dr["ProductID"];
```

This sample shows how the basic *DataRow* class needs indexers to access fields and casting of values to retrieve a typed value. This style of coding is prone to errors. *Typed DataSets* aim to prevent you from making errors in referencing fields and casting values by generating code, based on table and query definitions.

The DataSet Designer

Typed DataSets in Visual Studio are created using the DataSet Designer. The designer is invoked when you create a new *Typed DataSet*. To do this, add a new item of type *DataSet,* as shown in Figure 3-6.

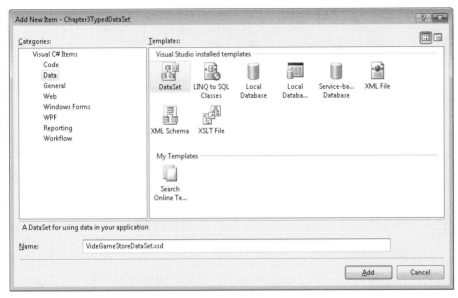

FIGURE 3-6 Adding a *Typed DataSet* to your project

After adding the item to your project, the designer opens automatically, showing you an empty design surface, as shown in Figure 3-7.

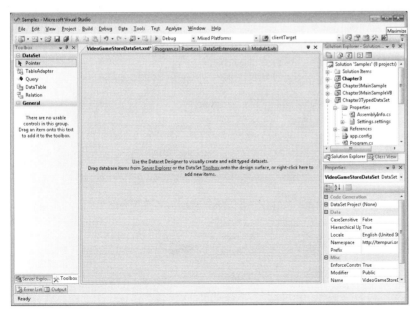

FIGURE 3-7 A new *DataSet* in the DataSet Designer

As indicated by the toolbox, a *Typed DataSet* consists of *TableAdapters*, queries, data tables, and relationships.

TABLEADAPTER

Dragging a *TableAdapter* from the toolbox onto the design surface triggers the TableAdapter Configuration Wizard, shown in Figure 3-8.

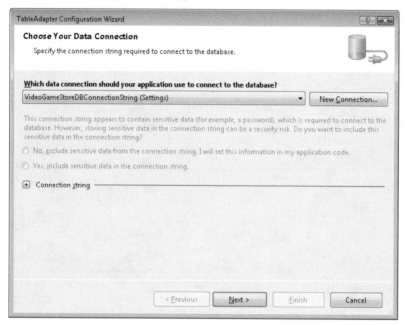

FIGURE 3-8 The TableAdapter Configuration Wizard

The wizard makes you specify a database connection first, so you select *VideoGameStoreDB* as your connection. Doing this automatically creates an entry in your configuration file, allowing the connection string to be modified when deploying the application to different machines. The entry created in the configuration file looks like this:

```
<connectionStrings>
    <add name="Chapter3TypedDataSet.Properties.Settings.
VideoGameStoreDBConnectionString"
        connectionString="Data Source=.;Initial Catalog=VideoGameStoreDB;Integrated
Security=True"
        providerName="System.Data.SqlClient" />
</connectionStrings>
```

Next, the Choose A Command Type page of the wizard, shown in Figure 3-9, asks you to define how you want to access the database.

You have the choice of any of the following:

- Defining a SQL statement
- Creating new stored procedures
- Using existing stored procedures

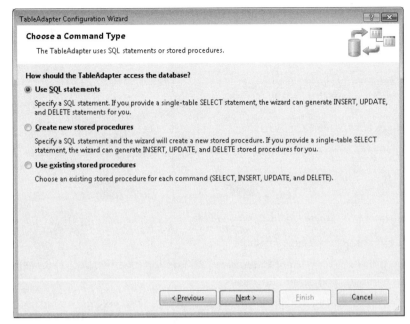

FIGURE 3-9 Specifying how the *TableAdapter* needs to access the database

When choosing for SQL statements, the Enter A SQL Statement page connects to an editor that allows you to specify the query used to retrieve data, see Figure 3-10. A query builder is also available for building more complex SQL statements.

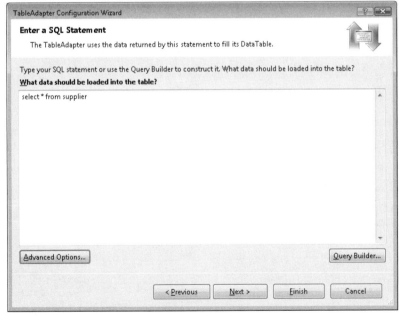

FIGURE 3-10 Specifying the SQL statement

Pressing Advanced Options opens a new window, named Advanced Options, that displays a number of significant settings, shown in Figure 3-11.

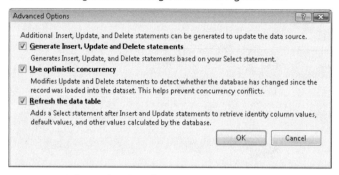

FIGURE 3-11 Advanced options for generating the *Typed DataSet*

All the following options are enabled by default:

- **Generate Insert, Update, and Delete Statements** This option uses the select statement to derive insert, update, and delete statements.

- **Use Optimistic Concurrency** This option influences the SQL statement generated for the first option. If enabled, the update and delete statements include a WHERE clause, which checks to see if the records was modified after being read from the database.

- **Refresh the DataTable** This option generates code that refreshes a data row after it has been committed to the database. This is especially useful if you're using the database for generating primary keys or have a timestamp column in your table to identify row versions.

After you choose the advanced options and set the SQL query, the Choose Methods to Generate page of the wizard (shown in Figure 3-12) allows you to choose and name the methods to be generated on the *TableAdapter*.

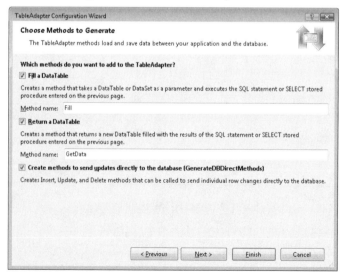

FIGURE 3-12 Choosing which methods to generate

- **Fill a *DataTable***   This option generates a method, with a name that you specify, that takes a *DataTable* as a parameter and loads the data into that table. This is usually used if you plan to have *DataSets* with multiple tables.

- **Return a *DataTable***   This option generates a method, with a name that you specify, that uses a SQL statement to build a new *DataTable* and return that *DataTable*.

- **Create Methods to Send Updates Directly to the Database**   This option creates additional methods on the *TableAdapter*, allowing you to insert, update, and delete data without using *DataRows*, but rather by passing each individual field as a parameter.

The wizard now generates the *TableAdapter* based in the information that you provided. It also automatically generates a *Typed DataTable* because the *TableAdapter* needs a datatable to hold the retrieved data, as shown in Figure 3-13.

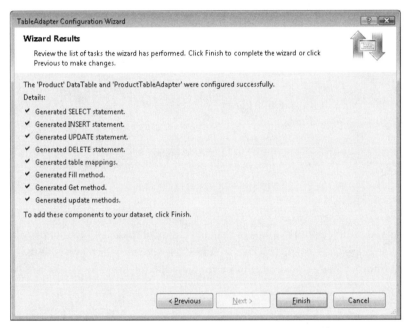

FIGURE 3-13 Generating the *TableAdapter* and the matching *DataTable*

The result is displayed on the design surface of the DataSet Designer, as shown in Figure 3-14.

An alternative way to achieve the same result would be to open Server Explorer; connect to the database; and drag a table, view, or stored procedure from Server Explorer onto the design surface.

By clicking on a column in the *DataTable*, you can inspect the properties in the Property windows.

You can add queries to a *TableAdapter* by right-clicking the *TableAdapter* and selecting Add Query. The query specified when adding queries to a *TableAdapter* can return any number of fields from the database up to the total that it holds. Specifying more fields results in an error, and specifying fewer leaves fields empty. Columns marked as mandatory should not be excluded from the query because a runtime error results.

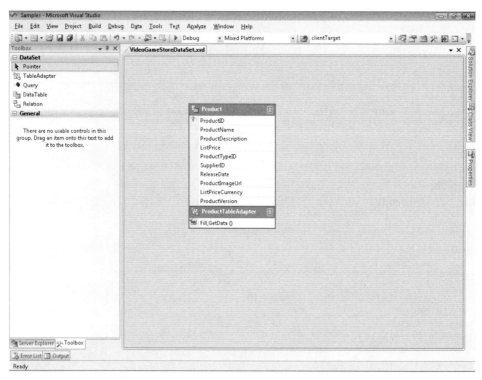

FIGURE 3-14 The *DataTable*, with the *TableAdapter*, on the design surface

QUERY

By using the *TableAdapter*, you can retrieve sets of data from the database, and the set of data is stored in a table. Using the *Query* item, you can create a *TableAdapter*, which implements SQL statements that return either a single value or perform an update, insert, or delete.

DATATABLE

When adding a *DataAdapter* to the *DataSet*, you automatically create a *DataTable* that matches the result of the *Select* query. It is also possible to define *DataTables* without a *TableAdapter*. To do this, drag a *DataTable* item from the toolbox onto the design surface and right-click the *DataTable* to add columns.

RELATIONSHIPS

DataTables can have relationships with other *DataTables* (or with themselves). When dragging tables from Server Explorer onto the design surface or when adding a new *TableAdapter*, the designer automatically checks for a relationship with another *DataTable*. If it detects a relationship, it adds the relationship to the *DataSet*. It uses the metadata from the database to do this. If you want to create a relationship manually, drag the *Relation* item from the toolbox onto the design surface.

Sample: Products and Suppliers

The following sample uses the *VideoGameStoreDB* database to build a *Typed DataSet* with products and suppliers. The goal is to create an application that prints all products per supplier to the console.

To do this, perform the following steps:

1. Create a console application named SupplierListing.

2. Add a *DataSet* named VideoGameStoreDataSet.

3. Open Server Explorer and add a data connection to *VideoGameStoreDB* (included on the companion CD), if not already present.

4. Drag the *Products* table onto the design surface.

5. Drag a *TableAdapter* from the toolbox onto the design surface. Doing this activates the TableAdapter Configuration Wizard.

6. In the wizard, when entering the SQL statement, select all fields except the *SupplierLocation* field.

Notice how the designer automatically detects the relationship between *Supplier* and *Product.*

You're ready to use the *DataSet.* Listing 3-4 shows how you can use the *Typed DataSet* to retrieve data. This involves the following steps:

1. Create an instance of the *DataSet.*

2. Create instances of the *TableAdapters* that you want to use to retrieve the data from the database.

3. Fill the tables in the *DataSet* using the *Fill* method in the *TableAdapter.*

The *DataSet* is now populated with data and you can iterate over the suppliers in the *Supplier* table. Notice how the *Typed DataSet* now has a property called *Supplier* and you don't need an indexer on the *Tables* property to access the table. Also, each row in the table is not of type *DataRow,* but rather of type *SupplierRow.*

Fields of the supplier are accessed using the *SupplierRow,* which offers properties for each column in the table.

A method has been generated to traverse the relationship between supplier and product. The *SupplierRow* offers a method named *GetProducts,* which returns an array of *ProductRow* objects.

LISTING 3-4 Using *Typed DataSets*

```vb
' VB
Public Sub Main(ByVal args() As String)
    Dim ds As VideoGameStoreDataSet = New VideoGameStoreDataSet
    Dim taProduct As VideoGameStoreDataSetTableAdapters.ProductTableAdapter = _
                    New VideoGameStoreDataSetTableAdapters.ProductTableAdapter
    Dim taSupplier As VideoGameStoreDataSetTableAdapters.SupplierTableAdapter = _
                    New VideoGameStoreDataSetTableAdapters.SupplierTableAdapter
    taProduct.Fill(ds.Product)
    taSupplier.Fill(ds.Supplier)
    For Each supplier As VideoGameStoreDataSet.SupplierRow In ds.Supplier
        Console.WriteLine("------------------------------")
        Console.WriteLine(("Supplier: " _
                    + (supplier.SupplierName + (" [" _
                    + (supplier.SupplierPhone + "]")))))
        Console.WriteLine("Products:")
        Dim products() As VideoGameStoreDataSet.ProductRow = _
    supplier.GetProductRows
        For Each product As VideoGameStoreDataSet.ProductRow In products
            Console.WriteLine(("   " + product.ProductName))
        Next
    Next
    Console.ReadLine()
End Sub
```

```csharp
// C#
static void Main( string[] args )
{
    VideoGameStoreDataSet ds = new VideoGameStoreDataSet ();

    VideoGameStoreDataSetTableAdapters.ProductTableAdapter taProduct =
        new VideoGameStoreDataSetTableAdapters.ProductTableAdapter ();
    VideoGameStoreDataSetTableAdapters.SupplierTableAdapter taSupplier =
        new VideoGameStoreDataSetTableAdapters.SupplierTableAdapter ();

    taProduct.Fill ( ds.Product );
    taSupplier.Fill ( ds.Supplier );

    foreach ( VideoGameStoreDataSet.SupplierRow supplier in ds.Supplier )
```

```
{
    Console.WriteLine ( "---------------------------------------" );
    Console.WriteLine ( "Supplier: " + supplier.SupplierName +
                        " [" + supplier.SupplierPhone + "]" );
    Console.WriteLine ( "Products:" );

VideoGameStoreDataSet.ProductRow[] products =
                                supplier.GetProductRows();
    foreach ( VideoGameStoreDataSet.ProductRow product in products )
    {
        Console.WriteLine ( "    " + product.ProductName );
    }
}

    Console.ReadLine ();
}
```

✔ **Quick Check**

   ■ Where does a *Typed DataSet* store connection information?

Quick Check Answer

   ■ A unique entry is created in the connection section of the configuration file.

LAB   **Using *Typed DataSets***

In this lab, you create a class library to read data into a *Typed DataSet* and use the generated classes to extract the information. You need the *VideoGameStoreDB* database to complete these exercises. You can install the solutions to these exercises from the Code folder on the companion CD.

EXERCISE 1   Create a *Typed DataSet* with Customer and Purchase Details

In this exercise, you build a class library that implements a data access layer using *Typed DataSets* and create the *DataSet*.

1.   Open a new class library project named: TypedDataAccess.
2.   Add a new item of *Typed DataSet,* named *CustomerDataSet*
3.   Use Server Explorer to connect to the *VideoGameStoreDB* database.
4.   Using the DataSet Designer and Server Explorer, add the *Customer* and *Purchase* tables to the design surface of the *CustomerDataSet* by dragging them from Server Explorer to the DataSet Designer.
5.   Notice how the relationship between the two tables is created automatically.

EXERCISE 2   Load Data into a *Typed DataSet*

In this exercise, you load data into the *DataSet* that you created in the previous exercise.

1.   Use the TypedDataAccess project created in Exercise 1, or copy the project from the solution on the companion CD, and add a class named *CustomerDB*.

2.   Add a method named *GetCustomers*, which returns a *CustomerDataSet*.

   Within the method, perform the following steps:

   a.   Create a *DataSet* of type *CustomerDataSet*.

   b.   Fill both the *Customer* and *Purchase* tables in the *DataSet* using the *TableAdapters*.

   c.   Return the *DataSet*.

   Your code should look like this:

```vb
' VB
Public Class CustomerDB

    Public Function GetCustomers() As CustomerDataSet
        Dim ds As New CustomerDataSet()

        Using cta = New CustomerDataSetTableAdapters.CustomerTableAdapter()
            Using pta = New CustomerDataSetTableAdapters.PurchaseTableAdapter()
                cta.Fill(ds.Customer)
                pta.Fill(ds.Purchase)
            End Using
        End Using
        Return ds
    End Function
End Class
```

```csharp
// C#
public class CustomerDB
{
    public CustomerDataSet GetCustomers()
    {
        CustomerDataSet ds = new CustomerDataSet ();
        using ( CustomerDataSetTableAdapters.CustomerTableAdapter cta =
            new CustomerDataSetTableAdapters.CustomerTableAdapter () )
        {
            using ( CustomerDataSetTableAdapters.PurchaseTableAdapter pta =
                new CustomerDataSetTableAdapters.PurchaseTableAdapter () )
            {
                cta.Fill ( ds.Customer );
                pta.Fill ( ds.Purchase );
            }
        }
```

```
        return ds;
    }
}
```

EXERCISE 3   Insert Data into a *Typed DataSet*

Continuing with the code from Exercise 2, you implement code to insert data into the *DataSet*.

1. Use the TypedDataAccess project created in Exercise 2, or copy the project from the solution on the companion CD. Assume that you need a method to add a customer to the *Customer* table, perhaps to reuse this method in a Web service. Add a method called *AddCustomer* to the *CustomerDB* class and let it take two parameters: an ID of type *Integer* and a name of type *String*.

2. Within this method, create a new customer datatable of type *CustomerDataTable*.

4. Add a new row to the table using the *AddCustomerRow* method.

5. Notice how the Intellisense helps you when adding a new row.

    Your code should look like this:

```vb
' VB
Public Sub AddCustomer(ByVal id As Integer, ByVal name As String)
    Dim ctbl = New CustomerDataSet.CustomerDataTable()
    ctbl.AddCustomerRow(name, Nothing, Nothing, Guid.Empty)
End Sub
```

```csharp
// C#
public void AddCustomer( int id, int name )
{
    CustomerDataSet.CustomerDataTable ctbl = new CustomerDataSet.CustomerDataTable ();
    ctbl.AddCustomerRow ( name, null, null, Guid.Empty );
}
```

Lesson Summary

- *Typed DataSets* are not part of the .NET Framework.
- *Typed DataSets* consist of code generated using the DataSet Designer in Visual Studio.
- The four elements of *Typed DataSets* are
    - DataAdapter
    - DataTable
    - Query
    - Relation
- A *Typed DataSet* contains properties for accessing the datatables in the *DataSet* in a strongly typed manner.
- A *Typed DataTable* contains properties for accessing rows in a strongly typed manner.

- A typed row contrains properties for accessing fields as properties in a strongly typed manner. It also contains methods for navigating relationships.
- Typed *TableAdapters* use a connection string that can be managed via the configuration file.

Lesson Review

You can use the following questions to test your knowledge of the information in Lesson 2, *"Typed DataSets."* The questions also are available on the companion CD of this book if you prefer to review them in electronic form.

NOTE ANSWERS

Answers to these questions and explanations of why each answer choice is correct or incorrect are located in the "Answers" section at the end of the book.

1. Which of the following statements is true? (Choose all that apply. Each answer is a separate solution.)

   A. *Typed DataSets* are part of the System.Data namespace in the .NET Framework.

   B. *Typed DataSets* are a Visual Studio feature for generating code.

   C. *Typed DataSets* work only on a SQL Server database.

   D. *Typed DataSets* have been around since the first version of Visual Studio.

2. Which statement is true?

   A. A *Typed DataSet* can contain data from only one data source.

   B. A typed *DataAdapter* uses a connection string that is stored in the application settings section of the configuration file.

   C. A typed *DataRow* contains properties for navigating relationships.

   D. A typed *DataAdapter* can optionally includes methods for accessing the database directly.

Chapter Review

To practice and reinforce the skills you learned in this chapter further, you can do any or all of the following:

- Review the chapter summary.
- Review the list of key terms introduced in this chapter.
- Complete the case scenarios. These scenarios set up real-world situations involving the topics of this chapter and ask you to create a solution.
- Complete the suggested practices.
- Take a practice test.

Chapter Summary

- *DataSets* and *DataTables* allow data to be kept in memory in a relational model, independent of the device used.
- A *DataSet* can maintain and validate relationships between *DataTables*.
- A *DataTable* consists of *DataColumns* and *DataRows*.
- A typed *DataTable* consists of *DataColumns* and typed *DataRows*.
- Typed *DataRows* offer properties to access fields and methods to navigate relationships.
- *TableAdapters* are used to load data into *DataTables*.
- Typed *TableAdapters* offer methods for loading data into typed *DataTables*.

Key Terms

Do you know what these key terms mean? You can check your answers by looking up the terms in the glossary at the end of the book.

- *Constraint*
- *DataColumn*
- *DataRelation*
- *DataRow*
- *DataSet*
- *DataTable*
- *Typed DataSet*

Case Scenario

In the following case scenario, you apply what you've learned about how to use *DataSets* to retrieve data from a database. You can find answers to the questions posed in this scenario in the "Answers" section at the end of this book.

Case Scenario: Designing Data Access

The company you work for has decided it needs to replace an existing VB6 application with a .NET Framework application. The application uses a relational database and you're asked to present a solution for accessing the data in the database. The application consists of a desktop application and a number of scheduled batch jobs.

In interviews, these people have said the following:

IT MANAGER

"We need to develop applications fast and with as few bugs as possible. Catching and fixing a bug early in the development cycle is 10 times cheaper than solving a bug in production code."

CFO

"One of the batches is the invoice batch. It is imperative that this batch performs well. We need to send out those invoices on the first day of the month."

QUESTION

Answer the following question for your manager

- What kind of data access technology should you use?

Suggested Practices

To help you master the exam objectives presented in this chapter, complete the following tasks.

Using ADO.NET in a Windows application

- **Practice 1** Use the *VideoGameStoreDB* database to create a Microsoft Windows application that uses a data adapter to fill a *DataTable* with products and bind the *DataTable* to a datagrid in the user interface

- **Practice 2** Use the *VideoGameStoreDB* database to create a Windows application that uses a typed *DataSet* data adapter to fill a typed *DataTable* with products and bind the *DataTable* to a datagrid in the user interface. Notice how the datagrid deals differently with this data source

Take a Practice Test

The practice tests on this book's companion CD offer many options. For example, you can test yourself on just the content covered in this chapter, or you can test yourself on the entire 70-561 certification exam content. You can set up the test so that it closely simulates the experience of taking a certification exam, or you can set it up in study mode, which allows you to look at the correct answers and explanations after you answer each question

> **MORE INFO**   **PRACTICE TESTS**
>
> For details about all the available practice test options, see the section entitled "How to Use the Practice Tests," in the Introduction of this book.

CHAPTER 4

Updating Data

Data adapters and table adapters are the core ADO.NET elements that assist not just reading data from the database but also updating data in the database. This chapter deals with the intricacies of implementing not just basic update scenarios but also with implementing transaction management to maintain data integrity and how to deal with exceptions that may occur in the update process.

Exam objectives in this chapter:

- Manage data by using the *DataAdapter* or the *TableAdapter*.
- Manage transactions.
- Manage data integrity.
- Update data.
- Manage exceptions when modifying data.

Lessons in this chapter:

Before You Begin

To complete the lessons in this chapter, you must have:

- A computer that meets or exceeds the minimum hardware requirements listed in the "Introduction" section at the beginning of the book
- Microsoft Visual Studio 2008 Professional Edition installed on your computer
- An understanding of Microsoft Visual Basic or C# syntax and familiarity with Microsoft .NET Framework version 3.5
- An understanding of relational data, transactions, and two-phase commit.

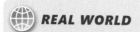

REAL WORLD

Mark Blomsma

Implementing scenarios for updating data in a database involves more than "executing a SQL insert statement." From an architecture point of view, you need a clear strategy for dealing with database interaction. You also need an architecture that allows you to be flexible in supporting both online applications as well as batch-oriented systems. I've worked on an application where we build an invoicing system where we created the user interface first. This leads to an application where most functions were scoped around a single invoice. Next, we started implementing the batches. Being concerned about code reuse, we of course reused the services we created for the user interface, which at a functional level gave us quick results. Our nonfunctional requirements related to performance were another matter, however. Running a batch with millions of invoices does not scale well if you create a database roundtrip for each invoice. After refactoring our code and setting the *SqlDataAdapter.BulkUpdate* property to 20000, allowing us to fire 20000 inserts into SQL Server in a single roundtrip, boosted performance by a factor of 100.

Lesson 1: Updating Data

There are many ways of updating data using ADO.NET. This lesson explains the core ADO.NET elements involved in performing updates. Higher levels of abstraction, such as LINQ to SQL and Entity Framework, use these elements while allowing you to program in an object-oriented manner.

> **After this lesson, you will be able to:**
> - Insert /Update/Delete data using a command
> - Insert /Update/Delete data using a *DataAdapter*
> - Insert/Update/Delete data using a *Typed DataSet*
> - Change the batch size of a bulk update
> - Update custom data types
> - Use stored procedures to update data
> - Use dynamic SQL to update data
>
> **Estimated lesson time: 45 minutes**

Insert /Update/Delete Data Using a Command

The *DbCommand* class is the ADO.NET base class that can be used to send a non-query SQL statement to the database. The *DbCommand* class represents a SQL statement or stored procedure to execute against a data source. It is a base class for database-specific classes that represent commands. Specific implementations include *SqlCommand, OledbCommand, OdbcCommand, OracleCommand*, and other database-specific vendor classes. The code here shows how to use *DbProviderFactory* to generate a database-independent command that fires a *DELETE* statement at the database:

```vb
' VB
Public Sub DeleteCustomer(ByVal id As Integer)
    ' Get connection string
    Dim css As ConnectionStringSettings
    css = ConfigurationManager.ConnectionStrings("VideoGameStoreDB")

    ' Get factory based on info on database provider
    Dim factory As DbProviderFactory
    factory = DbProviderFactories.GetFactory(css.ProviderName)
    ' Use using construct to ensure Dispose is called after completion
    Using conn As DbConnection = factory.CreateConnection
        conn.ConnectionString = css.ConnectionString
```

```
' Use using construct to ensure Dispose is called after completion
Using cmd As DbCommand = factory.CreateCommand()
    cmd.Connection = conn
    cmd.CommandType = CommandType.Text
    cmd.CommandText = "delete customer where customerID = @id"

    ' Create "id" parameter
    Dim paramID As DbParameter
    paramID = factory.CreateParameter()
    paramID.ParameterName = "@id"
    paramID.Value = id

    cmd.Parameters.Add(paramID)

    ' Open connection and execute query
    conn.Open()
    Dim count As Integer
    count = cmd.ExecuteNonQuery()
    conn.Close()

    If count < 1 Then
        Throw New ArgumentOutOfRangeException("id", "Customer not found.")
    End If

    End Using
End Using
End Sub


// C#
public void DeleteCustomer(int id)
{
    // Get connection string
    ConnectionStringSettings css =
            ConfigurationManager.ConnectionStrings["VideoGameStoreDB"];
    DbProviderFactory factory = DbProviderFactories.GetFactory ( css.ProviderName );

    // Use using construct to ensure Dispose is called after completion
    using ( DbConnection conn = factory.CreateConnection () )
    {
        conn.ConnectionString = css.ConnectionString;

        // Use using construct to ensure Dispose is called after completion
        using ( DbCommand cmd = factory.CreateCommand () )
        {
            cmd.Connection = conn;
            cmd.CommandType = CommandType.Text;
            cmd.CommandText = "delete customer where customerID = @id";
```

```
    // Create "id" parameter
    DbParameter paramID = factory.CreateParameter ();
    paramID.ParameterName = "@id";
    paramID.Value = id;
    cmd.Parameters.Add ( paramID );

    // Open connection and execute query
    conn.Open ();
    int count = cmd.ExecuteNonQuery ();
    conn.Close ();

    if ( count < 1 )
        throw new ArgumentOutOfRangeException ( "id", "Customer not found." );
    }
}
```

To avoid risk of SQL injection, it is recommended to use parameters rather than string concatenation. Malicious SQL code can be executed when using string concatenation; for instance, a user could enter a closing quote in an input field followed by a whole new SQL statement. Because the string is appended to a *SELECT* statement, the code is executed. The command object can also be used to execute a stored procedure. To execute a stored procedure, change the *CommandType* property to *CommandType.StoredProcedure* and assign the stored procedure name instead of assigning a SQL statement to the *CommandText* property.

> **MORE INFO   READ MORE ON SQL INJECTION**
>
> MSDN has a whole section on security and protection, including SQL Injection. Read more about this topic at *http://msdn.microsoft.com/en-us/library/ms161953.aspx*, or use Live Search to look for the keywords "Microsoft SQL Injection."

The previous code could also be implemented in a database-specific manner, as shown in the code sample here:

```vb
' VB

Public Sub DeleteCustomer(ByVal id As Integer)
    Dim css As ConnectionStringSettings
    css = ConfigurationManager.ConnectionStrings("VideoGameStoreDB")

    Using conn As SqlConnection = New SqlConnection()
        conn.ConnectionString = css.ConnectionString

        Using cmd As SqlCommand = New SqlCommand()
            cmd.Connection = conn
            cmd.CommandType = CommandType.Text
            cmd.CommandText = "delete customer where customerID = @id"
```

```
            cmd.Parameters.AddWithValue("@id", id)

            conn.Open()
            Dim count As Integer
            count = cmd.ExecuteNonQuery()
            conn.Close()

            If count < 1 Then
                Throw New ArgumentOutOfRangeException("id", "Customer not found.")
            End If

        End Using
    End Using
End Sub


// C#
public void DeleteCustomer( int id )
{
    ConnectionStringSettings css = ConfigurationManager.ConnectionStrings
            ["Samples.Properties.Settings.VideoGameStoreDB"];
    using ( SqlConnection conn = new SqlConnection ( css.ConnectionString ) )
    {
        using ( SqlCommand cmd = new SqlCommand () )
        {
            cmd.Connection = conn;
cmd.CommandType = CommandType.Text;
            cmd.CommandText = "delete customer where customerID = @id";

            SqlParameter paramID = new SqlParameter ( "@id", id );
            cmd.Parameters.Add ( paramID );

            conn.Open ();
            int count = cmd.ExecuteNonQuery ();
            conn.Close ();

            if ( count == -1 )
                throw new ArgumentOutOfRangeException ( "id", "Customer not found." );
        }
    }
}
```

Instead of using the *DbProviderFactory* the code decides the type of database it wants to connect to and instantiates a *SqlConnection* object. The same goes for the command object; rather than using the factory to create an instance of a *DbCommand* the code goes ahead and creates an instance of a *SqlCommand*.

Notice how the database-specific implementation offers overloaded constructors, which create much more compact code.

Update Data Using a *DataAdapter*

In Chapter 3, "DataSets," you saw how a *DataAdapter* can be used to retrieve data from the database and store the data in a *DataSet* or *DataTable*. A common scenario is to load data from a database into a *DataTable*, modify data in the user interface, and then persist the changes back to the database. The *DataAdapter* is capable not just of retrieving the data, but also of sending any changes back to the database. A common scenario is to use a command builder to create the commands used by the *DataAdapter* to update, insert, and delete data.

Using a Command Builder

DbCommandBuilder is a class that allows you to generate *DELETE*, *INSERT*, and *UPDATE* statements based on a provided *SELECT* statement. Going back to the previous sample of deleting a customer, the code could be rewritten to derive the *DELETE* statement from the *SELECT* statement, as shown in the code here:

```
' VB
Public Sub UpdateCustomer(ByVal id As Integer)
    Dim css As ConnectionStringSettings
    css = ConfigurationManager.ConnectionStrings("VideoGameStoreDB")

    Using conn As SqlConnection = New SqlConnection()
        conn.ConnectionString = css.ConnectionString

        Using cmd As SqlCommand = New SqlCommand("select customerID,
                customerName from customer", conn)

            Using adapter As SqlDataAdapter = New SqlDataAdapter(cmd)

                ' the SqlCommandBuilder will derive insert, update
                ' and delete commands and add them to the adapter
                Dim builder As SqlCommandBuilder = New SqlCommandBuilder(adapter)

                Dim dt As DataTable = New DataTable()

                adapter.Fill(dt)
                adapter.FillSchema(dt, SchemaType.Mapped)

                ' row 0 will now be changed
                dt.Rows(0)("CustomerName") = "Mark" + RandomNumber()

                ' send changes to database
                adapter.Update(dt)
```

```
        End Using

      End Using
    End Using
  End Using
End Sub


// C#
public void UpdateCustomer( int id )
{
    ConnectionStringSettings css = ConfigurationManager.ConnectionStrings
            ["VideoGameStoreDB"];
    using ( SqlConnection conn = new SqlConnection ( css.ConnectionString ) )
    {
        using ( SqlCommand cmd =
            new SqlCommand( "select customerID, customerName from customer" , conn) )
        {
            using ( SqlDataAdapter adapter = new SqlDataAdapter ( cmd ) )
            {
                // the SqlCommandBuilder will derive insert, update
                // and delete commands and add them to the adaper.
                SqlCommandBuilder builder
                        = new SqlCommandBuilder ( adapter );

                DataTable dt = new DataTable ();
                adapter.Fill ( dt );
                adapter.FillSchema ( dt, SchemaType.Mapped );

                // row 0 will be now changed
                dt.Rows[0]["CustomerName"] = "Mark" + RandomNumber();

                // send changes to database
                adapter.Update ( dt );

            }
        }
    }
}
```

The previous code shows *SqlCommand* being used to create a *SqlDataAdapter*. *SqlCommandBuilder* is then used to derive the *INSERT, UPDATE,* and *DELETE* statements and set those properties in the *DataAdapter*. After modifying data in the datatable, the updates can be sent back to the database simply by calling the *UPDATE* statement on the *DataAdapter*.

How the *UPDATE* and *DELETE* statements deal with concurrency issues depends on the table definition. If your table contains a *TimeStamp* column, then this column is used in the WHERE clause of the *UPDATE* and *DELETE* statements. If the table does not have such a column, then by default, all available fields are used in the WHERE clause and the original values of the fields are used to detect whether the data in the database has been changed by another user while the current data was disconnected.

Performing Bulk Updates

The *SqlDataAdapter* used in the previous sample is a specific implementation of the *DbDataAdapter*. Aside from implementing the default behavior of the base class in a Microsoft SQL Server–specific manner, it also offers a property called *BatchUpdateSize*. This property, which is set to 1 by default, sets how many SQL statements are sent to the database in a single batch. By defaulting to 1, it is set to open a connection, send one statement, and then close the connection. In batch scenarios, this can be a very costly way of interacting with the database. Imagine a data table with 10,000 new rows. With 10,000 round trips to the server running SQL Server, performance would be poor. By setting the *BatchUpdateSize* to 2,000, for example, only five batches of statements would be sent to the database.

Update Data Using a Table Adapter

Chapter 3 demonstrated the use of *Typed DataSets* for retrieving data from the database. Figure 3-13 showed that the code generated by the *Typed DataSet* includes *UPDATE*, *INSERT*, and *DELETE* statements. The generated statements can be used to perform an update on a *Typed DataSet* in a similar fashion as when using a plain *DataAdapter*.

Using the *VideoGameStoreDataSet,* as shown in Figure 4-1, you can write the following code to use a table adapter to send updates to the database:

```vb
' VB
' Create datasets and table adapters
Dim ds As New VideoGameStoreDataSet()

Dim taProduct As _
    New VideoGameStoreDataSetTableAdapters.ProductTableAdapter()
Dim taSupplier As _
    New VideoGameStoreDataSetTableAdapters.SupplierTableAdapter()

' Fill tables
taProduct.Fill(ds.Product)
taSupplier.Fill(ds.Supplier)

' Add new row to table
Dim product = ds.Product.NewProductRow()
product.SupplierRow = ds.Supplier(0)
product.ProductName = "Halo 6"
ds.Product.AddProductRow(product)

' Update the database using the table adapter
taProduct.Update(ds)
```

```csharp
// C#
// Create datasets and table adapters
VideoGameStoreDataSet ds = new VideoGameStoreDataSet ();

VideoGameStoreDataSetTableAdapters.ProductTableAdapter taProduct =
    new VideoGameStoreDataSetTableAdapters.ProductTableAdapter ();
VideoGameStoreDataSetTableAdapters.SupplierTableAdapter taSupplier =
    new VideoGameStoreDataSetTableAdapters.SupplierTableAdapter ();

// Fill tables
taProduct.Fill ( ds.Product );
taSupplier.Fill ( ds.Supplier );

// Add new row to table
VideoGameStoreDataSet.ProductRow product = ds.Product.NewProductRow ();
product.SupplierRow = ds.Supplier[0];
product.ProductName = "Halo 6";
ds.Product.AddProductRow ( product );

// Update the database using the table adapter
taProduct.Update ( ds );
```

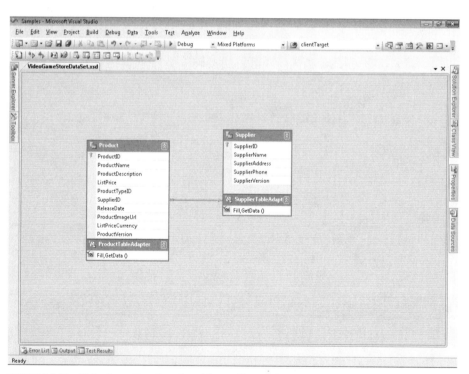

FIGURE 4-1 The *VideoGameStoreDataSet* with suppliers and products

Alternatively, when creating the *Typed DataSet*, the *GenerateDirectDBStatements* option generates typed *INSERT, UPDATE,* and *DELETE* statements on the table adapter, allowing the table adapter to be used to execute a direct statement without using the *DataSet* of *DataTable*. Because these become methods on the *DataAdapter,* Visual Studio offers Intellisense when using these methods, as shown in Figure 4-2.

```
taProduct.Insert(
```
int ProductTableAdapter.Insert (**string ProductName**, string ProductDescription, double ListPrice, int ProductTypeID,
                                int? SupplierID, DateTime? ReleaseDate, string ProductImageUrl, string ListPriceCurrency)

FIGURE 4-2 Direct database statement usage in Visual Studio

Updating Custom Types

SQL Server 2005 and later support the use of Common Language Runtime (CLR) types as column types. ADO.NET supports this feature through the *SqlClient* namespace and a *SqlCommand* or even a *DataAdapter UPDATE* statement can be used to update a custom type. DataSet Designer, however, does not support the use of custom types.

Because custom types are a SQL Server–specific feature, you need to use the *SqlCommand* class to create a command that can update a custom type. The code here shows how the *Supplier* table in the *VideoGameStoreDB* has a *Location* column of type *Point,* with *Point* being a user-defined type. Notice that the *UdtTypeName* property needs to be set on the location parameter:

```vb
' VB
Public Sub InsertSupplier(ByVal name As String, ByVal location As Point)
    ' Get connectionstring from configfile.
    Dim css As ConnectionStringSettings
    css = ConfigurationManager.ConnectionStrings("VideoGameStoreDB")

    ' Build database connection
    Using conn As SqlConnection = New SqlConnection()
        conn.ConnectionString = css.ConnectionString

        ' Build sql command
        Using cmd As SqlCommand = _
                New SqlCommand _
    ("insert into supplier (supplierName, supplierLocation) VALUES ( @name,
            @location )", conn)

            ' Add name parameter
            cmd.Parameters.AddWithValue("@name", name)

            ' Add location parameter
            Dim paramLocation As New SqlParameter("@location", location)
```

```
            paramLocation.UdtTypeName = "Point"
            cmd.Parameters.Add(paramLocation)

            ' Open connection and execute command
            conn.Open()
            Dim count As Integer
            count = cmd.ExecuteNonQuery()
            conn.Close()

        End Using
    End Using
End Sub


// C#
public void InsertSupplier(string name, Point location)
{
    // Get connectionstring from configfile.
    ConnectionStringSettings css = ConfigurationManager.ConnectionStrings
            ["Samples.Properties.Settings.VideoGameStoreDB"];

    // Build database connection
    using ( SqlConnection conn = new SqlConnection( css.ConnectionString ) )
    {
        // Build sql command
        using ( SqlCommand cmd = new SqlCommand() )
        {
            cmd.Connection = conn;

            cmd.CommandText =
        "insert into supplier (supplierName, supplierLocation) VALUES ( @name, @location ) ";

            // Add name parameter
            SqlParameter paramName = new SqlParameter( "@name", name );
            cmd.Parameters.Add( paramName );

            // Add location parameters
            SqlParameter paramLocation = new SqlParameter( "@location", location );
            paramLocation.UdtTypeName = "Point";
            cmd.Parameters.Add( paramLocation );

            // Open connection and execute command
            conn.Open();
            int count = cmd.ExecuteNonQuery();
            conn.Close();
        }
    }
}
```

Using Stored Procedures

Stored procedures provide an extra layer of abstraction between the database and your ADO.NET data access layer, allowing you to think of your database in terms of services instead of datatables. In ADO.NET, it is possible to use stored procedures instead of dynamic SQL statements to insert, update, and delete data. The *DbCommand* (or *SqlCommand* if you're using SQL Server) has a *CommandType* property that can be set to *StoredProcedure*, after which the *CommandText* is expected to contain the name of the stored procedure that needs to be called. DataSet Designer allows you to specify the stored procedures using a wizard. It even generates stored procedures for you if you want.

 Quick Check

- **What property on a *DataAdapter* becomes important when performing bulk updates on a SQL Server database?**

Quick Check Answer

- **The *UpdateBatchSize* property can be increased to minimize the number of round trips that are made when performing multiple updates.**

Sample: Updating the Database

It's time to look at a sample with more than a console application as a user interface. Listing 4-1 shows what is needed to implement a Windows Form application that reads products from *VideoGameStoreDB* and updates the database after changes have been made using a *DataGridView* control. The Winform controls for *DataAdapters* and *DataSets* are used to build the form.

LISTING 4-1 Updating the Database

```vb
' VB
Public Class Form1
    ' Handle Load event
    Private Sub Form1_Load(ByVal sender As System.Object, ByVal e As System.EventArgs)
            Handles MyBase.Load
      ' Use table adapter (control on form) to fill dataset (also a control on the form)
      Me.productTableAdapter.Fill( this.videoGameStoreDataSet.Product )
    End Sub

    ' Handle button click event
    Private Sub btnUpdate_Click (ByVal sender As System.Object, ByVal e As
            System.EventArgs) Handles MyBase.Load
      ' Use table adapter to write changes to the database
      Me.productTableAdapter.Update( videoGameStoreDataSet )
    End Sub
End Class
```

```csharp
// C#
public partial class Form1 : Form
{
    public Form1()
    {
        InitializeComponent();
    }

    private void Form1_Load( object sender, EventArgs e )
    {
        // Use table adapter (control on form) to fill dataset (also a control on the form)
        this.productTableAdapter.Fill( this.videoGameStoreDataSet.Product );
    }

    private void btnUpdate_Click( object sender, EventArgs e )
    {
        // Use table adapter to write changes to the database
        productTableAdapter.Update( videoGameStoreDataSet );
    }
}
```

Figure 4-3 shows the user interface of an application that displays all the rows in the Products table, allows insertion, updating, and deletion of these products, and features an Update button to send changes back to the database. Remember that the form is based on a *DataSet* that is a disconnected, in-memory representation of the data in the database. We need to use a table adapter to send changes back to the database.

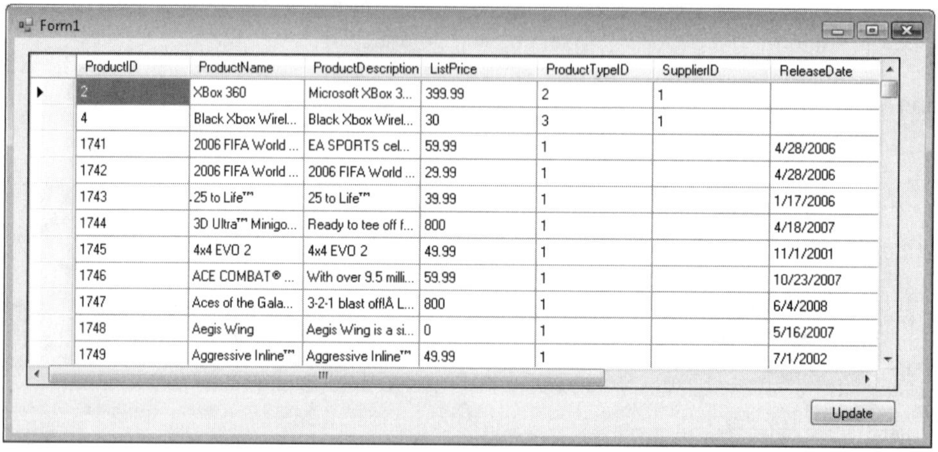

FIGURE 4-3 Insert, update, and delete entries in the *Products* table

The sample uses a *Typed DataSet* to manage the interaction with the database and to make it easy to bind the data in the user interface to the *DataGridView* control. The *DataSet* used in the sample is shown in Figure 4-4.

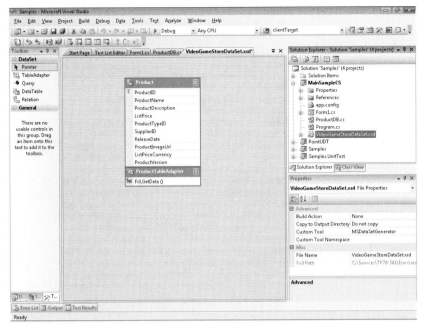

FIGURE 4-4 The *DataSet* contains just one table: Product.

The design view of the form in the sample application is shown in Figure 4-5. Notice the design time components at the bottom of the Form Designer.

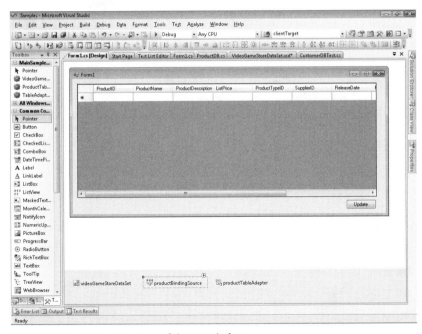

FIGURE 4-5 The *Designtime* view of the sample form

Let's look at the four steps needed to build this application.

1. Create the *Typed DataSet*

The *Typed DataSet* is created by adding a new item to the WinForm application of type *DataSet*. Then, using Server Explorer, you make a connection to the database and drag the *Product* table onto the DataSet Designer design surface. This generates the datatable definition and a default implementation for the *SELECT, INSERT, UPDATE,* and *DELETE* statements.

> **NOTE AUTOMATIC OPTIMISTIC LOCKING**
>
> Because the *Product* table contains a *ProductVersion* column of type *TimeStamp,* the code generator automatically uses the *ProductVersion* in the WHERE clause of the UPDATE and DELETE statements for the purpose of optimistic locking.

2. Add Controls to the Form

Add a new form to the project and add a *DataGridView* control and an Update button to the form.

3. Bind Data to the *DataGridView* Control

Use the smart tag to select a data source for the *DataGridView* control. The *Typed DataSet* shows up in the selector and the *Products* table can be selected, as shown in Figure 4-6.

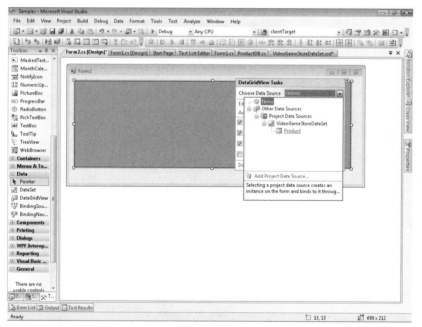

FIGURE 4-6 Select a data source for the *DataGridView.*

The *DataGridView* control now adds three design time components to the form: the *DataSet*, a *TableAdapter*, and a binding source. The classes all match the classes you've seen in this chapter and Chapter 3. At this point, code has been added to the form load event to retrieve data from the database and populate data in the *DataSet*, see Listing 4-1.

4. Update the Database

Finally, the code to send updates to the database needs to be implemented. The Update button, which we added in step 2, needs to implement the click event and call the *Update* method on the *DataAdapter,* as shown in Listing 4-1. Open the form in the Form Designer and double-click the Update button in the designer opens the code view of the form and adds the event handler automatically. Notice how all three design time components are accessible from the code within the form.

LAB   **Updating Data**

In this lab, you create a class library to update and delete data. You create a unit test to see if the code in the class library performs as expected. You need to have the *VideoGameStoreDB* database installed to perform these exercises, as each exercise builds on the previous one. You can install the files for this lab, including the complete solution containing the code for all the exercises, from the Code folder on the companion CD.

EXERCISE 1   Insert a Row Using a Non-query SQL Statement

In this exercise, you put an *INSERT* statement into the customer table. The *INSERT* statement modifies the customer entry and does not return any data.

1. Start a new Class Library project named DataAccess.

2. Add a connection string to the project settings named VideoGameStoreDB and have it contain a valid connection string to the *VideoGameStoreDB* database.

   Hint: Use the Settings tab in the Project Properties dialog box to do this.

3. Add an assembly reference to System.Configuration.dll.

4. Add a class named *CustomerDB*.

5. Add a method named *InsertCustomer* as follows:

   a. Let it have the parameters name of type string and details, also of type string.

   b. Create a reference to the connection string.

   c. Create a SQL connection.

   d. Create a SQL command using command parameters.

   e. Execute the command.

   Your code should look like this:

```vb
' VB
Public Sub InsertCustomer(ByVal name As String, ByVal details As String)
    Dim css As ConnectionStringSettings
    css = ConfigurationManager.ConnectionStrings("VideoGameStoreDB")
```

```
Using conn As SqlConnection = New SqlConnection(css.ConnectionString)

    Dim sql = "insert into customer (customername, customerdetails) values
            (@name, @details)"

    Using cmd As SqlCommand = New SqlCommand(sql, conn)

        cmd.Parameters.AddWithValue("name", name)
        cmd.Parameters.AddWithValue("details", details)
        conn.Open()
        cmd.ExecuteNonQuery()
        conn.Close()

    End Using
  End Using
End Sub

// C#
public void InsertCustomer( string name, string details )
{
    ConnectionStringSettings css =
        ConfigurationManager.ConnectionStrings["VideoGameStoreDB"];

    using ( SqlConnection conn = new SqlConnection( css.ConnectionString ) )
    {
        string sql = "insert into customer (customername, customerdetails)
                values (@name, @details)";
        using ( SqlCommand cmd = new SqlCommand( sql, conn ) )
        {
            cmd.Parameters.AddWithValue( "name", name );
            cmd.Parameters.AddWithValue( "details", details );
            conn.Open();
            cmd.ExecuteNonQuery();
            conn.Close();
        }
    }
}
```

6. Implement a new method named *GetCustomer,* which returns a *DataRow.* Have the method take the customer name as the parameter. Return null (or Nothing) if the customer is not found.

Your code should look like this:

```vb
' VB
Public Function GetCustomer(ByVal name As String) As DataRow
    Dim css As ConnectionStringSettings
    css = ConfigurationManager.ConnectionStrings("VideoGameStoreDB")

    Dim dt As New DataTable()

    Using conn As SqlConnection = New SqlConnection(css.ConnectionString)

        Dim sql = "select * from customer where customername = @name"

        Using cmd As SqlCommand = New SqlCommand(sql, conn)

            cmd.Parameters.AddWithValue("name", name)

            Using adapter As SqlDataAdapter = New SqlDataAdapter(cmd)
                conn.Open()
                adapter.Fill(dt)
                conn.Close()
            End Using

            If (dt.Rows.Count > 0) Then
                Return dt.Rows(0)
            Else
                Return Nothing
            End If

        End Using
    End Using
End Function
```

```csharp
// C#
public DataRow GetCustomer( string name )
{
    ConnectionStringSettings css =
        ConfigurationManager.ConnectionStrings["VideoGameStoreDB"];

    DataTable dt = new DataTable();

    using ( SqlConnection conn = new SqlConnection( css.ConnectionString ) )
    {
        string sql = "select * from customer where customername = @name";
        using ( SqlCommand cmd = new SqlCommand( sql, conn ) )
```

```
        {
            cmd.Parameters.AddWithValue( "name", name );
            using ( SqlDataAdapter adapter = new SqlDataAdapter( cmd ) )
            {
                conn.Open();
                adapter.Fill( dt );
                conn.Close();
            }
        }
    }
    if ( dt.Rows.Count > 0 )
    {
        return dt.Rows[0];
    }
    else
    {
        return null;
    }
}
```

7. Create a unit test by right-clicking the *InsertCustomer* method.

8. Implement the unit test by inserting a customer and then using the *GetCustomer* method to check whether the customer was stored successfully in the database.

   Your code should look like this:

```vb
' VB
<TestMethod()> _
Public Sub InsertCustomerTest()
    Dim target As CustomerDB = New CustomerDB()
    Dim name As String = "Blomsma"
    Dim details As String = "New customer, handle with care"
    target.InsertCustomer(name, details)

    Dim customer = target.GetCustomer("Blomsma")

    Assert.IsNotNull(customer)
End Sub
```

```csharp
// C#
[TestMethod()]
public void InsertCustomerTest()
{
    CustomerDB target = new CustomerDB();
    string name = "Blomsma";
    string details = "New customer, handle with care.";
    target.InsertCustomer( name, details );
```

```
        DataRow customer = target.GetCustomer( "Blomsma" );

        Assert.IsNotNull( customer );
    }
```

9. Run the unit test. Make sure to remove the customer manually if you run the test more than once.

EXERCISE 2 Update Using a *DataTable*

In this exercise, you update the customer table in the database using an instance of a *DataTable*. Continue by using your solution from Exercise 1, or by using the code that you installed from the companion CD.

1. Add a new item of type *DataSet*, named *CustomerDataSet,* to the DataAccess project.

2. In Server Explorer, open the *VideoGameStore* database and drag the *Customer* table onto the DataSet Designer surface.

3. Right-click CustomerTableAdapter and choose Configure.

4. Check Advanced Options to make sure that the Refresh Data Table option is selected.

5. Add a method to the *CustomerDB* class named *SaveCustomers* and pass CustomerDataTable as a parameter. Within the method, perform the following steps:

   a. Create an instance of *CustomerTableAdapter.*

   b. Use the adapter to update the database.

   Your code should look like this:

   ' **VB**
   ```vb
   Public Sub SaveCustomers(ByVal customers As CustomerDataSet.CustomerDataTable)
       Dim cta = New CustomerDataSetTableAdapters.CustomerTableAdapter()
       cta.Update(customers)
   End Sub
   ```

   // **C#**
   ```csharp
   public void SaveCustomers( CustomerDataSet.CustomerDataTable customers )
   {
       CustomerDataSetTableAdapters.CustomerTableAdapter cta =
           new CustomerDataSetTableAdapters.CustomerTableAdapter();

       cta.Update( customers );
   }
   ```

6. Create a unit test by right-clicking the *SaveCustomers* method. Add the test to the test project that you created in Exercise 1. Have the test create a *Customer* table with one entry, save the table, and check the database using the *GetCustomer* method.

Your code should look like this:

```vb
' VB
<TestMethod()> _
Public Sub SaveCustomersTest()
    Dim target As CustomerDB = New CustomerDB()
    Dim customers = new CustomerDataSet.CustomerDataTable()
    Customers.AddCustomerRow( "Blomsma", String.Empty, "New customer,
            handle with care", Guid.Empty )

    target.SaveCustomers(customers)

    Dim customer = target.GetCustomer("Blomsma")
    Assert.IsNotNull(customer)
End Sub
```

```csharp
// C#
[TestMethod()]
public void SaveCustomersTest()
{
    CustomerDB target = new CustomerDB();
    CustomerDataSet.CustomerDataTable customers = new CustomerDataSet.
            CustomerDataTable();
    customers.AddCustomerRow( "Blomsma",
        String.Empty,
        "New customer, handle with care.",
        Guid.Empty );
    target.SaveCustomers( customers );

    DataRow customer = target.GetCustomer( "Blomsma" );
    Assert.IsNotNull( customer );
}
```

7. Run the unit test. Make sure to remove the customer manually if you run the test more than once.

EXERCISE 3   Accommodate Bulk Updates

Now you expand the *SaveCustomers* method to accommodate bulk updates. Continue with your solution from Exercise 2, or use the code you installed from the companion CD.

1. Add a parameter to the method of type *integer* named *batchSize*.

2. *CustomerTableAdapter* does not expose the *BatchUpdateSize* property because this is a *SqlDataAdapter*-specific property. You need to expose this property on *CustomerTableAdapter* by opening *CustomerDataSet* in Dataset Designer and double-clicking *CustomerTableAdapter*. This creates a partial class entry for *CustomerTableAdapter*. Partial classes are great for adding custom code to designer-generated code.

3. In the partial class add a method named *SetBatchUpdateSize,* which takes one parameter of type *integer.* Within the method, perform the following steps:

   a. Obtain a reference to *SqlDataAdapter.*

   b. Set the *UpdateBatchSize* property as you want.

   Your code should look like this:

```vb
' VB
Partial Public Class ProductTableAdapter
    Public Sub SetBatchUpdateSize( batchSize as Integer )
        Me.Adapter.UpdateBatchSize = batchSize
    End Sub
End Class
```

```csharp
// C#
public partial class CustomerTableAdapter {

    public void SetBatchUpdateSize( int batchSize )
    {
        this.Adapter.UpdateBatchSize = batchSize;
    }
}
```

4. Change the *SaveCustomers* method to set the batch size.

   Your code should look like this:

```vb
' VB
Public Sub SaveCustomers(ByVal customers As CustomerDataSet.CustomerDataTable)
    Dim cta = New CustomerDataSetTableAdapters.CustomerTableAdapter()
    cta.SetBatchUpdateSize(batchSize)
    cta.Update(customers)
End Sub
```

```csharp
// C#
public void SaveCustomers( CustomerDataSet.CustomerDataTable customers,
        int batchSize )
{
    CustomerDataSetTableAdapters.CustomerTableAdapter cta =
        new CustomerDataSetTableAdapters.CustomerTableAdapter();


    cta.SetBatchUpdateSize( batchSize );
    cta.Update( customers );
}
```

5. Create a new unit test to test the batch update. Insert three new customers and set the batch size to 10.

Your code should look like this:

```vb
' VB
<TestMethod()> _
Public Sub SaveCustomersTest()
    Dim target As CustomerDB = New CustomerDB()
    Dim customers = new CustomerDataSet.CustomerDataTable()
    Customers.AddCustomerRow( "Blomsma", String.Empty, "New customer,
            handle with care", Guid.Empty )
    Customers.AddCustomerRow( "Wildermuth", String.Empty, "New customer,
            handle with care", Guid.Empty )
    Customers.AddCustomerRow( "Wightman", String.Empty, "New customer,
            handle with care", Guid.Empty )

    target.SaveCustomers(customers)

    Dim customer1 = target.GetCustomer("Blomsma")
    Assert.IsNotNull(customer1)
    Dim customer2 = target.GetCustomer("Wildermuth")
    Assert.IsNotNull(customer2)
    Dim customer3 = target.GetCustomer("Wightman")
    Assert.IsNotNull(customer3)
End Sub
```

```csharp
// C#
[TestMethod()]
public void SaveCustomersTest1()
{
    CustomerDB target = new CustomerDB();
    CustomerDataSet.CustomerDataTable customers = new CustomerDataSet.
            CustomerDataTable();
    customers.AddCustomerRow( "Blomsma",
        String.Empty,
        "New customer, handle with care.",
        Guid.Empty );
    customers.AddCustomerRow( "Wildermuth",
        String.Empty,
        "New customer, handle with care.",
        Guid.Empty );
    customers.AddCustomerRow( "Wightman",
        String.Empty,
        "New customer, handle with care.",
        Guid.Empty );
    target.SaveCustomers( customers, 10 );
```

```
    DataRow customer1 = target.GetCustomer( "Blomsma" );
    Assert.IsNotNull( customer1 );
    DataRow customer2 = target.GetCustomer( "Wildermuth" );
    Assert.IsNotNull( customer2 );
    DataRow customer3 = target.GetCustomer( "Wightman" );
    Assert.IsNotNull( customer3 );
}
```

6. The best way to see how the update batch size affects the database interaction is to run the test with the batch size set to 1 and then again with the size set to 10 and monitor the difference with the SQL Profiler.

Lesson Review

You can use the following questions to test your knowledge of the information in Lesson 1, "Updating Data." The questions also are available on the companion CD of this book if you prefer to review them in electronic form.

> **NOTE ANSWERS**
>
> Answers to these questions and explanations of why each answer choice is correct or incorrect are located in the "Answers" section at the end of the book.

1. Which of the following snippets is the best way to insert a row in the *Customer* table?

A.

```vb
' VB
Using conn As SqlConnection = new SqlConnection( connectionString )
    Dim sql As String = "insert into customer (customername, customerdetails)
            values (@name, @details)";
    Using cmd As SqlCommand = new SqlCommand( sql, conn )
        cmd.Parameters.AddWithValue( "name", "Blomsma" )
        cmd.Parameters.AddWithValue( "details", "New customer" )
        conn.Open()
        cmd.ExecuteNonQuery()
        conn.Close()
    End Using
End Using
```

```csharp
// C#
using ( SqlConnection conn = new SqlConnection( connectionString ) )
{
    string sql = "insert into customer (customername, customerdetails)
            values (@name, @details)";
    using ( SqlCommand cmd = new SqlCommand( sql, conn ) )
    {
        cmd.Parameters.AddWithValue( "name", "Blomsma" );
        cmd.Parameters.AddWithValue( "details", "New customer" );
```

```
        conn.Open();
        cmd.ExecuteNonQuery();
        conn.Close();
    }
}
```

B.

```vb
' VB
Using conn As SqlConnection = new SqlConnection( connectionString )
    Dim sql As String = "insert into customer (customername, customerdetails)
            values (@name, @details)";
    Using cmd As SqlCommand = new SqlCommand( sql, conn )
        cmd.Parameters.AddWithValue( "name", "Blomsma" )
        cmd.Parameters.AddWithValue( "details", "New customer" )
        conn.Open()
        cmd.ExecuteReader()
        conn.Close()
    End Using
End Using
```

```csharp
// C#
using ( SqlConnection conn = new SqlConnection( connectionString ) )
{
    string sql = "insert into customer (customername, customerdetails)
            values (@name, @details)";
    using ( SqlCommand cmd = new SqlCommand( sql, conn ) )
    {
        cmd.Parameters.AddWithValue( "name", "Blomsma" );
        cmd.Parameters.AddWithValue( "details", "New customer" );
        conn.Open();
        cmd.ExecuteReader();
        conn.Close();
    }
}
```

C.

```vb
' VB
Using conn As SqlConnection = new SqlConnection( connectionString )
    Dim sql As String = "insert into customer (customername, customerdetails)
            values (@name, @details)"
    Using cmd As SqlCommand = new SqlCommand( sql, conn ) )
        cmd.Parameters.AddWithValue( "name", "Blomsma" )
        cmd.Parameters.AddWithValue( "details", "New customer" )
        conn.Open()
```

```
        cmd.ExecuteXmlReader()
        conn.Close()
    End Using
End Using


// C#
using ( SqlConnection conn = new SqlConnection( connectionString ) )
{
    string sql = "insert into customer (customername, customerdetails)
            values (@name, @details)";
    using ( SqlCommand cmd = new SqlCommand( sql, conn ) )
    {
        cmd.Parameters.AddWithValue( "name", "Blomsma" );
        cmd.Parameters.AddWithValue( "details", "New customer" );
        conn.Open();
        cmd.ExecuteXmlReader();
        conn.Close();
    }
}
```

D.

```
' VB
Using conn As SqlConnection = new SqlConnection( connectionString )
    Dim sql As String = "insert into customer (customername, customerdetails)
            values ( " + name + ", " + details + " )"
    Using cmd As SqlCommand = new SqlCommand( sql, conn )
        conn.Open()
        cmd.ExecuteNonQuery()
        conn.Close()
    End Using
End Using


// C#
using ( SqlConnection conn = new SqlConnection( connectionString ) )
{
    string sql = "insert into customer (customername, customerdetails)
            values ( " + name + ", " + details + " )";
    using ( SqlCommand cmd = new SqlCommand( sql, conn ) )
    {
        conn.Open();
        cmd.ExecuteNonQuery();
        conn.Close();
    }
}
```

2. Which of the following statements is true?

    A. *UpdateBatchSize* is a property of *DbConnection.*

    B. *UpdateBatchSize* is a property of *SqlConnection.*

    C. *UpdateBatchSize* is a property of *DbDataAdapter.*

    D. *UpdateBatchSize* is a property of *SqlDataAdapter.*

Lesson 2: Data Integrity and Transactions

Using ADO.NET data integrity can be ensured at two levels. The first involves making sure the data in the *DataSet* is valid at all times. The second is to make sure that the consist state of the *DataSet* is stored correctly in the database. This last step needs to be managed when updating multiple items in a datastore within what is considered to be the same transaction.

> **After this lesson, you will be able to:**
> - Enforce constraints on data in a *DataSet*
> - Manage a transaction
> - Deal with concurrency
>
> **Estimated lesson time: 30 minutes**

Enforcing Data Integrity in a *DataSet*

Enforcing data integrity at *DataSet* level involves making sure that data is marked as invalid when it contains an error. To maintain this level of integrity, constraints, such as a foreign key constraint, can be added to a *DataTable*.

Constraints

Constraints are created at datatable level and are used along with the *PrimaryKey* property of the *DataTable* to maintain the integrity of the data within a *DataTable*. ADO.NET offers two kinds of constraints: the *ForeignKeyConstraint* and the *UniqueConstraint*. ADO.NET sometimes creates constraints automatically. When you create a *DataRelation,* for example, ADO.NET creates the corresponding *ForeignKeyConstraint,* and when you set the *Unique* property of a column to True, ADO.NET creates a *UniqueConstraint*.

FOREIGNKEYCONSTRAINT

A *ForeignKeyConstraint* sets up the relationship between either two *DataTables* or between individual rows in a single table. The constraint enforces that any values found in the specified columns of the child table must be present in the parent table. The properties of the *ForeignKeyConstraint* object are shown in Table 4-1.

TABLE 4-1 Properties of the *ForeignKeyConstraint* Class

PROPERTY	DESCRIPTION
AcceptRejectRule	Indicates the action that should take place across this constraint when *AcceptChanges* is invoked
Columns	Gets the child columns of this constraint
ConstraintName	The name of a constraint in the *ConstraintCollection*

TABLE 4-1 Properties of the *ForeignKeyConstraint* Class

PROPERTY	DESCRIPTION
DeleteRule	Gets or sets the action that occurs across this constraint when a row is deleted
RelatedColumns	The parent columns of this constraint
RelatedTable	Gets the parent table of this constraint
Table	Gets the child table of this constraint
UpdateRule	Gets or sets the action that occurs across this constraint on when a row is updated

The actions to be taken by the constraint are determined by three properties: *AcceptRejectRule, DeleteRule,* and *UpdateRule.* The possible values of the *AcceptRejectRule* are *Cascade* or *None.* The *DeleteRule* and *UpdateRule* properties can be set to *Cascade, None, SetDefault,* or *SetNull.*

A *ForeignKeyConstraint* needs to be created explicitly at run time. When using *Typed DataSets* and when creating a *DataRelation*, DataSet Designer automatically creates a *ForeignKeyConstraint.*

The code shown in Listing 4-2 shows how to create a relationship between two tables. The foreign key constraint is enabled, so only existing values for the *ContactType* field are allowed. It shows that the *BuildDataSetWithRelation* method creates two tables, adds them to the *DataSet* and then proceeds to build a *DataRelation* between the two tables. The relationship connects the *ContactType* field in *Contact* to the primary key in the *ContactTypes* table. By enabling constraints when creating the relationship, the foreign key constraint is automatically implemented, and adding data that holds a reference to a nonexisting *ContactTypes* entry causes an exception to be thrown. The correct implementation would be to add the *ContactTypes* entry before adding the *Contact* entry.

UNIQUECONSTRAINT

UniqueConstraint represents a restriction on a set of columns in which all values must be unique. It ensures that for each *DataRow* in a *DataTable,* the row contains a unique value for the specified *DataColumn* or combination of *DataColumns.*

The *PrimaryKey* property of the *DataTable* creates a special kind of *UniqueConstraint,* the primary difference being that the *PrimaryKey* column(s) can be passed to the *Find* method. The properties of a *UniqueConstraint* are shown in Table 4-2.

TABLE 4-2 Properties on the *UniqueConstraint* Class

PROPERTY	DESCRIPTION
Columns	The array of columns that this constraint affects
ConstraintName	The name of a constraint in the *ConstraintCollection*

TABLE 4-2 Properties on the *UniqueConstraint* Class

PROPERTY	DESCRIPTION
IsPrimaryKey	Gets a *boolean* value indicating whether or not the constraint is on a primary key
Table	Gets the table to which this constraint belongs

Listing 4-2 shows how to create a unique constraint within the BuildSupplierTable.

LISTING 4-2 Constraints

```
' VB
Public Function BuildDataSetWithRelation() As DataSet
    Dim ds As New DataSet
    Dim dtSupplier = BuildSupplierTable()
    Dim dtProduct = BuildProductTable()

    ds.Tables.Add(dtSupplier)
    ds.Tables.Add(dtProduct)

    Dim parent = dtSupplier.Columns("SupplierID")
    Dim child = dtProduct.Columns("SupplierID")

    Dim dr = New DataRelation("FK_Supplier2Product", _parent, child, True)
    ds.Relations.Add(dr)

    ' will fail because of FK constraint
    dtProduct.Rows.Add(New Object() {1, "Bill", "Malone", 1})

    ' succeeds because supplier exists
    dtSupplier.Rows.Add(New Object() {1, "Support/Helpdesk"})
    dtProduct.Rows.Add(New Object() {1, "Bill", "Malone", 1})

    Return ds

End Function

Public Function BuildSupplierTable() As DataTable
    Dim dt As New DataTable("Supplier")
    Dim key As DataColumn = dt.Columns.Add("SupplierID", GetType(Integer))
    Dim supplier As DataColumn = _
                dt.Columns.Add("SupplierName", GetType(String))
    Dim keys() As DataColumn = New DataColumn() {key}
    dt.PrimaryKey = keys
    dt.Constraints.Add(New UniqueConstraint( supplier ))
    Return dt
End Function
```

```vb
Public Function BuildProductTable() As DataTable
    Dim dt As New DataTable("Product")
    Dim key As DataColumn = dt.Columns.Add("ProductId", GetType(Integer))
    dt.Columns.Add("ProductName", GetType(String))
    dt.Columns.Add("SupplierID", GetType(Integer))
    Dim keys() As DataColumn = New DataColumn() {key}
    dt.PrimaryKey = keys
    Return dt
End Function
```

```csharp
// C#
private static DataSet BuildDataSetWithRelation()
{
    DataSet ds = new DataSet();
    DataTable dtProduct = BuildProductTable();
    DataTable dtSupplier = BuildSupplierTable();

    ds.Tables.Add(dtProduct);
    ds.Tables.Add(dtSupplier);

    DataColumn parent = dtSupplier.Columns["SupplierID"];
    DataColumn child = dtProduct.Columns["SupplierID"];

    DataRelation dr =
        new DataRelation( "FK_Supplier2Product", parent, child, true );
    ds.Relations.Add( dr );

    // next statement will fail at runtime because of FK constraint
    dtProduct.Rows.Add(new object[] { 1, "Halo 3", 1 });

    // next two statements succeed because supplier now exists
    dtSupplier.Rows.Add(new object[] { 1, "Microsoft" });
    dtProduct.Rows.Add(new object[] { 1, "Halo 3", 1 });
    return ds;
}

private static DataTable BuildSupplierTable()
{
    DataTable dt = new DataTable ( "Supplier" );
    DataColumn key = dt.Columns.Add ( "SupplierID", typeof ( int ) );
    dt.Columns.Add ( "SupplierName", typeof ( string ) );
    dt.PrimaryKey = new DataColumn[] { key };  // Set the PK
    dt.Constraints.Add(new UniqueConstraint(supplier));
    return dt;
}
```

```
private static DataTable BuildProductTable()
{
    DataTable dt = new DataTable ( "Product" );
    DataColumn key =
        dt.Columns.Add ( "ProductID", typeof ( int ) );
    dt.Columns.Add ( "ProductName", typeof ( string ) );
    dt.Columns.Add ( "SupplierID", typeof ( int ) );
    dt.PrimaryKey = new DataColumn[] { key };
    return dt;
}
```

Managing Transactions

Transactions are sequences of actions that need to either succeed or fail as a group. The most basic example of a transaction is a transfer of money between two bank accounts. The funds need to be subtracted from one account and added to another. Either both the subtraction and the addition succeed, or both fail. Any other scenario leads to an inconsistent state. ADO.NET offers a number of technologies to manage a transaction. It is possible to manage a transaction manually at connection level. You can manage it using the lightweight transaction manager or, if you're using multiple resources, you may choose to use a distributed transaction using the Distributed Transaction Coordinator (DTC).

MANUAL TRANSACTION MANAGEMENT

A *database transaction* can be managed manually by using the *DbTransaction* class or a derivative thereof. The transaction object mediates between your .NET Framework code and the underlying data source. There are three steps to follow when using a transaction: create the transaction, execute commands within the transaction, and commit (or roll back) the transaction.

By getting a connection to enlist in the transaction, the actions performed on that connection are managed by the transaction object. The code here shows a connection being opened. The *BeginTransaction()* method triggers the transaction and the code shows that you need only roll back the transaction in case of an exception:

```
' VB
Dim tx As DbTransaction
Try
    conn.Open()
    tx = conn.BeginTransaction()
    cmdDeleteOrders.ExecuteNonQuery()
    cmdDeleteCustomer.ExecuteNonQuery()
    tx.Commit()
    conn.Close()
Catch ex As Exception
    If tx Is Not Nothing Then
        tx.Rollback()
    End If
```

```
            If conn Is Not Nothing Then
                    If conn.State <> ConnectionState.Closed Then
                            Conn.Close()
                    End If
            End If
    End If
    End Try
```

```csharp
// C#
DbTransaction tx;
try
{
    conn.Open();
    tx = conn.BeginTransaction();
    cmdDeleteOrders.ExecuteNonQuery();
    cmdDeleteCustomer.ExecuteNonQuery();
    tx.Commit();
    conn.Close();
}
catch ( Exception exception )
{
    if ( tx != null )
    {
        tx.Rollback();
    }
    if ( conn != null )
    {
        if ( conn.State != ConnectionState.Closed )
        {
            conn.Close();
        }
    }
}
```

The exception handling can be simplified if the previous code is refactored as shown in this next code. The *using* statement calls *Dispose()* on the transaction object. The *Dispose* method checks to see if there are any uncommitted changes. If there are, it rolls back the transaction:

```vb
' VB
conn.Open()
Using tx As DbTransaction = conn.BeginTransaction()
    cmdDeleteOrders.ExecuteNonQuery()
    cmdDeleteCustomer.ExecuteNonQuery()
    tx.Commit()
    conn.Close()
End Using
```

```
// C#
conn.Open();
using ( DbTransaction tx = conn.BeginTransaction() )
{
    cmdDeleteOrders.ExecuteNonQuery();
    cmdDeleteCustomer.ExecuteNonQuery();
    tx.Commit();
    conn.Close();
}
```

Aside from beginning a new transaction, the *DbConnection* class also offers *EnlistTransaction*, a method for enlisting in a transaction that is already running. *EnlistTransaction* is used internally when a transaction is created within the context of an already-running transaction. This is sometimes referred to as a connection joining its ambient connection.

> **NOTE   DATA COMMANDS**
>
> Although it's theoretically possible to use data commands to execute *BeginTransaction* statements on the data source, executing such statements can be dangerous because the application and database engine transactions can get out of sync easily.

The isolation level is an important parameter when creating the transaction using *BeginTransaction*. The isolation level specifies the transaction-locking behavior for the connection. See Table 4-3 for a list of possible values for the *IsolationLevel* enumerator.

TABLE 4-3 Isolation Level for Transactions

VALUE	DESCRIPTION
Chaos	The pending changes from more highly isolated transactions cannot be overwritten.
ReadCommitted	Shared locks are held while the data is being read to avoid dirty reads, but the data can be changed before the end of the transaction, resulting in nonrepeatable reads or phantom data.
ReadUncommitted	A dirty read is possible, meaning that no shared locks are issued and no exclusive locks are honored.
RepeatableRead	Locks are placed on all data that is used in a query, preventing other users from updating the data. Prevents nonrepeatable reads, but phantom rows are still possible.
Serializable	A range lock is placed, preventing other users from updating or inserting rows into the locked data until the transaction is complete.

TABLE 4-3 Isolation Level for Transactions

VALUE	DESCRIPTION
Snapshot	Reduces blocking by storing a version of data that one application can read while another is modifying the same data. Indicates that from one transaction, you cannot see changes made in other transactions, even if you query again.
Unspecified	A different isolation level than the one specified is being used, but the level cannot be determined.

The *Transaction* class has a *static* property (*Shared* in Visual Basic) called *Current* that gives you access to the current transaction. The current transaction is known as the *ambient transaction*. This property is null if there is no ongoing transaction. You can access the *Current* property directly to change the transaction isolation level, roll back the transaction, or view the transaction status.

USING THE LIGHTWEIGHT TRANSACTION MANAGER

Managing transactions at connection level is convenient when all the code for updating a database is located within the same method. Once you get to the point where multiple methods open connections to the database and each needs to participate in a transaction, then you find yourself passing a transaction object as a parameter to each of these methods. This cluttering of method calls can be avoided using the Lightweight Transaction Manager (LTM). The LTM is used to manage a single transaction to a durable resource manager, such as SQL Server. Volatile resource managers, which are memory-based, can also be enlisted in a single transaction. The transaction managers are intended to be invisible to the developer, who never needs to write code to access them. The core interaction point between the developer and the LTM is the *TransactionScope* class, located in System.Transactions.dll. The *TransactionScope* class allows a developer to scope a number of methods within the transaction scope, and any connection used within the transaction scope automatically enlists itself in the transaction. Using the *using* construct, the transaction scope offers a very elegant solution for managing transactions. The code here shows how the *TransactionScope* class is used:

```vb
' VB
Public Sub DeleteCustomerWithOrders( customerId As Integer )

    Using tx As TransactionScope =
            New TransactionScope( TransactionScopeOption.Required )
        ' open connection
        ...
        ' delete orders for customer
        ...
        ' delete customer
        ...
        tx.Complete()
    End Using
End Sub
```

```csharp
// C#
public void DeleteCustomerWithOrders( int customerId )
{
    using ( TransactionScope tx =
            new TransactionScope( TransactionScopeOption.Required ) )
    {
        // open connection
        ...
        // delete orders for customer
        ...
        // delete customer
        ...
        tx.Complete();
    }
}
```

TransactionScope has a number of options that can be set when constructing an instance of the class. The first is *TransactionScopeOption,* which indicated whether the transaction scope should create a new transaction, enlist in an already running transaction, or suppress the actions within the scope by hiding them from an already-running, ambient transaction. The values for the *TransactionScopeOption* enumerator are displayed in Table 4-4. Aside from the scope option, *TransactionScope* also offers overloaded constructors for setting the transaction scope option, timeout, and the isolation level. (See Table 4-3 for a list of transaction scope options.)

TABLE 4-4 Transaction Scope Options

VALUE	DESCRIPTION
Required	A transaction is required by the scope. It uses an ambient transaction if one already exists. Otherwise, it creates a new transaction before entering the scope. This is the default value.
RequiresNew	A new transaction is always created for the scope.
Supress	The ambient transaction context is suppressed when creating the scope. All operations within the scope are performed without an ambient transaction context.

The LTM escalates the transaction to the DTC only when it needs to.

DISTRIBUTED TRANSACTIONS

The LTM works very well for scenarios where multiple updates need to be persisted to the same database. When updating multiple resources, a more advanced resource manager is needed to coordinate the transaction. This is the domain of the DTC, which can manage transaction across multiple resources. The wonderful thing about the DTC is that the interaction between the developer and the DTC is also managed using the *TransactionScope* class. In fact, the

LTM has the ability to detect that when a single resource is accessed, the LTM can handle the transaction and that when a second, different, resource is accessed, the transaction should be escalated to the DTC.

Escalation occurs in the following situations:

- At least one durable resource that does not support single-phase notifications is enlisted in the transaction.

- At least two durable resources that support single-phase notifications are enlisted in the transaction. For example, enlisting a single connection does not cause a transaction to be promoted. However, whenever you open a second connection to a database (causing the database to enlist), the System.Transactions infrastructure detects that it is the second durable resource in the transaction and escalates it to an DTC transaction.

- A request to marshal the transaction to a different application domain or different process is invoked; for example, the serialization of the transaction object across an application domain boundary. The transaction object is marshaled by value, meaning that any attempt to pass it across an application domain boundary (even in the same process) results in serialization of the transaction object. You can pass the transaction objects by making a call on a remote method that takes a *Transaction* as a parameter, or you can try to access a remote transactional-serviced component. This serializes the transaction object and results in an escalation, as when a transaction is serialized across an application domain. It is being distributed and the local transaction manager is no longer adequate.

The code below shows that a transaction is managed across multiple method calls. Each method individually manages its own connection and its own transaction, but by being placed inside the transaction scope the second method will trigger the DTC to take over transaction management from the LTM.

```vb
' VB
Public Sub DeleteCustomerWithOrders( customerId As Integer )
    Using ( TransactionScope tx = new TransactionScope() )

        DeleteOrders( customerId )

        ' at this point the LTM is managing the transaction

        DeleteCustomer( customerId )

        ' at this point the DTC is managing the transaction
        tx.Complete()
    End Using
End Sub
```

```csharp
// C#
public void DeleteCustomerWithOrders( int customerId )
{
    using ( TransactionScope tx = new TransactionScope() )
    {
        DeleteOrders( customerId );

        // at this point the LTM is managing the transaction

        DeleteCustomer( customerId );

        // at this point the DTC is managing the transaction
        tx.Complete();
    }
}
```

In the previous sample, as soon as the *DeleteCustomer* method opens a new connection to the same or a different database, the LTM hands off the transaction to the DTC. This is transparent for the developer. However, you incur a small performance penalty because activating the DTC introduces some overhead.

It is possible to monitor DTC transactions through Component Services. To monitor the DTC transaction, choose Start, Control Panel, Administrative Tools, Component Services. Then within the tool, choose Computers, My Computer, Distributed Transaction Coordinator, and Transaction Statistics. The screen that now opens shows the number of running, committed, and failed DTC transactions.

Different connections to the same database appear as different databases to the LTM resource manager and cause the LTM to escalate the transaction to the DTC. The same applies for different users (and different security contexts) that connect to the same database using integrated security. This is one of the reasons for choosing a fixed non-personal account for accessing a database from a Web site or application server, for example.

Therefore, if the orders and customers are in the same database in the previous example, then it would be good practice to avoid escalation to a distributed transaction and not to use the LTM or manage opening and closing the connection manually.

Sample: Deleting Products and Suppliers

The following sample uses the *VideoGameStoreDB* database to build a *Typed DataSet* with products and suppliers. The goal is to create an application that deletes a supplier and all his products.

1. Create a console application named *SupplierListing*.
2. Add a *DataSet* named *VideoGameStoreDataSet*.
3. Open Server Explorer and, if not present, add a data connection to the *VideoGameStoreDB* database (included on the companion CD to this book).
4. Drag the *Products* table onto the design surface.

5. Drag a table adapter from the toolbox onto the design surface. This action will invoke the Table Adapter Wizard. In the wizard, when entering the SQL statement, select all fields except the *SupplierLocation* field.

6. Check the designer surface. The designer has detected the relationship between Supplier and Product and added it to the *DataSet* automatically.

7. The relationship can be edited by double-clicking it in the designer. Change the relationship to Foreign Key Constraint and set the update rule to Cascade. This causes the *DataSet* to delete automatically any in-memory instances of Product.

8. Add a query on the *Supplier* table to retrieve a single Supplier by performing the following steps:

    a. Use the following query:

    ```
    SELECT SupplierID, SupplierName, SupplierAddress, SupplierPhone,
    SupplierVersion
    FROM Supplier
    WHERE SupplierID = @id
    ```

    b. Name the query "FillBySupplierID and GetDataBySupplierID."

9. Add a query on the *Product* table to retrieve products from a single supplier:

    a. Use the following query:

    ```
    SELECT ProductID, ProductName, ProductDescription, ListPrice,
    ProductTypeID, SupplierID, ReleaseDate, ProductImageUrl,
    ListPriceCurrency, ProductVersion

    FROM dbo.Product

    WHERE SupplierID = @id
    ```

    b. Name the query "FillBySupplierID and GetDataBySupplierID."

10. You're ready to use the *DataSet*. Listing 4-3 shows how you can use the *Typed DataSet* to delete data within the scope of a transaction. This involves the following steps:

    a. Create an instance of the *DataSet*.

    b. Create instances of the table adapters that you want to use to retrieve the data from the database.

    c. Fill the tables in the *DataSet* using the table adapter *FillBySupplierID* method.

The *DataSet* is now populated with data from a single supplier, and the supplier can be deleted using the *Delete* method. Notice that the products do not need to be deleted individually. The *DataSet* maintains the foreign constraint and automatically removes all products.

Until now, all changes have been applied on the in-memory store. A *TransactionScope* instance is created to manage the database transaction. Both table adapters are used to persist changes to the database. The *Complete* method on *TransactionScope* is called to signal the successful completion of the transaction.

LISTING 4-3 Using *Typed DataSets* to Delete Data in a Transaction

```vb
' VB
Public Sub DeleteSupplierWithProducts(ByVal supplierID As Integer)

    Dim ds As New VideoGameStoreDataSet()

    Dim sta As New VideoGameStoreDataSetTableAdapters.SupplierTableAdapter()
    Dim pta As New VideoGameStoreDataSetTableAdapters.ProductTableAdapter()

    sta.Fill(ds.Supplier, supplierID)
    pta.Fill(ds.Product, supplierID)

    If ds.Supplier.Count = 1 Then
        ' this will trigger cascaded delete
        ' on the in memory dataset
            ds.Supplier(0).Delete()

    End If

    Using scope As New TransactionScope()
        ' both adapters need to write
        ' changes to the database
        sta.Update(ds)
        pta.Update(ds)

        scope.Complete()
    End Using

End Sub
```

```csharp
// C#
public void DeleteSupplierWithProducts( int supplierID )
{
    VideoGameStoreDataSet ds = new VideoGameStoreDataSet();

    VideoGameStoreDataSetTableAdapters.SupplierTableAdapter sta
        = new VideoGameStoreDataSetTableAdapters.SupplierTableAdapter();
    VideoGameStoreDataSetTableAdapters.ProductTableAdapter pta
        = new VideoGameStoreDataSetTableAdapters.ProductTableAdapter();

    sta.FillBySupplierID( ds.Supplier, supplierID );
    pta.FillBySupplierID( ds.Product, supplierID );
```

```
    if ( ds.Supplier.Count == 1 )
    {
        // this will trigger cascaded delete
        // on the in memory dataset
        ds.Supplier[0].Delete();
    }

    using ( TransactionScope scope = new TransactionScope() )
    {
        // both adapters need to write
        // changes to the database
        sta.Update( ds );
        pta.Update( ds );

        scope.Complete();
    }
}
```

✔ **Quick Check**

- What happens if you forget to call *TransactionScope.Complete()* when implementing a transaction with a *using* construct?

Quick Check Answer

- When the *TransactionScope* object is disposed, it detects that the transaction was not completed and perform a rollback.

LAB   **Managing Transactions**

In this lab, you create a class library to insert data into a *Typed DataSet* and persist it to the database. You need the *VideoGameStoreDB* database to complete these exercises, and each exercise builds on the previous one. You can install the files for this lab, including the complete solution containing the code for all the exercises, from the Code folder on the companion CD.

EXERCISE 1   Create a Data Access Layer

In this exercise, you build a class library that implements a data access layer. You use a *Typed DataSet* to generate the majority of the code needed to interact with the database.

1. Open a new class library project named *TransactionalDataAccess*.
2. Add a new item of type *DataSet*, named *CustomerDataSet*.
3. Use Server Explorer to connect to the *VideoGameStoreDB* database.

4. Using DataSet Designer and Server Explorer, add the *Customer* and *Purchase* tables to the design surface of *CustomerDataSet* by dragging them from Server Explorer to DataSet Designer.

5. Notice how the relationship between the two tables is created automatically.

6. Add a new class named *CustomerDB* to the project.

7. Within the class, add a method named *CreateQuickPurchase*. Within the method, perform the following steps:

   a. Create an instance of *CustomerDataSet*.

   b. Add a row to the *Customer* table.

   c. Add a row to the *Purchase* table.

   d. Create and call a *SaveCustomer* method to write the customer changes to the database.

   e. Create and call a *SavePurchase* method to write the purchase changes to the database. Instead of saving purchases, have it throw an exception.

   Your code should look like this:

```vb
' VB
Public Sub CreateQuickPurchase(ByVal customerName As String,
        ByVal purchaseDetails As String)
    Dim ds As CustomerDataSet = New CustomerDataSet()

    Dim customer = ds.Customer.AddCustomerRow(customerName, "PO Box 999",
            "Chapter 2 Lesson 2", Guid.Empty)

    ds.Purchase.AddPurchaseRow(customer, DateTime.Today, purchaseDetails)

    SaveCustomer(ds)
    SavePurchase(ds)

End Sub

Private Sub SaveCustomer(ByVal ds As CustomerDataSet)
    Dim cta = New CustomerDataSetTableAdapters.CustomerTableAdapter()
    cta.Update(ds)
End Sub

Private Sub SavePurchase(ByVal ds As CustomerDataSet)
    ' fake an error in the update purchases action
    Throw New Exception("An error occurred while updating Purchases.")

    'Dim pta = New CustomerDataSetTableAdapters.PurchaseTableAdapter()
    'pta.Update(ds)
End Sub
```

```csharp
// C#
public void CreateQuickPurchase(string customerName, string purchaseDetails)
{
    CustomerDataSet ds = new CustomerDataSet();

    CustomerDataSet.CustomerRow customer =
        ds.Customer.AddCustomerRow( customerName, "PO Box 999",
                "Chapter 2 Lesson 2", Guid.Empty );
    ds.Purchase.AddPurchaseRow( customer, DateTime.Today, purchaseDetails );

    SaveCustomer( ds );
    SavePurchase( ds );

}

private static void SaveCustomer( CustomerDataSet ds )
{
    CustomerDataSetTableAdapters.CustomerTableAdapter cta =
        new CustomerDataSetTableAdapters.CustomerTableAdapter();
    cta.Update( ds );
}

private static void SavePurchase( CustomerDataSet ds )
{
    // fake an error in the update purchases action
    throw new Exception( "An error occurred while updating Purchases" );
}
```

8. Create a unit test to test the *CreateQuickPurchase* method.

   Your unit test should look like this:

```vb
' VB
<TestMethod()> _
    Public Sub CreateQuickPurchaseTest()
    Try
        Dim target As CustomerDB = New CustomerDB
        target.CreateQuickPurchase("Blomsma", "Pre-order Halo 7")
    Catch ex As Exception
        ' check that no data has been inserted
        Dim count = CountCustomers()
        If (count > 0) Then
            Assert.Fail("Transaction management not implemented correctly.")
        End If
    End Try
End Sub
```

```vb
Private Function CountCustomers() As Integer
    Dim connectionString As String _
    = "Data Source=.;Initial Catalog=VideoGameStoreDB;Integrated Security=True"
    Dim sql = "select count(*) from customer where customername = 'Blomsma'"
    Dim count = 0

    Using conn = New SqlConnection(connectionString)
        Using cmd = New SqlCommand(sql, conn)
            conn.Open()
            count = CType(cmd.ExecuteScalar(), Integer)
            conn.Close()
        End Using
    End Using
    Return count

End Function
```

```csharp
// C#
[TestMethod()]
public void CreateQuickPurchaseTest()
{
    try
    {
        CustomerDB target = new CustomerDB();
        target.CreateQuickPurchase( "Blomsma", "Pre-order Halo 7" );
    }
    catch ( Exception )
    {
        // check that no data has been inserted
        int count = CountCustomers();
        if ( count != 0 )
        {
            Assert.Fail( "Transaction management not implemented correctly." );
        }
    }
}

private static int CountCustomers()
{
    string connectionString = "Data Source=.;Initial Catalog=
            VideoGameStoreDB;Integrated Security=True";
    string sql = "select count(*) from customer where customername = 'Blomsma'";
    int count = 0;
```

```
using ( SqlConnection conn = new SqlConnection( connectionString ) )
{
    using ( SqlCommand cmd = new SqlCommand( sql, conn ) )
    {
        conn.Open();
        count = (int) cmd.ExecuteScalar();
        conn.Close();
    }
}
return count;
}
```

9. Run the unit test.

    Question: What data do you expect to see in the database? Check the *Customer* and *Purchase* tables in the database. Is it what you expected?

    Answer: Because there is no transaction management, the customer was stored, but the purchase was not.

EXERCISE 2   Implement Transaction Management

In this exercise, you implement transaction management using the *TransactionScope* class.

Continue by using the TransactionalDataAccess project created in Exercise 1, or by using the code that you installed from the companion CD.

1. Implement a transaction in the *CreateQuickPurchase* method with the *using* construct. You need to add a reference to the System.Transaction.dll file.

2. Call the *Complete* method on the transaction scope object.

    Your code should look like this:

```
' VB
Public Sub CreateQuickPurchase(ByVal customerName As String,
        ByVal purchaseDetails As String)
    Dim ds As CustomerDataSet = New CustomerDataSet()

    Dim customer = ds.Customer.AddCustomerRow(customerName, "PO Box 999",
            "Chapter 2 Lesson 2", Guid.Empty)

    ds.Purchase.AddPurchaseRow(customer, DateTime.Today, purchaseDetails)
    Using scope As New TransactionScope()
        SaveCustomer(ds)
        SavePurchase(ds)
    End Using

End Sub
```

```csharp
// C#
public void CreateQuickPurchase( string customerName, string purchaseDetails )
{
    CustomerDataSet ds = new CustomerDataSet();

    CustomerDataSet.CustomerRow customer =
        ds.Customer.AddCustomerRow( customerName,
                                    "PO Box 999",
                                    "Chapter 2 Lesson 2",
                                    Guid.Empty );
    ds.Purchase.AddPurchaseRow( customer, DateTime.Today, purchaseDetails );

    using ( TransactionScope scope = new TransactionScope() )
    {
        SaveCustomer( ds );
        SavePurchase( ds );
        scope.Complete();
    }
}
```

3. Run the unit test again and check the database.

This time, neither the customer nor the purchase has been persisted to the database.

EXERCISE 3   Implement a Distributed Transaction

The code created in Exercise 2 used the *TransactionScope* class to manage the transaction. This code allows the transaction to start as a lightweight transaction and be escalated to a distributed transaction when needed. Examine when this happens.

1. Add trace statements to the *CreateQuickPurchase* method, before *SaveCustomer,* after *SaveCustomer,* and after *SavePurchase.* Use the transaction information property on the current transaction to trace the local transaction identifier and the distributed transaction identifier.

Your code should look like this:

```vbnet
' VB
Public Sub CreateQuickPurchase(ByVal customerName As String,
        ByVal purchaseDetails As String)
    Dim ds As CustomerDataSet = New CustomerDataSet()

    Dim customer = ds.Customer.AddCustomerRow(customerName, "PO Box 999",
            "Chapter 2 Lesson 2", Guid.Empty)

    ds.Purchase.AddPurchaseRow(customer, DateTime.Today, purchaseDetails)
    Using scope As New TransactionScope()
```

```
        Dim current = Transaction.Current
        Trace.WriteLine("Local: " + current.TransactionInformation.
                LocalIdentifier)
        Trace.WriteLine("Distribution: " + current.TransactionInformation.
                DistributedIdentifier.ToString())

        SaveCustomer(ds)

        Trace.WriteLine("Local: " + current.TransactionInformation.
                LocalIdentifier)
        Trace.WriteLine("Distribution: " + current.TransactionInformation.
                DistributedIdentifier.ToString())

        SavePurchase(ds)

        Trace.WriteLine("Local: " + current.TransactionInformation.
                LocalIdentifier)
        Trace.WriteLine("Distribution: " + current.TransactionInformation.
                DistributedIdentifier.ToString())

    End Using

End Sub

// C#
public void CreateQuickPurchase( string customerName, string purchaseDetails )
{
    CustomerDataSet ds = new CustomerDataSet();

    CustomerDataSet.CustomerRow customer =
        ds.Customer.AddCustomerRow( customerName,
                                    "PO Box 999",
                                    "Chapter 2 Lesson 2",
                                    Guid.Empty );
    ds.Purchase.AddPurchaseRow( customer, DateTime.Today, purchaseDetails );

    using ( TransactionScope scope = new TransactionScope() )
    {
        Transaction current = Transaction.Current;
        Trace.WriteLine( "Local: " + current.TransactionInformation.
                LocalIdentifier );
        Trace.WriteLine( "Distributed: " + current.TransactionInformation.
                DistributedIdentifier );

        SaveCustomer( ds );
```

```
        Trace.WriteLine( "Local: " + current.TransactionInformation.
                LocalIdentifier );
        Trace.WriteLine( "Distributed: " + current.TransactionInformation.
                DistributedIdentifier );


        SavePurchase( ds );


        Trace.WriteLine( "Local: " + current.TransactionInformation.
                LocalIdentifier );
        Trace.WriteLine( "Distributed: " + current.TransactionInformation.
                DistributedIdentifier );


        // do not call complete to force rollback
        // scope.Complete();
    }
}
```

2. Look in the output window in Visual Studio and examine the traced information. Notice how the value of the distributed transaction identifier changes when the purchases get persisted to the database.

   You might want to run the code in the debugger if you find the output window too cluttered.

Lesson Summary

- Transactions can be managed at connection level using the *DbConnection* class, or derivative thereof, by the LTM or the DTC.

- The LTM automatically escalates a transaction to the DTC as soon as a second connection is opened.

- The DTC can manage transactions across multiple connections to either the same database or separate databases or resources.

Lesson Review

You can use the following questions to test your knowledge of the information in Lesson 2, "Data Integrity and Transactions." The questions also are available on the companion CD of this book if you prefer to review them in electronic form.

> **NOTE ANSWERS**
>
> Answers to these questions and explanations of why each answer choice is correct or incorrect are located in the "Answers" section at the end of the book.

1. Which of the following statements is true?

    A. The *DbConnection* class can be used to connect to any database.

    B. The *SqlConnection* class can be used to connect to a SQL Server database.

    C. The *DataAdapter* class serves as a bridge between a *DataSet* and a data source for retrieving and saving data.

    D. The *TableAdapter* provides communication between your application and a database.

2. Which of the following statements is true?

    A. The *DbTransaction* class can be used to manage a transaction on any database.

    B. The *SqlTransaction* class can be used to manage a transaction on a SQL Server database.

    C. The *DataAdapter* automatically applies a transaction when updating data.

    D. The *TableAdapter* automatically applies a transaction when updating data.

3. When disposing a *TransactionScope* instance, the transaction is rolled back if which of the following are true? (Choose all that apply.)

    A. There is no exception, and the *Complete* method has not been invoked.

    B. There is no exception, and the *Complete* method has been invoked.

    C. There is an exception, and the *Complete* method has not been invoked.

    D. There is an exception, and the *Complete* method has been invoked.

Chapter Review

To practice and reinforce the skills you learned in this chapter further, you can do any or all of the following:

- Review the chapter summary.
- Review the list of key terms introduced in this chapter.
- Complete the case scenario. This scenario sets up a real-world situation involving the topics of this chapter and asks you to create a solution.
- Complete the suggested practices.
- Take a practice test.

Chapter Summary

- Updating data can be performed using the *DbCommand* or derivative thereof class.
- Updating data can be performed using the *DataAdapter* class, allowing multiple changes in a *DataTable* or *DataSet* to be persisted.
- Updating *Typed DataSets* can be done using a *TableAdapter*.
- Transactions can be managed manually using a derivative of the *DbTransaction* class.
- Transactions can be managed using the LTM encapsulated in the *TransactionScope* class.
- Transactions can be escalated to the DTC when more than one resource or connection needs to be managed.

Key Terms

Do you know what these key terms mean? You can check your answers by looking up the terms in the glossary at the end of the book.

- Database transaction
- Distributed Transaction Coordinator (DTC)
- Lightweight Transaction Manager (LTM)

Case Scenario

In the following case scenario, you apply what you've learned about how to use *DataSets* to update data in a database. You can find answers to the questions posed in this scenario in the "Answers" section at the end of this book.

Case Scenario: Managing Transactions

The company you work for has decided it needs to replace an existing Visual Basic 6 application with a .NET application. The application uses multiple relational databases, and you're asked to present a solution for updating the data in the database. The system includes a few batch processes.

In interviews, these people have said the following:

IT MANAGER

"If we're upgrading anyway, then we want to improve the consistency of data. We've had some bugs in the past where orders that weren't placed by customers have been entered into the system."

CFO

"Consistency is more important than performance."

QUESTION

Answer the following question for your manager:

- What kind of transaction management technology should we use?

Suggested Practices

To help you master the exam objectives presented in this chapter, complete the following tasks.

- **Practice 1**   Use the *VideoGameStoreDB* database to create a Windows application that uses a *DataAdapter* to fill a datatable with products and bind the datatable to a data grid in the user interface. Now, add a button to the form that takes the datatable and persists any changes back to the database.

- **Practice 2**   Use the *VideoGameStoreDB* database to create a Windows application that uses a *Typed DataSet DataAdapter* to fill a typed datatable with products and bind the datatable to a data grid in the user interface. Add a button to save any changes in the grid and use *TableAdapters* to persist the changes back to the database.

Take a Practice Test

The practice tests on this book's companion CD offer many options. For example, you can test yourself on just the content covered in this chapter, or you can test yourself on the entire 70-561 certification exam content. You can set up the test so that it closely simulates the experience of taking a certification exam, or you can set it up in study mode, which allows you to look at the correct answers and explanations after you answer each question.

> *MORE INFO*   **PRACTICE TESTS**
>
> For details about all the available practice test options, see the section entitled "How to Use the Practice Tests," in the Introduction to this book.

CHAPTER 5

Synchronizing Data

As much as it feels like we are in an interconnected world, those connections can be tenuous and expensive. In the outside world, we are creating applications that rely on Internet connectivity, but what happens when we leave the coffee shop with our laptop? We may need a way of accessing our data even when we're far away from it. The farther the data gets from the source of the data (usually a database), the more you require a way to handle the synchronization of the data.

This holds true for the data center as well. The cost of going across the network to retrieve data on every request can be a burden to the overall system. That is where caching data can be a great solution. Caching data is simply making a copy of the data available locally where it is cheaper to access. But for data that is volatile, you need a way to keep local copies without living with stale data. Being able to have smart caching is crucial to this working. Knowing when a cache is invalid and spending the resource to reload it from the data source allows you to cache your data aggressively. This chapter specifically covers the problem of synchronizing data. Whether it is cached data or occasionally connected data, the problem is similar: knowing how to manage change. In the cached data scenario, you must know when to reload data that is stale. And in the occasionally connected data scenario, you must know how to synchronize and merge changes from both the local cache of data and the remote data source.

Exam objectives in this chapter:

- Monitor event notifications.
- Cache data.
- Manage update conflicts between online data and offline data.
- Partition data for synchronization.
- Implement Synchronization Services.

Lessons in this chapter:

Before You Begin

To complete the lessons in this chapter, you must have:

- A computer that meets or exceeds the minimum hardware requirements listed in the "Introduction" section at the beginning of the book
- Microsoft Visual Studio 2008 Professional edition installed on your computer
- An understanding of Microsoft Visual Basic or C# syntax and familiarity with Microsoft .NET Framework version 3.5
- The Microsoft Sync Framework installed on your computer

Lesson 1: Caching Data

Not all data is volatile. That should not come as much of a surprise to most of you, but if you look at the data strategies for most applications, you could surmise that most developers don't understand this basic idea. In many of those applications, every time data is needed, it's requested from the database. Although it makes sense to make sure that the latest data is available to the application, the underlying assumption is that the data you are working with is changing.

In most applications, it's important to understand what data is volatile and not volatile. For example, in a typical e-commerce application, much of the data is very static (like the product catalog); other data is less static (the inventory data); and the shopping cart data is very volatile. Interestingly, only the inventory data is truly the type of data that cannot be easily cached. The product catalog data is easily cached because it changes infrequently. The shopping cart data is easily cached because it is changed through a well-known process (that is, the visitor to a Web site adding something to the cart). Only the inventory data needs to be retrieved because it is needed to make sure that the data is not stale. Understanding and designing your data around this basic tenet of data caching is crucial to a good data cache strategy.

> **After this lesson, you will be able to:**
> - Determine what data to cache
> - Use Web Server–based caching
> - Use memory-based caching
>
> **Estimated lesson time: 30 minutes**

 REAL WORLD

Shawn Wildermuth

Before the .NET platform, I worked on a number of large-scale classic-ASP Web projects. In those days, we had to implement a lot of custom caching scenarios as the current databases we were using (Microsoft SQL Server 6.5 and SQL Server 7) just could not keep up with the tremendous demand we had for data delivery. Learning the types of data and the different scenarios for caching and when to cache was critical to these projects not breaking under the high loads we were delivering.

Much to my delight, when the original version of .NET Framework shipped, we could rely on built-in systems for cache management instead of building a lot of our own code to do the work. The problem was still determining how best to cache our data, but the underlying plumbing was already there once we determined the best way to handle caching.

Why Cache?

Regardless of your data source, retrieving data can be an expensive operation. This is especially true for large, busy databases, where your simple operation of retrieving data may be adding unnecessary load. The central idea about caching is simply that the closer the data is to where it is used, the more performance of the system in general increases. For example, in a Web application, you benefit if you keep your data on or near the Web server.

Boundaries are expensive. Whether it is the AppDomain, process, or network boundary; you pay a price for crossing that boundary. The closer to the data (and the fewer boundaries you cross), the less expensive the request for data is. Making intelligent decisions about when to cache data is a key to creating powerful, robust systems.

In addition, understanding how to cache data most effectively is crucial. You might think that it's most effective to cache your data in the form in which you use the data (for example, Business Objects, *DataSets,* and so on). But in fact, caching the *results* of the data use is a better approach more often. In ASP.NET, this is supported with page or control caching. Because ASP.NET builds Hypertext Markup Language (HTML), caching the resulting HTML for non-volatile data can increase the throughput of your Web application enormously.

> **MORE INFO   WEB PAGE CACHING**
>
> Web page caching is not covered specifically in this book. For information on Web server page and control caching, you should refer to the *MCAD/MCSD Self-Paced Training Kit: Developing Web Applications with Microsoft Visual Basic .NET and Microsoft Visual C# .NET, Second Edition* by Jeff Web (Microsoft Press, 2003). You can find information about this title online at *http://www.microsoft.com/mspress/books/6714.aspx.*

As mentioned in the introduction to this lesson, understand your data—know what data can be cached. The problem is that refreshing or invalidating caches can become more of a drain on a system than having no caching at all. Understand the nature of your data volatility and pick the right solution for your application.

Caching Options

The word *cache* implies different meanings to different people. Many developers I've talked with immediately try to find a class that will hold on to a cache of data for them instead of understanding that the purpose of caching may be simply to hold a reference to existing data. This may not work in all scenarios because the lifetime of objects is very different based on the type of application you are using. For example, in a Web application scenario, the lifetime of page or control objects is very transitory, so caching data at the page level is not effective. In contrast to Web applications, rich-client applications (including Windows Forms, Windows Presentation Foundation, and Silverlight), caching data as part of the application makes a lot more sense. Depending on the technology, you need to make that important decision of how to cache data effectively.

In addition, you want to understand the nature of your data to determine effective caching strategies for simple caches. This is often segmented into global or user-based caching. Global caches are effectively a set of caches that affect all users of an application, whereas user-level caches use specific data.

ASP.NET Caching

For ASP.NET-based projects, you have a wide variety of methods for handling caching. The nature of the data to cache determines which cache you use. The different caching mechanisms are enumerated in Table 5-1.

TABLE 5-1 ASP.NET Caching Mechanisms

CACHE TYPE	USE CASE
Cookies	Used to cache data that is user-specific and small. Commonly used to store tokens or keys to larger data stores, but some basic preferences can be stored there.
ViewState	Page-level cache implemented as a hidden form element on the page sent to the client. Often used as a temporary cache to prevent retrieval from other data stores. Sent back to Page during Postbacks. Bloats the size of the HTML markup. Useful for stateless storage of data on a per-page/per-control basis.
Session	Browser-session-based cache (for example, every browser visitor gets his or her own cache) of arbitrary objects. By default, memory based on the Web server can be configured for cross-machine persistence.
Cache	In-memory, per-application cache of arbitrary objects.

In Web scenarios, you can choose from each of these methodologies for different reasons. Picking the right cache can make a big difference in the overall performance of your Web application. For example, for small pieces of data that you want to access in the browser, cookies are the obvious choice because the client-side code has access to the cookies. On the other side of the spectrum, when you need to cache data that is useful to every user (such as a product catalog), the *Cache* class is great for an application-level cache. Let's discuss the cache types one at a time.

Cookies

Using cookies makes it fairly trivial to set data on the server that gets accessed from the client. Although this is not exactly caching, it has some overlap with the use-case of storing data for use later in the application. To manipulate the cookies in ASP.NET, you use the *Response* object's Cookie collection to add or remove *HttpCookie* objects like so:

```
' VB
' Store the user's favorite color
Dim cookie As New HttpCookie("favColor", "#0000FF")

' Add it
Response.Cookies.Add(cookie)
```

```
// C#
// Store the user's favorite color
HttpCookie cookie = new HttpCookie("favColor", "#0000FF");

// Add it
Response.Cookies.Add(cookie);
```

On the client, it's a bit more difficult because JavaScript gives you the cookies only as a single string. You can use a simple function to find each individual cookie, as shown here:

```
// JavaScript
function setColor() {
  var color = getCookie("favColor");
  if (color != null) {
    document.body.style.backgroundColor = color;
  }
}

function getCookie(name) {
  var value = document.cookie.match('(^|;) ?' + name + '=([^;]*)(;|$)');

  if (value) {
    return unescape(value[2]);
  }
  else {
    return null;
  }
}
```

ViewState

In contrast to Cookies, ViewState allows you to store data in the markup of a page. This allows you to save a state without causing a burden on the server for that state (or even requiring the user to come back to the same server in load-balancing scenarios). The problem with this approach is that the size of the corresponding markup is bloated. ViewState is a useful tool, but using it wisely, to keep the size of the markup pages as small as possible, is an art. In addition, ViewState is encrypted so it is only useful for saving states that you need to use when a page posts back to the server. The client code (for example, JavaScript) does not have access to the ViewState because it can't decrypt it.

ViewState uses a simple key/value pair to store data:

```
' VB
ViewState("favoriteColor") = "#8080FF"
```

```
// C#
ViewState["favoriteColor"] = "#8080FF";
```

In the markup of the page, this turns into a hidden input element that has all the ViewState objects for the page encrypted:

```
<input type="hidden"
    name="__VIEWSTATE"
    id="__VIEWSTATE"
    value="/wEPDwULLTE5MzY3OTc2NzYPFgIeDWZhdm9yaXRlQ29sb3IFByM4MDgwRkZkZO+ArSsCpqg
        VDfIpvy7FzW6TWsGt" />
```

Once placed in ViewState, you can access it on subsequent postbacks because it is part of the request. To access it, you can use the *ViewState* object and supply the key:

```
if (IsPostBack)
{
  theDiv.Style[HtmlTextWriterStyle.BackgroundColor] = (string)
        ViewState["favoriteColor"];
}
```

One requirement is that any object you place in ViewState must support serialization (marking it with the *SerializationAttribute* is often adequate). But this means that some types can't be used in ViewState. For example, suppose that you try to store a *WizardStep* object (which is part of the ASP.NET Wizard framework) in ViewState like so:

```
ViewState["currentWizardStep"] = new WizardStep();
```

It throws an exception at run time with the error:

```
Type 'System.Web.UI.WebControls.WizardStep' in Assembly 'System.Web, Version=2.0.0.0,
Culture=neutral, PublicKeyToken=b03f5f7f11d50a3a' is not marked as serializable.
```

The reason for this is that the *WizardStep* class isn't marked as serializable, so the ASP.NET framework doesn't have the information it needs to store it.

Finally, you must be aware of the size of the object in ViewState. In this code, you saw a ViewState with a minimum of data in it (the example showed storage of a string, but the ViewState in the markup also contained data that other controls inserted so the size is not indicative of how large simple strings are or could be). It's often easy to think to use ViewState for simple storage of data (for example, *DataSets* or collections of objects), but in those cases, the ViewState becomes huge. *DataSets* are particularly troublesome because of their tightly coupled nature. You might think it would be a good idea to store an individual *DataRow* in ViewState because that is just a single row of data. The problem with that approach is that the *DataRow* refers to the *DataTable*, which refers to the *DataSet*, which in turn refers to all *DataTables*. Storing a *DataRow* in ViewState invariably stores the entire *DataSet* in ViewState, which can be a huge amount of data. Looking at the resulting page size when you are developing using ViewState becomes a required task to help fine-tune the page size.

Session

Every time a user visits your Web application, the server creates a unique number for that individual browser instance that is communicated back and forth to the client. This unique number is called the SessionID. This allows the server to create a temporary store of cached data for the user called Session State. By default, Session State is stored in memory on the server, although you can configure it to use SQL Server or a service called State Server to allow for a cross-machine Session State. In any of these cases, Session State is used to store data whose life is limited to the browser session with time-out (typically 20 minutes). If the user closes his or her browser or waits too long, any data in the Session State is gone. Session state is a good solution for storing a user-specific transient state that is too big to include in ViewState.

Session State uses the same key/value pairing that ViewState uses:

```vb
' VB
Session("favoriteColor") = "#8080FF"
```

```csharp
// C#
Session["favoriteColor"] = "#8080FF";
```

Also like ViewState, you can store only data that is serializable. Retrieving Session data is achieved using the same key/value pairing as ViewState:

```vb
' VB
If IsPostBack Then
  theDiv.Style(HtmlTextWriterStyle.BackgroundColor) = CStr(Session("favoriteColor"))
End If
```

```csharp
// C#
if (IsPostBack)
{
  theDiv.Style[HtmlTextWriterStyle.BackgroundColor] = (string)Session["favoriteColor"];
}
```

The caveat about using Session State is that retrieving on every page can cause a large load on servers. In that case, you should be aware of what pages in ASP.NET require the data in Session and enable Session for only those pages specifically. You can specify in the Web.config file that all pages do not enable Session State:

```xml
<configuration>
  <system.Web>
    <pages enableSessionState="false">
      <!-- ... -->
    </pages>
  </system.Web>
</configuration>
```

Then you should specifically allow it only on pages that require it:

```
<%@ Page Language="C#"
        AutoEventWireup="true"
        CodeBehind="Default.aspx.cs"
        Inherits="TestCaching._Default"
        EnableSessionState="True" %>
```

Alternatively, you can specify that Session can only be read, not changed, which makes it more efficient:

```
<%@ Page Language="C#"
        AutoEventWireup="true"
        CodeBehind="Default.aspx.cs"
        Inherits="TestCaching._Default"
        EnableSessionState="ReadOnly" %>
```

Cache

The last type of ASP.NET caching is application-level caching using the *Cache* class. Unlike the other types of Web caching, application-level caches are shared among all users of a Web application. This means that caching for one user can improve the experience for other users.

Like ViewState and Session State, discussed previously, Cache can be accessed using a simple key/value pairing with the indexer:

```
' VB
Cache("highlightColor") = "#8080FF"
```

```
// C#
Cache["highlightColor"] = "#8080FF";
```

Also like ViewState and Session State, you can store only data that is serializable. Retrieving Cache data is likewise performed using the key/value pairing:

```
' VB
If IsPostBack Then
   theDiv.Style(HtmlTextWriterStyle.BackgroundColor) = CStr(Cache("highlightColor"))
End If
```

```
// C#
if (IsPostBack)
{
   theDiv.Style[HtmlTextWriterStyle.BackgroundColor] = (string)Cache["highlightColor"];
}
```

Because this data is at the application level, you have a lot more control over the way that data is cached. If you use the *Cache.Insert* method instead of the indexer, you are presented with several ways to control the cached item, including absolute expiration, sliding expiration, and cache dependency. Absolute expiration is specifying a specific date and time that an item expires. You can do that by specifying a specific *DateTime* object in the fourth parameter (in which case the fifth parameter must be *Cache.NoSlidingExpiration*), as shown here:

```vb
' VB
Cache.Insert("highlightColor", _
            "#8080FF", _
            Nothing, _
            DateTime.Today.AddDays(1), _
            Cache.NoSlidingExpiration)
```

```csharp
// C#
Cache.Insert("highlightColor",
            "#8080FF",
            null,
            DateTime.Today.AddDays(1),
            Cache.NoSlidingExpiration);
```

Absolute expiration means that no matter how many times the cache is accessed, it always expires at a very specific time. In contrast, the sliding expiration gets renewed every time it is accessed. You can specify a sliding expiration with a *TimeSpan* in the fifth parameter (making the fourth parameter *Cache.NoAbsoluteExpiration*):

```vb
' VB
Cache.Insert("highlightColor", _
            "#8080FF", _
            Nothing, _
            Cache.NoAbsoluteExpiration, _
            TimeSpan.FromMinutes(2))
```

```csharp
// C#
Cache.Insert("highlightColor",
            "#8080FF",
            null,
            Cache.NoAbsoluteExpiration,
            TimeSpan.FromMinutes(2));
```

In addition to cache length, you can specify a cache dependency. But what is a cache dependency? Let's look at the problem first. Cached data can be volatile. You might need to cache the data aggressively, but as it changes, you always want the latest version of the data. One approach to solving this issue is to make a very short expiration to refresh the cache (functionally, like polling for the updates). The problem is that tuning this to coincide with changes is too difficult: either you're reloading the cache too often or not often enough. Cache dependencies mean to solve this problem by creating a way to create a dependency on an external resource (like files or SQL Server data) and let the resource alert the cache to new data. There are two types of *CacheDependency* classes: file cache dependencies and SQL Server cache dependencies.

The *CacheDependency* class does simple file/directory cache dependencies for you. To use it, you can specify a file path to a file that you are using. For example, here it is loading some text from a file and then creating a *CacheDependency* object with that same file path:

```vb
' VB
Dim colorFromFile As String = File.ReadAllText(filePath)

' Create a dependency to the file
Dim dependency As New CacheDependency(filePath)

' Cache the Data
Cache.Insert("highlightColor", _
         "#8080FF", _
         dependency)
```

```csharp
// C#
string colorFromFile = File.ReadAllText(filePath);

// Create a dependency to the file
CacheDependency dependency = new CacheDependency(filePath);

// Cache the Data
Cache.Insert("highlightColor",
         colorFromFile,
         dependency);
```

What this does is monitor the file. When it changes in any way, the cache entry is invalidated so that when it's requested again, the cache retrieves it from the original source. This works for files, sets of files, or directories using different overloads of the *CacheDependency* class.

Another type of cache dependency that is interesting is the *SqlCacheDependency*. This type of cache depends on SQL Server data. In this type of dependency, you can specify a table name to depend on to invalidate the cache. In SQL Server 2005 and later, you can also specify a specific query to depend on instead of just table names. This type of dependency polls the database periodically (based on a configuration setting) to test if changes have happened. If they have, the cached item is invalidated.

To start, you need to configure the Web site's Web.config file to support SQL Server–based cache dependency:

```xml
<?xml version="1.0"?>
<configuration>
  <!-- ... -->

  <connectionStrings>
    <add name="Northwind"
        connectionString="..."
        providerName="System.Data.SqlClient" />
  </connectionStrings>
```

```
   <system.Web>
     <!-- ... -->

     <caching>
       <sqlCacheDependency pollTime="15000"
                            enabled="true">
         <databases>
           <add connectionStringName="Northwind" name="Northwind" />
         </databases>
       </sqlCacheDependency>
     </caching>

   </system.Web>
</configuration>
```

By including the caching block inside your Web.config file, you are setting up the database and polling frequency for checking the dependency (although in SQL Server 2005 and later, it uses a callback mechanism instead of actually polling). Once this is set up, you can use the *SqlCacheDependency* object when storing an object into the cache:

```
' VB
Dim dependency As SqlCacheDependency = Nothing

' Try and create the dependency and if it fails because
' of set up failing, set up the database/table and try again
Do While dependency Is Nothing
Try
        ' Try and create the Dependency, if the database
        ' or table are not setup, it will throw an exception
        dependency = New SqlCacheDependency("Northwind", "Products")
Catch dbex As DatabaseNotEnabledForNotificationException
        ' Setup the database for SQL Notifications
        SqlCacheDependencyAdmin.EnableNotifications(connectionString)
Catch tblex As TableNotEnabledForNotificationException
        ' Setup the Table for Notifications
        SqlCacheDependencyAdmin.EnableTableForNotifications(connectionString,
            "Products")
End Try
Loop

' Add item to the Cache
Cache.Insert("Products", GetProducts(), dependency)

// C#
SqlCacheDependency dependency = null;

// Try and create the dependency and if it fails because
// of set up failing, set up the database/table and try again
```

```
while (dependency == null)
{
  try
  {
    // Try and create the Dependency, if the database
    // or table are not setup, it will throw an exception
    dependency = new SqlCacheDependency("Northwind", "Products");
  }
  catch (DatabaseNotEnabledForNotificationException)
  {
    // Setup the database for SQL Notifications
    SqlCacheDependencyAdmin.EnableNotifications(connectionString);
  }
  catch (TableNotEnabledForNotificationException)
  {
    // Setup the Table for Notifications
    SqlCacheDependencyAdmin.EnableTableForNotifications(connectionString, "Products");
  }
}


// Add item to the Cache
Cache.Insert("Products", GetProducts(), dependency);
```

When using the *SqlCacheDependency* object, you must be able to handle exceptions that are thrown when the dependencies are not enabled at the server level. This code starts with a *while* loop to allow for the dependency to be retried when the database and/or table are not enabled. In those cases you would use the *SqlCacheDependencyAdmin* class to enable notifications and try the dependency again. Once the dependency is created, your code falls out of the *while* loop to the code that inserts into the cache using the *SqlCacheDepenency* class.

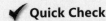 **Quick Check**

- What class do you use to ensure that a cache of data is updated if the data in a SQL Server database changes?

Quick Check Answer

- *SqlCacheDependency*

Desktop Caching

Unlike caching on the server, caching in desktop applications is much more straightforward. In most desktop applications, you have control over a process and do not have to deal with stateless communication with a server. For this reason, you can simply cache data on the desktop, either in memory or by persisting it locally.

In-memory caching is as simple as holding on to references to data instead of retrieving them from a remote machine (for example, a Web service or a database) on every access. In most cases, this sort of caching is organically how you build most desktop applications. You retrieve data, show it to the user, and hold on to the data. Because your applications are long-lived, holding on to the data is simple.

Being able to use cache dependencies would be a great benefit, but because the *Cache* class (and its dependencies) actually live in the System.Web assembly, they are difficult to include in your desktop applications. You should avoid using the *System.Web.Cache* class to cache data outside ASP.NET because that class does not exist in some .NET Framework versions (such as the client-SKU of the .NET Framework 3.5).

Finally, you can save your cached data locally between invocations of your application. There are many ways to save a wide variety of data in your application. For example, if you create a *DataTable* to hold some data that you need to cache, you can use this pattern of loading on startup and saving at shutdown:

```vb
' VB
Private myData As New DataTable()
Private ReadOnly FILENAME As String = "mycache.xml"

Private Sub Form1_Load(ByVal sender As Object, ByVal e As EventArgs)
  If File.Exists(FILENAME) Then
    myData.ReadXml(FILENAME)
  End If
End Sub

Private Sub Form1_FormClosing(ByVal sender As Object, ByVal e As FormClosingEventArgs)
  If myData.Rows.Count > 0 Then
    myData.WriteXml(FILENAME, XmlWriteMode.WriteSchema)
  End If
End Sub
```

```csharp
// C#
DataTable myData = new DataTable();
readonly string FILENAME = @"mycache.xml";

private void Form1_Load(object sender, EventArgs e)
{
  if (File.Exists(FILENAME))
  {
    myData.ReadXml(FILENAME);
  }
}
```

```
private void Form1_FormClosing(object sender, FormClosingEventArgs e)
{
  if (myData.Rows.Count > 0)
  {
    myData.WriteXml(FILENAME, XmlWriteMode.WriteSchema);
  }
}
```

In this code, you load the file (if it exists) in the *Loaded* event of your desktop application. Then, on the *FormClosing* event, you save the file if any data already exists. The details of how you save data is not nearly as important as the pattern of caching the data based on startup and shutdown.

LAB   Caching Data

In this lab, you cache some data using the *Cache* class and use *SqlCacheDependency* to make the cache refresh on a change to the database. All the lab files can be installed from the Code folder on the companion CD. To start, you need to have a copy of the Lab1 project in the Chapter 5 folder. Depending on which language you choose to use (Visual Basic or C#), the project file is either in the Chapter5/Cs folder or the Chapter5/Vb folder. Open the Exercise1_Before's Lab1.sln file to open the project in Visual Studio.

EXERCISE 1   Using the Cache Class

In this exercise, you take an existing Web project and add caching for the database data.

1. Once you have the project open, press F5 to run the project in Visual Studio so that you can see the simple Web page that is displaying XBox game data. Click Refresh to see that every time someone visits this page, the status message states that you are retrieving the data from the database. Close the browser and return to Visual Studio.

2. Right-click the default.aspx page in Project Explorer and select View Code to see the implementation page (which has the extension.cs or .vb, depending on your choice of language).

3. Just inside the class declaration, create a new read-only string called *CacheKey* and assign it *MYCACHEKEY* as a value. You use this as the key to the Cache for the data you are storing, as shown here:

   ```
   ' VB
   Private ReadOnly CacheKey As String = "MYPRODUCTLIST"

   // C#
   readonly string CacheKey = "MYPRODUCTLIST";
   ```

4. Next, find the *GetProduct* method of the implementation class.

5. Near the end of the method, find the return keyword and just before the results are returned, put the data in the cache using the *Cache* class, and the *CacheKey* that you created.

6. Next, you need to check for the cache so at the top of the method, create an *if* statement that checks to see if the *Cache* contains an entry using the *Cache* key (by checking for *NULL*).

7. Inside the body of the *if* statement, set the *Text* property of the statusLabel to Retrieved From Cache to show the user that the data came from the cache, not the database.

8. Next, cast the entry for *CacheKey* in the *Cache* and return it.

9. In the *else* part of the *if* statement, surround the existing database implementation that was already in the method. The resulting method should look like this:

```vb
' VB
Private Function GetProducts() As List(Of Product)

    If Cache(CacheKey) IsNot Nothing Then
        statusLabel.Text = "Loaded from Cache"
        Return CType(Cache(CacheKey), List(Of Product))

    Else

        statusLabel.Text = "Loaded data from database"

        Using ctx As New ProductModelConnection()

            Dim cutoffDate As New DateTime(2007, 12, 31)

            ' Create query
            Dim qry = From g In ctx.Product _
                        Where g.ReleaseDate > cutoffDate _
                        Order By g.ReleaseDate _
                        Select g

            ' Retrieve the list from the database
            Dim results As List(Of Product) = qry.ToList()

            ' Add to cache before returning it
            Cache(CacheKey) = results

            ' Return the Results
            Return results

        End Using

    End If

End Function
```

```csharp
// C#
List<Product> GetProducts()
{
  if (Cache[CacheKey] != null)
  {
    statusLabel.Text = "Loaded from Cache";
    return (List<Product>)Cache[CacheKey];
  }
  else
  {
    statusLabel.Text = "Loaded data from database";
    using (ProductModelConnection ctx = new ProductModelConnection())
    {
      DateTime cutoffDate = new DateTime(2007, 12, 31);

      // Create query
      var qry = from g in ctx.Product
                where g.ReleaseDate > cutoffDate
                orderby g.ReleaseDate
                select g;

      // Retrieve the list from the database
      List<Product> results = qry.ToList();

      // Add to cache before returning it
      Cache[CacheKey] = results;

      // Return the results
      return results;
    }
  }
}
```

10. Run the application, and click Refresh to see that every time you visit the page after the first invocation, you are using the version from the cache.

EXERCISE 2   Using the *SqlCacheDependency* Class

In this exercise, you create a *SqlCacheDependency* object that causes the cache to become invalidated once the data is changed.

1. Before you can add the code for the *SqlCacheDependency* object, you must add the configuration to the Web project to support *SqlCacheDepenedency* objects. Open the Web.config file to start this process.

2. Find the *system.Web* ending tag in the configuration file.

3. Create a new *caching* element tag.

4. Inside the new tag, create a *sqlCacheDependency* tag.

5. Add an *enabled* attribute to the *sqlCacheDependency* tag and set it to True.

6. Add a *polltime* attribute to the *sqlCacheDependency* tag and set it to 1000 for a 1-second poll time. This poll time is high, but for your example, it's easier to test using that setting.

7. Inside the *sqlCacheDependency* tag, create a new *database* tag.

8. Inside the *database* tag, create a new *add* tag.

9. In the *add* tag, add a *connectionStringName* attribute and a *name* attribute and set them both to *Products*. Your new section should look like this:

```
<caching>
  <sqlCacheDependency pollTime="1000" enabled="true">
    <databases>
      <add name="Products" connectionStringName="Products" />
    </databases>
  </sqlCacheDependency>
</caching>
```

10. Next, find the *connectionStrings* tag inside the configuration file.

11. Create a new *add* tag inside the *connectionStrings* tag.

12. Inside the *add* tag, add a name attribute and set it to *Products* (to match up with the *connectionStringName* from the caching block shown previously).

13. Also inside the *add* tag, add a *connectionString* attribute and set it to the connection string for the database that hosts the *VideoGameStore* data.

14. Again, inside the *add* tag, add a *providerName* attribute and set it to *System.Data.SqlClient*. Your connection string section should look like this (note the project already had a connection string for the Entity Framework model but you can't re-use that one):

```
<add name="Products"
        connectionString="Server=localhost;Initial Catalog=VideoGameStore;
                          Integrated Security=True;"
        providerName="System.Data.SqlClient" />
```

15. Return back to the implementation file for the Default.aspx page.

16. Create a new method called *AddToCache* accepting a *List of Products* as a parameter.

17. Inside the new method create a new local variable named *connString* of type string and assign it by looking up the *Products* connection string in the configuration file (using the *ConnectionManager.ConnectionStrings* property).

18. Create a new local variable called *dep* of type *SqlCacheDependency* and assign a *NULL* reference (or Nothing in Visual Basic) to it.

19. Create a *while* (or *do while* in Visual Basic) loop to repeat while the new *dep* variable is *NULL* (or *Nothing* in VB).

20. Inside the *while* loop, create a *try* block (of a *try/catch* statement) and inside that, set the *dep* local variable by assigning it a new *SqlCacheDependency,* specifying *Products* as the *databaseEntryName* (to match the name in the Web.config file) and *Product* for the table name to match the table from which you are caching data.

21. Create a *catch* block attached to the *try* section to handle the *DatabaseNotEnabled ForNotification* exception.

22. Inside this *catch* block, call the *EnableNotifications* static (or *Shared* in VB) method for the *SqlCacheDependencyAdmin* class, specifying the *connString* local variable to enable notifications for the database if it hasn't been enabled already.

23. Create another *catch* block to handle the *TableNotEnabledForNotification* exception (resulting in two *catch* blocks for the one *try* block).

24. Inside the new *catch* block, call the *EnableTableForNotifications* static method for the *SqlCacheDependencyAdmin* class, specifying the *Product* table to allow notifications for that table.

25. Now that you have a valid *SqlCacheDependency* object, you use it to insert the item into the cache. After the *while* block, call the *Insert* method of the *Cache* class specifying the *CacheKey,* the *Products* parameter of this method, and the new dependency object you created. The new *AddToCache* method should look like this:

```
' VB
Private Sub AddToCache(ByVal products As List(Of Product))

    Dim connString As String = ConfigurationManager.ConnectionStrings("Products").
        ConnectionString

    Dim dep As SqlCacheDependency = Nothing

    Do While dep Is Nothing

      Try
        dep = New SqlCacheDependency("Products", "Product")
      Catch e1 As DatabaseNotEnabledForNotificationException
        SqlCacheDependencyAdmin.EnableNotifications(connString)
      Catch e2 As TableNotEnabledForNotificationException
        SqlCacheDependencyAdmin.EnableTableForNotifications(connString, "Product")
      End Try

    Loop

    Cache.Insert(CacheKey, products, dep)

  End Sub
```

```csharp
// C#
    void AddToCache(List<Product> products)
    {
        string connString = ConfigurationManager.ConnectionStrings["Products"].
            ConnectionString;

        SqlCacheDependency dep = null;

        while (dep == null)
        {
            try
            {
                dep = new SqlCacheDependency("Products", "Product");
            }
            catch (DatabaseNotEnabledForNotificationException)
            {
                SqlCacheDependencyAdmin.EnableNotifications(connString);
            }
            catch (TableNotEnabledForNotificationException)
            {
                SqlCacheDependencyAdmin.EnableTableForNotifications(connString,
                    "Product");
            }
        }

        Cache.Insert(CacheKey, products, dep);
    }
```

26. Inside the *GetProducts* method, find the line where you added the *results* into the cache with the *CacheKey* and replace it with a call to *AddToCache* like so:

```vb
' VB
' Add to cache before returning it
AddToCache(results)
```

```csharp
// C#
// Add to cache before returning it
AddToCache(results);
```

27. Compile and run the application. Click Refresh to see that you are pulling the data from the cache after the first run.

28. Without closing the browser or stopping debugging, return to Visual Studio.

29. If the Server Explorer is not already shown, from the main menu, select View, Server Explorer.

30. Find the server in your server list (or add it manually using Server Explorer) and navigate to the *VideoGameStore* database.

31. Open the *Tables* node on the server and right-click the *Product* table and select Show Table Data to open the actual data in the table.

32. Change any data in the table (it does not have to be one of the rows shown on your Web page because *SqlCacheDependency* is working on changes at the table level in this case).

33. Once you change and commit the change, go back to the Web page and refresh the browser to see that the data came from the database because the cache was invalidated when the table changed.

Lesson Summary

- Caching data is important in a variety of scenarios.
- In Web applications, you have different caching tools for caching data depending on the type of data.
- Using the *Cache* class for caching application data allows you to gain the benefit of caching with full control over how the caches are invalidated.
- You can use sliding or fixed expirations for caching with the *Cache* class.
- You can use the *SqlCacheDependency* class to control invalidating the cache once the underlying database data changes.

Lesson Review

Use the following questions to test your knowledge of the information in Lesson 1, "Caching Data." The questions are also available on the companion CD if you prefer to review them in electronic form.

> **NOTE ANSWERS**
>
> Answers to these questions and explanations of why each answer choice is correct or incorrect are located in the "Answers" section at the end of the book.

1. What should you use for user-based data caching for very small pieces of data in a Web application?

    A. Session State

    B. Cookies

    C. ViewState

    D. Cache

2. Why would you avoid using Session State for caching?

    A. Data is user-based.

    B. Data is large.

    C. Data is application-based.

    D. Data is used across pages.

3. What would you use to create a cache of application-based database data that must invalidate the cache as the underlying data changes?

   A. Cache with a sliding expiration

   B. Session State

   C. Cache with a fixed expiration

   D. Cache with *SqlCacheDependency*

Lesson 2: Microsoft Sync Framework

When dealing with data, there are times when simple caching just is not good enough. Caching read-only data works well, but if you are working with volatile data, the caching mechanism needs to be expanded to support synchronization of the data. The problem is exacerbated by changes to the cache and the backing data store. The need to not only keep these caches in sync but also to handle merging changes becomes a difficult problem to solve. Finally, in some situations, you also need to be able to have an offline experience for your application that makes the change management timeline become longer and longer. Long-lived change management is a particularly difficult problem to solve as well. These problems are ones that the Microsoft Sync Framework is made to solve.

> **After this lesson, you will be able to:**
> - Understand when to use the Microsoft Sync Framework
> - Create and use an offline cache of data using the Sync Services for ADO.NET
> - Manage synchronization between the data source and the offline cache
>
> **Estimated lesson time: 30 minutes**

What Is the Microsoft Sync Framework?

The Microsoft Sync Framework is a broad set of tools to allow for a variety of synchronization scenarios. It allows for synchronization over virtually any scenario. This including roaming with data, taking data offline, and sharing data. The framework supports the ability to write custom providers to synchronize data across any type of device and any protocol. To support common use cases, the Microsoft Sync Framework includes several prebuilt providers:

- Sync Services for ADO.NET, to synchronize ADO.NET data
- Sync Services for File Systems, to synchronize files and directory structures
- Sync Services for FeedSync, to synchronize RSS/ATOM feeds

Providers and Participants

These providers are built on top of the Microsoft Sync Framework. Each provider is capable of creating a replica of data in a specific scenario. A replica is a set of data that is to be kept in sync with another set of data in a separate place. For example, you might have a phone with contacts. The provider is able to create a replica of the contact data for the phone that might also be housed on your laptop. If the data stored in the replica is in a different schema than another replica, the provider does the mapping between the schemas.

Synchronization involves two types of data: data and metadata. The data is the actual items to be synchronized. The metadata is the data that helps determine how the synchronization occurs. Metadata includes information like date-time stamps, versions, or simply publishing

IDs. It's this metadata that makes the job of synchronizing the data across disparate devices possible, as seen in Figure 5-1.

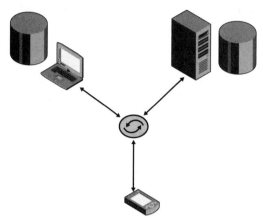

FIGURE 5-1 Participant types

The provider model is a peer-to-peer relationship. Each peer in a synchronization relationship is called *participants*. Participants may be computers, handheld devices, or even Web services. Each participant must be able to at least return information. In addition, each participant may be able to handle the metadata as well for the synchronization. Participants are categorized into three types based on their ability to deal with metadata:

- **Full** Can store data and metadata as well as code that performs the actual synchronization in the form of a Sync Service.
- **Partial** Can store data and metadata but cannot host code or applications to perform the synchronization.
- **Simple** Can only provide data. They do not store data or metadata.

When initiating a synchronization session, all three types of participants can be part of the session, but a session requires at least one Full participant so that the code can be executed that compares the metadata to determine how the synchronization will be performed.

Architecture

For each type of synchronization, Microsoft Sync Services requires a Sync Services Provider, which is a set of classes that wrap the base libraries in the Microsoft Sync Framework. These providers handle the communication of data and metadata during a session, as shown in Figure 5-2.

The synchronization involves both the data (in the data source) and the metadata. The metadata typically involves several types of information about the data in the data source:

- **Versions** Information that is used to determine when an item changed. This could be a simple auto-numbered version (for example, like a SQL Server *rowversion* element) or a computed version (an auto-incremented large integer version).

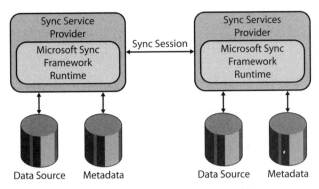

FIGURE 5-2 Microsoft Synchronization Services architecture

- **Knowledge**   A compact representation of the changes in the provider. This is an efficient way to pass change information to help reconciliation of the changes across sources in the Sync Session.
- **Tombstones**   Information about items that have been deleted. Because deletions are absent, tombstones are a list of items that have been deleted since the last synchronization.

This metadata is used to instantiate a synchronization session where a source and destination discuss the changes and reconcile them (if possible). During a synchronization session, a source and destination communicate changes on both sides of the synchronization to determine how to merge changes. The flow of a synchronization session between a source and destination is shown in Figure 5-3.

Although you will learn the overall structure of Microsoft Sync Framework, this training kit focuses on the Sync Services for ADO.NET.

Using the Sync Services for ADO.NET

Because a very common method of synchronization is the synchronization of database data, Microsoft includes Sync Services for ADO.NET as a provider for handling synchronization between two data sources. The Sync Services for ADO.NET provide tools in Visual Studio to support generating the local replica for applications. To do this, it creates a local SQL Server Compact edition database (.sdf) file for the local cache of data to be synchronized. This provides a simple way to make an occasionally offline application that handles synchronization when it has access to the database server. In addition, these tools generate SQL Server scripts to support the metadata (row versioning and tombstones) as well as to write a wrapper around the provider to do the synchronization. This does not mean you have to use these tools to generate all this code. Sync Services for ADO.NET also provides the underlying providers for SQL Server and SQL Server Compact edition to make this possible. You can decide to write the sync providers manually if you like, but because it is more usual to use the toolset, this chapter covers the tools instead.

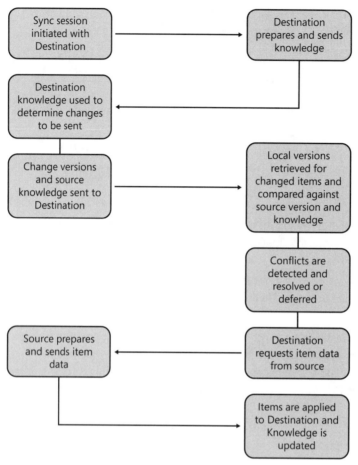

FIGURE 5-3 Synchronization flow

Enabling Sync Services for ADO.NET

If you are starting with a standard Windows Forms application, you can add support for Sync Services by adding a new item to your project called Local Database Cache, by right-clicking your project and selecting Add New Item..., as shown in Figure 5-4.

Once you add this item to your project, this opens the Configure Data Synchronization dialog box, where you can pick your local and remote data sources as well as shape what data you want to cache, as shown in Figure 5-5.

In this dialog box, you select (or create) a server connection. By default the client connection will be a SQL Server Compact edition (.sdf) file. This will create a new local database for the local cache in your application.

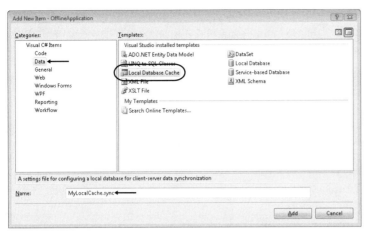

FIGURE 5-4 Adding a local database cache

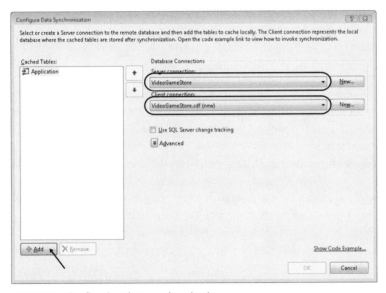

FIGURE 5-5 Configuring data synchronization

NOTE **CHANGES FOR SQL SERVER 2008**

If you are using SQL Server 2008, notice that the Use SQL Server Change Tracking check box is selected. If you leave this option enabled, you do not need to specify any of the table-level change tracking discussed in the next few sections.

Before you can complete the dialog box, you need to add cached tables by using the Add button. This opens the Configure Tables For Offline Use dialog box, which you can use to pick and configure each of these tables, as shown in Figure 5-6.

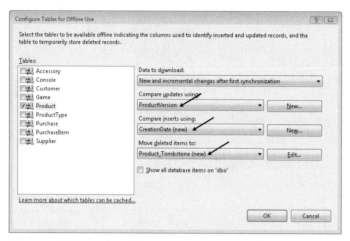

FIGURE 5-6 Table configuration

This dialog box lets you select what tables in the server database to synchronize (for example, if you want to make a copy of in the local cache database). In addition, you can pick how the sync framework performs the synchronization. In general, this dialog box shows you the changes it wants to make to the server schema to support synchronization. This metadata is required to monitor changes and often requires these schema changes. For example, once the *Product* table is selected, there are selectors for comparing updates, inserts, and deletes (as tombstones). The inserts and deletes are marked as (New) to signify that the tools want to modify the schema to support this change. In addition to the schema changes, the synchronization framework adds triggers to the database to support tracking the metadata. The schema changes are added to your project as two SQL scripts—one that modifies the schema and one that removes those modifications. These are useful as the application is deployed because the local changes that the tools make should never be performed on a production machine during development.

SQL Server Timestamp or Rowversion Columns

You should notice that the Compare Updates Using: drop-down list in the Configure Tables For Offline Use does not show a (New) designation. Because the *Product* table already contains a Rowversion column, the tools are attempting to reuse this for change tracking. Although this seems like the right thing to do, it presents a problem. The existing version of the Sync Services for ADO.NET (v1.0) tries to only load new data into the replica based on a recent version of the Rowversion column using @@DBTS.

This means that existing data will never be added to the replica because it has an older *Rowversion* value. To work around this, you should always create a new column called LastEditDate using a *DateTime* value. This is merely a workaround, because the *DateTime* value for versioning may cause unintended side effects (as *DateTime* isn't precise enough for high-volume transactional systems).

Finally, the tools create a local *Typed DataSet* that queries the local cache directly, as seen in Figure 5-7.

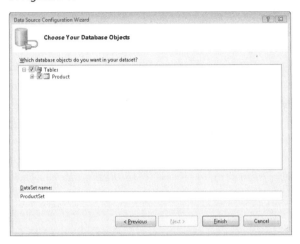

FIGURE 5-7 Adding a *Typed DataSet*

In this last dialog box, you pick the tables to include in the *Typed DataSet* (typically all the tables). This results in changes to your project, as shown in Figure 5-8.

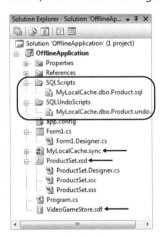

FIGURE 5-8 Project changes

The changes include two script folders for the changes to the server schema and an undo script to reverse those changes. In addition, a .sync file represents the different classes that are generated for synchronization, a .xsd file represents the *Typed DataSet* for the replica data, and a SQL Server Compact edition database (.sdf) file contains the replica data.

Synchronizing Data

Now that you have a project that has enabled synchronization, you use the generated classes to work with the Microsoft Sync Framework. Part of the code that was generated for you in the Local Database Cache item was a *Typed DataSet* that already has *TableAdapters* for loading data directly from the replica. In fact, you can load data directly just using the default behavior of the *TableAdapters* like so:

```vb
' VB
Private data As New ProductSet()
Private ta As New ProductSetTableAdapters.ProductTableAdapter()

Private Sub Form1_Load(ByVal sender As Object, ByVal e As EventArgs)
  ' Fill from the Table Adapter
  ' (directly from the replica)
  ta.Fill(data.Product)

  ' Bind to your UI
  dataGridView1.DataSource = data.Product
End Sub
```

```csharp
// C#
ProductSet data = new ProductSet();
ProductSetTableAdapters.ProductTableAdapter ta =
  new ProductSetTableAdapters.ProductTableAdapter();

private void Form1_Load(object sender, EventArgs e)
{
  // Fill from the Table Adapter
  // (directly from the replica)
  ta.Fill(data.Product);

  // Bind to your UI
  dataGridView1.DataSource = data.Product;
}
```

When you run this code, instead of pulling from the server, it pulls directly from the prepopulated replica (the replica was created during the generation process). If you change the server now and run the project, you get the stale data from your replica. One of the generated classes is one that derives from the *SyncAgent* class and provides a starting point to start a synchronization session as seen here:

```vb
' VB
Dim agent As New MyLocalCacheSyncAgent()
agent.Synchronize()
```

```csharp
// C#
MyLocalCacheSyncAgent agent = new MyLocalCacheSyncAgent();
agent.Synchronize();
```

The *MyLocalCacheSyncAgent* class is the one that derives from the *SyncAgent* class that performs the synchronization. During the synchronization, the Sync Framework calls the server to get a list of changes and merges them with local changes to the replica (the SQL Server CE database). Once the synchronization is complete, you need to reload your data from the replica by using the *TableAdapter* (or whatever you end up using for data access) to load the local data store. The synchronization does not happen between your in-memory data and the server, but with the replica and the synchronization partner (the server, in this case). Though not shown in the previous example, the *Synchronize* method actually returns a *SyncStatistics* object that contains data about the results of the synchronization. For example:

```vb
' VB
Dim stats As SyncStatistics = agent.Synchronize()
Dim msg As String = String.Concat("Changes Found: ", stats.DownloadChangesApplied)
MessageBox.Show(msg)
```

```csharp
// C#
SyncStatistics stats = agent.Synchronize();
string msg = string.Concat("Changes Found: ", stats.DownloadChangesApplied);
MessageBox.Show(msg);
```

The *SyncStatistics* class supports properties to report information about the changes, including the synchronization time and the number of download and upload changes that were applied or failed. This object can be useful in sharing that information with the user about the synchronization process effectiveness.

You may have noticed that I said that during the synchronization session, the Sync Framework calls to the server to get a list of changes and merges them with your local changes. This is correct; the synchronization is one-way by default. However, you can change this behavior if you want. The *SyncAgent* class supports a *Configuration* property that holds information about each table that will be synchronized. Each of these tables supports a *SyncDirection* enumeration that describes how the synchronization should happen. The valid values of the *SyncDirection* enumeration are shown in Table 5-2.

TABLE 5-2 *SyncDirection* Values

VALUE	MEANING
DownloadOnly	Synchronization is pulled from the source of the data. No local versions are uploaded.
UploadOnly	Synchronization is pushed to the source of the data. No server versions are downloaded.
Snapshot	A full copy of the server data is brought down. No real synchronization happens.
Bidirectional	Synchronization is pulled and pushed to the source of the data. This is a full synchronization.

To change the synchronization code to allow for a full bidirectional synchronization, you can set the *SyncDirection* of each table that requires it. For example:

```
' VB
Dim agent As New MyLocalCacheSyncAgent()
agent.Configuration.SyncTables("Product").SyncDirection = SyncDirection.Bidirectional
Dim stats As SyncStatistics = agent.Synchronize()
```

```
// C#
MyLocalCacheSyncAgent agent = new MyLocalCacheSyncAgent();
agent.Configuration.SyncTables["Product"].SyncDirection = SyncDirection.Bidirectional;
SyncStatistics stats = agent.Synchronize();
```

Using the *SyncTables* collections of the configuration is not even necessary in this case because each table specified in the local database cache has a property defined in the *SyncAgent* class. So you can just use the typed *SyncTable* called *Product* on the generated *SyncAgent* class (called *MyLocalCacheSyncAgent* in this example) like so:

```
' VB
Dim agent As New MyLocalCacheSyncAgent()
agent.Product.SyncDirection = SyncDirection.Bidirectional
Dim stats As SyncStatistics = agent.Synchronize()
```

```
// C#
MyLocalCacheSyncAgent agent = new MyLocalCacheSyncAgent();
agent.Product.SyncDirection = SyncDirection.Bidirectional;
SyncStatistics stats = agent.Synchronize();
```

 Quick Check

- What kind of synchronizations does the Microsoft Sync Framework support?

Quick Check Answers

- *UploadOnly, DownloadOnly, Snapshot,* and *Bidirectional.*

Using Sync Services for ADO.NET

To become more proficient in the use of the Microsoft Sync Framework, you should build a simple application that demonstrates the basics of offline synchronization. This lab gets you comfortable with the basics. All the lab files can be installed from the Code folder on the companion CD. To start, you need to have a copy of the LocalCacheApplication project in the Chapter 5 folder. Depending on which language you choose to use (Visual Basic or C#), it is either in the Chapter5/Lesson1/Exercise1/Cs folder or the Chapter5/Lesson1/Exercise1/Vb folder. Please open the Exercise1_Before's LocalCacheApplication.sln file to open the project in Visual Studio.

EXERCISE 1   Add Sync Services to a Project

In this exercise, you add a local database cache to your project.

1. In Solution Explorer, right-click the project and select Add, New Item....

2. In the Add New Item... dialog box, in tree view, select the Data node and find the Local Database Cache item. Name the item **MyCache.sync**, as shown in Figure 5-9.

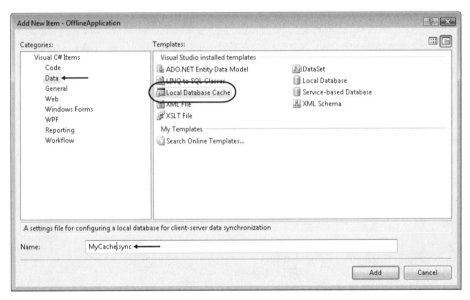

FIGURE 5-9 Adding a local database cache

3. Once you name the Local Database Cache, the Configure Data Synchronization dialog box appears. In this dialog box, pick a server connection (probably *VideoGameStore* from labs in earlier chapters). This prepopulates a client connection for you, as shown in Figure 5-10.

4. Click Add to add to the Cached Tables list. The Configure Tables For Offline Use dialog box opens.

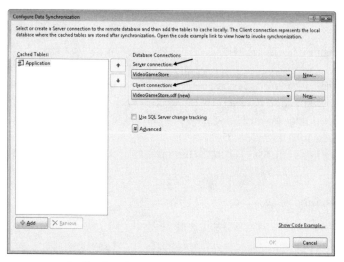

FIGURE 5-10 Configuring data synchronization

5. In this dialog box, click the *Product* table.

6. While *Product* is checked, you should see the values on the right side of the dialog box fill with default values. Note that the Compare Inserts Using: and Move Deleted Items To: drop-down lists both end in "(new)" to indicate that it will be inserting a new column and table to manage this metadata. The dialog box should now look like Figure 5-11.

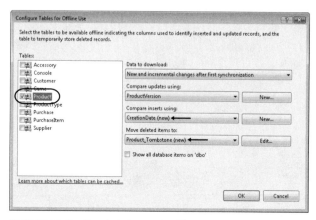

FIGURE 5-11 Configuring change tracking

7. Click New to create a new column (instead of the ProductVersion column). This opens the New Data Column On Server dialog box.

8. While in the New Data Column On Server dialog box, change the new column name to ChangeDate and the datatype to DateTime by making selections from the drop-down lists, as shown in Figure 5-12.

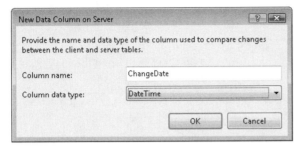

FIGURE 5-12 Adding a Server Column for synchronization

9. Click OK to return to the Configure Tables For Offline Use dialog box.

10. Click OK to return to the Configure Data Synchronization dialog box.

11. Click OK.

12. When the confirmation dialog box to create the SQL scripts appears, click OK to close it. The Data Source Configuration Wizard opens, which you use to add a *Typed DataSet* to your project that matches the replica database.

13. Click the check box next to the Tables item in the tree control to include all the tables (in this case, there's only one).

14. Change the name of the *Typed DataSet* to **ProductSet**, as shown in Figure 5-13.

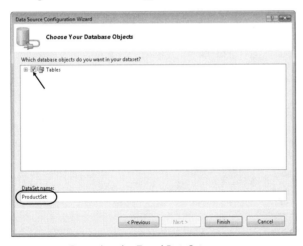

FIGURE 5-13 Preparing the *Typed DataSet*

15. Click Finish to create the *Typed DataSet*.

16. Confirm that several files have been added to the project, including App.config, MyCache.sln, ProductSet.xsd, and VideoGameStore.sdf, as well as two directories for SQL Scripts (SQLScripts and SQLUndoScripts).

EXERCISE 2   Bind Data

In this exercise, you bind your data from the replica to your user interface.

1. If it is not open, double-click the Form1.vb/Form1.cs file to open the main form for the application in design mode.

2. Open the Data Sources window (you can use SHIFT+ALT+D to show the window if it is not available).

3. Notice that the *ProductSet* dataset has already been added as a data source.

4. Click the + sign on the *ProductSet* to see the *Product* table.

5. Click on the *Product* table, as shown in Figure 5-14.

FIGURE: 5-14 The *ProductSet* in the Data Sources window

6. Use the Product drop-down list to change it from DataGridView to None.

7. Drag the *Product* table onto the *Grid* on Form1 to data-bind it to the *DataSource* automatically. Your Form1 designer should have columns defined for the *Grid* and a number of objects added at the bottom of the form, as shown in Figure 5-15.

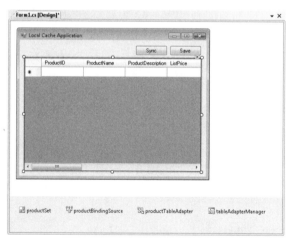

FIGURE 5-15 Your form after you drag the *DataSource*

8. Double-click the title bar of the Form1 to create a handler for the *Loaded* event of the form.

9. The code view appears, where you can see the call to the *Fill* method of the *productTableAdapter*. That's the line of code that fills in the data from the replica.

10. Run the application to see that the application is now showing data.

11. Close the application and return to Visual Studio.

12. Find the *Click* handler of the *saveButton*.

13. Add the following code to validate the data and save it to the replica database:

```vb
' VB
Validate()
ProductBindingSource.EndEdit()
TableAdapterManager.UpdateAll(ProductSet)
MessageBox.Show("Saved")
```

```csharp
// C#
Validate();
productBindingSource.EndEdit();
tableAdapterManager.UpdateAll(this.productSet);
MessageBox.Show("Saved");
```

14. Run the application and change some data.

15. Click Save.

16. Close and rerun the application to see that the changes were saved.

17. Close the application again and return to Visual Studio.

EXERCISE 3 Add Synchronization Support

So far, you have saved data to the local SQL Server Compact edition (.sdf) file, and those changes have not been propagated to the server. To do this, you must initiate a synchronization session. In this exercise, you add synchronization to your application.

1. In the code view of the Form1 file, find the *Click* handler for the *syncButton*.

2. In the handler, create a new instance of the synchronization agent class (*MyCacheSyncAgent*) called *agent*.

3. Create a variable called *stats* of type *SyncStatistics*. You may need to include (or import in Visual Basic) the *Microsoft.Synchronization.Data* namespace.

4. Assign the *stats* variable by calling the agent's *Synchronize* method.

5. Call the *MessageBox.Show* method, including a string that includes the phrase "Sync Complete" and the number of *DownloadChangesApplied*.

6. Finally, update the *Product* table of the *ProductSet* dataset by using the Form1
productTableAdapter member's *Fill* method to fill the *Product* table of the *ProductSet*.
The resulting *Click* handler of the *SyncButton* should look like this:

```vb
' VB
  Private Sub syncButton_Click(ByVal sender As System.Object, _
                            ByVal e As System.EventArgs) Handles syncButton.
Click
    Dim agent As New MyCacheSyncAgent()
    Dim stats As SyncStatistics = agent.Synchronize()
    MessageBox.Show(String.Concat("Sync Complete: #/Items Changed: ", stats.
          DownloadChangesApplied))
    Me.ProductTableAdapter.Fill(Me.ProductSet.Product)
  End Sub
```

```csharp
// C#
private void syncButton_Click(object sender, EventArgs e)
{
  MyCacheSyncAgent agent = new MyCacheSyncAgent();
  SyncStatistics stats = agent.Synchronize();
  MessageBox.Show(string.Concat("Sync Complete: #/Items Changed: ", stats.
        DownloadChangesApplied));
  this.productTableAdapter.Fill(this.productSet.Product);
}
```

7. In Visual Studio, use Server Explorer to open the *Product* table of *VideoGameStore*.

8. Edit one of the *ProductNames* in the table.

9. Run the application.

10. Notice that your change isn't shown in the data because you are still using data from
the old replica.

11. Click Sync to get the changes from the server.

> **NOTE**
>
> Step 11 is using the default behavior of only pulling down changes, so your changes will
> not be propagated to the server.

12. Notice that the change you made on the server is now shown on the client.

Lesson Summary

- The Microsoft Sync Framework allows you to perform synchronization in a variety of
scenarios.

- The Microsoft Sync Framework allows for three types of synchronization partners: Full,
Partial, or Simple.

- The Sync Services for ADO.NET, a set of tools over the Microsoft Sync Framework, allows you to create offline replicas of database data and synchronize database data.
- Adding support for offline data is handled by adding a local database cache to any .NET project.

Lesson Review

Use the following questions to test your knowledge of the information in Lesson 2, "Microsoft Sync Framework." The questions are also available on the companion CD if you prefer to review them in electronic form.

> *NOTE* **ANSWERS**
>
> Answers to these questions and explanations of why each answer choice is correct or incorrect are located in the "Answers" section at the end of the book.

1. What type of participant only supports providing data to a synchronization session?
    - **A.** Simple.
    - **B.** Full.
    - **C.** Partial.
    - **D.** None—they all support more than just providing data to a synchronization session.

2. What type of metadata must be stored about data to enable synchronization? (Each answer forms a complete solution. Choose all that apply.)
    - **A.** Source of the data
    - **B.** Tombstones
    - **C.** Versions
    - **D.** Data schema

3. What type of project item do you need to add to a .NET project to support Sync Services for ADO.NET?
    - **A.** *Typed DataSets*
    - **B.** Entity Framework Model
    - **C.** Database Files
    - **D.** Local Database Cache

Chapter Review

To practice and reinforce the skills you learned in this chapter further, you can perform the following tasks:

- Review the chapter summary.
- Review the list of key terms introduced in this chapter.
- Complete the case scenarios. These scenarios set up real-world situations involving the topics in this chapter and ask you to create a solution.
- Complete the suggested practices.
- Take a practice test.

Chapter Summary

- Synchronization of data, whether it is database data or caching of data in your applications, is a key feature of many programming projects.
- Learning the full breadth of database-caching options can help you create rich, scalable applications.
- Using the Microsoft Sync Framework (and the Sync Services for ADO.NET) is a compelling way to enable synchronized data in an application.

Key Terms

Do you know what these key terms mean? You can check your answers by looking up the terms in the glossary at the end of the book.

- Cache
- Participant
- Replica
- Synchronization

Case Scenarios

In the following case scenarios, you apply what you have learned about configuring Internet protocol addressing. You can find answers to these questions in the "Answers" section at the end of this book.

Case Scenario 1: Supporting an Offline Client

You are a lead developer for a company that has a large sales staff. You have been responsible for a desktop application where your sales staff keeps a list of their prospect pipeline. Your manager comes to you because too many of the salespeople have been complaining that they must constantly find public network access points to use the application and would like a solution that works without an Internet connection. Currently, the application uses virtual private network (VPN) access and ADO.NET to connect directly to the database servers. Answer the following questions.

1. What technology should you use to support an offline version of the prospect application?

2. How will changes be merged on the server and on the client?

Case Scenario 2: Improving Web Application Performance

You are the developer responsible for a small Web application that allows users to check for the current inventory stock counts at a small tire business. As the business has grown and the number of users of the application has increased, the load on the database has affected the performance of each page request. Answer the following questions.

1. How can you solve the performance problems?

2. The DBA is concerned that any solution you find will cause the users to get stale data. How do you counter that argument?

Suggested Practices

To help you master the exam objectives presented in this chapter, complete the following tasks.

Caching Data

- **Practice 1**   Take an existing Web application and determine how to cache every different type of data into solutions, including Cookies, ViewState, Session State, and Cache.

- **Practice 2**   Find places in a current application to implement the *SqlCacheDependency* object.

Microsoft Sync Framework

- **Practice 1**   Add a local database cache to an existing desktop application.

Take a Practice Test

The practice tests on this book's companion CD offer many options. For example, you can test yourself on just one exam objective, or you can test yourself on all of the 70-561 exam content. You can set up the test so that it closely simulates the experience of taking a certification exam, or you can set it up in study mode so that you can look at the correct answers and explanations after you answer each question.

> **MORE INFO   PRACTICE TESTS**
>
> For details about all the practice test options available, see the section entitled "How to Use the Practice Tests," in the Introduction to this book.

CHAPTER 6

Introducing LINQ

Developers use queries all the time. You might not think of searching through in-memory objects as "querying," but it is. In Microsoft .NET Framework 3.5 (more specifically, in Microsoft C# 3.0 and Microsoft Visual Basic 9), Microsoft supplies developers with Language Integrated Query (LINQ), a new tool for defining queries across many different disciplines. This chapter introduces you to LINQ and explains how it can be used against simple CLR objects. After you understand this basic use, the rest of the book builds upon the basics to explain how LINQ is integrated into a number of different data technologies.

Exam objective in this chapter:

- Query data sources by using LINQ.
- Transform data by using LINQ.

Lessons in this chapter:

Before You Begin

To complete the lessons in this chapter, you must have:

- A computer that meets or exceeds the minimum hardware requirements listed in the "Introduction" section at the beginning of the book
- Microsoft Visual Studio 2008 Professional Edition installed on your computer
- An understanding of Visual Basic 9 or C# 3.0 syntax, including a basic understanding of extension methods and lambda functions.

In addition, a familiarity with the .NET Framework version 3.5 is helpful.

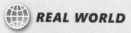 **REAL WORLD**

Shawn Wildermuth

Ok, I'll admit it. I was not much of a fan of LINQ when it first appeared. All the early demos seemed to indicate that LINQ was a new Object-Relational Mapper (ORM) from Microsoft. That space is already pretty crowded, so I held my breath until it got a little more mature before I investigated further. Much to my surprise, LINQ had very little to do with database mapping. In fact, LINQ was about defining and executing query semantics in code. That was certainly worth my time. For me, LINQ represents a way to think about filtering, ordering, and shaping data. I now use this throughout my codebase, from replacements of simple foreach (or ForEach in Visual Basic) constructs to complex shaping of results in Web services and data tiers.

Lesson 1: Constructing Queries with LINQ

Creating queries in LINQ is a fairly straightforward process of defining the expressions that define the nature of your operation. These expressions may be performing filtering, ordering, shaping, grouping, calculations, or other actions. Combining these expressions to create a query requires that you understand the basic underpinnings of LINQ and how it actually works. It is of no use simply to know how to make it do what you want. Understanding why it works that way is crucial to real understanding.

After this lesson, you will be able to:

- Create a query using the *IEnumerable* extension method syntax
- Create a query using the language-level LINQ syntax

Estimated lesson time: 30 minutes

Why LINQ?

In software development, the data is the main consideration. For the beginning programmer, it may seem that the world is about data entry, but at some point, it's important to be able to evaluate data. That's what queries are all about.

For databases, the most prevalent solution has been Structured Query Language (SQL), regardless of vendor. The idea behind SQL was to provide a common way to describe the type of operation that the user wanted to perform. For example:

```
SELECT CustomerID, CompanyName
  FROM Customers
WHERE Country = 'Canada'
ORDER BY CompanyName
```

SQL provides a simple, text-based syntax to describe the parts of a query operation (for example, *SELECT, FROM, WHERE, ORDER BY,* and other statements). Whether you are using SQL Server, Oracle, DB2, or even many desktop databases, the SQL syntax is strikingly similar. The basic framework of SQL was to provide a way to communicate the same ideas across different data technologies so that every vendor did not invent its own strategy for the basics of query. This is important for databases, but what about the rest of the development ecosystem?

Quering database data is an obvious need, but you have to deal with other data, too. You need a solution that works with data as disparate as object graphs, Extensible Markup Language (XML) data, Web service results, and JavaScript Object Notation (JSON). You need to have a way to think about querying in a generalized way across the different sorts of data you see as a developer. That's the purpose of LINQ. The query semantics are integrated into the languages, and it is extensible to other types of data. .NET Framework 3.5 supports LINQ against different sources including database targets, XML, and in-memory objects in the form of LINQ providers. These providers are LINQ to SQL, LINQ to XML, and LINQ to

Objects. In addition, Microsoft supports LINQ for Entities to allow queries against the Entity Framework (available as part of .NET Framework 3.5 SP1).

LINQ is designed so that anyone can support LINQ against data as they see fit. Many projects have included support for LINQ in nontraditional scenarios such as LINQ to Amazon and LINQ to Flickr, as well as more traditional scenarios such as third-party data frameworks (NHibernate.LINQ and LLBLGen Pro's LINQ support). There is power in defining LINQ as the basic language of query semantics.

LINQ provides a basic grammar to outline the way a query is composed. Unlike in SQL, this syntax is not text-based, which means LINQ is type-safe and compiler-validated. For example, if you use the previous query in a simple .NET Framework application, your ADO.NET code might look like this:

```vb
' VB
Using conn As New SqlConnection()
  Using cmd As SqlCommand = conn.CreateCommand

    cmd.CommandText = "SELECT CustomerID, CompanyName " + _
                      "  FROM Customers " + _
                      " WHERE Country = 'Canada'" + _
                      " ORDER BY CompanyName"


    ' ...


  End Using
End Using
```

```csharp
// C#
using (SqlConnection conn = new SqlConnection(connString))
using (SqlCommand cmd = conn.CreateCommand())
{
  // SQL is Text, no way for the compiler to validate the query
  cmd.CommandText = @"SELECT CustomerID, CompanyName
                    FROM Customers
                    WHERE Country = 'Canada'
                    ORDER BY CompanyName";

  // ...

}
```

LINQ allows you to do this same work but use language-level semantics for defining your query and have it validated during compilation. Here is LINQ to SQL code that does the same thing:

```vb
' VB
Using ctx = New NorthwindDataContext
```

```
Dim query = From c In ctx.Customers _
            Where c.Country = "Canada" _
            Order By c.CompanyName _
            Select New With {c.CompanyName, c.ContactName}

End Using
```

```
// C#
using (NorthwindDataContext ctx = new NorthwindDataContext())
{
  var query = from c in ctx.Customers
              where c.Country == "Canada"
              orderby c.ContactName
              select new { c.CustomerID, c.CompanyName };

  // ...
}
```

The parts of the query syntax (for example, *from*, *where*, *orderby*) are integrated into the language itself. This allows you to create queries more organically than with textual SQL. This is the power of LINQ.

A quick view of this example might give the impression that LINQ is just pushing database querying into the language. That would be incorrect. In fact, the purpose of LINQ is to provide a mechanism to construct queries that can be used across different problem domains.

LINQ Basics

Take a simple task as an example. Assume that you have a list of strings that represent the names to be displayed on a page. For our example, assume that you need to take this list of names and find all the names that start with a particular letter. Before LINQ, you might take this list and use *foreach* (or *ForEach* in Visual Basic) syntax to create a new list of strings to use for the page, as shown here:

```
' VB
Dim names() As String = { "Adam", "Edward", "Phillip", _
                          "Andrew", "Bob", "Pete", "Amy" }

Dim pageNames As New ArrayList()

For Each name As String In names
  If name.StartsWith("A") Then
        pageNames.Add(name)
  End If
Next name

' ...
```

```csharp
// C#
string[] names = new string[] { "Adam", "Edward", "Phillip",
                                "Andrew", "Bob", "Pete", "Amy" };

ArrayList pageNames = new ArrayList();

foreach (string name in names)
{
  if (name.StartsWith("A")) pageNames.Add(name);
}

// ...
```

This code works because you can use the *foreach* keyword to enumerate easily through the list of of names defined in the code. Interestingly, the *foreach* keyword requires that the items to be enumerated support a basic interface, *IEnumerable*. The *IEnumerable* interface specifies a way to get an enumerator object that can enumerate the list (in a forward-only fashion). That interface contract defines the requirements for what *foreach* does.

The same holds true for LINQ. LINQ requires a basic interface to specify the basic operations for queries (including *select, where,* and *orderby*). This interface is the *IEnumerable<T>* interface (*IEnumerable(Of T)* in Visual Basic). The *IEnumerable<T>* interface itself is a simple extension of the *IEnumerable* interface to support enumerators that are type-safe. *IEnumerable<T>* is the interface that LINQ extends by adding extension methods for the query operations. These extension methods are part of the *Enumerable* class in the *System.Linq* namespace. The *Enumerable* class exposes these extension methods once you add the *System.Linq* namespace to your file/project. Because it uses extension methods to add this functionality, most .NET Framework collections now support this new interface. Here is that earlier example, with the extension methods to perform the same work:

```vb
' VB
' using System.Linq
Dim names() As String = { "Adam", "Edward", "Phillip", _
                          "Andrew", "Bob", "Pete", "Amy" }

Dim pageNames() As String = _
    names.Where( _
              Function(name) name.StartsWith("A") _
          ).ToArray()

' ...
```

```csharp
// C#
// using System.Linq
string[] names = new string[] { "Adam", "Edward", "Phillip",
                                "Andrew", "Bob", "Pete", "Amy" };
```

```
string[] pageNames = names.Where(name => name.StartsWith("A")).ToArray();
```

```
// ...
```

Because the string array supports the *IEnumerable<T>* interface, it has the *Where* extension method added to support filtering the results. In this example, you are specifying a lambda to denote the actual query syntax (to find strings that start with the letter *A*). Finally you are calling *ToArray* to execute the query and return an array of strings. This works because the *Where* extension method returns an *IEnumerable<T>* reference. It's only when you actually execute the query that the query instructions (in this case, the *Where* extension method) are applied against the collection. This is a key idea that is important to understand. The fact that you are calling *ToArray* at the end of the query should be an afterthought. For example, you can create the query and keep a reference to it for use later in your application:

```vb
' VB
Dim names As List(Of String) = New List(Of String) ( _
          New String() {"Adam", "Edward", "Phillip", _
                        "Andrew", "Bob", "Pete", "Amy"})

Dim query = names.Where(Function(name) name.StartsWith("A"))
```

```csharp
// C#
List<string> names = new List<string>
                     {
                         "Adam", "Edward", "Phillip",
                         "Andrew", "Bob", "Pete", "Amy"
                     };

var query = names.Where(name => name.StartsWith("A"));
```

Now with the query, you can execute the query (by calling *ToArray*) to get the names that match the query:

```vb
' VB
' Returns Adam, Andrew and Amy
Dim aNames() As String = query.ToArray()
```

```csharp
// C#
// Returns Adam, Andrew and Amy
string[] aNames = query.ToArray();
```

What if you add a new name to the names collection and execute *ToArray* again? Will you get the same result, or will it actually re-execute the query? Here's the result:

```vb
' VB
' Add a new Name
names.Add("Alex")
```

```
' Returns Adam, Andrew, Amy and Alex
aNames = query.ToArray()
```

```
// C#
// Add a new Name
names.Add("Alex");
```

```
// Returns Adam, Andrew, Amy and Alex
aNames = query.ToArray();
```

When you call *ToArray* the second time, the query is executed again. This is called *deferred execution*. The *Where* method you used earlier defined a query with a filter. When you are ready, you can call one of the execution methods (for example, any method that returns results instead of an instance of *IEnumerable<T>*).

So far you have used only a single extension method to specify your query. You can chain them together to create more complex queries. Any query that returns an *IEnumerable<T>* instance supports this. For example:

```
' VB
Dim query = names.Where(Function(name) name.StartsWith("A")) _
                 .OrderBy(Function(name) name)

Dim pageNames() As String = query.ToArray()
```

```
// C#
var query = names.Where(name => name.StartsWith("A"))
                 .OrderBy(name => name);

string[] pageNames = query.ToArray();
```

In this example, you're still using the *Where* extension method to specify a lambda that is used to define the filter, but in addition, you're adding an *OrderBy* extension method to sort the results that you get back from the *Where* extension method.

Using the extension methods works, but the code is more verbose than you'd likely want. The multiple lambdas do not necessarily make the code clearer, especially as the query operations become more complex. That's where LINQ can be a key asset.

It's hard to define LINQ. Much of what you have seen so far is really LINQ. The support for *IEnumerable<T>* allows for a very expressive way to define queries. To complete the circle, LINQ defines new language-level support for this mechanism. For example, you can replicate the previous query by using the language-level integration like so:

```
' VB
Dim query = From name In names _
            Where name.StartsWith("A") _
            Order By name _
            Select name
```

```
Dim aNames() As String = query.ToArray()

// C#
var query = from name in names
            where name.StartsWith("A")
            orderby name
            select name;

string[] aNames = query.ToArray();
```

The syntax of the language integration is meant to look like SQL but it's not directly analogous to SQL. It may be just syntactic sugar[1], but it is a sweet treat to use. If you look back to the earlier example using the *foreach* syntax, you can draw the same parallel. Before *foreach* (before .NET Framework for most developers), you used the *for* keyword to perform looping (whether it was Visual Basic, C++, Java, JavaScript, or other languages):

```
// JavaScript
var someCollection = new Array();
// Fill the collection

// Using the for keyword to loop
for (var x = 0; x < 100; x++) {
  var item = someCollection(x);
}
```

The addition of the *foreach* keyword was a shortcut for collections that were enumerable. The *for* keyword version of this code is not much longer than the *foreach* version, but it is a lot cleaner. Defining temporary variables (in this case, the *x* variable) simply to allow you to loop was unnecessary and cluttered up the code.

 **Quick Check**

- What is the interface that is required for a collection to support LINQ?

Quick Check Answer

- The *IEnumerable<T>* (or *IEnumerable(Of T)* in Visual Basic) is required to support LINQ. Most common collections (generic and nongeneric) now support this interface when used on .NET Framework 3.5).

As you saw in earlier examples, LINQ doesn't require any language changes to work. You can use extension methods to do most of the work. But LINQ's language-level integration makes the code that much cleaner.

---

[1] *http://en.wikipedia.org/wiki/Syntactic_sugar*

Your First LINQ Query

Now that you have enough background, you can start using LINQ in some code. For the rest of the chapter, you will work with a simple set of data. This data is a set of XBox 360 console games that include information such as name, description, price, and rating. For these examples, when you create a new instance of the *GameList,* it will already be full of *Game* data for you. The class diagram for this data is shown in Figure 6-1.

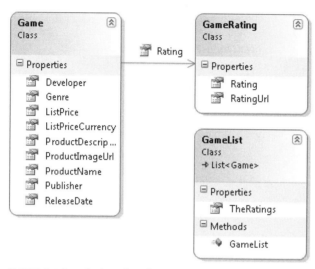

FIGURE 6-1 Sample data class diagram

The example project can be installed from the Code folder on the companion CD. If you want to follow along, in the \Chapter6 folder, open the folder based on your language (for example, cs == C#, vb == Visual Basic) and open the Example1_Before folder. The project is called Example1. This project is a simple console application with the *Game* data already added to the project.

To start your LINQ statement, create an instance of the *GameList* class inside the static *Main* method. You might need to add a *using* (or *imports*) statement to bring in the *VideoGames* namespace:

```vb
' VB
Imports VideoGames

Namespace Example1
  Friend Class Program
    Shared Sub Main(ByVal args() As String)

      Dim games As New GameList()

    End Sub
  End Class
End Namespace
```

```
// C#
using VideoGames;

namespace Example1
{
  class Program
  {
    static void Main(string[] args)
    {
      GameList games = new GameList();
    }
  }
}
```

This *GameList* class inherits from *List<Game>*, so it's a generic collection of *Game* objects. Because the *List<T>* (*List(Of T)* in Visual Basic) generic collection supports *IEnumerable<T>*, you can use LINQ to get data about the games. Next, create a new variable called *query* and assign it by using the LINQ syntax to simply retrieve all the results of the collection. You can start the query by specifying *from g in games,* which indicates the sequence and a range variable for the query. In this example, *games* is the sequence for the query (the object that supports enumeration) and *g* is the range variable. A range variable is a temporary variable that is used to indicate the enumerated instances. In other words, the *g* represents each game as the query executes.

Next, you can simply specify select *g* to indicate that you want to return the results of the query as *Game* instances. Your query should look like so:

```
' VB
Dim query = From g In games _
            Select g
```

```
// C#
var query = from g in games
            select g;
```

Next, execute the query to see the results. To do this, use the *foreach* syntax to walk through the results and display them in the Console. To do this, create the *foreach* statement specifying a new temporary variable for each *Game* in the result called *game* and call the query's *ToList* method to return a list of the results. Remember that the query is not actually executed until you call this method. Inside the *foreach*, write each game's *ProductName* to the console and then call *Console.ReadLine()* afterwards to make sure you can see the result in the console. Your code should look something like this:

```
' VB
Dim results As List(Of Game) = query.ToList()

For Each game As Game In results
  Console.WriteLine(game.ProductName)
Next game
```

```
Console.WriteLine(String.Concat("Count: ", results.Count))
Console.ReadLine()
```

```
// C#
List<Game> results = query.ToList();

foreach (Game game in results)
{
    Console.WriteLine(game.ProductName);
}

Console.WriteLine(string.Concat("Count: ", results.Count));
Console.ReadLine();
```

If you run the application, you should see a long list of games listed in the console window (as shown in Figure 6-2).

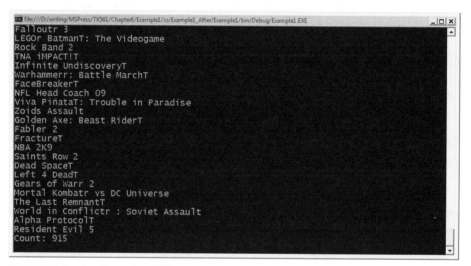

FIGURE 6-2 Results of your first LINQ query

In this first query, you returned all the results. You can make this query more interesting if you like. First, create a simple filter. If you go back to the LINQ query and add a line before the *select* line, you can return only the games that are in the "Action" genre. You can do that by adding a WHERE clause testing each game's *Genre* property, as shown here:

```
' VB
Dim query = From g In games _
            Where g.Genre = "Action" _
            Select g
```

```
// C#
var query = from g in games
```

```
        where g.Genre == "Action"
        select g;
```

If you rerun the application, your results now return only *Game* objects that have *Action* as their *Genre*. (Note that the number of results has changed.) Next, you can sort the result by adding a new line specifying the *orderby* statement. For example, you can order them by the release date, as shown here:

' VB
```
Dim query = From g In games _
            Where g.Genre = "Action" _
            Order By g.ReleaseDate _
            Select g
```

// C#
```
var query = from g in games
            where g.Genre == "Action"
            orderby g.ReleaseDate
            select g;
```

Rerun the application to see the results sorted by the release date. Finally, make one more change. To be able to filter out titles that might not be appropriate for children, add a new part of the WHERE clause to select only ratings that are not mature. It might not seem simple because the *Rating* property of the *Game* class is not a primitive type but instead is an instance of the *GameRating* class. LINQ doesn't care that it isn't primitive, you can walk down the object graph and simply test for the *Rating* properties of the *Game* class and the *GameRating* class. In addition, you can simply add this new part of the filter to the WHERE clause using standard-language logical operators. The completed query can be seen here:

' VB
```
Dim query = From g In games _
            Where g.Genre = "Action" AndAlso _
                g.GameRating.Name <> "MA (Mature)" _
            Order By g.ReleaseDate _
            Select g
```

// C#
```
var query = from g in games
            where g.Genre == "Action" &&
                g.GameRating.Name != "MA (Mature)"
            orderby g.ReleaseDate
            select g;
```

If you run the application again, you see that games with any mature content have been removed. Next, let's look at the breadth of LINQ expressions.

Expressions

In the section entitled "Your First LINQ Query," earlier in this lesson, you saw that a query is just a list of instructions and that the query can be reused and returns different results if the underlying data has changed. This works because each LINQ query contains an internal list of operations (called *expressions*) that it uses to execute a query. This set of operations in fact is called the Expression Tree. It represents a graph of expressions that are used in your LINQ queries.

Each expression in the tree is essentially an expression type (that matches an extension method) and a lambda that represents the nature of the expression. Most of the expressions pertinent to LINQ are specified as extension methods (specified in the *System.Linq.Enumerable* class) to the *IEnumerable<T>* interface. All these extension methods are listed in Table 6-1.

TABLE 6-1 LINQ *IEnumerable<T>* Extension Methods

EXTENSION METHOD	PURPOSE
Aggregate	Creates accumulations over a sequence of values
All<T>	Tests all elements in the sequence against a criteria and returns True if all members satisfy the criteria
Any	Tests all elements in the sequence against a criteria and returns True if any of the members satisfy the criteria
AsEnumerable<T>	Returns an *IEnumerable<T>* for the sequence
Average	Performs an aggregation to determine the average value in a sequence
Cast<T>	Allows up casting and down casting to different *IEnumerable<T>* instances
Concat<T>	Combines two sequences sequentially
Contains	Determines if a particular item is contained in the sequence
Count	Returns the number of elements in a sequence
DefaultIfEmpty	Returns the sequence or a default value if the sequence is empty
Distinct	Returns unique instances from the collection
ElementAt<T>	Returns a specific member of the sequence
ElementAtOrDefault(of	Returns a specific member of the sequence or a default value if the member is null or invalid
Empty<T>	Returns an empty sequence of the correct specified type
Except	Returns a sequence which contains the members of two sequences that differ
First	Returns the first member of a sequence

TABLE 6-1 LINQ *IEnumerable<T>* Extension Methods

EXTENSION METHOD	PURPOSE
FirstOrDefault	Returns the first member of a sequence or a default value if the first member is null or invalid
GroupBy	Provides grouping support for the sequence
GroupJoin	Performs a join and then groups the resulting sequence
Intersect	Returns a sequence which contains the members of two sequences which are the same
Join	Correlates two sequences by key values of individual members of the sequences
Last	Returns the last member of a sequence
LastOrDefault	Returns the last member of a sequence or a default value if the last member is not valid
LongCount	Returns the number of items in a sequence, supporting a 64-bit number for the number in the sequence
Max	Performs an aggregation to determine the largest value in a sequence
Min	Performs an aggregation to determine the smallest value in a sequence
OfType<T>	Returns a sequence that contains the members of a sequence whose type matches the specified type
OrderBy	Performs an ascending sort on a sequence of values
OrderByDescending	Performs a descending sort on a sequence of values
Reverse<T>	Returns a sequence whose order is opposite its current order
Select	Performs a projection of the sequence
SelectMany	Performs a cross-join across two sequences returning a flat sequence including both sequences
SequenceEqual	Compares two sequences to determine equality
Single	Returns a specific member of a sequence
SingleOrDefault	Returns a specific member of a sequence or a default value if the member is not valid
Skip<T>	Returns a sequence skipping a specified number of members at the beginning the sequence
SkipWhile	Returns a sequence skipping all members based on specific criteria in a sequential group of members

TABLE 6-1 LINQ *IEnumerable<T>* Extension Methods

EXTENSION METHOD	PURPOSE
Sum	Performs an aggregation to determine the sum of values in a sequence
Take<T>	Returns a sequence with a specified number of members
TakeWhile	Returns a sequence that satisfy a specific criteria in a sequential group of members
ThenBy	Performs a ascending sort on a sequence by a secondary sort (where the primary sort is dictated by an ORDERBY clause)
ThenByDescending	Performs a descending sort on a sequence by a secondary sort (where the primary sort is dictated by an ORDERBY clause)
ToArray<T>	Executes the query and returns a typed *Array* as the result
ToDictionary<T>	Executes the query and returns a typed *Dictionary<TKey,TElement>* as the result
ToList(Of)	Executes the query and returns a typed *List<T>* as the result
ToLookup	Executes the query and returns a typed *Lookup<TKey, TElement>* as the result
Union	Performs a merge of two sequences, allowing duplicate values
Where	Filters the sequence by specific criteria

For C# and Visual Basic, language-level keywords are used to create LINQ queries. The breadth of the language integration depends on the language. Table 6-2 compares the C# and Visual Basic language keyword support.

TABLE 6-2 Language Keywords

	C# EQUIVALENT	VISUAL BASIC EQUIVALENT
Data Source	*From*	*From*
Filtering	*Where*	*Where*
Sort, Ascending	*Orderby*	*Order By*
Sort, Descending	*orderby ... descending*	*Order By ... Descending*
Joining	*Join*	*Join*
Grouping	*group ... by*	*Group ... By*
	-or-	*-or-*
	group ... by ... into	*Group ... By ... Into*
Cross Joins	*join ... in ... on ... equals ... into*	*Group Join ... In ... On ...*

TABLE 6-2 Language Keywords

	C# EQUIVALENT	VISUAL BASIC EQUIVALENT
Skip	N/A	*Skip*
SkipWhile	N/A	*Skip While*
Take	N/A	*Take*
TakeWhile	N/A	*Take While*
All (Aggregation)	N/A	*Aggregate … In … Into All(…)*
Any (Aggregation)	N/A	*Aggregate … In … Into Any()*
Average (Aggregation)	N/A	*Aggregate … In … Into Average()*
Count (Aggregation)	N/A	*Aggregate … In … Into Count()*
LongCount (Aggregation)	N/A	*Aggregate … In … Into LongCount()*
Min (Aggregation)	N/A	*Aggregate … In … Into Min()*
Max (Aggregation)	N/A	*Aggregate … In … Into Max()*
Sum (Aggregation)	N/A	*Aggregate … In … Into Sum()*

Table 6-2 implies that the LINQ support in C# is weaker than in Visual Basic, but in fact the languages are equal in their LINQ support. The reason that Visual Basic has more keywords is that the lambda syntax in Visual Basic is more verbose than in C#, so mixing lambdas with the language-level integration in C# is more natural. The Visual Basic support helps limit the need for the lambda support. For example, here is a more complex query in both languages:

```vb
' VB
Dim games As New GameList()

' Skip the first 25 and return the next 25
Dim query = From game In games _
            Where game.Genre = "Action" And _
                game.GameRating.Name <> "MA (Mature)" _
            Select game _
            Skip 25 _
            Take 25

Dim sportsGames As List(Of Game) = query.ToList()
```

```csharp
// C#
GameList games = new GameList();

var query = from game in games
            where game.Genre == "Action" &&
```

```
                game.GameRating.Name != "MA (Mature)"
            select game;

// Skip the first 25 and return the next 25
List<Game> sportsGames = query.Skip(25).Take(25).ToList();
```

Although the Visual Basic version is able to put the language integration directly into the query, the C# version has to place those elements as extension methods on the query. There are benefits to both approaches. The important piece of information to take from this example is that everything is possible with both languages, it's just a matter of how it is performed.

 **Quick Check**

- What are the two required parts of a language-integrated LINQ query?

Quick Check Answer

- Every query using language integration must have *from* and *select* sections.

Query Execution

Now that you've constructed a query, you probably noticed that the earlier example used the *ToList* method to return a list of results. In addition, the earlier example used the *ToArray* method to return a simple array of results. Each of these methods causes the query to actually enumerate the sequence and execute the expression tree to determine the results. As was hinted in Table 6-1, you can use a number of different methods to enumerate the values.

First, use the simple execution methods, *ToList* and *ToArray*. Both of these methods return a flat collection of the results. Note that the returned values of these methods are typed to the type of objects in the query:

```
' VB
Dim results As List(Of Game) = query.ToList()
Dim arrayResults() As Game = query.ToArray()
```

```
// C#
List<Game> results = query.ToList();
Game[] arrayResults = query.ToArray();
```

In the case where you need results that you can look up by key, you can use the *ToDictionary* (for one-to-one mapping of keys to objects) or *ToLookup* (for one-to-many mapping of keys to collection of objects). First, the *ToDictionary* method requires that you supply a lambda function that returns the key from your object (for example, the *ProductName* in this collection):

```
' VB
Dim dictGames As Dictionary(Of String, Game) = _
    query.ToDictionary(Function(game) game.ProductName )

Dim gyruss As Game = dictGames("Gyruss")
```

```
// C#
Dictionary<string, Game> dictGames =
        query.ToDictionary(game => { return game.ProductName; });

Game gyruss = dictGames["Gyruss"];
```

Second is using the *ToLookup* method, which instead of creating one-to-one mapping creates a mapping of values that can return a collection of elements. Like *ToDictionary*, *ToLookup* requires a lambda function to specify what the key is. In this example, you are returning the *Genre* so you get a lookup for all the games in each *Genre*. The resulting lookup supports access via an indexer but instead of returning a *Game* object, it returns an *IEnumerable<Game>* collection that contains all the games in a particular genre:

```
' VB
Dim lookupGames As ILookup(Of String, Game) = _
  query.ToLookup(Function(game) game.Genre )

Dim actionGames As IEnumerable(Of Game) = lookupGames("Action")
```

```
// C#
ILookup<string, Game> lookupGames =
  query.ToLookup(game => { return game.Genre; });

IEnumerable<Game> actionGames = lookupGames["Action"];
```

You can also retrieve only a single element of the result using the single-item methods, such as *First, Last,* and *ElementAt:*

```
' VB
Dim firstGame As Game = query.First()
Dim lastGame As Game = query.Last()
Dim fifthGame As Game = query.ElementAt(4)
```

```
// C#
Game firstGame = query.First();
Game lastGame = query.Last();
Game fifthGame = query.ElementAt(4);
```

Each of these methods also supports a version that returns the element or a default value (null for objects and default values for primitive values). For example:

```
' VB
Dim firstGame As Game = query.FirstOrDefault()
Dim lastGame As Game = query.LastOrDefault()
Dim fifthGame As Game = query.ElementAtOrDefault(4)
```

```
// C#
Game firstGame = query.FirstOrDefault();
Game lastGame = query.LastOrDefault();
Game fifthGame = query.ElementAtOrDefault(4);
```

There are times where you want to calculate a result instead of returning a sequence of items. These extension methods support simple execution or an optional lambda to determine how to perform the aggregation. For example, the *Count* method can be used like so:

```vb
' VB
Dim count As Integer = query.Count()
Dim teenCount As Integer = _
  query.Count(Function(game) game.GameRating = ESRBRating.T)
```

```csharp
// C#
int count = query.Count();
int teenCount = query.Count(game => game.GameRating == ESRBRating.T);
```

This works for the range of aggregators (*Min, Max,* and *Average*):

```vb
' VB
Dim minPrice As Decimal = query.Min(Function(game) game.ListPrice)
Dim latestRelease As DateTime = query.Max(Function(game) game.ReleaseDate)
Dim avgPrice As Decimal = query.Average(Function(game) game.ListPrice)
```

```csharp
// C#
decimal minPrice = query.Min(game => game.ListPrice);
DateTime latestRelease = query.Max(game => game.ReleaseDate);
decimal avgPrice = query.Average(game => game.ListPrice);
```

LAB   Simple LINQ Queries

In this lab, you construct a simple query and execute the query to get the results. All the lab files can be installed from the Code folder on the companion CD. To start, you need to have a copy of the Lab1 project in the Chapter6 folder. Depending on which language you choose to use, it will be either in the Chapter6/Cs folder or the Chapter6/Vb folder. Please open the Lab1_Before's Lab1.sln file to open the project in Visual Studio.

EXERCISE 1   Constructing a Simple Query

In this exercise, you construct a basic LINQ query to prepare to query against a type-safe collection of data.

1. Open the main code file for the project (for C#, it is Program.cs; for Visual Basic, it is Module1.vb).

2. Inside the *Main* method, create an instance of the *GameList* class called games. Also, add a reference to the *GameList* namespace to the top of the file, as shown here:

```vb
' VB
Imports Lab1.VideoGames

Module Module1
```

```
    Sub Main()

        Dim games As New GameList

    End Sub

End Module

// C#
...
using VideoGames;

namespace Lab1
{
  class Program
  {
    static void Main(string[] args)
    {
      GameList games = new GameList();
    }
  }
}
```

3. Inside the *Main* method, create an instance of the *GameList* class called games. Also, add a reference to the *GameList* namespace to the top of the file, as shown here:

```
' VB
Dim query = From g In games _
            Select g
// C#
var query = from g in games
            select g;
```

4. Add a filter by using LINQ's *Where* statement. Filter the games by only retrieving games whose *ProductName* starts with the letter *A*:

```
' VB
Dim query = From g In games _
            Where g.ProductName.StartsWith("A") _
            Select g
// C#
var query = from g in games
            where g.ProductName.StartsWith("A")
            select g;
```

5. Order the query by using LINQ's *OrderBy* statement, arranging the results by their *ProductName*, in descending order:

```
' VB
Dim query = From g In games _
```

```
                    Order By g.ProductName Descending _
                    Where g.ProductName.StartsWith("A") _
                    Select g
// C#
var query = from g in games
            orderby g.ProductName descending
            where g.ProductName.StartsWith("A")
            select g;
```

6. Compile the application to make sure that everything was typed correctly.

EXERCISE 2 Retrieving Results

Now that you have a query, retrieve a result.

1. Just after the creation of the query from Exercise 1, create a new typed list containing *Game* objects called results and assign it a value by calling the query's *ToList* method:

```
' VB
Dim result As List(Of Game) = query.ToList()

// C#
List<Game> results = query.ToList();
```

2. Create a *foreach* (or *For Each*) statement and iterate through each game in the results like so:

```
' VB
For Each aGame As Game In result
Next

// C#
foreach (Game aGame in results)
{
}
```

3. Inside the *foreach* statement, write out to the Console the *ProductName* of each game:

```
' VB
For Each aGame As Game In result

    Console.WriteLine(aGame.ProductName)

Next

// C#
foreach (Game aGame in results)
{
    Console.WriteLine(aGame.ProductName);
}
```

4. To enable you to see the results when you run the application, add a call to Console. ReadLine to the end of the code inside the *Main* method. Your completed *Main* method should look like so:

```vb
' VB
Sub Main()

  Dim games As New GameList

  Dim query = From g In games _
              Order By g.ProductName Descending _
              Where g.ProductName.StartsWith("A") _
              Select g

  Dim result As List(Of Game) = query.ToList()

  For Each aGame As Game In result

    Console.WriteLine(aGame.ProductName)

  Next

  Console.ReadLine()

End Sub
```

```csharp
// C#
static void Main(string[] args)
{
  GameList games = new GameList();

  var query = from g in games
              orderby g.ProductName descending
              where g.ProductName.StartsWith("A")
              select g;

  List<Game> results = query.ToList();

  foreach (Game aGame in results)
  {
    Console.WriteLine(aGame.ProductName);
  }

  Console.ReadLine();
}
```

5. Run the application to see the games listed.

EXERCISE 3   Limiting Results

Now that you have retrieved basic results from your query, refactor it to return only some of the results. This is ordinarily used to page pieces of the result to the client.

1. Take the existing application and comment out the construction of the *results* variable.

2. Add a new typed list of games and when assigning it, instead of calling the query's *ToList* method, first call the *Take* method, specifying 10 for the number of results to return.

3. Immediately after the *Take* method, call the *ToList* method to return the list as shown here:

```
' VB
'Dim result As List(Of Game) = query.ToList()
Dim result As List(Of Game) = query.Take(10).ToList()
```

```
// C#
//List<Game> results = query.ToList();
List<Game> results = query.Take(10).ToList();
```

4. Run the application again to show that only the first 10 results are returned.

Lesson Summary

- LINQ is powered by the *IEnumerable<>* interface, which supports the bulk of the functionality inside LINQ.

- LINQ queries allow you to specify a set of expressions that are calculated over a list of data, not just the execution of that search.

- LINQ queries can be reused.

- The language integration of LINQ allows you to specify queries directly in language code.

- The *IEnumerable<>* extension methods allow you to perform all the same code that a LINQ query can, but in a more readable fashion.

Lesson Review

You can use the following questions to test your knowledge of the information in Lesson 1, "Constructing Queries with LINQ." The questions also are available on the companion CD of this book if you prefer to review them in electronic form.

> **NOTE   ANSWERS**
>
> Answers to these questions and explanations of why each answer choice is correct or incorrect are located in the "Answers" section at the end of the book.

1. Which LINQ statement defines the data source and range variable in a LINQ query?

   A. *from* in C#; *From* in Visual Basic

   B. *select* in C#; *Select* in Visual Basic

   C. *join* in C#; *Join* in Visual Basic

   D. *where* in C#; *Where* in Visual Basic

2. Which query expression is used to limit the number of results?

   A. *Skip*

   B. *Take*

   C. *Where*

   D. *Select*

3. Which interface defines the basic extension methods for LINQ?

   A. *IEnumerable<T> (IEnumerable(Of T) in Visual Basic)*

   B. *IList*

   C. *IEnumerable*

   D. *IQueryable<T> (IQueryable(Of T) in Visual Basic)*

Lesson 2: Shaping Results with LINQ

So far, this chapter has covered how to create and execute queries. Now you shape the results you get back from those queries. This includes changing the nature of the results you retrieve, such as simple results, projection, and anonymous types.

After this lesson, you will be able to:
- Return a set of primitive results from a query
- Project results into new types
- Create on-the-fly types from the results of a query

Estimated lesson time: 30 minutes

Retrieving Primitive Results

Up to now, you've looked at querying types and returning the types that matched the query. For example:

```vb
' VB
Dim query = From g In games _
            Where g.Genre = "Action" _
            Select g

Dim results as List(Of Game) = query.ToList()
```

```csharp
// C#
var query = from g in games
            where g.Genre == "Action"
            select g;

List<Game> results = query.ToList();
```

By using the *select* (or *Select* in Visual Basic) statement, you are specifying what to return in the query. In this example, you are simply returning instances of the *Game* class that match the query (for example, whose *Genre* is *Action*). But what if you really wanted to just get a list of the product names? You can do that by instructing the *select* statement to return the value of the property when the query is executed:

```vb
' VB
Dim query = From g In games _
            Where g.Genre = "Action" _
            Select g.ProductName

Dim results As List(Of String) = query.ToList()
```

```
// C#
var query = from g in games
            where g.Genre == "Action"
            select g.ProductName;

List<string> results = query.ToList();
```

Note that because you're returning a primitive value instead of an instance of your *Game* class, the return value has changed. *ProductName* is a string property; therefore, your results must be using the type of string. This is true for any type. The content of the *select* statement defines what form the results from the query take.

 Quick Check

- What are LINQ projections used for?

Quick Check Answer

- LINQ projections are used to shape the result of the query. Projections do not change the selected items in a query, only how those items are returned to the user of the query.

Projecting Results into Types

Primitive types meet your needs in some situations, but sometimes you need something more powerful. Much as a SQL query allows you to shape your results to return only the columns in the database that are needed, LINQ supports the same idea. In LINQ, this is called *projection*. Take this simple example. Consider this structure, which represents only the most basic data about a particular game:

```
' VB
Public Structure GameInfo
  Public Name As String
  Public Price As Decimal
  Public Rating As ESRBRating
End Structure
```

```
// C#
public struct GameInfo
{
    public string Name;
    public decimal Price;
    public ESRBRating Rating;
}
```

When you construct your query, you can have your *select* statement create a new instance of this structure and fill it when the query is executed:

```
'VB
Dim query = From g In games _
            Where g.Genre = "Action" _
            Select New GameInfo() With _
            { _
              .Name = g.ProductName, _
              .Price = g.ListPrice, _
              .Rating = g.GameRating _
            }

Dim results As List(Of GameInfo) = query.ToList()
```

```
// C#
var query = from g in games
            where g.Genre == "Action"
            select new GameInfo()
            {
                Name = g.ProductName,
                Price = g.ListPrice,
                Rating = g.GameRating
            };

List<GameInfo> results = query.ToList();
```

This code projects the results into a new type. This allows you to create smaller surface area on data that you are passing out of the LINQ query. Note that the return type (as in the earlier example) has also changed to the new data type that is being returned. This technique is not limited to structures or small types. You could also use it to create new instances of the *Game* class that filtered out the properties that you did not want the consumers of the results to access. For example:

```
' VB
Dim query = From g In games _
            Where g.Genre = "Action" _
            Select New Game() With _
            { _
              .ProductName = g.ProductName, _
              .ListPrice = g.ListPrice, _
              .GameRating = g.GameRating _
            }

Dim results As List(Of Game) = query.ToList()
```

```
// C#
var query = from g in games
            where g.Genre == "Action"
            select new Game()
            {
                ProductName = g.ProductName,
                ListPrice = g.ListPrice,
                GameRating = g.GameRating
            };


List<Game> results = query.ToList();
```

In this example, you are creating a new instance of the *Game* class for every result but filling in only the data that you want returned. This is a common way to filter out sensitive or protected data that the consumer of the data might not need or have the right to see.

Projecting Results into Anonymous Types

Using projection to fill in types is tremendously useful, but there are occasions where you want to be able to create temporary data types that are shaped for a specific need. This is actually more analogous to the SQL example because they return simple values. Using projection into anonymous types allows you to craft types on the fly that contain only the data you want:

```
' VB
Dim query = From g In games _
            Where g.Genre = "Action" _
            Select New With _
            { _
                .Name = g.ProductName, _
                .Price = g.ListPrice _
            }


Dim results = query.ToList()
```

```
// C#
var query = from g in games
            where g.Genre == "Action"
            select new
            {
                Name = g.ProductName,
                Price = g.ListPrice
            };


var results = query.ToList();
```

By using the *anonymous type* syntax, you can project your results into new types that are defined on the fly. Because the types are anonymous, you must infer the variable type (using *var* in C# or *Dim* in Visual Basic). In this way, you can make simple temporary types or complex object models that use the projection features of LINQ. For example, you could create a more complex anonymous type by supporting a nested type, as follows:

```vb
' VB
Dim query = From g In games _
            Where g.Genre = "Action" _
            Select New With _
            { _
              .Name = g.ProductName, _
              .Price = g.ListPrice, _
              .PubInfo = New With _
              { _
                .Publisher = g.Publisher, _
                .Developer = g.Developer _
              } _
            }

Dim results = query.ToList()
```

```csharp
// C#
var query = from g in games
            where g.Genre == "Action"
            select new
            {
              Name = g.ProductName,
              Price = g.ListPrice,
              PubInfo = new
              {
                Publisher = g.Publisher,
                Developer = g.Developer
              }
            };

var results = query.ToList();
```

Joining with LINQ

In addition to simple shaping, LINQ supports combining two disparate data sources into a single LINQ query. This is done by using the *join* syntax in LINQ. Next you'll walk through a simple example.

First, consider the following structure and collection:

```vb
' VB
Public Structure CurrencyType
  Public Currency As String
```

```vbnet
    Public Symbol As String
    Public isPrefix As Boolean
End Structure

Public Class CurrencyTypeList
  Inherits List(Of CurrencyType)

  Public Sub New()
        Add(New CurrencyType() With {.Currency = "USD", _
                                .isPrefix = True, _
                                .Symbol = "$"})
        Add(New CurrencyType() With {.Currency = "MS Points", _
                                .isPrefix = False, _
                                .Symbol = " Points"})
      End Sub
  End Class
```

```csharp
// C#
public struct CurrencyType
{
  public string Currency;
  public string Symbol;
  public bool isPrefix;
}

public class CurrencyTypeList : List<CurrencyType>
{
  public CurrencyTypeList()
  {
    Add(new CurrencyType() { Currency = "USD",
                             isPrefix = true,
                             Symbol = "$" });
    Add(new CurrencyType() { Currency = "MS Points",
                             isPrefix = false,
                             Symbol = " Points" });
  }
}
```

The *CurrencyType* is a simple structure that contains information used to format the currency for a *Game*. The *CurrencyTypeList* is a simple list of *CurrencyTypes*. You can join this list to your *GameList* class to get information about the *Currency* used for each game. The simplest way to join two data sources is to use multiple *from* statements and the *where* statement:

```vbnet
' VB
Dim games As New GameList()
Dim currencies As New CurrencyTypeList()
```

```
Dim query = From g In games _
            From c In currencies _
            Where g.ListPriceCurrency = c.Currency _
            Select New With _
            { _
              .Name = g.ProductName, _
              .ListPrice = g.ListPrice, _
              .Currency = g.ListPriceCurrency, _
              .CurrencySymbol = c.Symbol, _
              .IsCurrencySymbolPrefixed = c.isPrefix _
            }

Dim results = query.ToList()

// C#
GameList games = new GameList();
CurrencyTypeList currencies = new CurrencyTypeList();

var query = from g in games
            from c in currencies
            where g.ListPriceCurrency == c.Currency
            select new
            {
              Name = g.ProductName,
              ListPrice = g.ListPrice,
              Currency = g.ListPriceCurrency,
              CurrencySymbol = c.Symbol,
              IsCurrencySymbolPrefixed = c.isPrefix
            };

var results = query.ToList();
```

In this example, you are joining the *GameList* and *CurrencyTypeList* data sources and using both in your projection. Because there are two data sources, the LINQ query expects that the WHERE clause includes a lambda function that defines how the two pieces of data are linked. In addition, the LINQ syntax supports a real *join* statement that supports more control than the simple syntax:

```
' VB
Dim query = From g In games _
            Join c In currencies _
                On g.ListPriceCurrency Equals c.Currency _
            Where g.Genre = "Action" _
            Select New With _
            { _
              .Name = g.ProductName, _
              .ListPrice = g.ListPrice, _
```

```
            .Currency = g.ListPriceCurrency, _
            .CurrencySymbol = c.Symbol, _
            .IsCurrencySymbolPrefixed = c.isPrefix _
        }
```

```
// C#
var query = from g in games
            join c in currencies
                on g.ListPriceCurrency equals c.Currency
            where g.Genre == "Action"
            select new
            {
                Name = g.ProductName,
                ListPrice = g.ListPrice,
                Currency = g.ListPriceCurrency,
                CurrencySymbol = c.Symbol,
                IsCurrencySymbolPrefixed = c.isPrefix
            };
```

The *join* statement allows you to create the data source ("c in currencies") as you would in the *from* statement, but then it defines the relationship using the *on* statement. Note that in this syntax, the qualifier to link the two properties (in this case, *ListPriceCurrency* and *Currency*) is the *equals* statement, not the *equal* operator ("==" in C#; "=" in Visual Basic).

Grouping with LINQ

The last feature of LINQ discussed in this chapter is the support for grouping in LINQ. Grouping allows you to create hierarchies of data based on common data. To use grouping, you would use the *group* statement. The *group* statement allows you to specify a criterion for how to do the grouping (the *by* keyword) and then a name to call the group (after the *into* keyword). For example, if you take your list of games and want to arrange it by genre, you can do so with the following code:

```
' VB
Dim query = From g In games _
            Group g By g.Genre Into genres = Group _
            Select genres

Dim results = query.ToList()
```

```
// C#
var query = from g in games
            group g by g.Genre into genres
            select genres;

var results = query.ToList();
```

In this example, you are creating groups of *Game* objects that are separated by the *Genre* they specify. In the *select* statement, you specify a new range variable to retrieve the grouped results. Notice that variable inference is used to retrieve the results, but what form do the results come in? Each result is an instance of the *IGrouping<>* interface. Therefore you can change your results to a *List<>* of our *IGrouping* interface like so:

```
' VB
Dim results As List(Of IGrouping(Of String, Game)) = query.ToList()
```

```
// C#
List<IGrouping<string, Game>> results = query.ToList();
```

The returned list contains instances of the *IGrouping<>* interface. The generic types included in the interface are the type of the key and the type of the group's collection. The *IGrouping<>* interface supports two generic parameters. The first of these (called *Key*) specifies the Type of the key; the second is the type that is stored in the group. In addition, the *IGrouping<>* interface implements the *IEnumerable<>* interface for the data type specified in the second parameter of the *IGrouping<>* interface. This means you can go through each group, get the key, and enumerate the items in that group, as follows:

```
' VB
For Each group As IGrouping(Of String, Game) In results

    Console.WriteLine(String.Concat("Group: ", group.Key))

    For Each game As Game In group
            Console.WriteLine(game.ProductName)
    Next game

Next group
```

```
// C#
foreach (IGrouping<string, Game> group in results)
{
    Console.WriteLine(string.Concat("Group: ", group.Key));

    foreach (Game game in group)
    {
        Console.WriteLine(game.ProductName);
    }
}
```

In this example, you go through each group and show the *Key,* and then you go through the group's collection (remember, it implements *IEnumerable<Game>* in this case) and can show each game in that group.

When grouping, the order of the groups and the items in each group is specified by multiple ordering statements. The general rule of thumb is to control the order of items in a group by ordering before the group statement, and control the order of the groups by using ordering after the group, as seen here:

```vb
' VB
Dim query = From g In games _
            Order By g.ReleaseDate Descending _
            Group g By g.Genre Into genres = Group _
            Order By Genre _
            Select genres
```

```csharp
// C#
var query = from g in games
            orderby g.ReleaseDate descending
            group g by g.Genre into genres
            orderby genres.Key
            select genres;
```

Note that the first ordering statement will order the *Game* objects, whereas the second ordering statement orders the groups themselves. The syntax of the second ordering statement is different for C# and Visual Basic. In C#, you specify the group you created and order by the key of the group, whereas in Visual Basic, you specify the property name that you used to do the ordering (*Genre*) to perform the same ordering.

 **Quick Check**

- What are joins used for in LINQ?

Quick Check Answer

- Joins allow you to combine two different data sources into a single query to be treated as a single data source.

LAB **Shaping Results**

In this lab, you take an existing query and change it to shape the result of the query. To start, you need to have the a copy of the Lab2 project in the Chapter6 folder. Depending on which language you choose to use, it is in either the Chapter6/Cs folder or the Chapter6/Vb folder. Please open the Lab2_Before's Lab2.sln file to open the project in Visual Studio.

EXERCISE 1 Retrieving a List of Strings

In this exercise, you project into a simple typed collection.

1. Open the main code file for the project (for C#, it is Program.cs; for Visual Basic, it is Module1.vb).

2. Notice that there is already a set of code similar to the simple LINQ queries in the lab from Lesson 1.

3. Take the existing LINQ query and change the *select* statement so that it returns a list of *ProductName* items instead:

```vb
' VB
Dim query = From g In games _
            Where g.ReleaseDate < DateTime.Today _
            Order By g.ReleaseDate _
            Select g.ProductName
```

```csharp
// C#
var query = from g in games
            where g.ReleaseDate < DateTime.Today
            orderby g.ReleaseDate
            select g.ProductName;
```

4. You should notice that the execution of the query is using type inference (*var* in C#; *Dim* in Visual Basic), so you do not have to change the code when you shape the result.

5. In the *foreach* loop, change the result variable to be a typed variable by specifying *String* for the type (instead of the inferred type).

6. Change the code inside the *foreach* loop to simply write out each result instead of calling the result's *ProductName*:

```vb
' VB
For Each result As String In results
   Console.WriteLine(result)
Next result
```
```csharp
// C#
foreach (String result in results)
{
   Console.WriteLine(result);
}
```

If you run the program now, you see that it is returning simple strings instead of *Game* objects.

EXERCISE 2   Projecting a Result into a Specific Type

Continuing from the last exercise, you project your results into a known class.

1. In Visual Studio, from the main menu, select Project, Add New Item… to add a new class to the project.

2. Select the *Class* type of project item and name the new class *GameInfo.cs* or *GameInfo. vb* depending on the language you are using.

3. Inside the new class file that you have created, make sure the new class is public by adding the appropriate keyword, if necessary.

4 Next, add a public property called *Name* of type *String*.

5. Add a new public property called *Release* of type *DateTime*. Your class should look like so:

```vb
' VB
Public Class GameInfo

  Private _name As String
  Public Property Name() As String
    Get
      Return _name
    End Get
    Set(ByVal value As String)
      _name = value
    End Set
  End Property


  Private _release As DateTime
  Public Property NewProperty() As String
    Get
      Return _release
    End Get
    Set(ByVal value As String)
      _release = value
    End Set
  End Property

End Class
```

```csharp
// C#
public class GameInfo
{
  public String Name { get; set; }
  public DateTime Release { get; set; }
}
```

6. Go back to the original source file and project results into this new type.

You can do this by changing the *select* statement to create a new instance of the *GameInfo* class setting the *Name* and *Release* with the *ProductName* and *ReleaseDate* properties like so:

```vb
' VB
Dim query = From g In games _
            Where g.ReleaseDate < DateTime.Today _
            Order By g.ReleaseDate _
```

```
                        Select New GameInfo With _
                        { _
                          .Name = g.ProductName, _
                          .Release = g.ReleaseDate _
                        }
```

```
// C#
var query = from g in games
            where g.ReleaseDate < DateTime.Today
            orderby g.ReleaseDate
            select new GameInfo
            {
                Name = g.ProductName,
                Release = g.ReleaseDate
            };
```

7. Change your *foreach* loop to take the *GameInfo* type instead of a *String*.

8. Change the call to write to the console to use the new *Name* property of *GameInfo,* as shown here:

```
' VB
For Each result As GameInfo In results
    Console.WriteLine(result.Name)
Next result
```

```
// C#
foreach (GameInfo result in results)
{
    Console.WriteLine(result.Name);
}
```

If you run the application again, you see the same results, but we're getting the results from a list of a concrete class instead a list of primitive types.

EXERCISE 3   Projecting a Result into an Anonymous Type

Next, you change your query to use an anonymous type instead of the concrete one you used in the last exercise.

1. In the LINQ query, remove the type name from the projection to change the type to an anonymous type as follows:

```
' VB
Dim query = From g In games _
                Where g.ReleaseDate < DateTime.Today _
                Order By g.ReleaseDate _
```

```
           Select New With _
           { _
             .Name = g.ProductName, _
             .Release = g.ReleaseDate _
           }
```

```
// C#
var query = from g in games
            where g.ReleaseDate < DateTime.Today
            orderby g.ReleaseDate
            select new
            {
              Name = g.ProductName,
              Release = g.ReleaseDate
            };
```

2. You need to change your *foreach* statement to take the anonymous type. To do this, change the strongly typed variable to an inferred one (like the one you had when you started):

```
' VB
For Each result In results
  Console.WriteLine(result.Name)
Next result
```

```
// C#
foreach (var result in results)
{
  Console.WriteLine(result.Name);
}
```

3. Run the application and see that you are still getting the same result, but you are using an anonymous type. Note that you didn't need to change the call to Console.WriteLine because the anonymous type named the property *Name* for you.

4. Add a new property to the anonymous type called *Description* and assign it to the *ProductDescription* type, as shown here:

```
' VB
Dim query = From g In games _
            Where g.ReleaseDate < DateTime.Today _
            Order By g.ReleaseDate _
            Select New With _
            { _
              .Name = g.ProductName, _
              .Release = g.ReleaseDate, _
              .Description = g.ProductDescription _
            }
```

```
// C#
var query = from g in games
               where g.ReleaseDate < DateTime.Today
               orderby g.ReleaseDate
               select new
               {
                  Name = g.ProductName,
                  Release = g.ReleaseDate,
                  Description = g.ProductDescription
               };
```

5. In your *foreach* loop, change the Console.WriteLine code to write out the *Description* property:

```
' VB
For Each result In results
   Console.WriteLine(result.Description)
Next result
```

```
// C#
foreach (var result in results)
{
   Console.WriteLine(result.Description);
}
```

6. Run the application to see how the descriptions are now being shown.

Lesson Summary

- Projection allows you to shape your results in the select portion of the LINQ query.
- You can project into simple, existing, or anonymous types.
- LINQ allows you to shape your results into groups.
- You can also combine two different sources in LINQ using the *join* statement.

Lesson Review

You can use the following questions to test your knowledge of the information in Lesson 2, "Shaping Results with LINQ." The questions also are available on the companion CD of this book if you prefer to review them in electronic form.

NOTE ANSWERS

Answers to these questions and explanations of why each answer choice is correct or incorrect are located in the "Answers" section at the end of the book.

1. What LINQ expressions are used to shape results in a query? (Choose all that apply. Each answer forms a complete solution.)

   A. *where* in C#; *Where* in Visual Basic

   B. *select* in C#; *Select* in Visual Basic

   C. *join* in C#; *Join* in Visual Basic

   D. *group* in C#; *Group* in Visual Basic

2. What types of shapes can LINQ query results be shaped into? (Choose all that apply. Each answer forms a complete solution.)

   A. Collections of primitive types

   B. Collections of complex types

   C. Single types

   D. Collections of anonymous types

3. Which LINQ statement is used to merge two data sources to perform queries?

   A. *where* in C#; *Where* in Visual Basic

   B. *select* in C#; *Select* in Visual Basic

   C. *join* in C#; *Join* in Visual Basic

   D. *group* in C#; *Group* in Visual Basic

4. Which LINQ keyword is used to categorize results in a query?

   A. *where* in C#; *Where* in Visual Basic

   B. *select* in C#; *Select* in Visual Basic

   C. *join* in C#; *Join* in Visual Basic

   D. *group* in C#; *Group* in Visual Basic

Chapter Review

To practice and reinforce the skills you learned in this chapter further, you can do any or all of the following:

- Review the chapter summary.
- Review the list of key terms introduced in this chapter.
- Complete the case scenarios. These scenarios set up real-world situations involving the topics of this chapter and ask you to create a solution.
- Complete the suggested practices.
- Take a practice test.

Chapter Summary

- LINQ is a key technology for defining queries across a variety of different types of data, including in-memory objects, databases, and XML.
- The language integration of LINQ enables it to create most queries in a type-safe, readable form.
- Expression trees are important to the way LINQ works in that lambda expressions are stored as a set of criteria to perform against data sources.
- LINQ supports the ability to shape the data that is returned from a query and is not limited to the same form as the data source.
- By providing joining and grouping, LINQ supports a rich way to get at the right data in your application without having to shape the data source.

Key Terms

Do you know what these key terms mean? You can check your answers by looking up the terms in the glossary at the end of the book.

- Data source
- Expression
- Expression Tree
- LINQ
- Projection

Case Scenario

In the following case scenario, you apply what you've learned about how to create queries with LINQ. You can find answers to the questions posed in this scenario in the "Answers" section at the end of this book.

Case Scenario: Designing a Demonstration Program

Trey Research is designing a new application that provides a dashboard for users currently logged onto their system. The dashboard provides the user the ability to search and sort the information shown on the screen at once. The existing dashboard already has the user data in memory, but the searching and sorting needs to be designed.

QUESTIONS

Answer the following questions for your manager:

1. How can we create several standard sorts and filter combinations? Is this something that can be hard-wired into the code?

2. Should we devise our own query language to specify the filters and searches? Why or why not?

Suggested Practices

To help you master the exam objectives presented in this chapter, complete the following tasks.

Introducing LINQ

- **Practice 1**   Create a Microsoft Windows application that shows all the processes on a particular machine. Use LINQ to query the process list that is returned by System. Environment's Process class.

- **Practice 2**   Expand on the examples in the Lesson 2 lab to add grouping to the games by *Genre*.

- **Practice 3**   Take an existing use of nested *foreach* calls in an existing project and refactor it using LINQ to filter the data.

Take a Practice Test

The practice tests on this book's companion CD offer many options. For example, you can test yourself on just the content covered in this chapter, or you can test yourself on the entire 70-561 certification exam content. You can set up the test so that it closely simulates the experience of taking a certification exam, or you can set it up in study mode, which allows you to look at the correct answers and explanations after you answer each question.

> **MORE INFO**   **PRACTICE TESTS**
>
> For details about all the available practice test options, see the section entitled "How to Use the Practice Tests," in the Introduction to this book.

CHAPTER 7

XML

Although the focus of this training kit is to prepare you as a developer for dealing with database data, sometimes that data needs to be dealt with in other formats. Extensible Markup Language (XML) is one such format. In this chapter, you delve into two particular areas of XML integration, including using XML with *DataSets* and querying XML with Language Integrated Query (LINQ).

Exam objective in this chapter:

- Handle special data types.

Lessons in this chapter:

Before You Begin

To complete the lessons in this chapter, you must have:

- A computer that meets or exceeds the minimum hardware requirements listed in the "Introduction" section at the beginning of the book
- Microsoft Visual Studio 2008 Professional edition installed on your computer
- An understanding of Microsoft Visual Basic or C# syntax and familiarity with the Microsoft .NET Framework version 3.5

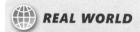

REAL WORLD

Shawn Wildermuth

In the early days of *DataSet,* I was very enamoured with them. After working with *RecordSets* in my ADO days, I found *DataSets* to be a fantastic bit of code. They allowed me to deal with multiple types of interrelated data. My earliest blog that was running .NET code (*http://adoguy.com*) was in fact running completely on a *DataSet*. Because I was the only one who changed data, using the *DataSet* integration to save out the *DataSet* as XML every time I added a blog entry or some other part of my site was really simple. In fact although other sites were being plagued with problems like SQL injection attacks, my site kept humming along since I was working with the data without an actual database. I don't necessarily recommend this practice, but it helped me understand the power of saving the *DataSet* as an XML file between sessions as well as caching the *DataSet* in memory for very fast access to the data.

Lesson 1: *DataSets* and XML

As we have seen in Chapter 3, *"DataSets,"* *DataSets* are powerful objects that can be used in a variety of scenarios. In addition, XML represents structured storage for data. Luckily, *DataSets* support several key pieces of functionality to load and save as XML data. In this lesson, you learn how to read and write *DataSets* as XML, as well as how to use DiffGrams (a special type of XML serialization that is useful for saving change state). Finally, you learn how to customize the XML generation by the *DataSet*.

> **After this lesson, you will be able to:**
> - Write a *DataSet* as XML
> - Read *DataSet* XML into a *DataSet*
> - Work with DiffGrams
> - Customize XML Serialization
>
> **Estimated lesson time: 45 minutes**

Writing a *DataSet* as XML

Once you have gotten the grasp of how to work with *DataSets* in your .NET Framework applications, it seems a shame to leave all that data only for use either in-memory or in the database. In fact, it would be downright helpful if we could save that data to disk. That is where writing *DataSets* as XML comes into play.

For example, let's assume we've created a simple two-table *DataSet* like so:

```vb
' VB
Dim ds As New DataSet()

Dim connString As String = "Server=.;Database=VideoGameStore;" + _
                    "Integrated Security=true;"

Using conn As New SqlConnection(connString)
Using cmd As SqlCommand = conn.CreateCommand()

  cmd.CommandText = "SELECT * FROM Product;" & _
                "SELECT * FROM ProductType;"

  Dim da As New SqlDataAdapter(cmd)

  ' Map the results to the Tables
  da.TableMappings.Add("Table", "Product")
  da.TableMappings.Add("Table1", "ProductType")
```

```
' Fill the data
da.Fill(ds)

End Using
End Using

// C#
DataSet ds = new DataSet();

string connString = @"Server=.;Database=VideoGameStore;
                      Integrated Security=true;";

using (SqlConnection conn = new SqlConnection(connString))
using (SqlCommand cmd = conn.CreateCommand())
{
  cmd.CommandText = @"SELECT * FROM Product;
                      SELECT * FROM ProductType;";

  SqlDataAdapter da = new SqlDataAdapter(cmd);

  // Map the results to the Tables
  da.TableMappings.Add("Table", "Product");
  da.TableMappings.Add("Table1", "ProductType");

  // Fill the data
  da.Fill(ds);
}
```

After running this simple code, you end up with a *DataSet* that contains two tables. The *DataSet* classes supports a method called *WriteXml*, whose job it is to write the data inside a *DataSet* as XML. In its simpliest form, you can write out a file of XML like so:

```
' VB
ds.WriteXml("..\..\product.xml")
```

```
// C#
ds.WriteXml(@"product.xml");
```

This simple method call results in a very simple form of XML. This form starts with an element based on the *DataSetName* of the *DataSet* (*NewDataSet* by default). Next, each table is serialized as a set of elements and each column in each table is a child element of the table. Each table's types are serialized as siblings of each other. For example, this is your simple Product.xml file:

```
<?xml version="1.0" standalone="yes"?>
<NewDataSet>
  <Product>
    <ProductID>2</ProductID>
```

```
        <ProductName>XBox 360</ProductName>
        <ProductDescription>Microsoft XBox 360 Standard</ProductDescription>
        <ListPrice>399.99</ListPrice>
        <ProductTypeID>2</ProductTypeID>
        <SupplierID>1</SupplierID>
        <ProductImageUrl>images/noimage.jpg</ProductImageUrl>
        <ListPriceCurrency>USD</ListPriceCurrency>
        <ProductVersion>AAAAAAAAB90=</ProductVersion>
    </Product>

    <!-- ... -->

    <ProductType>
      <ProductTypeID>3</ProductTypeID>
      <ProductTypeName>Accessory</ProductTypeName>
      <ProductTypeDescription>Video Game Accessory</ProductTypeDescription>
    </ProductType>
</NewDataSet>
```

If you don't want to write the contents as XML directly but instead just want to retrieve a string that contains the XML representation, you can also use the *GetXml* method to retrieve the XML as follows:

' VB
```
Dim xml as string = ds.GetXml()
```

// C#
```
string xml = ds.GetXml();
```

The *GetXml* method in the *DataSet* is rarely used because it does not support any of the advanced features of the XML serialization. Instead, you could use *WriteXml* but instead of specifying a filename, you can use one of the classes that can be written to directly (for example, *Stream, XmlWriter,* or *TextWriter*). For example, to write out the *DataSet* into a *MemoryStream,* you could use the following code:

' VB
```
Dim strm As New MemoryStream()
ds.WriteXml(strm)
```

// C#
```
MemoryStream strm = new MemoryStream();
ds.WriteXml(strm);
```

In addition, the *WriteXml* accepts as a second parameter an *XmlWriteMode* enumeration. This enumeration is detailed in Table 7-1.

TABLE 7-1 *XmlWriteMode* Enumeration

VALUE	MEANING
XmlWriteMode.DiffGram	The format of the XML is a DiffGram (explained in the next section).
XmlWriteMode.IgnoreSchema	The XML is written without an inline schema (the default behavior).
XmlWriteMode.WriteSchema	Include the schema (for example, .xsd) as an inline schema in the XML document (also explained in the next section).

XML Serialization and *DataSets*

*D*ataSets can be serialized using XML serialization but often the results are confusing to those using these two technologies together for the first time. Although XML Serialization is used in a variety of situations, the most common situation is in ASP.NET Web Services (also called ASMX Web Services).

When *DataSets* are serialized using XML serialization, the *DataSet* determines how to perform the serialization. By default, the *DataSet* is serialized as a DiffGram, which is a useful but noninteroperable format. To control the format of the XML, you can either use the *WriteXml/GetXml* methods of the *DataSet* to manage the XML directly or you can use a *XmlDataDocument* method to wrap the *DataSet*, which always returns a simple version of the XML when serialized.

Reading XML with a *DataSet*

Much like writing data in a *DataSet*, reading is simple using the *ReadXml* method. Loading a *DataSet* with XML can be as simple as the following code:

```vb
' VB
Dim mySet as new DataSet()
mySet.ReadXml("products.xml")
```

```csharp
// C#
DataSet mySet = new DataSet();
mySet.ReadXml("products.xml");
```

What does the *ReadXml* method actually do? It attempts to categorize all elements with the same name in a *DataTable*. It also attempts to create relationships between elements based upon descendent/ascendant relationships in the XML. Although this approach isn't flawless, it does help create relational versions of hierarchies quite well. Be aware that some complex XML schemas do not map into the *DataSet;* therefore, not every XML file can be loaded into a *DataSet.*

What is not obvious from the code examples so far is that *ReadXml* does not automatically clear itself between calls to *ReadXml.* This may imply that when you call *ReadXml,* you should clear the *DataSet* with its *Clear* method, but in fact it opens up an additional piece of important functionality: data merging. If you call *ReadXml* multiple times you can merge data from disperate sources into a single *DataSet* like so:

```
' VB
' Get First Set of Data
mySet.ReadXml("BadDataSet.xml")

' Get More data and add it to the existing data
mySet.ReadXml("Another.xml")
```

```
// C#
// Get First Set of Data
mySet.ReadXml(@"BadDataSet.xml");

// Get More data and add it to the existing data
mySet.ReadXml(@"Another.xml");
```

The *ReadXml* can accept XML from other sources than from file names directly. To do this, you can supply a *Stream, TextReader,* or *XmlReader* object as follows:

```
' VB
Dim stream As Stream = GetFromStream()
mySet.ReadXml(stream)

Dim rdr As XmlReader = GetXmlReader()
mySet.ReadXml(rdr)

Dim text As TextReader = GetTextReader()
mySet.ReadXml(text)
```

```
// C#
Stream stream = GetFromStream();
mySet.ReadXml(stream);

XmlReader rdr = GetXmlReader();
mySet.ReadXml(rdr);

TextReader text = GetTextReader();
mySet.ReadXml(text);
```

These four methods for loading XML should allow you to load XML into a *DataSet* from any source, whether it be in-memory, Web Service, REST API, object serialization, or an actual file.

Like its *WriteXml* brethren, the *ReadXml* method has an enumeration to control how the reading is handled. By default, the code attempts to do the right thing when determining how to read the XML into the *DataSet* but the *XmlReadMode* enumeration (shown in Table 7-2) offers ways to specify how you want the read to be performed, as shown here:

```vb
' VB
Dim mySet As New DataSet()
mySet.ReadXml("product.xml", XmlReadMode.Auto)
```

```csharp
// C#
DataSet mySet = new DataSet();
mySet.ReadXml(@"product.xml", XmlReadMode.Auto);
```

TABLE 7-2 *XmlReadMode* Enumeration

VALUE	MEANING
XmlReadMode.Auto	Attempts to determine from the XML the best way to read the data. This is the default behavior.
XmlReadMode.ReadSchema	Reads any inline XML schema into the *DataSet*. New schema elements are merged with an existing *DataSet* schema but an exception is thrown on duplicate schema elements.
XmlReadMode.IgnoreSchema	Ignores inline XML schema. Any elements that are not already part of the *DataSet* are ignored.
XmlReadMode.InferSchema	Any inline XML schema are ignored and the *DataSet* schema are inferred by the structure of the XML.
XmlReadMode.DiffGram	Reads the XML as a DiffGram merging changes into the *DataSet*. See the section entitled "Using DiffGrams," later in this lesson, for further explanation.
XmlReadMode.Fragment	Reads XML as an XML fragment and uses any inline schema to define the schema. Otherwise, it infers the schema.
XmlReadMode.InferTypedSchema	Works like *XmlReadMode.InferSchema* but attempts to infer strong types (for example, making XML dates into .NET *DateTime* structures). If it cannot determine the types, it infers them as strings.

Using the *XmlReadMode* enumeration, you can control the way that the tables and relationships are created in the *DataSet*. Alternatively, you can use XML schema to define the layout and only use *XmlReadMode.Ignore* schema as you'll see in the next section.

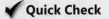

Quick Check

- Can you read an XML file directly from a file path using the *DataSet*?

Quick Check Answer

- Yes. The *DataSet.ReadXml* method has an overload that supports specifying a file name.

DataSets and XML Schema

The fact that you can describe the schema in terms of an XML Schema Definition (XSD) is implied by the way that *Typed DataSets* work (as explained in Chapter 3). The format of the raw design document for *Typed DataSets* is an .xsd document. This means that there is a mapping of a *DataSet* schema to an XML schema.

When working with the *DataSet* class (or the *DataTable* class) you are using the underlying schema that is embedded into the *DataSet*. This schema is not an XML schema but a *DataSet* schema. What is useful is communicating the *DataSet* schema as an XML schema. To do this, you can use the *ReadXmlSchema* and *WriteXmlSchema* methods of the *DataSet*. You can take any *DataSet* and write out an XSD simply by calling the *WriteXmlSchema* method like so:

```
' VB
someSet.WriteXmlSchema("someSet.xsd")
```

```
// C#
someSet.WriteXmlSchema("someSet.xsd");
```

The *WriteXmlSchema* method supports *Stream, TextWriter,* and *XmlWriter* like its *WriteXml* brethren as well. You can control some of the generation of your XML schemas by using the *Namespace* properties on the *DataSet*, *DataTable,* and *DataColumn* classes. Specifying the Namespace indicates that the *DataTable's* contents should be created in their own XML namespace. When the XML Schema (.xsd) is created, the elements in the *DataTable* will be created in that XML namespace as shown:

```
' VB
Dim someSet As New DataSet("Library")
someSet.Namespace = "http://microsoft.com/tk561"


' Create the Book table
Dim bookTable As DataTable = someSet.Tables.Add("Book")
bookTable.Namespace = "http://microsoft.com/tk561"
bookTable.Columns.Add("id", GetType(Integer))
bookTable.Columns("id").Namespace = "http://microsoft.com/tk561"
bookTable.Columns.Add("name", GetType(String))
bookTable.Columns("name").Namespace = "http://microsoft.com/tk561"


someSet.WriteXmlSchema("someSet.xsd")
```

```
// C#
DataSet someSet = new DataSet("Library");
someSet.Namespace = "http://microsoft.com/tk561";

// Create the Book table
DataTable bookTable = someSet.Tables.Add("Book");
bookTable.Namespace = "http://microsoft.com/tk561";
bookTable.Columns.Add("id", typeof(int));
bookTable.Columns["id"].Namespace = "http://microsoft.com/tk561";
bookTable.Columns.Add("name", typeof(string));
bookTable.Columns["name"].Namespace = "http://microsoft.com/tk561";

someSet.WriteXmlSchema("someSet.xsd");
```

In addition to *Namespace*, you can control the namespace prefix for the elements in the XML by specifying the prefix as well. Instead of generating a random prefix, using the *Prefix* property will force the specific prefix to be used, for example:

```
' VB
ds.Namespace = "http://microsoft.com/tk561"
ds.Prefix = "my"
```

```
// C#
ds.Namespace = "http://microsoft.com/tk561";
ds.Prefix = "my";
```

When you specify the namespace and the prefix, you design the default namespace like so:

```
<?xml version="1.0" standalone="yes"?>
<my:NewDataSet xmlns:my="http://microsoft.com/tk561">
  <!-- ... -->
</my:NewDataSet>
```

You can also write out the schema when you call *WriteXml* directly. In that case, if you use the *WriteXmlMode.WriteSchema* enumerated value, you get your XML schema written inline as part of the larger XML document. This option is interesting if you are working with external clients who need to understand the structure of your schema in a way that is not a platform-specific way. Because XML schema is used in a variety of platforms, using XML schema can help non–.NET Framework client make sense of your XML documents.

The support is not limited to only writing XML schema; you can also use it to load your *DataSet* schema. Defining *DataSet* schemas can be done in a variety of ways. You could write terse code like this:

```
' VB
Dim someSet As New DataSet("Library")

' Create the Book table
Dim bookTable As DataTable = someSet.Tables.Add("Book")
```

```vbnet
bookTable.Columns.Add("id", GetType(Integer))
bookTable.Columns.Add("name", GetType(String))
bookTable.Constraints.Add("PK_Book", bookTable.Columns("id"), True)

' Create the Shelf table
Dim shelfTable As DataTable = someSet.Tables.Add("Shelf")
shelfTable.Columns.Add("id", GetType(Integer))
shelfTable.Columns.Add("name", GetType(String))
shelfTable.Constraints.Add("PK_Shelf", bookTable.Columns("id"), True)

' Create the Collection table
Dim collectionTable As DataTable = someSet.Tables.Add("Collection")
collectionTable.Columns.Add("id", GetType(Integer))
collectionTable.Constraints.Add("PK_Book", bookTable.Columns("id"), True)

' Create Relationships
someSet.Relations.Add(collectionTable.Columns("id"), shelfTable.Columns("id"))
someSet.Relations.Add(collectionTable.Columns("id"), bookTable.Columns("id"))
someSet.Relations.Add(shelfTable.Columns("id"), bookTable.Columns("id"))
```

```csharp
// C#
DataSet someSet = new DataSet("Library");

// Create the Book table
DataTable bookTable = someSet.Tables.Add("Book");
bookTable.Columns.Add("id", typeof(int));
bookTable.Columns.Add("name", typeof(string));
bookTable.Constraints.Add("PK_Book", bookTable.Columns["id"], true);

// Create the Shelf table
DataTable shelfTable = someSet.Tables.Add("Shelf");
shelfTable.Columns.Add("id", typeof(int));
shelfTable.Columns.Add("name", typeof(string));
shelfTable.Constraints.Add("PK_Shelf", bookTable.Columns["id"], true);

// Create the Collection table
DataTable collectionTable = someSet.Tables.Add("Collection");
collectionTable.Columns.Add("id", typeof(int));
collectionTable.Constraints.Add("PK_Book", bookTable.Columns["id"], true);

// Create Relationships
someSet.Relations.Add(collectionTable.Columns["id"], shelfTable.Columns["id"]);
someSet.Relations.Add(collectionTable.Columns["id"], bookTable.Columns["id"]);
someSet.Relations.Add(shelfTable.Columns["id"], bookTable.Columns["id"]);
```

You could also specify this same schema using an XML Schema Document (.xsd) like so:

```
<?xml version="1.0" standalone="yes"?>
<xs:schema id="Library"
           xmlns=""
           xmlns:xs="http://www.w3.org/2001/XMLSchema"
           xmlns:msdata="urn:schemas-microsoft-com:xml-msdata">
  <xs:element name="Library"
              msdata:IsDataSet="true"
              msdata:UseCurrentLocale="true">
    <xs:complexType>
      <xs:choice minOccurs="0"
                 maxOccurs="unbounded">
        <xs:element name="Book">
          <xs:complexType>
            <xs:sequence>
              <xs:element name="id"
                          type="xs:int" />
              <xs:element name="name"
                          type="xs:string"
                          minOccurs="0" />
            </xs:sequence>
          </xs:complexType>
        </xs:element>
        <xs:element name="Shelf">
          <xs:complexType>
            <xs:sequence>
              <xs:element name="id"
                          type="xs:int" />
              <xs:element name="name"
                          type="xs:string"
                          minOccurs="0" />
            </xs:sequence>
          </xs:complexType>
        </xs:element>
        <xs:element name="Collection">
          <xs:complexType>
            <xs:sequence>
              <xs:element name="id"
                          type="xs:int" />
            </xs:sequence>
          </xs:complexType>
        </xs:element>
      </xs:choice>
    </xs:complexType>
    <xs:unique name="PK_Book"
               msdata:PrimaryKey="true">
```

```
      <xs:selector xpath=".//Book" />
      <xs:field xpath="id" />
    </xs:unique>
    <xs:unique name="PK_Shelf"
                msdata:PrimaryKey="true">
      <xs:selector xpath=".//Shelf" />
      <xs:field xpath="id" />
    </xs:unique>
    <xs:unique name="Collection_PK_Book"
                msdata:ConstraintName="PK_Book"
                msdata:PrimaryKey="true">
      <xs:selector xpath=".//Collection" />
      <xs:field xpath="id" />
    </xs:unique>
    <xs:keyref name="Relation1"
                refer="Collection_PK_Book">
      <xs:selector xpath=".//Shelf" />
      <xs:field xpath="id" />
    </xs:keyref>
    <xs:keyref name="Relation3"
                refer="PK_Shelf">
      <xs:selector xpath=".//Book" />
      <xs:field xpath="id" />
    </xs:keyref>
    <xs:keyref name="Relation2"
                refer="Collection_PK_Book">
      <xs:selector xpath=".//Book" />
      <xs:field xpath="id" />
    </xs:keyref>
  </xs:element>
</xs:schema>
```

If you have an XML schema that describes the structure of your data, you can use the *ReadXmlSchema* method of the *DataSet* to read the schema document and create your *DataSet* schema like so:

```
' VB
Dim mySet As New DataSet()

' Get First Set of Data
mySet.ReadXmlSchema("SomeDataSet.xsd")
```

```
// C#
DataSet mySet = new DataSet();

// Get First Set of Data
mySet.ReadXmlSchema("SomeDataSet.xsd");
```

By calling the *ReadXmlSchema* method, the *DataSets* are loaded with the schema in the .xsd file. Alternatively, you can use the *XmlRead* method with the *XmlReadMode.ReadSchema* enumerated value to read an XML document with an inline schema, as shown here:

```
' VB
Dim schemaSet As New DataSet()
schemaSet.ReadXml("SomeData.xsd", XmlReadMode.ReadSchema)
```

```
// C#
DataSet schemaSet = new DataSet();
schemaSet.ReadXml("SomeData.xsd", XmlReadMode.ReadSchema);
```

Customizing XML Serialization

As you saw in the section entitled "Writing a *DataSet* as XML," earlier in this lesson, you can use *WriteXml* to save your *DataSets* to XML, but the format of the XML is a bit basic. For example, look at the example used previously:

```
<?xml version="1.0" standalone="yes"?>
<NewDataSet>
  <Product>
    <ProductID>2</ProductID>
    <ProductName>XBox 360</ProductName>
    <ProductDescription>Microsoft XBox 360 Standard</ProductDescription>
    <ListPrice>399.99</ListPrice>
    <ProductTypeID>2</ProductTypeID>
    <SupplierID>1</SupplierID>
    <ProductImageUrl>images/noimage.jpg</ProductImageUrl>
    <ListPriceCurrency>USD</ListPriceCurrency>
    <ProductVersion>AAAAAAAAB90=</ProductVersion>
  </Product>

  <!-- ... -->

  <ProductType>
    <ProductTypeID>3</ProductTypeID>
    <ProductTypeName>Accessory</ProductTypeName>
    <ProductTypeDescription>Video Game Accessory</ProductTypeDescription>
  </ProductType>
</NewDataSet>
```

First, notice that each column in each table is written out as a nested element. Although this is useful for some work, you may want to change the way that columns are serialized. To do this, you can specify the *ColumnMapping* property of the *DataColumn* to one of the values in the *MappingType* enumeration. Table 7-3 details the behavior of the *MappingType* enumeration.

TABLE 7-3 The *MappingType* Enumeration

VALUE	MEANING
MappingType.Element	Maps the *DataColumn* to a simple element in the XML. This is the default value.
MappingType.Attribute	Maps the *DataColumn* to an attribute on the table's element.
MappingType.Hidden	Does not serialize the *DataColumn* when writing out to XML.
MappingType.SimpleContent	Writes the *DataColumn* to the content inside the table's element in the XML. Only one column can be specified as *Simple Content*.

For example, suppose that you change the columns of your Product table to use the *MappingType.Attribute* to change your serialization to attributes on the table element like so:

```vb
' VB
Dim products As DataTable = ds.Tables("Product")
For Each column As DataColumn In products.Columns
  column.ColumnMapping = MappingType.Attribute
Next column
```

```csharp
// C#
DataTable products = ds.Tables["Product"];
foreach (DataColumn column in products.Columns)
{
  column.ColumnMapping = MappingType.Attribute;
}
```

It would make our resulting XML look like this:

```xml
<?xml version="1.0" standalone="yes"?>
<NewDataSet>
  <Product ProductID="2"
          ProductName="XBox 360"
          ProductDescription="Microsoft XBox 360 Standard"
          ListPrice="399.99"
          ProductTypeID="2"
          SupplierID="1"
          ProductImageUrl="images/noimage.jpg"
          ListPriceCurrency="USD"
          ProductVersion="AAAAAAAAB90=" />
  <!-- ... -->
</NewDataSet>
```

In addition, you can change the fact that related tables are written out as siblings in the XML file. To do this, you must have a relationship between two tables. You can specify a the *DataRelation.IsNested* property to make the related entities created as nested elements instead of the default behavior. For example:

```vb
' VB
Dim rel As DataRelation = ds.Relations.Add( _
  ds.Tables("ProductType").Columns("ProductTypeID"), _
  ds.Tables("Product").Columns("ProductTypeID"))

' Change Nesting
rel.Nested = True
```

```csharp
// C#
DataRelation rel = ds.Relations.Add(
  ds.Tables["ProductType"].Columns["ProductTypeID"],
  ds.Tables["Product"].Columns["ProductTypeID"]);

// Change Nesting
rel.Nested = true;
```

When you specify the relationship nesting, your resulting XML looks like so:

```xml
<?xml version="1.0" standalone="yes"?>
<NewDataSet>
  <ProductType>
    <ProductTypeID>1</ProductTypeID>
    <ProductTypeName>Game</ProductTypeName>
    <ProductTypeDescription>Video Game</ProductTypeDescription>
    <Product>
      <ProductID>1741</ProductID>
      <ProductName>2006 FIFA World Cup™</ProductName>
      <ProductDescription>EA SPORTS celebrates the world's largest sporting event
          with the only official and exclusive licensed video game for the 2006
          FIFA World Cup Germany.</ProductDescription>
      <ListPrice>59.99</ListPrice>
      <ProductTypeID>1</ProductTypeID>
      <ReleaseDate>2006-04-28T00:00:00-04:00</ReleaseDate>
      <ProductImageUrl>http://www.xbox.com/NR/rdonlyres/A9C63C71-CFAD-4A87-A01B-
          048701B3DE25/0/box2006fifaworldcup.jpg</ProductImageUrl>
      <ListPriceCurrency>USD</ListPriceCurrency>
      <ProductVersion>AAAAAAAAB98=</ProductVersion>
    </Product>
  </ProductType>
</NewDataSet>
```

You'll notice that *ProductType* is the parent in this case because the relationship is set up with *ProductType* as the parent row. If this were switched, the order of the nested would be the inverse.

Using DiffGrams

DataSets are not simple data structures. One of the major features that *DataSets* support is the ability to learn about the changes of specific pieces of data. In fact, each column in each row can have two copies of data: the original version of the data as retrieved (usually from a database), as well as a modified version of the data. In concurrency scenarios, it is useful to know what the original and modified version of each piece of data so you can perform intelligent updating of data to a data source. When you are working with *DataSets* locally, this information is used by *DataAdapters* to know how to perform updates to the database. One way of sharing this information is by use of a *DataSet* XML format called *DiffGrams*.

There are scenarios where you may want to save this information with your *DataSet*. For example, you could save a *DataSet* as XML (including the change information) if you are not quite ready to update the data (like intermittent network connections) but you don't want to have to keep the application in memory. This is where the DiffGram support can be very powerful.

DiffGrams and Web Services

Unlike most scenarios where you are saving data to a file or a stream of some kind, when you use *DataSets* with ASP.NET Web Services, the *DataSet* itself controls the type of serialization that is used. If you simply try and return *DataSets* from Web Services, you will soon find that the default serialization format in that case is a DiffGram. This is not necessarily an issue, but if you are using a Web Service for its ability to interoperate with other systems, only .NET systems can make sense of the DiffGram format.

To change this, you can either write out the XML using *XmlWrite* to a *MemoryStream* or to wrap the *DataSet* with a *XmlDataDocument*, which normalizes the serialization for you.

When you use a *DataSet* to read or write XML, you have the option of use DiffGrams as your XML format. By calling the *WriteXml* method using *XmlWriteMode.DiffGram*, your XML serialization is in a very specific format that only *DataSets* can understand. This format includes the change information about the data. For example, you can take your *DataSet* filled with *Product* data, change some columns, and then save it as a DiffGram, as shown here:

```
' VB
Dim row As DataRow = ds.Tables("Product").Rows(0)
row("ReleaseDate") = DateTime.Today
row("ListPrice") = 29.99D

' Write out the XML
ds.WriteXml("products.xml", XmlWriteMode.DiffGram)
```

```
// C#
DataRow row = ds.Tables["Product"].Rows[0];
row["ReleaseDate"] = DateTime.Today;
row["ListPrice"] = 29.99M;


// Write out the XML
ds.WriteXml("products.xml", XmlWriteMode.DiffGram);
```

When you write out the Products.xml file, it's in the form of a DiffGram. The DiffGram format extends the basic XML to include some *DataSet*-specific attributes so that when read into a *DataSet*, the state of the modified rows is preserved. For example, here is the Product.xml file that was produced by the code example (throughout these code samples, significant parts of the code are shown in bold):

```
<?xml version="1.0" standalone="yes"?>
<diffgr:diffgram xmlns:msdata="urn:schemas-microsoft-com:xml-msdata"
                 xmlns:diffgr="urn:schemas-microsoft-com:xml-diffgram-v1">
  <NewDataSet>
    <Product diffgr:id="Product1"
             msdata:rowOrder="0"
             diffgr:hasChanges="modified">
      <ProductID>2</ProductID>
      <ProductName>XBox 360</ProductName>
      <ProductDescription>Microsoft XBox 360 Standard</ProductDescription>
      <ListPrice>29.99</ListPrice>
      <ProductTypeID>2</ProductTypeID>
      <SupplierID>1</SupplierID>
      <ReleaseDate>2008-08-27T00:00:00-04:00</ReleaseDate>
      <ProductImageUrl>images/noimage.jpg</ProductImageUrl>
      <ListPriceCurrency>USD</ListPriceCurrency>
      <ProductVersion>AAAAAAAAB90=</ProductVersion>
    </Product>
    <Product diffgr:id="Product2"
             msdata:rowOrder="1">
      <ProductID>4</ProductID>
      <ProductName>Black Xbox Wireless Controller</ProductName>
      <ProductDescription>Black Xbox Wireless Controller</ProductDescription>
      <ListPrice>25</ListPrice>
      <ProductTypeID>3</ProductTypeID>
      <SupplierID>1</SupplierID>
      <ProductImageUrl>images/noimage.jpg</ProductImageUrl>
      <ListPriceCurrency>USD</ListPriceCurrency>
      <ProductVersion>AAAAAAAAB94=</ProductVersion>
    </Product>
  </NewDataSet>
  <diffgr:before>
    <Product diffgr:id="Product1" msdata:rowOrder="0">
```

```
  <ProductID>2</ProductID>
  <ProductName>XBox 360</ProductName>
  <ProductDescription>Microsoft XBox 360 Standard</ProductDescription>
  <ListPrice>399.99</ListPrice>
  <ProductTypeID>2</ProductTypeID>
  <SupplierID>1</SupplierID>
  <ProductImageUrl>images/noimage.jpg</ProductImageUrl>
  <ListPriceCurrency>USD</ListPriceCurrency>
  <ProductVersion>AAAAAAAAB90=</ProductVersion>
  </Product>
  </diffgr:before>
</diffgr:diffgram>
```

Note that the first *Product* element has *diffgr:hasChanges="modified"* added to the element. This tells the *DataSet* when you read back this XML file that that specific *Product* row is modified. In addition, the *diffgr:before* element is added to the format to show the original value of the changed rows as shown at the bottom of the XML.

Writing out a DiffGram writes all the data, not just the changed data. In scenarios where you want to be able to write out just the changes, you should call *DataSet.GetChanges()* before you write out the XML, like so:

```
' VB
Dim changesOnly As DataSet = ds.GetChanges()
changesOnly.WriteXml("products.xml", XmlWriteMode.DiffGram)


// C#
DataSet changesOnly = ds.GetChanges();
changesOnly.WriteXml("products.xml", XmlWriteMode.DiffGram);
```

Finally, you can read back in the changes that you wrote out as a DiffGram using the *ReadXml* method and the *ReadXmlMode.DiffGram* value:

```
' VB
changedSet.ReadXml("products.xml", XmlReadMode.DiffGram)


// C#
changedSet.ReadXml("products.xml", XmlReadMode.DiffGram);
```

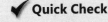 **Quick Check**

- Does a DiffGram contain only the changed rows of a *DataSet*?

Quick Check Answer

- No. When you save a *DataSet* as a DiffGram, it saves all the data, changes and all, by default. If you want to save just the changes (for example, if you want to save the changes to send it to a Web Service) you call *DataSet.GetChanges()* first to create a *DataSet* with only the changes.

Work with *DataSets* and XML

In this lab, you save and load data with XML.

EXERCISE 1   Create a *DataSet*

In this exercise, you create a *DataSet* in preparation for saving and loading the *DataSet* as XML.

1. Create a new Console project using Visual Studio 2008.

2. Open the main project file (Program.cs in C# or Module1.vb in Visual Basic).

3. Find the *Main* method and create a new *DataSet* called *theSet*.

4. Create a new *DataTable* by adding a new table called Game in the new *DataSet* and save the new table in a new local variable.

5. Create a new column on the new *DataTable* called *GameID* and specify the type of Integer (or int) as the column type.

6. Specify the *AutoIncrement* property to True on the new column.

7. Create two more columns:

   - Name, of type *string*.

   - Price, of type *decimal*.

   Your code so far should look something like this:

```vb
' VB
Sub Main()

    Dim theSet As New DataSet()

    ' Setup the Game Table
    Dim games As DataTable = theSet.Tables.Add("Game")
    games.Columns.Add("GameID", GetType(Integer))
    games.Columns("GameID").AutoIncrement = True
    games.Columns.Add("Name", GetType(String))
    games.Columns.Add("Price", GetType(Decimal))

End Sub
```

```csharp
// C#
static void Main(string[] args)
{
    DataSet theSet = new DataSet();

    // Setup the Game Table
    DataTable games = theSet.Tables.Add("Game");
    games.Columns.Add("GameID", typeof(int));
    games.Columns["GameID"].AutoIncrement = true;
    games.Columns.Add("Name", typeof(string));
    games.Columns.Add("Price", typeof(decimal));
}
```

8. Add new rows to the new table by using the *NewRow* method and setting the Name and Price columns using the following values:

- "Gears of War 2" and 59.99
- "MLB 2009" and 59.99

This code should look like so:

```vb
' VB
Dim newGame As DataRow = games.NewRow()
newGame("Name") = "Gears of War 2"
newGame("Price") = 59.99D
games.Rows.Add(newGame)
newGame = games.NewRow()
newGame("Name") = "MLB 2009"
newGame("Price") = 59.99D
games.Rows.Add(newGame)
```

```csharp
// C#
DataRow newGame = games.NewRow();
newGame["Name"] = "Gears of War 2";
newGame["Price"] = 59.99M;
games.Rows.Add(newGame);
newGame = games.NewRow();
newGame["Name"] = "MLB 2009";
newGame["Price"] = 59.99M;
games.Rows.Add(newGame);
```

9. Using the table named Game, iterate through the table's rows to write out the GameID, Name, and Price using *Console.WriteLine*.

10. After the iteration, call *Console.ReadLine* to force the console to stay open, as shown here:

```vb
' VB
For Each game As DataRow In theSet.Tables("Game").Rows
  Console.WriteLine("({0}): {1} - {2}", _
                    game("GameID"),
                    game("Name"),
                    game("Price"))
Next game

' Wait for Return
Console.ReadLine()
```

```csharp
// C#
foreach (DataRow game in theSet.Tables["Game"].Rows)
{
  Console.WriteLine("({0}): {1} - {2}",
    game["GameID"],
```

```
    game["Name"],
    game["Price"]);
}


// Wait for Return
Console.ReadLine();
```

11. Run the application to make sure that the project can create the data and show it in
    the console.

EXERCISE 2   Save *DataSet* to XML

In this exercise, add a new line just before the call to *ReadLine()* to save your data.

1. Add a call to *DataSet*.SaveXml specifying Games.xml as the name and also specifying
   XmlWriteMode.WriteSchema to include the schema in the new XML document:

   ```
   ' VB
   theSet.WriteXml("games.xml", XmlWriteMode.WriteSchema)
   ```

   ```
   // C#
   theSet.WriteXml("games.xml", XmlWriteMode.WriteSchema);
   ```

2. Run the application to see that it is creating the data.

3. Close the application and open the Games.xml file in your Bin/Debug directory of your
   new project. It should look something like this:

   ```
   <?xml version="1.0" standalone="yes"?>
   <NewDataSet>
     <xs:schema id="NewDataSet"
                xmlns=""
                xmlns:xs="http://www.w3.org/2001/XMLSchema"
                xmlns:msdata="urn:schemas-microsoft-com:xml-msdata">
       <xs:element name="NewDataSet"
                   msdata:IsDataSet="true"
                   msdata:UseCurrentLocale="true">
         <xs:complexType>
           <xs:choice minOccurs="0"
                      maxOccurs="unbounded">
             <xs:element name="Game">
               <xs:complexType>
                 <xs:sequence>
                   <xs:element name="GameID"
                               msdata:AutoIncrement="true"
                               type="xs:int"
                               minOccurs="0" />
                   <xs:element name="Name"
                               type="xs:string"
                               minOccurs="0" />
   ```

```
            <xs:element name="Price"
                            type="xs:decimal"
                            minOccurs="0" />
                </xs:sequence>
            </xs:complexType>
        </xs:element>
    </xs:choice>
</xs:complexType>
</xs:element>
</xs:schema>
<Game>
    <GameID>0</GameID>
    <Name>Gears of War 2</Name>
    <Price>59.99</Price>
</Game>
<Game>
    <GameID>1</GameID>
    <Name>MLB 2009</Name>
    <Price>59.99</Price>
</Game>
</NewDataSet>
```

EXERCISE 3   Read *DataSet* from XML

Now that you're saving data, try and load the data in this exercise.

1. Just before you create the Game table, create an *if* statement to test for the *File.Exists* method on the Game.xml file. You may need to add a reference to the *System.IO* namespace to get *File.Exists()* to work.

2. After that *if* statement, call the *DataSet*'s *ReadXml* method, specifying Game.xml as the file name and *XmlReadMode.ReadSchema* as the second parameter.

3. After the reading of Game.xml, you can skip all the code up to displaying it in the console. To do this, create an *else* block after the *if* block and put all the code in creating the schema and data inside this block.

    Your code should now look like this:

```vb
' VB
If File.Exists("games.xml") Then
  theSet.ReadXml("games.xml")
Else

  ' Setup the Game Table
  Dim games As DataTable = theSet.Tables.Add("Game")
  games.Columns.Add("GameID", GetType(Integer))
  games.Columns("GameID").AutoIncrement = True
  games.Columns.Add("Name", GetType(String))
  games.Columns.Add("Price", GetType(Decimal))
```

```
' Add some data
Dim newGame As DataRow = games.NewRow()
newGame("Name") = "Gears of War 2"
newGame("Price") = 59.99D
games.Rows.Add(newGame)
newGame = games.NewRow()
newGame("Name") = "MLB 2009"
newGame("Price") = 59.99D
games.Rows.Add(newGame)
End If


// C#
if (File.Exists("games.xml"))
{
   theSet.ReadXml("games.xml");
}
else
{

   // Setup the Game Table
   DataTable games = theSet.Tables.Add("Game");
   games.Columns.Add("GameID", typeof(int));
   games.Columns["GameID"].AutoIncrement = true;
   games.Columns.Add("Name", typeof(string));
   games.Columns.Add("Price", typeof(decimal));

   // Add some data
   DataRow newGame = games.NewRow();
   newGame["Name"] = "Gears of War 2";
   newGame["Price"] = 59.99M;
   games.Rows.Add(newGame);
   newGame = games.NewRow();
   newGame["Name"] = "MLB 2009";
   newGame["Price"] = 59.99M;
   games.Rows.Add(newGame);
}
```

4. Run the application. If the Game.xml file exists, your new code reads that code instead of re-creating the data.

Lesson Summary

- The *DataSet* and *DataTable* classes can be used directly to load and save XML data.
- Using the *XmlReadMode* and *XmlWriteMode* enumerations can be helpful in determining how the creation or parsing of the XML is done by the *DataSet/DataTable*.

- DiffGrams are a powerful way to format *DataSet* change data into an XML format that can be used to retain change state across instances of *DataSets*.
- You can load a *DataSet* with XML schema to prepopulate the structure of a *DataSet*.
- You have some power (with limitations) to define how the XML serialization is performed through customizing the columns and relationships in a *DataSet*.

Lesson Review

You can use the following questions to test your knowledge of the information in Lesson 1, "*DataSets* and XML." The questions also are available on the companion CD of this book if you prefer to review them in electronic form.

> **NOTE ANSWERS**
>
> Answers to these questions and explanations of why each answer choice is correct or incorrect are located in the "Answers" section at the end of the book.

1. Which types of XML can be parsed by a *DataSet* or *DataTable* using the *ReadXml* method? (Each answer forms a complete solution. Choose all that apply.)

   A. XML fragments

   B. XML Schema Documents

   C. DiffGrams

   D. XML documents with inline schemas

2. Which of these statements regarding DiffGrams is true?

   A. DiffGrams are understood in a variety of platforms and languages.

   B. DiffGrams include only information about changes to a *DataSet*.

   C. DiffGrams contain all the information in a *DataSet,* including change information.

   D. DiffGrams are the default format of XML when using *DataSet.WriteXml*.

3. In what ways can you customize the way that *DataSet.WriteXml* creates the XML? (Each answer forms a complete solution. Choose all that apply.)

   A. Specify whether a field is an element or an attribute.

   B. Specify how whitespace formatting is handled.

   C. Specify that the *DataSet* should be created as an XML fragment.

   D. Hide parts of the *DataSet* from the XML file.

Lesson 2: Querying XML with LINQ

Chapter 6, "Introducing LINQ," described LINQ as a standard way to create queries in .NET Framework version 3.5. In this chapter, that discussion continues by using some of the same techniques to create queries against XML. Although not necessarily a replacement for XML-based techniques like XPath or even XQuery, the LINQ support for XML provides an extension of the common syntax for queries. This lesson introduces you to the new queryable XML classes, as well as show you how to use them to create your own LINQ queries against XML data.

> **After this lesson, you will be able to:**
> - Parse XML using the lightweight XML LINQ classes.
> - Create LINQ queries against XML documents.
>
> **Estimated lesson time: 30 minutes**

Introducing Queryable XML Classes

From its earliest days, the .NET Framework included implicit support for XML using the *System.Xml* namespace. This namespace included support for basic parsing and complex manipulation of XML using XPath and XSLT. Although the new XML classes that support LINQ are not meant to be a complete replacement for all XML use-cases, they do provide a lighter-weight alternative to these classes.

These new classes can be found in the *System.Xml.Linq* namespace. Each of these classes represents a different piece of the XML story. Unlike the old classes, which all started with the prefix of *Xml*, each of these classes starts with just the letter *X*. For readers who are familiar with the *System.Xml* classes, Table 7-4 shows a comparison of the new classes and their *System.Xml* counterparts so you can determine where to use which class. If you do not see a particular class in Table 7-4, that means there is not a counterpart class in the queryable XML classes.

TABLE 7-4 *System.Xml.Linq* Counterpart Classes

SYSTEM.XML.LINQ CLASS	SYSTEM.XML CLASS
XDocument	*XmlDocument*
XElement	*XmlElement*
XAttribute	*XmlAttribute*
XNode	*XmlNode*
XName	No equivalent; uses strings or *XmlNameTables*
XNamespace	No equivalent; uses *XmlNameTables*
XCData	*XmlCDataSection*
XText	*XmlText*

Typically you parse existing XML using these classes. This usually starts by creating an *XDocument* object and either loading or parsing XML. Loading builds an *XDocument* from a current document or Uniform Resource Identifier (URI), whereas *Parse* takes an in-memory string of XML and creates the document by parsing the result. For example:

```vb
' VB
Dim doc As XDocument = XDocument.Load("..\..\games.xml")
Dim parsedDoc As XDocument = XDocument.Parse("<Foo></Foo>")
```

```csharp
// C#
XDocument doc = XDocument.Load(@"..\..\games.xml");
XDocument parsedDoc = XDocument.Parse("<Foo></Foo>");
```

You can also construct an *XDocument* by creating in-line XML. In Visual Basic, this can be done with a language feature called XML Literals as shown here:

```vb
' VB
Dim xml = <?xml version="1.0"?>
          <Foo>
            <Bar id="1">Quux</Bar>
          </Foo>
```

Note that in Visual Basic, you can use actual in-line XML. The datatype of the *xml* variable is *XDocument*. If you remove the version information from the inline XML, it types this object as an *XElement* (or an XML Fragment). This is a little more complex in C# because it does not support XML literals, but the *XML Linq* family of classes supports daisy-chaining constructors so you can approximate the construction to show some level of structure. For example:

```csharp
// C#
XDocument memoryDoc =
  new XDocument(
    new XElement("Foo",
      new XElement("Bar",
        new XAttribute("id", "1"),
        new XText("Quux"))));
```

In both of these examples, the resulting *XDocument* contains the same XML. The basic class that is used in queryable XML is the *XNode* class. It represents any part of the XML tree. In fact, each of the part classes (for example, *XDocument*, *XElement*, and *XAttribute*) derive directly from *XNode*. The *XNode* class contains the basic interface for walking the XML tree. This includes basic navigation like *NextNode* and *PreviousNode* properties, as well as retrieval of related methods that return collections like *Nodes*, *Ancestors*, and *Descendants*. Using these, you can perform simple tranversal of the XML tree, as shown here:

```vb
' VB
For Each node As XNode In memoryDoc.Nodes()
  Console.WriteLine(node.NodeType)
Next node
```

```vbnet
For Each node As XNode In memoryDoc.Descendants()
  Console.WriteLine(node.NodeType)
Next node

For Each node As XNode In memoryDoc.Ancestors()
  Console.WriteLine(node.NodeType)
Next node
```

```csharp
// C#
foreach (XNode node in memoryDoc.Nodes())
{
  Console.WriteLine(node.NodeType);
}

foreach (XNode node in memoryDoc.Descendants())
{
  Console.WriteLine(node.NodeType);
}

foreach (XNode node in memoryDoc.Ancestors())
{
  Console.WriteLine(node.NodeType);
}
```

These methods support simple searching as well, because they allow you to specify names to find and return such as those shown here:

```vbnet
' VB
For Each node As XNode In memoryDoc.Descendants("Game")
  Console.WriteLine(node.NodeType)
Next node
```

```csharp
// C#
foreach (XNode node in memoryDoc.Descendants("Game"))
{
  Console.WriteLine(node.NodeType);
}
```

Using these methods we can search using plain old Common Language Runtime (CLR) code, but the code can be terse. Delving into the contents of the XML document using these methods works, but using LINQ is often a better option.

Constructing a Query

Constructing queries against the LINQ-enabled XML classes is simple but may not seem as straightforward. For example, you cannot issue a query directly against the *XDocument* class or any of the XML classes. That is because none of these classes directly support the *IEnumerable<T>* class, which was explained in Chapter 6. To query the XML, you need collections to search against. This is where you can use any of the methods that return collections. For example you can use the *Descendants* method of the *XDocument* class to query against, as shown here:

```vb
' VB
Dim doc As XDocument = XDocument.Load("games.xml")

Dim qry = From g In doc.Descendants("Game") _
        Select g

Dim games As List(Of XElement) = qry.ToList()
```

```csharp
// C#
XDocument doc = XDocument.Load(@"games.xml");

var qry = from g in doc.Descendants("Game")
        select g;

List<XElement> games = qry.ToList();
```

This example simply shows that you are first retrieving all the descendants from the *XDocument* that are *XElements* of type *Game*. You are simply creating an empty query in this example and returning all the results. But more common would be to actually create a filter (using the WHERE clause). Because *XElement* isn't strongly typed as simple objects would be, you need to use the application programming interface (API) of *XElement* to get at the contents you want. In this example, you look in each *Game* element and find all the ones who have an attribute called *Genre* whose value is *Sports:*

```vb
' VB
Dim qry = From g In doc.Descendants("Game") _
        Where g.Attribute("Genre").Value = "Sports" _
        Select g
```

```csharp
// C#
var qry = from g in doc.Descendants("Game")
        where g.Attribute("Genre").Value == "Sports"
        select g;
```

This example uses the *Attribute* method to find and return the *Genre* attribute; then you can compare against the *Value* of the attribute. The only issue with this approach is that attribute may or may not exist on a particular *XElement*. If the attribute is not required, the query fails because the call to the *Value* property results in a *NullReferenceException*. To get around this, you can test for the attribute first as shown here:

```vb
' VB
Dim qry = From g In doc.Descendants("Game") _
        Where g.Attribute("Genre") IsNot Nothing AndAlso _
            g.Attribute("Genre").Value = "Sports" _
        Select g
```

```csharp
// C#
var qry = from g in doc.Descendants("Game")
          where g.Attribute("Genre") != null &&
                g.Attribute("Genre").Value == "Sports"
          select g;
```

This allows you to perform complex filtering, but it also works for ordering or any other function of the query. Now that you have the results, the next section explains how to work with them.

Quick Check

- How do you query against XML documents with optional elements?

Quick Check Answer

- To query with optional elements, you must protect against asking for the value of an element that does not exist by checking for that existence first.

Working with Results

Unlike other uses for LINQ, using LINQ against XML requires you to get used to dealing with untyped data. As you saw in the queries in the previous section, you have to delve into the data by using different methods for getting at the actual values inside the XML. This holds true for results as well.

The problem is that most of the work that you are going to do with the results involves issues like data binding that usually work better on a property basis (for example, calling a property on a class to get data). This means when you issue queries against XML, it is often best to shape your results into a form that is easier to handle. This means projection into new types (anonymous or static). For example, you could shape your results into a simple anonymous type, as shown here:

```vb
' VB
Dim qry = From g In doc.Descendants("Game") _
          Where g.Attribute("Genre") IsNot Nothing AndAlso _
                g.Attribute("Genre").Value = "Sports" _
          Select New With _
          { _
            .Name = g.Attribute("ProductName").Value, _
            .Genre = g.Attribute("Genre").Value _
          }
```

```csharp
// C#
var qry = from g in doc.Descendants("Game")
          where g.Attribute("Genre") != null &&
                g.Attribute("Genre").Value == "Sports"
          select new
          {
            Name = g.Attribute("ProductName").Value,
            Genre = g.Attribute("Genre").Value
          };
```

This works well to create on-the-fly types for your code. More normally, you would project them into known types that are easier to work with (because you can pass them to methods and similar items):

```vb
' VB
Dim qry = From g In doc.Descendants("Game") _
          Where g.Attribute("Genre") IsNot Nothing AndAlso _
                g.Attribute("Genre").Value = "Sports" _
          Select New GameInfo With _
          { _
            .Name = g.Attribute("ProductName").Value, _
            .Genre = g.Attribute("Genre").Value _
          }
```

```csharp
// C#
var qry = from g in doc.Descendants("Game")
          where g.Attribute("Genre") != null &&
                g.Attribute("Genre").Value == "Sports"
          select new GameInfo()
          {
            Name = g.Attribute("ProductName").Value,
            Genre = g.Attribute("Genre").Value
          };
```

As with the WHERE clauses that you saw in the previous section, you need to make sure that attributes exist when you are using projection:

```vb
' VB
Dim qry = From g In doc.Descendants("Game") _
          Where g.Attribute("Genre") IsNot Nothing AndAlso _
                g.Attribute("Genre").Value = "Sports" _
          Select New GameInfo With _
            { _
              .Name = g.Attribute("ProductName").Value, _
              .Genre = g.Attribute("Genre").Value, _
              .Publisher = If(g.Attribute("Publisher") IsNot Nothing, _
                            g.Attribute("Publisher").Value, _
                            "") _
            }
```

```csharp
// C#
var qry = from g in doc.Descendants("Game")
          where g.Attribute("Genre") != null &&
                g.Attribute("Genre").Value == "Sports"
          select new GameInfo()
          {
            Name = g.Attribute("ProductName").Value,
            Genre = g.Attribute("Genre").Value,
            Publisher = (g.Attribute("Publisher") != null ?
                        g.Attribute("Publisher").Value :
                        "")
          };
```

Finally, because you are dealing with all string data in the XML, you have to convert some values from strings to their correct data types. For example, if you are projecting into a class that takes a *DateTime*, you need to convert it during the projection, as shown here:

```vb
' VB
Dim qry = From g In doc.Descendants("Game") _
          Where g.Attribute("Genre") IsNot Nothing AndAlso _
                g.Attribute("Genre").Value = "Sports" _
          Select New GameInfo With _
            { _
              .Name = g.Attribute("ProductName").Value, _
              .Genre = g.Attribute("Genre").Value, _
              .Publisher = If(g.Attribute("Publisher") IsNot Nothing, _
                            g.Attribute("Publisher").Value, _
                            ""), _
              .Release = DateTime.Parse(g.Attribute("ReleaseDate").Value)
            }
```

```csharp
// C#
var qry = from g in doc.Descendants("Game")
          where g.Attribute("Genre") != null &&
                g.Attribute("Genre").Value == "Sports"
          select new GameInfo()
          {
            Name = g.Attribute("ProductName").Value,
            Genre = g.Attribute("Genre").Value,
            Publisher = (g.Attribute("Publisher") != null ?
                        g.Attribute("Publisher").Value :
                        ""),
            Release = DateTime.Parse(g.Attribute("ReleaseDate").Value)
          };
```

In this lab, you write and execute a query against a simple XML document.

EXERCISE 1   Creating a LINQ to XML Query

In this exercise, you create a query against an XML document.

1. In Visual Studio 2008, create a new .NET Framework 3.5 Console project called Lab2.

2. From the Project menu, select Add Existing Item … to add an existing file to your project.

3. Navigate to the location where you installed the code from the companion CD and find the Games.xml file. (You may need to change the file type in the file dialog to Data Files to see the .xml files.)

4. Open the main file in the new project (Program.cs in C# or Module1.vb in Visual Basic) and find the *Main* method (or *Function* in Visual Basic).

5. Inside *Main,* create a variable called *doc* of type *XDocument* and set it by calling *XDocument.Load,* specifying the path to the Games.xml file (usually ".\.\.\Games.xml"). You may need to add a *using* statement in C# (or *Imports* in Visual Basic) to *System. Xml.Linq* to resolve *XDocument,* as follows:

```
' VB
Dim doc As XDocument = XDocument.Load("../../games.xml")
```

```
// C#
XDocument doc = XDocument.Load("..\\..\\games.xml");
```

6. Create a new LINQ query by searching for the descendants of the document named "Game" and choosing only the games who have the *Genre* of "Family". Your query may look something like this:

```
' VB
Dim qry = From g In doc.Descendants("Game") _
          Where g.Attribute("Genre").Value = "Family" _
          Order By g.Attribute("ReleaseDate").Value Descending _
          Select g
```

```
// C#
var qry = from g in doc.Descendants("Game")
          where g.Attribute("Genre").Value == "Family"
          orderby g.Attribute("ReleaseDate").Value descending
          select g;
```

7. Create a new type-inferred variable by executing the query using its *ToArray* method.

8. Walk through the new array and write out to the console the *Attribute* called "ProductName".

9. After the iteration, call *Console.ReadLine* to force the console to stay open:

```vb
' VB
Dim games = qry.ToArray()

For Each game In games
  Console.WriteLine(game.Attribute("ProductName").Value)
Next game

Console.ReadLine()
```

```csharp
// C#
var games = qry.ToArray();

foreach (var game in games)
{
  Console.WriteLine(game.Attribute("ProductName").Value);
}

Console.ReadLine();
```

10. Run the application to show all the *Family*-themed games listed in your console.

EXERCISE 2   Returning a Simple Value List

Because Exercise 1 returns a list of *XElements* instead of something that is more consumable, in this exercise, refactor the code to return a simple list of strings instead.

1. Change the "select" part of your LINQ query to return the value of the *ProductName* attribute like so:

```vb
' VB
Dim qry = From g In doc.Descendants("Game") _
          Where g.Attribute("Genre").Value = "Family" _
          Order By g.Attribute("ReleaseDate").Value Descending _
          Select g.Attribute("ProductName").Value
```

```csharp
// C#
var qry = from g in doc.Descendants("Game")
          where g.Attribute("Genre").Value == "Family"
          orderby g.Attribute("ReleaseDate").Value descending
          select g.Attribute("ProductName").Value;
```

2. Go to the *for/each* loop and change what is written to the Console to the result of the iteration like so:

```vb
' VB
For Each game In games
  Console.WriteLine(game)
Next game
```

```
// C#
foreach (var game in games)
{
    Console.WriteLine(game);
}
```

3. Run the application to show all the *Family*-themed games listed in your console.

EXERCISE 3 Project Results into Types

In this exercise, refactor the code again to return a complex type instead of a single value.

1. To start, return to the LINQ query and change the 'select' part of the query to return an anonymous type that has a string called *Name* and a decimal value called *Price*.

2. When setting the *Name*, use the value of the *ProductName* attribute.

3. When setting *Price*, use the decimal class's *Parse* method to convert the string representation into a decimal value. Your query should resemble this code:

```
' VB
Dim qry = From g In doc.Descendants("Game") _
            Where g.Attribute("Genre").Value = "Family" _
            Order By g.Attribute("ReleaseDate").Value Descending _
            Select New With _
            { _
              .Name = g.Attribute("ProductName").Value, _
              .Price = Decimal.Parse(g.Attribute("ListPrice").Value) _
            }
```

```
// C#
var qry = from g in doc.Descendants("Game")
            where g.Attribute("Genre").Value == "Family"
            orderby g.Attribute("ReleaseDate").Value descending
            select new
            {
              Name = g.Attribute("ProductName").Value,
              Price = decimal.Parse(g.Attribute("ListPrice").Value)
            };
```

4. Go to the *for/each* loop and change what is written to the Console to the *Name* property of the result of the iteration like so:

```
' VB
For Each game In games
  Console.WriteLine(game.Name)
Next game
```

```
// C#
foreach (var game in games)
{
  Console.WriteLine(game.Name);
}
```

5. Run the application to show all the *Family*-themed games listed in your console.

Lesson Summary

- The LINQ XML classes represent a lighter-weight, though less-feature-rich, way of working with XML data in your .NET Framework applications.

- You can use LINQ to create queries against XML data.

- Using projection can simplify the consumption of results from a XML LINQ query.

Lesson Review

You can use the following questions to test your knowledge of the information in Lesson 2, "Querying XML with LINQ." The questions also are available on the companion CD of this book if you prefer to review them in electronic form.

> **NOTE ANSWERS**
>
> Answers to these questions and explanations of why each answer choice is correct or incorrect are located in the "Answers" section at the end of the book.

1. Which features do the XML LINQ classes support? (Each answer forms a complete solution. Choose all that apply.)

    A. Parsing XML

    B. XSL Transformations

    C. XPath

    D. XML Tree Traversal

2. Which datatype are attribute values in XML LINQ classes?

    A. Always *strings*

    B. Depends on their datatype in XSD

    C. Always *objects*

    D. *XValues*

Chapter Review

To practice and reinforce the skills you learned in this chapter further, you can do any or all of the following:

- Review the chapter summary.
- Review the list of key terms introduced in this chapter.
- Complete the case scenario. This scenario sets up a real-world situation involving the topics of this chapter and asks you to create a solution.
- Complete the suggested practices.
- Take a practice test.

Chapter Summary

- The *DataSets* classes provide straightforward access to saving and loading data as XML.
- *DataSets* support inferring or reading XML schemas.
- *DataSets* allow you to customize XML generation.
- Using LINQ is a robust way to query over XML-based data.
- Constructing LINQ queries over XML is similar with object-based LINQ but you need to navigate to specific attributes and elements in the query.
- Retrieving results from XML-based LINQ queries involves some projection to work around the type-less construction of XML.

Key Terms

Do you know what these key terms mean? You can check your answers by looking up the terms in the glossary at the end of the book.

- Extensible Markup Language (XML)
- XML Schema Document (XSD)

Case Scenario

In the following case scenario, you apply what you've learned about how to use XML in your data scenarios. You can find answers to the questions posed in this scenario in the "Answers" section at the end of this book.

Case Scenario: Use DiffGrams for Change Management

You are in a department that is responsible for a number of small applications to support your sales staff. Because your salespeople are often in the field, they use a virtual private network (VPN) to tunnel into your enterprise to access data.

Your main application follows a sale through the pipeline from initial lead to completed sale. Wireless connectivity is becoming ubiquitous, but it is not quite there yet. Your salespeople are frustrated because sometimes they cannot get access to their sales lead information because they can't connect to the system. You've been tasked with solving the problem.

QUESTIONS

Answer the following questions for your manager:

1. How can we give the salespeople access to data when they are offline?

2. Can they change data when they are offline?

Suggested Practices

To help you master the exam objectives presented in this chapter, complete the following tasks.

Handle special datatypes

- **Practice 1** Create an offline application using *DataSets* and XML data.

- **Practice 2** Write a Web Service that queries an XML data source (for example, Amazon's Web Service) using LINQ to XML.

Take a Practice Test

The practice tests on this book's companion CD offer many options. For example, you can test yourself on just the content covered in this chapter, or you can test yourself on the entire 70-561 certification exam content. You can set up the test so that it closely simulates the experience of taking a certification exam, or you can set it up in study mode, which allows you to look at the correct answers and explanations after you answer each question.

> **MORE INFO** **PRACTICE TESTS**
>
> For details about all the available practice test options, see the section entitled "How to Use the Practice Tests," in the Introduction to this book.

CHAPTER 8

LINQ to SQL

A new data access technology has been released with the introduction of Microsoft .NET Framework 3.5: LINQ to SQL. Language Integrated Query (LINQ) is an extensible language enhancement to both VB.NET and C#, allowing a developer to embed comprehensive queries directly in code, where the query is recognized, type-checked, and compiled by the compiler. LINQ to SQL is an implementation of an extension, allowing access to relational databases using the LINQ syntax. This chapter introduces LINQ to SQL; deals with reading, updating, mapping, and projecting data; and touches on expression trees, the inner workings of LINQ to SQL.

Exam objectives in this chapter:

- Query data sources using LINQ.
- Transform data by using LINQ.

Lessons in this chapter:

Before You Begin

To complete the lessons in this chapter, you must have:

- A computer that meets or exceeds the minimum hardware requirements listed in the "Introduction" section at the beginning of the book
- Microsoft Visual Studio 2008 Professional edition installed on your computer
- An understanding of Microsoft Visual Basic or C# syntax and familiarity with .NET Framework version 3.5

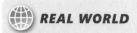

Lesson 1: Introduction to LINQ to SQL

As described in Chapter 6, "Introducing LINQ," LINQ has multiple providers, each of which allows integration of queries against a data source from within a LINQ-enabled language. C# and VB.NET are LINQ-enabled as of .NET Framework 3.5, but any language can use the infrastructure of the Common Language Runtime (CLR) to offer LINQ. Microsoft offers three providers for implementing LINQ-based data access to relational databases: LINQ to DataSets, LINQ to Entities, and the topic of this chapter, LINQ to SQL.

> **After this lesson, you will be able to:**
> - Insert /Update/Delete data using a command
> - Insert /Update/Delete data using a data adapter
> - Insert/Update/Delete data using a *Typed DataSet*
> - Change the batch size of a bulk update
> - Update custom data types
> - Use stored procedures to update data
> - Use dynamic SQL to update data
>
> **Estimated lesson time: 45 minutes**

LINQ to SQL Overview

LINQ to SQL allows a developer to embed queries in C# and VB.NET to access Microsoft SQL Server. Figure 8-1 shows the relationship between LINQ to SQL and its cousins, LINQ to DataSets, LINQ to Entities, LINQ to Objects, and LINQ to XML.

> **NOTE**
> The LINQ to SQL implementation provided by Microsoft is targeted at SQL Server databases, but any database vendor can implement a LINQ provider to its database, and there are open source projects that implement LINQ to MySQL, Progress, Oracle, and DB2.

To get a taste for LINQ to SQL, look at the following query, which uses the *VideoGameStore* database to select all customers starting with the letter *A*:

```vb
' VB
Dim db As New VideoGameStoreDBDataContext()

Dim query = From c In db.Customers _
        Where c.CustomerName.StartsWith("A") _
        Select c
```

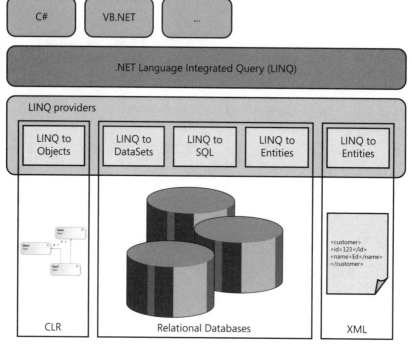

FIGURE 8-1 LINQ to SQL is one of the LINQ providers for relational data.

```
// C#
var db = new VideoGameStoreDBDataContext();

var query = from c in db.Customers
            where c.CustomerName.StartsWith( "A" )
            select c;
```

Any LINQ to SQL query uses a *DataContext* on which the query is performed, a query to define the selection that needs to occur on one or more tables and a result.

DataContext

The first step in the previous example creates a *VideoGameStoreDBContext*. *VideoGameStoreDB* is a class that inherits from *System.Data.Linq.DataContext*. *DataContext* is the source of all entities mapped over a database connection. It tracks changes that you made to all retrieved entities and maintains an identity cache that guarantees that entities retrieved more than one time are represented by using the same object instance.

In general, a *DataContext* instance is designed to last for one "unit of work"; however, your application defines that term. A *DataContext* is lightweight and is not expensive to create. A typical LINQ to SQL application creates *DataContext* instances at method scope or as a member of short-lived classes that represent a logical set of related database operations.

A *DataContext* can be used as a class in code, or the LINQ to SQL Designer in Visual Studio can be used to design a context which inherits from *DataContext*.

The *DataContext* is built on top of the standard ADO.NET classes, so managing connections can be left to the *DataContext* class, or an ADO.NET DbConnection can be used to create a *DataContext*.

It is possible to specify a connection when creating a *DataContext*. Therefore, it is also possible to share a connection across multiple contexts. One or more LINQ to SQL units of work can be placed inside a *TransactionScope* to enforce transactional integrity. See Chapter 4, "Updating Data," for more information on ADO.NET transactions.

DataContext can be used to work in a connected mode, but it also can work in a disconnected mode, where objects can be attached to the context after having been disconnected. You learn more about connected and disconnected mode in Lesson 2, "Updating Data."

Mapping

The result of the query needs to be mapped onto classes. There are two ways of implementing mapping:

- Using attributes
- Using an Extensible Markup Language (XML) mapping file

The first approach can be implemented manually, or the LINQ to SQL Designer can be used to create code that generates classes with attributes.

The code sample here shows the implementation of a *Supplier* class. The class has been adorned with attributes to supply the LINQ to SQL provider with information on how to map a column in the database to a class and field in C# / VB.NET.

The *TableAttribute* is used at class level to specify which database table the class needs to be mapped on, and the *ColumnAttribute* is used at property level to specify which column in the table the property needs to map on:

```vb
' VB
<Table(Name:="Supplier")> _
Public Class Supplier
    Private _id As Integer
    <Column(Name:="SupplierID")> _
    Public Property ID() As Integer
        Get
            Return _id
        End Get
        Set(ByVal value As Integer)
            _id = value
        End Set
    End Property
End Property
```

```
        Private _name As String
        <Column(Name:="SupplierName")> _
        Public Property Name() As String
            Get
                Return _name
            End Get
            Set(ByVal value As String)
                _name = value
            End Set
        End Property
    End Class


    Public Function GetSuppliers(ByVal name As String) As List(Of Supplier)
        Dim conn As New SqlConnection( cConnectionString )

        Dim db As New DataContext(conn)

        Dim Suppliers = db.GetTable(Of Supplier)()

        Dim query = From s In Suppliers _
                    Where s.Name = name _
                    Select s

        Return query.ToList()
    End Function


    // C#
    [Table(Name="Supplier")]
    public class Supplier
    {
        [Column(Name="SupplierID")]
        public int ID { get; set; }
        [Column(Name="SupplierName")]
        public string Name { get; set; }
    }


    public List<Supplier> GetSuppliers(string name)
    {
        SqlConnection conn = new SqlConnection( cConnectionString );

        var db = new DataContext( conn );

        Table<Supplier> Suppliers = db.GetTable<Supplier>();
```

```
    var query = from s in Suppliers
              where s.Name == name
              select s;

    return query.ToList();
}
```

This sample also demonstrates the use of a traditional ADO.NET *SqlConnection* object to specify to which database *DataContext* needs to connect.

Alternatively, the mapping can be specified in an XML mapping file. This allows for an implementation, also referred to as Plain Old CLR Objects (POCO). The advantage of an external mapping file is that any CLR object can be used, so it also works for any existing classes without the need to modify them. The code here demonstrates the use of the mapping file. Notice the absence of attributes on the *Supplier* class:

```
' VB
Public Class Supplier
    Private _id As Integer
    Public Property ID() As Integer
        Get
            Return _id
        End Get
        Set(ByVal value As Integer)
            _id = value
        End Set
    End Property

    Private _name As String
    Public Property Name() As String
        Get
            Return _name
        End Get
        Set(ByVal value As String)
            _name = value
        End Set
    End Property
End Class

Public Function GetSuppliers(ByVal name As String) As List(Of Supplier)
    Dim conn As New SqlConnection( cConnectionString )

    Dim xms = XmlMappingSource.FromUrl( "mapping.xml" )

    Dim db As New DataContext(conn, xms)

    Dim Suppliers = db.GetTable(Of Supplier)()
```

```vbnet
    Dim query = From s In Suppliers _
                Where s.Name = name _
                Select s

    Return query.ToList()
End Function
```

```csharp
// C#
public class Supplier
{
    public int ID { get; set; }
    public string Name { get; set; }
}

public List<Supplier> GetSuppliers( string name )
{
    SqlConnection conn = new SqlConnection( cConnectionString );

    XmlMappingSource xms = XmlMappingSource.FromUrl( "mapping.xml" );

    var db = new DataContext( conn, xms );

    Table<Supplier> Suppliers = db.GetTable<Supplier>();

    var query = from s in Suppliers
                where s.Name == name
                select s;

    return query.ToList();
}
```

The XML file contains the mapping between the database table and the CLR type:

```xml
<?xml version="1.0" encoding="utf-8"?>
<Database Name="VideoGameStoreDB"
          xmlns="http://schemas.microsoft.com/linqtosql/mapping/2007">
  <Table Name="dbo.Supplier" Member="Supplier">
    <Type Name="Supplier">
      <Column Name="SupplierID" Member="ID" />
      <Column Name="SupplierName" Member="Name"  />
    </Type>
  </Table>
</Database>
```

Creating a mapping document manually is a time-consuming, error-prone activity. Visual Studio includes a command-line tool named SQLMetal.exe that can be used to generate the mapping file based on a database schema.

Querying

The LINQ to SQL query is no different than any other LINQ query. The compiler parses the query, performs type checking, and compiles the query into an expression tree. For LINQ to SQL, the expression tree is then parsed into a SQL statement. The SQL statement is executed when the results of the query are accessed:

```vb
' VB
Public Function GetSuppliers(ByVal name As String) As List(Of Supplier)
    Dim conn As New SqlConnection( cConnectionString )

    Dim xms = XmlMappingSource.FromUrl( "mapping.xml" )

    Dim db As New DataContext(conn, xms)

    Dim Suppliers = db.GetTable(Of Supplier)()

    Dim query = From s In Suppliers _
                Where s.Name = name _
                Select s

    Return query.ToList()
End Function
```

```csharp
// C#
public List<Supplier> GetSuppliers( string name )
{
    SqlConnection conn = new SqlConnection( cConnectionString );

    XmlMappingSource xms = XmlMappingSource.FromUrl( "mapping.xml" );

    var db = new DataContext( conn, xms );

    Table<Supplier> Suppliers = db.GetTable<Supplier>();

    var query = from s in Suppliers
                where s.Name == name
                select s;

    return query.ToList();
}
```

In this sample, the variable *query* contains a reference to a *DataQuery* object that implements *IQueryably*. The SQL statement is not executed against the database until the *ToList()* function is called and the result of the query is retrieved and used to build a generic list of suppliers.

LINQ to SQL Designer

The LINQ to SQL Designer is a code-generating designer in Visual Studio that helps create classes and mappings to the classes. By dragging and dropping tables or stored procedures onto a design surface, this designer generates classes using mapping attributes to map tables and columns to the classes.

The generated classes are partial classes and can be extended, allowing for custom code to be added to the classes. A number of partial methods are also generated, allowing an event-like extensibility. For instance, for a *Customer* class with a *City* property, there are two partial methods: *OnCustomerCityChanging* and *OnCustomerCityChanged*. These methods allow custom code to be implemented and executed just before the property changes and right after the property has been changed.

A named context is also created, offering properties for every table in the context. The named context knows which connection string to use, so when using the context, the developer need not worry about the connection string.

The LINQ to SQL Designer is also capable of wrapping stored procedures, effectively allowing a stored procedure to be called directly on the data context as a method.

> **NOTE** **UDTS NOT SUPPORTED BY DESIGNER**
>
> The LINQ to SQL Designer does not support the use of user defined types (UDTs) as a column type.

 Quick Check

- Name the three ways to build a database connection using a *DataContext*.

Quick Check Answers

1. Provide the *DataContext* constructor with a connection string.

2. Provide the *DataContext* constructor with an ADO.NET *DbConnection* object.

3. Use the LINQ to SQL Designer to create a class that inherits from *DataContext* and hide the connection from you, allowing you to specify the connection string in the configuration file.

Sample: Using the LINQ to SQL Designer

It's time to look at how to use the LINQ to SQL Designer: The following steps demonstrate how to use it to generate code that allows access to the *VideoGameStoreDB* database.

1. In Visual Studio, start a new library project.

2. Add a new item to the project by right-clicking the project in the Solution Explorer and select Add New Item.

3. Next, choose for the Data category. Figure 8-2 shows the dialog box for selecting the LINQ to SQL Classes template.

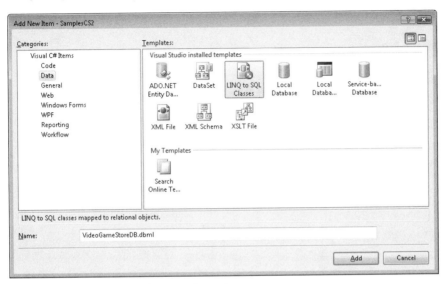

FIGURE 8-2 Add LINQ to SQL classes to the project.

4. Choose the 'LINQ to SQL Classes' template and name it **VideoGameStoreDB.dbml.** A new file is now added to the project and the LINQ to SQL Designer opens in Visual Studio, as shown in Figure 8-3.

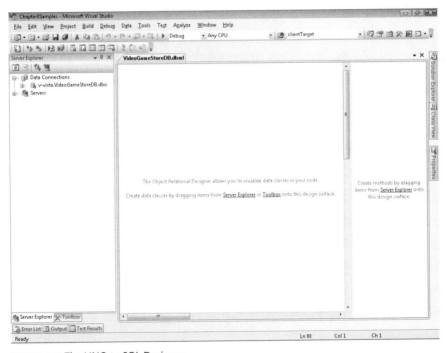

FIGURE 8-3 The LINQ to SQL Designer

5. Now that the LINQ to SQL Designer is open, the Server Explorer can be used to drag tables and stored procedures from the data connection onto the design surface.

Figure 8-4 shows the Product and ProductType tables on the design surface. Notice that the designer automatically perceives the foreign key relationship between Product and ProductType.

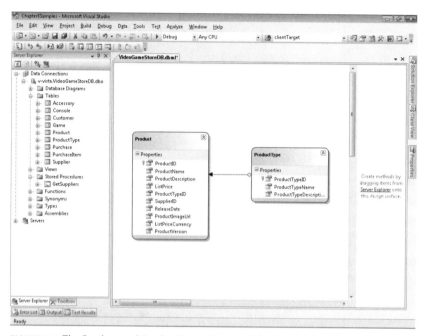

FIGURE 8-4 The Product and ProductType tables, and their relationship

6. By dragging tables from the data source to the design surface, the designer picks up what the data source is and generates code to set the connection string of *DataContext* automatically to that data source. Because *DataContext* can connect to only a single database, it stands to reason that the classes in a single Database Model (DBML) file all need to map to the same database. While adding the tables to the design surface, the designer automatically generates classes for a typed *DataContext*. The next step is to create a method that searches for products from a specific type, where the type name needs to contain a specific text. The following method does just that:

```vb
' VB
Public Function FindProducts(ByVal typename As String) As List(Of Product)
    Dim db = New VideoGameStoreDBDataContext()

    Dim query = From p In db.Products _
                Where p.ProductType.ProductTypeName Like typename _
                Select p

    Return query.ToList()
End Function
```

```csharp
// C#
public List<Product> FindProducts( string typename )
{
    var db = new VideoGameStoreDBDataContext();

    var query = from p in db.Products
                where p.ProductType.ProductTypeName.Contains( typename )
                select p;

    return query.ToList();
}
```

Notice the slight difference between VB.NET and C#. In VB.NET, there is an extra keyword, *LIKE*, whereas C# requires the use of the extension method *Contains*.

7. Now create a unit test, set a breakpoint on the line containing the return statement, and call the *FindProducts* method. Now look in the locals window to see the value of *query*. As shown in Figure 8-5, the debugger shows the SQL statement that the LINQ to SQL provider has generated based on the expression that has been assigned to the *query* variable. That SQL statement is executed against the database the moment that the *ToList()* method is called.

FIGURE 8-5 The debugger shows the generated SQL statement

LAB   **Using LINQ to SQL**

In this lab, you create a class library to retrieve data from the *VideoGameStoreDB* database using the LINQ to SQL Designer. You create a function to retrieve data and build a unit test to see if the code in the class library performs as expected. You need to have the *VideoGame-StoreDB* database installed to perform these exercises. Each exercise builds on the previous one. You can install the complete solution containing the code for all the exercises from the Code folder on the companion CD.

EXERCISE 1   Build a Model

In this exercise, you create a class library that implements a data access strategy based on LINQ to SQL.

1. Start a new Class Library project named *DataAccess*.

2. Add a new item of type *LINQ to SQL classes* to the project and name it **VideoGameStoreDB.dbml.**

3. Open the Server Explorer, add a data connection to the *VideoGameStoreDB* database, expand the database node, and browse to the tables in the database.

4. Drag the Customer, Purchase, PurchaseItem, and Product tables onto the design surface.

    Your designer should look as shown here.

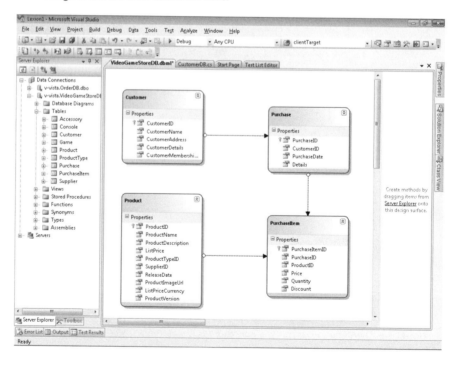

EXERCISE 2   Using the Model to Retrieve Data

In this exercise, you continue with the solution from Exercise 1. Alternatively, you can use the code for Exercise 1 from the companion CD. The aim of this exercise is to implement a search algorithm for finding customers in the *VideoGameStoreDB* database.

1. Add a class to the project named *CustomerDB*.

2. Add a method to the class named *FindCustomers* by performing the following steps:

    a. Let it have the parameter *productName (string)*;

    b. Create an instance of *VideoGameStoreDBDataContext*;

    c. Create a query to select all customer objects that have purchased a product with the specified parameter, productName;

    d. Use the query to return a generic list of customers;

    e. Add a trace statement to output the query to the Output window.

Your code should look like this:

```vb
' VB
Public Function FindCustomers(ByVal productName As String) As List(Of Customer)
    Dim db = New VideoGameStoreDBDataContext()

    Dim query = From c In db.Customers _
                Join pu In db.Purchases On c.CustomerID Equals pu.CustomerID _
                Join i In db.PurchaseItems On pu.PurchaseID Equals i.PurchaseID _
                Join p In db.Products On i.ProductID Equals p.ProductID _
                Where p.ProductName Like productName _
                Select c

    Return query.ToList()
End Function
```

```csharp
// C#
public class CustomerDB
{
public List<Customer> FindCustomers( string productName )
{
    var db = new VideoGameStoreDBDataContext();

    var query = from c in db.Customers
                join pu in db.Purchases on c.CustomerID equals pu.CustomerID
                join i in db.PurchaseItems on pu.PurchaseID equals i.PurchaseID
                join p in db.Products on i.ProductID equals p.ProductID
                where p.ProductName.Contains( productName )
                select c;
```

```
        Trace.WriteLine( query.ToString() );

        return query.ToList();
    }
}
```

3. Create a unit test by right-clicking the *FindCustomer* method.

4. Implement the unit test by searching for any customer that ordered a product named *Halo*. There are no results because the Purchases table is empty. We get back to this in Lesson 2.

   Your code should look like this:

   ```
   ' VB
   <TestMethod()> _
   Public Sub FindCustomersTest()
       Dim target As CustomerDB = New CustomerDB()
       Dim productName As String = "Halo"

       Dim actual As List(Of Customer)
       actual = target.FindCustomers(productName)

       Assert.AreEqual(0, actual.Count)
   End Sub
   ```

   ```
   // C#
    [TestMethod()]
   public void FindCustomersTest()
   {
       CustomerDB target = new CustomerDB();
       string productName = "Halo";

       List<Customer> actual;
       actual = target.FindCustomers( productName );

       Assert.AreEqual( 0, actual.Count );  // no purchases in the database
   }
   ```

Lesson Summary

- LINQ to SQL consists of an extension to LINQ where the expression embedded in the C# or VB.NET language is evaluated at run time to create a SQL statement.
- LINQ to SQL allows for embedding type-safe SQL statement generation.
- The LINQ to SQL Designer in Visual Studio helps generate classes to facilitate type-safe database querying.

Lesson Review

You can use the following questions to test your knowledge of the information in Lesson 1, "Introduction to LINQ to SQL." The questions also are available on the companion CD of this book if you prefer to review them in electronic form.

> **NOTE ANSWERS**
>
> Answers to these questions and explanations of why each answer choice is correct or incorrect are located in the "Answers" section at the end of the book.

1. LINQ to SQL is which of the following?

   A. A code generation feature of Visual Studio

   B. A CLR feature for connecting to SQL Server

   C. A feature of SQL Server for allowing C# to maximize performance

   D. A feature of SQL Server for allowing VB.NET to maximize performance

2. Which of the following statements is true?

   A. *CommitChanges* is a method of *SqlDataContext.*

   B. *CommitChanges* is a method of *DataContext.*

   C. *CommitChanges* is a method of *DbDataContext.*

   D. *CommitChanges* is a method of *OleDbDataContext.*

3. Which of the following statements is true?

   A. LINQ to SQL works with any database.

   B. LINQ to SQL works with SQL Server.

   C. LINQ to SQL is a CLR feature.

   D. LINQ to SQL is a SQL Server feature.

Lesson 2: Updating Data

In this lesson, we examine the options for updating data in a SQL Server database using LINQ to SQL. Both dynamic SQL and stored procedures can be used to achieve a database update.

> **After this lesson, you will be able to:**
> - Use LINQ to SQL to update data
> - Use stored procedures in combination with LINQ to SQL
>
> **Estimated lesson time: 30 minutes**

Using Dynamic SQL to Update Data

The LINQ to SQL providers for SQL Server examine the managed code query and use the available information to build a SQL statement dynamically. This statement is performed on the database, resulting in a collection of managed objects. Retrieving data is usually paired with updating data, and performing updated LINQ to SQL supports two scenarios: connected mode and disconnected mode.

Updating Data in Connected Mode

In addition to managing the connection to a specific SQL Server database, the *DataContext* implements a service known as *object tracking*. Object tracking is the change tracking system that LINQ to SQL provides to detect whether an object has been changed after it has been retrieved from the database.

When working with object tracking, it is important to realize that *DataContext* needs to be aware of every insert, update, and delete to generate the appropriate SQL statement.

In connected mode, all the tracking is performed by the data context. In disconnected mode, things get a little more complicated. The code here shows how to have *DataContext* track changes on a collection of data and write the updates to the database:

```vb
' VB
Public Sub UpdateProducts()

    Using db As New VideoGameStoreDBDataContext()

        Dim query = From p In db.Products _
                    Select p

        For Each product In query
            product.ListPrice = product.ListPrice * 1.1
            If product.ListPrice > 400 Then
                db.Products.DeleteOnSubmit(product)
            End If
        Next
```

```vbnet
        Dim newProduct = New Product With { _
        .ProductName = "Travian", _
        .ProductDescription = "Online Game", _
        .ListPrice = 20, _
        .ListPriceCurrency = "$", _
        .ProductTypeID = 1 _
        }

        db.Products.InsertOnSubmit(newProduct)

        db.SubmitChanges()
    End Using

End Sub
```

```csharp
// C#
public void UpdateProducts()
{
    using ( var db = new VideoGameStoreDBDataContext() )
    {
        var query =  from p in db.Products
                     select p;

        foreach(var product in query)
        {
            product.ListPrice = product.ListPrice * 1.1;
            if ( product.ListPrice > 400 )
            {
                db.Products.DeleteOnSubmit( product );
            }
        }

        ProductType game = (from pt in db.ProductTypes
                            where pt.ProductTypeName == "Game"
                            select pt).Single();

        Product newProduct = new Product()
        {
            ProductName = "Travian",
            ListPrice = 20,
            ProductType = game,
            ProductDescription = "Online Game",
            ProductTypeID = 1,
            ListPriceCurrency = "$"
        };
        newProduct.ListPrice = 5;
```

```
        db.Products.InsertOnSubmit( newProduct );
        db.SubmitChanges();
    }
}
```

This code shows how to use *VideoGameStoreDataContext* to query a list of products. Next, the price for each product is increased by 10 percent and any product that costs more than $400 is deleted. Finally, a new product is added. A number of dynamic SQL statements are generated, which are described in the next sections.

SELECT STATEMENT

The generated *SELECT* statement looks as follows:

```
SELECT [t0].[ProductID], [t0].[ProductName], [t0].[ProductDescription],
[t0].[ListPrice], [t0].[ProductTypeID], [t0].[SupplierID], [t0].[ReleaseDate],
[t0].[ProductImageUrl], [t0].[ListPriceCurrency], [t0].[ProductVersion]
FROM [dbo].[Product] AS [t0]
```

UPDATE STATEMENT

For each product, a variation of the following *UPDATE* statement is executed when SubmitChanges is called. Notice that the query uses the timestamp (= row version) on the product object in the WHERE clause to implement optimistic concurrency. A *SELECT* statement is generated to update the *timestamp* property of the product after the product has been updated:

```
exec sp_executesql N'UPDATE [dbo].[Product]
SET [ListPrice] = @p2
WHERE ([ProductID] = @p0) AND ([ProductVersion] = @p1)

SELECT [t1].[ProductVersion]
FROM [dbo].[Product] AS [t1]
WHERE ((@@ROWCOUNT) > 0) AND ([t1].[ProductID] = @p3)',
N'@p0 int,@p1 timestamp,@p2 float,
@p3 int',@p0=4,@p1=0x0000000000001696,@p2=39.930000000000007,@p3=4

SELECT [t1].[ProductVersion]'
FROM [dbo].[Product] AS [t1]
WHERE ((@@ROWCOUNT) > 0) AND ([t1].[ProductID] = @p3)',
N'@p0 int,@p1 timestamp,@p2 float,
@p3 int',@p0=4,@p1=0x0000000000001696,@p2=39.930000000000007,@p3=4
```

DELETE STATEMENT

The generated *DELETE* statement looks as follows:

```
exec sp_executesql N'DELETE FROM [dbo].[Product] WHERE ([ProductID] = @p0) AND
([ProductVersion] = @p1)',N'@p0 int,@p1 timestamp',@p0=2,@p1=0x00000000000019A1
```

INSERT STATEMENT

Again, notice that after the *INSERT* statement, the table is queried to return the timestamp of the product:

```
exec sp_executesql N'INSERT INTO [dbo].[Product]([ProductName], [ProductDescription],
[ListPrice], [ProductTypeID], [SupplierID], [ReleaseDate], [ProductImageUrl],
[ListPriceCurrency])
VALUES (@p0, @p1, @p2, @p3, @p4, @p5, @p6, @p7)

SELECT [t0].[ProductID], [t0].[ProductVersion]
FROM [dbo].[Product] AS [t0]
WHERE [t0].[ProductID] = (SCOPE_IDENTITY())',N'@p0 nvarchar(7),@p1 nvarchar(11),
@p2 float,@p3 int,@p4 int,@p5 datetime,@p6 nvarchar(4000),
@p7 nvarchar(1)',@p0=N'Travian',
@p1=N'Online Game',@p2=5,@p3=1,@p4=NULL,@p5=NULL,@p6=NULL,@p7=N'$'
```

Note that *SubmitChanges* first executes all *INSERT* statements, then all *UPDATE* statements, and finally all *DELETE* statements. The updates are not performed as a single transaction. If transactional behavior is needed, then the *SubmitChanges* method needs to be placed within a *TransactionScope*. See Chapter 4 for more information on implementing transactions.

> **NOTE** **DISABLE OBJECT TRACKING**
>
> The object tracking service can be disabled if you intend to perform read-only actions with your *DataContext*. To disable object tracking, use the *ObjectTrackingEnabled* property on the *DataContext* and set it to False.

Updating Data in Disconnected Mode

It is not always possible to select and update data using the same *DataContext* instance. A service-oriented application is most likely to have services where one service returns a collection of objects and a different service that updates the database based on a collection of objects. The complexity now lies in how to track changes. The solution lies in telling *DataContext* which action you wish to perform on an object, or collection of objects.

Updating Disconnected Data

To update a row in the database, an object can be reconnected to a *DataContext* using the *Attach* method. After attaching the object the *SubmitChanges* method can be called to generate dynamically the SQL statement needed to perform the update on the database, as shown in the following code:

```
' VB
Public Sub UpdateProducts( ByVal products As List<Product> )
    Using db = new VideoGameStoreDBDataContext()
        db.Products.AttachAll( products )
```

```
      db.SubmitChanges()
   End Using
End Sub
```

```
// C#
public void UpdateProducts( List<Product> products )
{
    using ( var db = new VideoGameStoreDBDataContext() )
    {
        db.Products.AttachAll( products );
        db.SubmitChanges();
    }
}
```

Deleting Disconnected Data

DataContext has no implicit way of detecting which objects in a collection need to be deleted. The only way to have *DataContext* delete rows in the database is to tell *DataContext* which objects need to be deleted using the *DeleteOnSubmit* or *DeleteAllOnSubmit* method, as shown in the following code:

```
' VB
Public Sub DeleteProducts( ByVal products As List<Product> )
   Using db = new VideoGameStoreDBDataContext()
       db.Products.DeleteAllOnSubmit( products )
       db.SubmitChanges()
   End Using
End Sub
```

```
// C#
public void DeleteProducts( List<Product> products )
{
    using ( var db = new VideoGameStoreDBDataContext() )
    {
        db.Products.DeleteAllOnSubmit( products );
        db.SubmitChanges();
    }
}
```

Inserting Disconnected Data

Again, *DataContext* has no way of implicitly detecting which objects are new and need to be inserted, rather than updated. The *InsertOnSubmit* and *InsertAllOnSubmit* methods are used for indicating which objects need to be inserted into the database, as shown in the following code:

```
' VB
Public Sub InsertProducts( ByVal products As List<Product> )
   Using db = new VideoGameStoreDBDataContext()
```

```
        db.Products.InsertAllOnSubmit( products )
        db.SubmitChanges()
    End Using
End Sub

// C#
public void InsertProducts( List<Product> products )
{
    using ( var db = new VideoGameStoreDBDataContext() )
    {
        db.Products.InsertAllOnSubmit( products );
        db.SubmitChanges();
    }
}
```

Designing Disconnected Services

The previous sections show the code needed to have LINQ to SQL perform inserts, updates, and deletes in a disconnect scenario. Implementing three separate services makes it hard to manage transactions across these three services. A common solution is to add a state property on the entity object that can be used to track whether an object is new or needs to be deleted. This allows for a single service to be implemented, in which the service iterates over the collection of objects and based on the state property to insert, attach, or delete an object.

Using Stored Procedures

In addition to being able to generate dynamic SQL statements, the LINQ to SQL provider is capable of mapping stored procedures. This is fully supported by the LINQ to SQL Designer.

The LINQ to SQL Designer allows you to drag stored procedures from the Server Explorer window onto the surface of the designer. Using this technique, SELECT, INSERT, UPDATE, and DELETE stored procedures can be added to the data context.

Figure 8-6 shows the LINQ to SQL design surface in Visual Studio; the Server Explorer is docked to the left side of the window. Within the LINQ to SQL design surface the right side of the surface shows the stored procedures that are mapped to this data context.

Stored procedures can be selected from the Server Explorer and dragged to the design surface, adding the procedure to the list of available procedures.

The LINQ to SQL Designer is not able to determine whether a stored procedure is related in any way to one of the existing types in the data context. This needs to be configured explicitly.

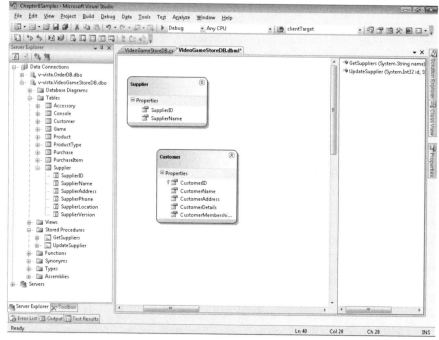

FIGURE 8-6 Mapping stored procedures using the LINQ to SQL Designer

The stored procedure has a *Return Type* property, which by default is set to Auto Generated Type, meaning that a new unique type is generated. However, this can be changed into any of the tables on the design surface. Note that the columns returned by the stored procedure must match with the columns of the table for the mapping to succeed.

It is also possible to use stored procedures to perform inserts, updates, and deletes. Figure 8-6 shows that a stored procedure, UpdateSupplier, has been added to the data context. The *Update* property of the Supplier table needs to be changed for any update on the Supplier table to be performed using that stored procedure (rather than dynamic SQL). Figure 8-7 shows how the behavior of the generated code for updates can be modified to map to the stored procedure. Each parameter of the stored procedure needs to be mapped to a property on the class.

After mapping the stored procedure, the table in the data context can be used in the same manner as before, but now, instead of generating dynamic SQL when calling the *SubmitChanges* method, the LINQ to SQL provider calls the specified stored procedure.

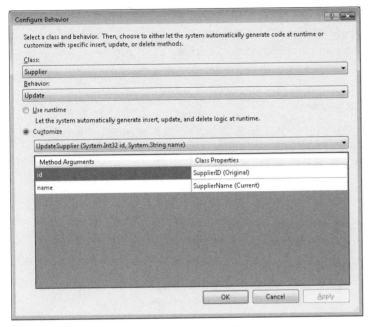

FIGURE 8-7 Mapping parameters to class properties.

Sample: Adding Customers

The following sample uses the *VideoGameStoreDB* database to create a data context and add a customer using a stored procedure. Perform the following steps:

1. Create a console application named *AddCustomer*.

2. Add a LINQ to SQL data context named *VideoGameStoreDB*.

3. Open Server Explorer and, if not present, add a data connection to the *VideoGameStoreDB* database (included on the companion CD).

4. Drag the customer table onto the design surface. Remove all properties except *CustomerID* and *CustomerName*.

5. Create a stored procedure named *AddCustomer* as follows:

```
CREATE PROCEDURE dbo.AddCustomer
  (
  @name nvarchar(50),
  @id int OUTPUT
  )
AS
BEGIN
  INSERT INTO Customer (CustomerName)
  VALUES (@name)

  SELECT @id = SCOPE_IDENTITY()
END
```

6. Drag the stored procedure from Server Explorer to the right side of the LINQ to SQL Designer.

7. Change the *Return Type* property of the stored procedure to *Customer.*

8. Change the *Insert* property of the Customer table to map to the AddCustomer stored procedure. Map the *CustomerID* property to the *id* parameter and *CustomerName* property to the *name* parameter.

9. In the *Main* method of the program, add code to retrieve a name from the command line and use the name to add a customer entry. Output the customer identity after you're done. Your code should look like this:

```vb
' VB
Module Module1

    Sub Main()
        Console.Write("Enter the name of the customer: ")
        Dim name = Console.ReadLine()

        Dim c = New Customer() With {.CustomerName = name}

        Using db = New VideoGameStoreDBDataContext()
            db.Customers.InsertOnSubmit(c)
            db.SubmitChanges()
        End Using

        Console.WriteLine("Customer with id {0} added.", c.CustomerID)
        Console.ReadLine()
    End Sub

End Module
```

```csharp
// C#
class Program
{
    static void Main( string[] args )
    {
        Console.Write( "Enter the name of the customer: " );
        string name = Console.ReadLine();

        Customer c = new Customer() { CustomerName = name };

        using ( var db = new VideoGameStoreDBDataContext() )
        {
            db.Customers.InsertOnSubmit( c );
            db.SubmitChanges();
        }
```

```
            Console.WriteLine( "Customer with id {0} added.", c.CustomerID );
            Console.ReadLine();
        }
    }
```

 Quick Check

- How do you manage transactions when using LINQ to SQL?

Quick Check Answer

- Use the *TransactionScope* class to wrap all database actions within a single transaction. This causes all changes performed within the *SubmitChanges()* method to be rolled back if any of the updates fail.

LAB   Inserting Data Using LINQ to SQL

In this lab, you create a class library to insert data into the database using LINQ to SQL. You insert a new customer with a new purchase. In the second exercise, you expand on the first exercise and use a stored procedure for inserting the purchase details. You need the *VideoGameStoreDB* database to complete these exercises. That, as well as the sources to the solutions to these exercises, can be installed from the Code folder on the companion CD.

EXERCISE 1   Insert a New Customer with Purchase

In this exercise, you create a *CreateQuickPurchase* method that takes two parameters, *customerName* and *purchaseDetails*, and persist these two objects to the database using a LINQ to SQL data context.

1. Open a new class library project named *DataAccess*.
2. Add a new item of type *LINQ to SQL classes,* named *VideoGameStoreDB*.
3. Use Server Explorer to connect to the *VideoGameStoreDB* database.
4. Using the DataSet Designer and Server Explorer, add the Customer and Purchase table to the design surface of *VideoGameStoreDB* by dragging them from Server Explorer to the LINQ to SQL Designer.

   Notice how the relationship between the two tables is created automatically.
5. Add a new class named *CustomerDB* to the project.
6. Within the class, add a method named *CreateQuickPurchase*. Within the method, perform the following steps:

   a. Create an instance of a new customer and initialize its properties.
   b. Create an instance of a new purchase and initialize its properties.

c. Create a *DataContext*.

d. Create a *TransactionScope*. To do this, you need to add an assembly reference to System.Transactions.dll.

e. Update the database within the *TransactionScope*. Don't forget to call the *Complete* method when doing this.

Your code should look like this:

```vb
' VB
Imports System.Transactions

Public Class CustomerDB
    Public Sub CreateQuickPurchase(ByVal customerName As String, _
                                     ByVal purchaseDetails As String)
        Dim customer = New Customer() With { _
        .CustomerName = customerName, _
        .CustomerAddress = "PO Box 999", _
        .CustomerDetails = "Chapter 8 Lesson 2" _
        }

        Dim purchase = New Purchase() With { _
        .Details = purchaseDetails, _
        .PurchaseDate = DateTime.Now, _
        .Customer = customer _
        }

        Using db = New VideoGameStoreDBDataContext()
            Using ts = New TransactionScope()
                db.Customers.InsertOnSubmit(customer)
                db.Purchases.InsertOnSubmit(purchase)
                ts.Complete()
            End Using
        End Using
    End Sub
End Class
```

```csharp
// C#
public class CustomerDB
{
    public void CreateQuickPurchase( string customerName, string purchaseDetails )
    {
        var customer = new Customer()
        {
            CustomerName = customerName,
            CustomerAddress = "PO BOX 999",
            CustomerDetails = "Chapter 8 Lesson 2"
        };
```

```
        var purchase = new Purchase()
        {
            Details = purchaseDetails,
            PurchaseDate = DateTime.Now,
            Customer = customer
        };

        using ( var db = new VideoGameStoreDBDataContext() )
        {
            using ( var ts = new TransactionScope() )
            {
                db.Customers.InsertOnSubmit( customer );
                db.Purchases.InsertOnSubmit( purchase );
                db.SubmitChanges();
                ts.Complete();
            }
        }
    }
}
```

7. Create a unit test to test the *CreateQuickPurchase* method.

Your unit test should look like this:

```
' VB
<TestMethod()> _
    Public Sub CreateQuickPurchaseTest()
    Dim target As CustomerDB = New CustomerDB ' TODO: Initialize to an
        appropriate value
    target.CreateQuickPurchase("Blomsma", "Pre-order Halo 7")
End Sub
```

```
// C#
[TestMethod()]
public void CreateQuickPurchaseTest()
{
    CustomerDB target = new CustomerDB();
    target.CreateQuickPurchase( "Blomsma", "Pre-order Halo 7" );
}
```

8. Run the unit test, and check the contents of the database using Server Explorer.

EXERCISE 2   Using Stored Procedures

In this exercise, you continue with the code from Exercise 1 and add the use of a stored procedure for updating the purchase. Use the DataAccess project created in Exercise 1, or copy the project from the solution on the companion CD.

1. Create a new stored procedure named *AddPurchase*. It should look like this:

```
CREATE PROCEDURE dbo.AddPurchase
    (
@customerID int,
@purchaseDate datetime,
@purchaseDetails ntext,
@purchaseID int OUTPUT
    )
AS
BEGIN
INSERT INTO Purchase (CustomerID, PurchaseDate, Details)
VALUES (@customerID, @purchaseDate, @purchaseDetails)

SELECT @purchaseID = SCOPE_IDENTITY()
END
```

2. Open the VideoGameStoreDB.dbml file.

3. Drag the AddPurchase stored procedure from Server Explorer onto the right side of the LINQ to SQL Designer.

4. Change the *Update* property on the *Purchase* class to map to the AddPurchase stored procedure.

5. Run the unit test again and check the database.

6. Now start SQL Profiler. The profiler can be accessed from the Tools menu in the Microsoft SQL Server Management.

7. Start a new trace.

8. Run the unit test again and check the SQL statements executed against the database. Notice that the AddPurchase stored procedure is used to insert the purchase.

Lesson Summary

- LINQ expressions lead to dynamically generated SQL statements that are executed against a SQL Server database.
- The LINQ to SQL Designer supports mapping of objects to stored procedures, as well as mapping of objects to tables.

Lesson Review

You can use the following questions to test your knowledge of the information in Lesson 2, "Updating Data." The questions also are available on the companion CD of this book if you prefer to review them in electronic form.

1. Which of the following is true?

   A. *DataContext.SubmitChanges()* performs all database updates in a single transaction.

   B. *DataContext.SubmitChanges()* performs all *INSERT* statements in a single transaction.

   C. *DataContext.SubmitChanges()* never deletes rows in the database; it only performs updates.

   D. *DataContext.SubmitChanges()* does not roll back changes if an error occurs.

2. Which of the following statements are true? (Choose all that apply.)

   A. LINQ to SQL can track changes in connected mode.

   B. LINQ to SQL can track changes in connected mode only when using the *DataContext.Attach* method.

   C. LINQ to SQL can track changes in disconnected mode only when using the *DataContext.Attach* method.

   D. LINQ to SQL can track changes in disconnected mode.

Chapter Review

To practice and reinforce the skills you learned in this chapter further, you can do any or all of the following:

- Review the chapter summary.
- Review the list of key terms introduced in this chapter.
- Complete the case scenario. This scenario sets up a real-world situation involving the topics of this chapter and asks you to create a solution.
- Complete the suggested practices.
- Take a practice test.

Chapter Summary

- LINQ to SQL is an implementation of an extension, allowing access to relational databases using the LINQ syntax.
- LINQ to SQL helps developers to implement a data access layer using a visual designer that helps map database tables to CLR objects.
- LINQ to SQL can generate dynamic SQL statements to query and update a SQL Server database.
- LINQ to SQL offers support for mapping *UPDATE, INSERT,* and *DELETE* statements to stored procedures.

Key Terms

Do you know what these key terms mean? You can check your answers by looking up the terms in the glossary at the end of the book.

- CLR
- Database transaction
- LINQ

Case Scenario

In the following case scenario, you apply what you've learned about how to use *LINQ to SQL* to retrieve data from a database. You can find answers to the questions posed in this scenario in the "Answers" section at the end of this book.

Case Scenario: Implementing a Data Access Layer

The company you work for has decided that it wants to develop a couple of support tools for monitoring an enterprise application.

In interviews, these people have made the following statements:

IT MANAGER

"We have a huge investment in our enterprise resource planning system, but we need a couple of easy-to-maintain tools for monitoring some of the tables in the database and performing some basic maintenance tasks. The application uses a SQL Server database."

CFO

"These tools are for maintenance only and should be easy and cheap to develop."

QUESTION

Answer the following question for your manager:

- What kind of technology should we use for implementing data access to the database?

Suggested Practices

To help you master the exam objectives presented in this chapter, complete the following tasks.

Using LINQ to SQL in a Windows Application

- **Practice 1**   Use the *VideoGameStoreDB* database to create a Microsoft Windows application that uses LINQ to SQL to retrieve a list of products and bind the list to a *DataGrid* in the user interface. Add a button to the form that takes the list and persists any changes back to the database.

- **Practice 2**   Expand on Practice 1 to support inserts and deletes. Implement a custom property on the generated *Product* class using the partial class (double-click the class in the LINQ to SQL Designer) and use it to track changes to the object.

Take a Practice Test

The practice tests on this book's companion CD offer many options. For example, you can test yourself on just the content covered in this chapter, or you can test yourself on the entire 70-561 certification exam content. You can set up the test so that it closely simulates the experience of taking a certification exam, or you can set it up in study mode, which allows you to look at the correct answers and explanations after you answer each question.

> **NOTE   PRACTICE TESTS**
>
> For details about all the available practice test options, see the section entitled "How to Use the Practice Tests," in the Introduction to this book.

CHAPTER 9

Using the Entity Framework

For many, this book may be just an introduction to the ADO.NET Entity Framework. It is worth taking a moment to step back and look at what the Entity Framework is, what it does, and why it is useful. We do that in this chapter. The answer to why it is useful should become clear as the chapter progresses.

In essence, the Entity Framework is an evolution of the way data and data structures are consumed, handled, and manipulated. A data consumer would normally require a working knowledge of the Entity-Relationship schematic in its native form to understand how to access and manipulate it. This means, for example, that the relationship between a Product table and a Customer table would need to be understood and navigated at query level to join the tables based upon a key of some kind to consume the data. An *Entity Data Model (EDM)* is generated by the Entity Framework based upon selected database entities, from which point instead of accessing and querying the data model, the EDM is accessed and queried instead.

This chapter examines how to use the Entity Framework to generate and implement an EDM and how to query the model.

Exam objectives in this chapter:

- Define and implement an EDM.
- Query data by using Object Services.
- Map data by using the EntitySQL language.
- Access entity data by using the EntityClient Provider.

Lesson in this chapter:

Before You Begin

To complete the lessons in this chapter, you must have:

- A computer that meets or exceeds the minimum hardware requirements listed in the Introduction section at the beginning of the book

- Microsoft Visual Studio 2008 Professional edition installed on your computer, along with the Microsoft .NET Framework 3.5 (Service Pack 1)

- An understanding of Microsoft Visual Basic or C# syntax and familiarity with .NET Framework 3.5 (Service Pack 1)

- A relational database, such as a recent version of Microsoft SQL Server

 REAL WORLD

James Wightman

When I first demonstrated the ADO.NET Entity Framework to a highly esteemed colleague—and close friend—I watched as his eyes darted across the monitor, taking in the reams of new information I was providing. Although he was initially impressed with the rapidity and ease with which I was generating an EDM, his look quickly turned to awe when I began bashing out object queries using LINQ to Entities and EntitySQL to interrogate the entities.

"It would take weeks to generate this kind of object model by hand," he said. And he was right. Then he continued, "And you still wouldn't get it right the first time!." Rapidly creating a high-performance EDM is the very least of the tricks the Entity Framework has up its sleeve, as this chapter shows.

Lesson 1: Generating and Querying an Entity Data Model

Using the ADO.NET Entity Framework to generate a queryable and updateable EDM opens the door to the world of Object Relational Mapping to the Visual Studio age. In theory, the developer could stop at generating the EDM and use it successfully and productively in its standard, generated form. The Entity Framework offers much more than this, however. It offers customization, optimization, and extensibility features that change it from merely a useful technology to an essential one.

> **After this lesson, you will be able to:**
> - Describe the Entity Framework and why it is used
> - Generate and update the EDM
> - Use Object Services to query the EDM
> - Use the *EntityClient* provider to access Entity data
>
> **Estimated lesson time: 60 minutes**

Defining the Entity Data Model

There are two methods available to generate an EDM. For those wishing to stay within Visual Studio, an ADO.NET EDM item can be added to a project. If a command-line approach is preferred, the EDM Generator tool can be used. Both methods are perfectly valid ways to generate an EDM and have the same result.

The first method requires adding a new project item to a project in Visual Studio. Figure 9-1 shows the Add New Item window, which is accessed by right-clicking the project in Solution Explorer and selecting Add, New Item.

Once you click Add, the Entity Data Model Wizard opens, which provides easy configuration of the EDM to be generated. The EDM is created in the project as a .edmx file. At this point, you can choose an empty model, which allows you to define the EDM manually. However, choosing the Generate From Database option moves the wizard to the next page, entitled 'Choose your Data Connection', where a data connection can be specified.

This page highlights a new concept that requires discussion—the *Entity* connection string. The majority of the *Entity* connection string is used to provide connection information to the data source, which means that part of the value is easily recognizable. The additional key-value pair in use is the metadata key, as shown here:

```
metadata=res://*/VideoGameStoreDb.csdl|res://*/VideoGameStoreDb.ssdl|res
://*/VideoGameStoreDb.msl;provider=System.Data.SqlClient;provider
connection string="Data Source=JIM-PC;Initial
Catalog=VideoGameStoreDB;Integrated Security=True"
```

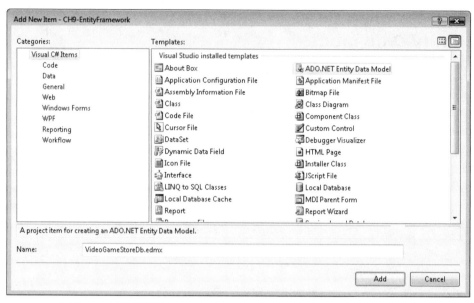

FIGURE 9-1 Adding an ADO.NET EDM to a project

Three metadata files are required to support an EDM, and they get configured as the model is generated. The three metadata files are incredibly important because they are fundamental to the operation of the EDM. They are described in Table 9-1.

TABLE 9-1 EDM Metadata

METADATA SPECIFICATION	DESCRIPTION
CSDL	This specification uses the *Conceptual Schema Definition Language (CSDL)*, which is used to define the entities, associations, sets, and containers of the object model.
SSDL	This metadata uses the *Store Schema Definition Language (SSDL)* to describe the storage container, which is used to persist data for applications using the generated EDM.
MSL	This metadata uses the *Mapping Specification Language (MSL)* and serves as the bridge between the CSDL and SSDL metadata. The MSL metadata maps the declarations in the CSDL file to tables defined in the SSDL file.

It is worth identifying at this point that the Entity Framework metadata artifacts listed in Table 9-1 are stored inside the EDMX file and are not generally viewable.

The generated metadata is relatively straightforward, however—the following snippet shows an example of the CSDL file, which in this case is the definition for the *VideoGameStoreDB Accessory* entity type, as follows:

```
<EntityType Name="Accessory">
    <Key>
       <PropertyRef Name="ProductID" />
    </Key>
    <Property Name="ProductID" Type="Int32" Nullable="false" />
    <Property Name="SystemName" Type="String" Nullable="false"
    MaxLength="100" Unicode="true" FixedLength="false" />
    <NavigationProperty Name="Product"
        Relationship="EdmGenModel.FK_Accessory_Product" FromRole="Accessory"
        ToRole="Product" />
</EntityType>
```

This example shows part of the SSDL file:

```
<EntityType Name="Accessory">
   <Key>
        <PropertyRef Name="ProductID" />
</Key>
<Property Name="ProductID" Type="int" Nullable="false" />
<Property Name="SystemName" Type="nvarchar" Nullable="false"
    MaxLength="100" />
    </EntityType>
```

Finally, this example shows the MSL file:

```
<EntitySetMapping Name="Accessory" StoreEntitySet="Accessory"
   TypeName="EdmGenModel.Accessory">
<ScalarProperty Name="ProductID" ColumnName="ProductID" />
<ScalarProperty Name="SystemName" ColumnName="SystemName" />
   </EntitySetMapping>
```

Notice how, in the previous metadata samples, the MSL metadata is used to map the CSDL definition to the SSDL definition.

The final page of the Entity Data Model Wizard provides the facility to select the database objects that are required in the EDM. In most cases, all the database objects get selected to be included in the model. This page also allows the configuration of the *Model* namespace. Once you click Finish, Visual Studio adds all necessary assembly references, generates the EDM, and opens the model in graphical format in the designer window. The EDM diagram for *VideoGameStoreDb* is shown as Figure 9-2, in the Data Model Designer.

With a properly designed and implemented database, the Entity Data Model wizard should easily identify the relationships between tables. If, after reviewing the model, there is an *Association* or *Entity* missing, the Entity Framework Designer toolbox can be used to add them.

When working with the Entity Framework Designer, a new window is available called the Model Browser. Figure 9-3 shows the Model Browser window.

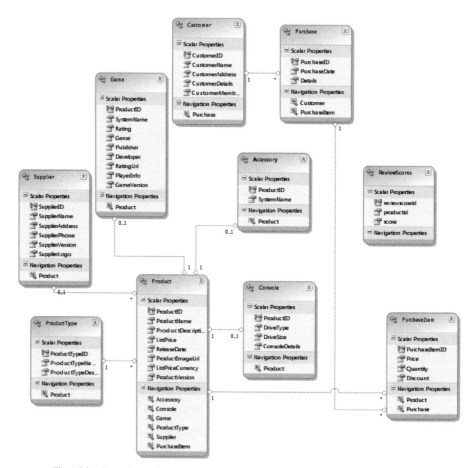

FIGURE 9-2 The *VideoGameStoreDb* EDM diagram

FIGURE 9-3 The Model Browser

Similar to Solution Explorer and the Class View, every type of object in the EDM can be accessed via the Model Browser. In addition, the model data store can be viewed and examined from this window.

The EDM designer is a very important tool for populating and configuring the Data Model, but it is also used for the purposes of updating and validating the Data Model against the data store. Right-clicking the objects shown in the Model Browser yields a context menu that provides the option to update the model from the database and validate the entity.

By right-clicking an entity in the EDM designer, the context menu offers further configuration options and access to underlying model information. This includes showing the mapping details of how an entity maps a database table, as shown in Figure 9-4.

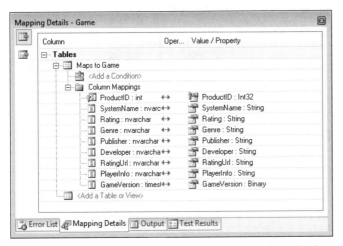

FIGURE 9-4 Showing the mapping between the EDM and the database

The same context menu also offers the ability to update the model from the database and to validate the model.

Notice how the Mapping Details window in Figure 9-4 has a row called <Add a Condition>. This row can be used to set a condition that filters the data available to the entity. With the *Game* entity, for example, one might wish to add a condition constricting the type of *Genre* values allowed. It is essentially a WHERE clause to filter the data.

Before looking at some of the different methods available to query the EDM, let's look at the other method of generating an EDM from the command line—the EdmGen tool.

Using the EDM Generator Tool

The use of the EDM Generator command-line tool offers more control over EDM generation through a series of options. The tool itself can be found in the Microsoft.NET/Framework/v3.5 directory beneath the Windows folder. It is also accessible from the Visual Studio 2008 command prompt. Figure 9-5 shows the output from executing EdmGen.exe/help, which lists the command-line switches available for use.

FIGURE 9-5 Listing the EdmGen command-line options

A /mode: value must be supplied to the tool. This can be one of the following five values, depending on the type of operation required:

- **/mode:ValidateArtifacts**   This mode is used to validate the .csdl, .ssdl, and .msl metadata files. Any errors or warnings are displayed as they are found. This mode requires at least the /inssdl or /incsdl argument. If /inmsl is specified, the /inssdl and /incsdl arguments are also required.

- **/mode:FullGeneration**   This mode uses the database connection information specified in the /connectionstring option and generates the .csdl, .ssdl, and .msl metadata files, in addition to an object layer and view files. Use of this option requires a /connectionstring argument and either the /project argument or all of the /outssdl, /outcsdl, /outmsdl, /outobjectlayer, /outviews, /namespace, and /entitycontainer arguments so the content is stored in files.

- **/mode:FromSSDLGeneration**   This mode generates .csdl and .msl files, source code, and views based upon the metadata in the the specified .ssdl file. The /inssdl argument and either the /project argument or all of the /outcsdl, /outmsl, /outobjectlayer, /outviews, /namespace, and /entitycontainer arguments are required.

- **/mode:EntityClassGeneration**   This mode creates a source code file that holds the classes generated from the .csdl file. This option requires the /incsdl argument and either the /project argument or the /outobjectlayer argument, with an optional /language argument.

- **/mode:ViewGeneration**   This mode creates a source code file that contains the views generated from the .csdl, .ssdl, and .msl files. The */inssdl, /incsdl,* and */inmsl* arguments, and either the */project* or */outviews* argument, with an optional */language* argument, are required.

Quite a few arguments are available for use in conjunction with the */mode* parameter. The most interesting of these are presented in the following list:

- **/p[roject]:<string>**   This option specifies a project name, which is used as the basis for the default namespace, the name of the EDM files, the name of object source file, and the name of the view generation source file. Also, the entity container name is set to *<project>Context.*

- **/prov[ider]:<string>**   Specifies the name of the data provider to be used to generate the .ssdl file. The default provider is *System.Data.SqlClient.*

- **/c[onnectionstring]:<connection string>**   Provides the connection string for the data source.

- **/incsdl:<file>**   Specifies the .csdl metadata file or the name of the directory that contains the .csdl files. Multiple */incsdl* values can be specified to use multiple directories or multiple CSDL files.

- **/refcsdl:<file>**   Indicates the additional .csdl file or files used to resolve any references in the */incsdl* specified file. The */refcsdl* file contains types that the source .csdl file depends upon. Again, multiple instances of the argument can be used.

- **/inmsl:<file>**   Specifies the .msl file or the name of a directory containing MSDL files. This parameter can be specified multiple times.

- **/inssdl:<file>**   Specifies the .ssdl file or the name of a directory containing the .ssdl file.

- **/outcsdl:<file>**   Specifies the name of the .csdl file to be created.

- **/outmsl:<file>**   Specifies the name of the .msl file to be created.

- **/outssdl:<file>**   Specifies the name of the .ssdl file to be created.

- **/outobjectlayer:<file>**   Specifies the name of the source code file that contains the objects generated from the .csdl file.

- **/outviews:<file>**   Specifies the name of the source code file that contains the generated views.

- **/language:[VB|CSharp]**   Specifies the language (Visual Basic or C#) for the generated source code files. The default is C#.

- **/namespace:<string>**   Specifies the model namespace that should be used. The namespace is set in the .csdl file when running */mode:FullGeneration* or */mode:FromSSDLGeneration.* The namespace is not used with */mode:EntityClassGeneration.*

- **/entitycontainer:<string>**   Specifies the name to give to the *<EntityContainer>* element in generated EDM metadata files.

It is useful at this point to look at a few examples of how to use the EdmGen tool to generate and validate an EDM and the underlying files.

To generate an EDM using the EdmGen tool, the */mode:FullGeneration* value should be provided, along with parameters for the database connection string and values to identify where the output from the generation should be directed. This can be a project or a series of files. Use of this option requires a */connectionstring* argument and either the */project* argument or all of the */outssdl, /outcsdl, /outmsdl, /outobjectlayer, /outviews, /namespace,* and */entitycontainer* arguments so the content is stored in files.

The following example performs a full generation of the EDM with the */project* parameter set ready for inclusion in a Console application project:

```
edmgen.exe /mode:FullGeneration /connectionstring:"Data Source=jim-pc;
Initial Catalog=VideoGameStoreDB;Integrated Security=True"
/project:EdmGenModel
```

The output from this command follows:

```
Microsoft (R) EdmGen version 3.5.0.0
Copyright (C) 2008 Microsoft Corporation. All rights reserved.

Loading database information...
Writing ssdl file...
Creating conceptual layer from storage layer...
Writing msl file...
Writing csdl file...
Writing object layer file...
Writing views file...

Generation Complete -- 0 errors, 2 warnings
```

Looking inside the directory, the EdmGen tool has generated a series of files that make up the EDM, ready for inclusion in a Visual Studio project:

```
EdmGenModel.csdl
EdmGenModel.msl
EdmGenModel.ObjectLayer.cs
EdmGenModel.ssdl
EdmGenModel.Views.cs
```

The EdmGen tool can be used again to validate the generated EDM metadata files, although of course the syntax is slightly different:

```
edmgen.exe /mode:ValidateArtifacts /inssdl:EdmGenModel.ssdl
/incsdl:EdmGenModel.csdl /inmsl:EdmGenModel.msl
```

The output from this command being executed is a list of errors and warnings related to the relevant metadata file. If there are no errors and no warnings, that information is also given.

The final two examples demonstrate how to use the EdmGen tool to generate source code that can be used in a Visual Studio project to access the EDM through code. The */mode* switches of interest are */mode:EntityClassGeneration* and */mode:ViewGeneration*.

The *EntityClassGeneration* mode generates source code containing the object classes that are generated from the CSDL metafile:

```
edmgen.exe /mode:EntityClassGeneration /incsdl:EdmGenModel.csdl
/project:VideoGameStoreObjectModel /language:CSharp
```

This command yields a new file in the directory called VideoGameStoreObject Model.ObjectLayer.cs, which can be imported into a C# project ready for use.

Finally, the */mode:ViewGeneration* mode is used to generate the source code containing the view generated from SSDL, CSDL, and MSL metadata files:

```
edmgen.exe /mode:ViewGeneration /incsdl:EdmGenModel.csdl
/inssdl:EdmGenModel.ssdl /inmsl:EdmGenModel.msl
/project:VideoGameStoreView /language:CSharp
```

Running this command writes a file called VideoGameStoreView.Views.cs file, which again is ready to be included and used in a Visual Studio project file. The story doesn't end there, however. To use the EDM in code, after importing all generated files, a number of additional steps are required, as follows:

1. Add assembly references for System.Data.Entity.dll and System.Runtime.Serialization.dll.

2. In Solution Explorer, use the Properties window to set the *Copy To Output Directory* property to *Copy If Newer* for the .csdl, .ssdl, and .msl files.

3. Add an Application Configuration file and insert a connection string to point to the metadata files and the data source. It should look similar to this:

```
<add name="VideoGameStoreModelContext"
connectionString="metadata=.\VideoGameStoreModel.csdl|.\VideoGameStoreModel.ssdl|.
\VideoGameStoreModel.msl;provider=System.Data.SqlClient;provider
connection string=&quot;Data Source=JIM-PC;Initial
Catalog=VideoGameStoreDB;Integrated
Security=True;MultipleActiveResultSets=True&quot;"
providerName="System.Data.EntityClient" />
```

4. Finally, add the following using/Imports directives to the main code file:

```
' VB
Imports System
Imports System.Linq
Imports System.Collections.Generic
Imports System.Text
Imports System.Data
Imports System.Data.Common
Imports System.Data.Objects
Imports System.Data.Objects.DataClasses

// C#
using System;
using System.Linq;
```

```
using System.Collections.Generic;
using System.Text;
using System.Data;
using System.Data.Common;
using System.Data.Objects;
using System.Data.Objects.DataClasses
```

Once the EDM is generated, a number of different options are available to query and manipulate it. The next section examines these methods.

Using Object Services to Query Data

Object Services is a feature of the ADO.NET Entity Framework used to perform *CREATE, READ, UPDATE, DELETE* (CRUD) operations against generated EDM types, where data is expressed as instances of entity types that are strongly typed Common Language Runtime (CLR) objects. Object Services supports *LINQ to Entities* queries, EntitySQL queries, and Query Builder methods.

At the heart of Object Services is the *ObjectContext* class, which contains an *EntityConnection* (for the EDM to connect to the database), the model metadata (as a *MetadataWorkspace* object) and an *ObjectStateManager* that monitors objects during *CREATE, UPDATE,* or *DELETE* operations. To perform querying of the EDM using Object Services, a reference to an EDM *ObjectContext* is required. Queries can then be executed against *ObjectContext*.

Querying Data as Objects

EntitySQL is a version of SQL that is used specifically to query an EDM. EntitySQL can be used with both Object Services and the *EntityClient* provider (more details about *EntityClient* are given later in this lesson). Although syntactically similar to Transact-SQL (T-SQL), it is tailored to query and update objects specifically. EntitySQL is used by building string-based queries, much as one might query a database; instead of tables and columns, however, an EntitySQL statement references entities in the EDM.

A simple example might be useful at this point. Using *VideoGameStoreDb*, the following code queries the EDM using the *ObjectQuery* class to retrieve a collection of products where the *ProductName* begins with 'g':

```vb
' VB
Dim theContext As VideoGameStoreDBEntities = New _
    VideoGameStoreDBEntities()

Dim productQuery As ObjectQuery(Of Product) = theContext.Product _
    .Where("it.ProductName like 'g%'")

For Each aProduct As Product In productQuery
    System.Console.WriteLine(aProduct.ProductName)
Next

System.Console.ReadKey()
```

```
// C#
VideoGameStoreDBEntities theContext = new VideoGameStoreDBEntities();

ObjectQuery<Product> productQuery = theContext.Product
      .Where("it.ProductName like 'g%'");

foreach (Product aProduct in productQuery)
{
    System.Console.WriteLine(aProduct.ProductName);
}

System.Console.ReadKey();
```

The second method of querying the object model is to use LINQ to Entities. Of the three methods, LINQ to Entities is probably the best because it offers features such as query validation. The following code snippet demonstrates the use of a LINQ to Entities query to retrieve a list of products from the *VideoGameStoreDb* EDM where the *ProductName* begins with 'g':

```
' VB
Dim products As ObjectQuery(Of Product) = theContext.Product

Dim productsQuery = _
    From product In products _
    Where product.ProductName.StartsWith("g") _
    Select product

For Each result As Product In productsQuery
    System.Console.WriteLine("Product Name:" & result.ProductName)
Next

System.Console.ReadKey()
```

```
// C#
ObjectQuery<Product> theProducts = theContext.Product;

var theProductsQuery = from product in theProducts
                where product.ProductName.StartsWith("g")
                select product;

foreach (Product result in theProductsQuery)
{
    System.Console.WriteLine("Product Name: " + result.ProductName);
}

System.Console.ReadKey();
```

Although using LINQ to Entities is not always possible or ideal, it is a very simple and effective way of querying an EDM. An alternative to doing this is to use Object Services, but this time using the Query Builder feature of the *ObjectQuery* class. *ObjectQuery* exposes the following Query Builder methods, presented in Table 9-2, with the EntitySQL equivalent.

TABLE 9-2 *ObjectQuery* syntax vs. *EntitySQL* syntax

OBJECTQUERY METHOD	ENTITYSQL STATEMENT
Distinct	DISTINCT
Except	EXCEPT
GroupBy	GROUP BY
Intersect	INTERSECT
OfType	OFTYPE
OrderBy	ORDER BY
Select	SELECT
SelectValue	SELECT VALUE
Skip	SKIP
Top	TOP and LIMIT
Union	UNION
UnionAll	UNION ALL
Where	WHERE

The following code shows a simple example that shows how to use a Query Builder query:

```vb
' VB
Dim queryBuilderProductQuery As ObjectQuery(Of Product) = _
    theContext.Product

' Iterate through the collection of Product items.
For Each result As Product In queryBuilderProductQuery
    System.Console.WriteLine("Product Name:" & result.ProductName)
Next

System.Console.ReadKey()
```

```csharp
// C#
ObjectQuery<Product> queryBuilderProductQuery = theContext.Product;

foreach (Product result in productQuery)
{
    System.Console.WriteLine("Product Name: " + result.ProductName);
}

System.Console.ReadKey();
```

Object queries support *projections,* which return data that cannot be easily expressed as entity types. The *ObjectQuery* class uses the *DbDataRecord* type for projections that return non-entity types, which can be either nested results or anonymous types. Simple types such as *Int32* and *String* are used with projections that return single property values. The *Select Query Builder* method returns an *ObjectQuery* that returns a collection of *DbDataRecord* objects when executed. Both LINQ to Entities and EntitySQL support query projection.

When a query is executed, only explicitly requested objects are returned as part of the results. Any related table is still accessible; however, because relationship objects that represent these associations are returned as a part of the results. These relationships can be navigated using *Navigation Properties,* though in an explicit manner.

Alternative methods of using referenced objects include using query paths or loading the related object by accessing the *Navigation Properties.* Using LINQ to Entities, a query path is specified within the query using the *.Include* syntax; when using EntitySQL, the *Include* property of *ObjectQuery* is used. The following code snippet demonstrates the use of the *.Include* syntax when using LINQ to Entities and the use of a *Navigation Property* and the *Load()* method:

```vb
' VB
Dim theContext As VideoGameStoreDBEntities = New _
    VideoGameStoreDBEntities()

Dim productQuery As ObjectQuery(Of Product) = theContext.Product _
    .Include("Game")

For Each theProduct As Product In productQuery
    If (Not (theProduct.Game) Is Nothing) Then
        System.Console.WriteLine(theProduct.Game.Developer)
    End If
Next

Dim productQueryUsingNavigationProperty As _
    ObjectQuery(OfProduct) = theContext.Product

For Each theProduct As Product In _
    productQueryUsingNavigationProperty
    theProduct.GameReference.Load(MergeOption.AppendOnly)
    If (Not (theProduct.Game) Is Nothing) Then
        System.Console.WriteLine(theProduct.Game.Developer)
    End If
Next
System.Console.ReadKey()
```

```csharp
// C#
VideoGameStoreDBEntities theContext = new
    VideoGameStoreDBEntities();
```

```
ObjectQuery<Product> theProductQuery = theContext.Product
    .Include("Game");

foreach (Product theProduct in theProductQuery)
{
    if (theProduct.Game!=null)
        System.Console.WriteLine(theProduct.Game.Developer);
}


ObjectQuery productQueryUsingNavigationProperty<Product> =
    theContext.Product;

foreach (Product theProduct in productQueryUsingNavigationProperty)
{
    theProduct.GameReference.Load(MergeOption.AppendOnly);
    if (aProduct.Game!=null)
        System.Console.WriteLine(aProduct.Game.Developer);
}


System.Console.ReadKey();
```

Updating Data in the Object Model

The uses for an EDM would be fairly restricted if it could be queried but not updated. Fortunately, the Entity Framework architecture and implementation offers the ability to make changes to the data in the EDM that can be propagated to the data store on request.

Updating data is performed through the *ObjectContext,* perhaps unsurprisingly, because as described earlier in the chapter, *ObjectContext* is the heart of the Entity Framework. *ObjectContext,* as the abstraction of the data store, manages changes performed against the EDM data—that is, *INSERT, UPDATE,* and *DELETE* operations included in the type of changes that are managed.

Once any modifications have been made, the *SaveChanges()* method of the *ObjectContext* class is called to execute the data operation against the underlying data store. The following code snippet demonstrates how a simple *INSERT, UPDATE,* or *DELETE* operation can be performed:

```
' VB
Using theContext As VideoGameStoreDBEntities = New _
    VideoGameStoreDBEntities()

    ' Inserting a new Product
    Dim aNewProduct As Product = New Product()
    aNewProduct.ProductName = "Metal Gear Solid 4: Guns of the " & _
        "Patriots"
    aNewProduct.ProductDescription = "MGS 4 Comes to the XBOX 360"
```

```vb
aNewProduct.ProductType = _
    theContext.ProductType.First(Function(pt) _
    pt.ProductTypeName = "Game")
aNewProduct.ListPriceCurrency = "USD"
theContext.AddToProduct(aNewProduct)

theContext.SaveChanges()

' Updating an existing Product
Dim anExistingProduct As Product = _
    theContext.Product.First(Function(p) p.ProductName = "Gears of " & _
    War®")
anExistingProduct.ListPrice = 29.99

' Deleting a Product
Dim productForDeletion As Product = _
    theContext.Product.First(Function(p) p.ProductName = "Metal Gear " & _
        Solid 4: Guns of the Patriots")
theContext.DeleteObject(productForDeletion)

theContext.SaveChanges()
End Using

System.Console.ReadKey()
```

```csharp
// C#
using (VideoGameStoreDBEntities theContext = new
    VideoGameStoreDBEntities())
{
    // Inserting a new Product
    Product aNewProduct = new Product();
    aNewProduct.ProductName = "Metal Gear Solid 4: Guns of the Patriots";
    aNewProduct.ProductDescription = "MGS 4 Comes to the XBOX 360";
    aNewProduct.ProductType = theContext.ProductType.First(pt =>
        pt.ProductTypeName == "Game");
    aNewProduct.ListPriceCurrency = "USD";
    theContext.AddToProduct(aNewProduct);

    theContext.SaveChanges();

    // Updating an existing Product
    Product anExistingProduct = theContext.Product.First(p => p.ProductName
        == "Gears of War®");
    anExistingProduct.ListPrice = 29.99;
```

```
    // Deleting a Product
    Product productForDeletion = theContext.Product.First(p => p.ProductName
        == "Metal Gear Solid 4: Guns of the Patriots");

    theContext.DeleteObject(productForDeletion);

    theContext.SaveChanges();
}

System.Console.ReadKey();
```

The underlying SQL statements used to update the data store are generated automatically when the EDM is generated. If desired, the EDM can be modified to execute a stored procedure to perform an *INSERT, UPDATE,* or *DELETE* operation. The stored procedure should be imported into the EDM for it to be available for use. Figure 9-6 shows how stored procedure mapping can be performed through the EDM Designer.

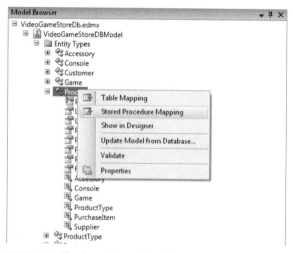

FIGURE 9-6 The Stored Procedure Mapping option in the Model Browser

Choosing the Stored Procedure Mapping option opens the Mapping Details window, shown in Figure 9-7.

As can be seen in Figure 9-7, the *Insert, Update* and *Delete* functions can be selected, which map the operations to the relevant stored procedures in the data store.

Let's take a moment and briefly discuss concurrency. By default, the Entity Framework defines the EDM in a way such that checks are not made against the data store when changes are saved. This is an example of an optimistic concurrency model. To specify that an entity should check for concurrency before updating the data store, the EDM Designer can be used to select the relevant exposed *Entity* (such as *ProductName*) and edit the properties using the Property Editor window. The *ConcurrencyMode* value can be selected, which also updates the underlying CSDL metadata.

FIGURE 9-7 The Mapping Details window

Alternatively, for fans of metadata, an additional attribute should be added to the CSDL metadata. This attribute is *ConcurrencyMode,* and its value should be set to *Fixed:*

```
<Property Name="ProductName" Type="String" Nullable="false" MaxLength="100"
Unicode="true" FixedLength="false" ConcurrencyMode="fixed" />
```

Customizing Objects

Types that are defined in an EDM expose only properties, which serve as an abstraction of the data source entities. When data classes are generated by the EDM tools, they are specified as partial classes; this allows additional partial class declarations to be created that expose additional custom properties and custom methods as required. Because of the use of partial classes, the additional code can reside in an entirely separate class file so that if the EDM gets updated or regenerated, the code is not overwritten or lost.

In addition, the behavior of a number of Object Services operations can be customized and added to. There are two ways to do this: by handling events raised by Object Services or by implementing additional partial methods that are executed when properties change. These are as follows:

- **OnPropertyChanging and OnPropertyChanged** These partial methods, located on generated data classes, are called by Object Services when a property is changed.

- **SavingChanges** This event is raised just before changes cached in the object context are written back to the underlying data source.

- **OnContextCreated** This partial method is located on the model's *EntityContainer* and is called whenever an *ObjectContext* is created.

- **AssociationChanged** This event is raised when a relationship between two objects changes.

Custom Data Classes

Custom data classes are created by inheriting from the *EntityObject* or *ComplexObject* class or by implementing a number of custom data class interfaces. The custom data class must keep the *ObjectContext* informed of changes. This is provided for and can be leveraged thanks to the inheritance from the *EntityObject* or *ComplexObject* base classes.

The custom class name and member property names must match the entity type and property names that are defined in the CSDL file of the EDM. For each of the entity type properties defined in the CSDL, there must be an associated property in the custom data class. On the other hand, the custom data class can have additional properties that don't map back to a property in the CSDL. Attributes must be applied to custom data classes and properties to provide an explicit mapping between the objects and the CSDL.

Finally, when inheriting from *EntityObject*, complex types must be implemented by inheriting from *ComplexObject*.

Using the *EntityClient* Data Provider

Using the *EntityClient* data provider is very similar to using any other data provider, such as *System.Data.SqlClient*. The *System.Data.EntityClient* objects inherit from classes in the *System.Data.Common* namespace. Data providers and the *System.Data.Common* namespace are discussed in depth in Chapter 2, "Selecting and Querying Data."

The *EntityClient* namespace contains a number of classes that should by now look familiar, to provide the capability of querying an EDM. These classes are

- **EntityConnection (inherits from *DbConnection*)**   Creates a connection to the EDM. An *EntityConnection* is instantiated with a specially formatted connection string in the format *name=contextname*. For the sample *VideoGameStoreDBEntities* context, this would be *name=VideoGameStoreDBEntities*. As with any other *DbConnection* implementation, the *Open()* method must be called to initialize the connection.

- **EntityCommand (inherits from *DbCommand*)**   The *EntityCommand* class should look very familiar: it offers similar members to the *SqlCommand* class implementation of *DbCommand*. The same *CommandType* enumeration is available to execute stored procedures, text, or open a table directly. The major difference is that any queries executed by the *EntityCommand* must use EntitySQL.

- **EntityDataReader (inherits from *DbDataReader*)**   The *EntityDataReader* class is used to read data from the EDM in a forward-only and unbuffered manner.

- **EntityTransaction (inherits from *DbTransaction*)**   An *EntityTransaction* servers as a wrapper for the underlying data provider's transaction object.

The following code demonstrates how to use the previously described *EntityClient* classes to connect to an *EntityDataModel* and query it to return the results:

```
' VB
Dim theEntityConnection As EntityConnection = New _
    EntityConnection("name=VideoGameStoreDBEntities")

theEntityConnection.Open()
```

```vb
Dim theCommand As EntityCommand = New EntityCommand()
theCommand.Connection = theEntityConnection
theCommand.CommandType = System.Data.CommandType.Text
theCommand.CommandText = "SELECT VALUE p.ProductName FROM " & _
    VideoGameStoreDBEntities.Product as p"

Dim theReader As EntityDataReader = _
    theCommand.ExecuteReader(CommandBehavior.SequentialAccess)

While theReader.Read()
    System.Console.WriteLine(theReader(0).ToString())
End While

System.Console.ReadKey()
```

```csharp
// C#
EntityConnection theEntityConnection = new
EntityConnection("name=VideoGameStoreDBEntities");

theEntityConnection.Open();

EntityCommand theCommand = new EntityCommand();
theCommand.Connection = theEntityConnection;
theCommand.CommandType = System.Data.CommandType.Text;
theCommand.CommandText = "SELECT VALUE p.ProductName FROM
    VideoGameStoreDBEntities.Product as p";

EntityDataReader theReader = theCommand.ExecuteReader(
    CommandBehavior.SequentialAccess);

while (theReader.Read())
{
    System.Console.WriteLine(theReader[0].ToString());
}

System.Console.ReadKey();
```

LAB   Using the Entity Framework

In this lab, you begin by creating a console application and using the Entity Framework to generate an *EntityDataModel* of the *VideoGameStoreDB* database. You then write a series of queries to use against the EDM, using LINQ to Entities and EntitySQL, to retrieve sets of data and output them to the console. Each exercise builds on the previous one.

As with the previous exercises, you need to have *VideoGameStoreDB* installed. You can install the files for this lab, including the complete solution containing the code for all the exercises, from the Code folder on the companion CD.

EXERCISE 1   Generating an Entity Data Model

In this exercise, you use the Edm Generator command-line tool to generate an EDM.

1. Using the EDM Generator tool against the *VideoGameStoreDB* database, generate the following:

   a. The Conceptual Schema Definition Language (.csdl) file

   b. The Store Schema Definition Language (.ssdl) file

   c. The Mapping Specification Language (.msl) file

   d. The ObjectLayer source code file

   e. The Views source code file

2. Import the files into a new Console Application project using Visual Studio and configure the project to use the Entity Framework.

   Your command-line command should look like this (obviously your connection string will differ from this one):

```
edmgen.exe /mode:FullGeneration /connectionstring:"Data Source=jim-
    pc;Initial Catalog=VideoGameStoreDB;Integrated Security=True"
    /project:VideoGameStore
```

EXERCISE 2   Querying an Entity Data Model

In this exercise, you use the *ObjectQuery* class with LINQ to Entities and EntitySQL to query the EDM created in Exercise 1.

1. Open the Console Application project you created in Exercise 1.

2. Query the EDM by performing the following steps:

   a. Using LINQ to Entities, select data from the *Product* entity where the *ProductName* value starts with 'ac'.

   b. Output the results to the console.

   c. Using EntitySQL, select data from the *Product* entity where the *ProductName* value starts with 'ac'.

   d. Output the results to the console.

   Your code should look like this:

```
' VB
Dim theContext As VideoGameStoreModelContext = New _
    VideoGameStoreModelContext()
```

```vbnet
' Using LINQ to Entities
Dim theProductQuery As Object = From prod In theContext.Product _
    Where prod.ProductName.StartsWith("ac") _
    Select prod

System.Console.WriteLine("LINQ to Entities:" + vbCrLf + vbCrLf)
For Each aProduct As Product In theProductQuery
    System.Console.WriteLine(aProduct.ProductName)
Next

System.Console.WriteLine(vbCrLf + vbCrLf + "EntitySQL:" + vbCrLf + _
    vbCrLf)

Dim theSecondProductsQuery As ObjectQuery(Of Product) = _
    theContext.Product _
    .Where("it.ProductName like 'ac%'")

For Each aProduct As Product In theSecondProductsQuery
    System.Console.WriteLine(aProduct.ProductName)
Next
```

```csharp
// C#
VideoGameStoreModelContext theContext = new
    VideoGameStoreModelContext();

// Using LINQ to Entities
var theProductQuery = from prod in theContext.Product
    where prod.ProductName.StartsWith("ac")
    select prod;

System.Console.WriteLine("LINQ to Entities:\n\n");

foreach (Product aProduct in theProductQuery)
{
    System.Console.WriteLine(aProduct.ProductName);
}

System.Console.WriteLine("\n\nEntitySQL:\n\n");

ObjectQuery<Product> theSecondProductsQuery = theContext.Product
    .Where("it.ProductName like 'ac%'");

foreach (Product aProduct in theSecondProductsQuery)
{
    System.Console.WriteLine(aProduct.ProductName);
}
```

Lesson Summary

- Generating an EDM using the EDM Generator tool is quick and easy.
- Entities are created for each compatible object in the data source.
- LINQ to Entities is an incredibly easy way to query an EDM.
- *EntitySQL* syntax is very similar to that of traditional SQL.
- Querying an EDM can be performed in very few lines of code.

Lesson Review

You can use the following questions to test your knowledge of the information in Lesson 1, "Generating and Querying an Entity Data Model." The questions also are available on the companion CD of this book if you prefer to review them in electronic form.

> **NOTE ANSWERS**
>
> Answers to these questions and explanations of why each answer choice is correct or incorrect are located in the "Answers" section at the end of the book.

1. What is the CSDL metadata file used for?

   A. It is used to store the *Entity* state temporarily when updating the EDM.

   B. It is used to persist data for applications using the generated EDM.

   C. It maps conceptual entities to data source entities.

   D. It defines the entities, associations, sets, and containers of the object model.

2. What is the MSL file used for?

   A. It is used to persist data for applications using the generated EDM.

   B. It maps conceptual entities to data source entities.

   C. It defines the entities, associations, sets, and containers of the object model.

   D. It is a source code file which provides model interaction.

3. Which of the following LINQ to Entity queries is correct?

   A.

   ```
   ' VB
   Dim theProductQuery As Object = From prod In theContext.Product _
       Where prod.ProductName.StartsWith("ac") _
       Select prod

   // C#
   var theProductQuery = from prod in theContext.Product
       where prod.ProductName.StartsWith("ac")
       select prod;
   ```

B.

```vb
' VB
Dim theProductQuery As Object = From prod In Product _
    Where prod.ProductName.StartsWith("ac") _
    Select prod
```

```csharp
// C#
var theProductQuery = from prod in Product
    where prod.ProductName.StartsWith("ac")
    select prod;
```

C.

```vb
' VB
Dim theProductQuery As Object = From prod In theContext.Product _
    Where prod.ProductName.BeginsWith("ac") _
    Select prod
```

```csharp
// C#
var theProductQuery = from prod in theContext.Product
    where prod.ProductName.BeginsWith("ac")
    select prod;
```

D.

```vb
' VB
Dim theProductQuery As Object = From prod In theContext.Product _
    Where prod.ProductName.StartsWith("ac") _
    Select Product
```

```csharp
// C#
var theProductQuery = from prod in theContext.Product
    where prod.ProductName.StartsWith("ac")
    select Product;
```

4. Which of the following Object Services queries is correct?

A.

```vb
' VB
Dim theSecondProductsQuery As EntityQuery(Of Product) = _
    theContext.Product _
    .Where("it.ProductName like 'ac%'")
```

```csharp
// C#
EntityQuery<Product> theSecondProductsQuery = theContext.Product
    .Where("it.ProductName like 'ac%'");
```

B.

```vb
' VB
Dim theSecondProductsQuery As ObjectQuery(Of Product) = _
    theContext.Product _
    .Where("it.ProductName like 'ac%'")
```

```csharp
// C#
ObjectQuery<Product> theSecondProductsQuery = theContext.Product
    .Where("it.ProductName like 'ac%'");
```

C.

```vb
' VB
Dim theSecondProductsQuery As ObjectQuery = _
    theContext.Product _
    .Where("it.ProductName like 'ac%'")
```

```csharp
// C#
ObjectQuery theSecondProductsQuery = theContext.Product
    .Where("it.ProductName like 'ac%'");
```

D.

```vb
' VB
Dim theSecondProductsQuery As ObjectQuery(Of Product) = _
    theContext.Product _
    .Where("ProductName like 'ac%'")
```

```csharp
// C#
ObjectQuery<Product> theSecondProductsQuery = theContext.Product
    .Where("ProductName like 'ac%'");
```

Chapter Review

To practice and reinforce the skills you learned in this chapter further, you can do any or all of the following:

- Review the chapter summary.
- Review the list of key terms introduced in this chapter.
- Complete the case scenario. This scenario sets up a real-world situation involving the topics of this chapter and asks you to create a solution.
- Complete the suggested practices.
- Take a practice test.

Chapter Summary

- It is possible to generate an EDM using the Visual Studio EDM Wizard or the command line using the EDM Generator tool.
- The Entity Framework uses three metadata files used to define the EDM. These are the Conceptual Schema Definition Language (CSDL) files, the Store Schema Definition Language (SSDL) file, and the Mapping Specification Language (MSL) file.
- The *EntityClient* data provider can be used to query the EDM and provides a familiar *SqlClient*-like interface with which to work.
- The LINQ implementation for use with an EDM is called LINQ to Entities.
- The EDM can be queried using the *ObjectQuery* class.
- EntitySQL is a special kind of structured query language to use for querying entities.

Key Terms

Do you know what these key terms mean? You can check your answers by looking up the terms in the glossary at the end of the book.

- Conceptual Schema Definition Language (CSDL)
- Entity Data Model (EDM)
- LINQ to Entities
- Mapping Specification Language (MSL)
- Object Services
- Store Schema Definition Language (SSDL)

Case Scenario

In the following case scenario, you apply what you've learned about the Entity Framework. You can find answers to the questions posed in this scenario in the "Answers" section at the end of this book.

Case Scenario: Rapid Prototyping Featuring Reusable Code

A major deadline is looming at the large IT consulting company where you work. Your line manager asks you to get involved with the project, a new customer relationship management system. Your manager asks for the best of both worlds: a prototype containing reusable code. Without a detailed requirements specification, a prototype is required, and because time is short before the deadline, she also stipulates that at least some of the prototype code must be reusable for the finished application. The company database administrator has given you access to a SQL Server database that contains the best estimate of the tables required.

QUESTION

Answer the following question for your manager:

- How can we approach this problem and produce a prototype in the short term but reuse the code in the finished application?

Suggested Practice

To help you master the exam objectives presented in this chapter, complete the following task.

- **Practice 1** Practice using the Entity Framework to generate an EDM with the Visual Studio Data Model Wizard and the EDM Generator command-line tool. Implement querying of the EDM using the different methods available, including LINQ to Entities, EntitySQL, and the *EntityClient* namespace.

Take a Practice Test

The practice tests on this book's companion CD offer many options. For example, you can test yourself on just the content covered in this chapter, or you can test yourself on the entire 70-561 certification exam content. You can set up the test so that it closely simulates the experience of taking a certification exam, or you can set it up in study mode, which allows you to look at the correct answers and explanations after you answer each question.

> **MORE INFO** **PRACTICE TESTS**
>
> For details about all the available practice test options, see the section entitled "How to Use the Practice Tests," in the Introduction to this book.

CHAPTER 10

ADO.NET Data Services

The world is not as simple as it once was. It used to be that all your applications ran on the desktop inside your company's enterprise. That was an easier world in which to develop software. With the ubiquity of both portable devices and Internet access, you are responsible for making your data available to a wider audience than ever. This may mean developing a variety of different types of clients: desktop, smart, Web, device, and so on. But with these different types of clients, accessing data becomes a key strategy to allow you to deal with data without reinventing it for every client.

A common strategy to retrieve data across an Internet connection is to use Web Services. ASP.NET's Web Services and the Windows Communication Framework (WCF) are both solid choices for creating these layers for this new world of application. But there is a problem with this approach. Let's take a simple example of an ASP.NET Web Service that is going to expose some customer data:

```vb
' VB
<WebService(Namespace := "http://customersite.org/")> _
Public Class CustomerService
        Inherits System.Web.Services.WebService


  <WebMethod> _
  Public Function GetCustomers() As Customer()
        Return DataAccess.GetCustomers()
  End Function

End Class
```

```csharp
// C#
[WebService(Namespace = "http://customersite.org/")]
public class CustomerService : System.Web.Services.WebService
{

  [WebMethod]
  public Customer[] GetCustomers()
  {
    return DataAccess.GetCustomers();
  }
}
```

This Web Service is simple. It exposes the customers as a Web Service call so that the client code can retrieve the data across an Internet connection. The code looks innocent enough, but the problem lurks in this Web Service over time. The call to *GetCustomers* works for some parts of an application, but not others (or for your application, but perhaps not the next application). Eventually most of these Web Services end up looking like this:

```vb
' VB
<WebService(Namespace := "http://customersite.org/")> _
Public Class CustomerService
        Inherits System.Web.Services.WebService

  <WebMethod> _
  Public Function GetCustomers() As Customer()
        Return DataAccess.GetCustomers()
  End Function

  <WebMethod> _
  Public Function GetCustomersByName() As Customer()
        Return DataAccess.GetCustomersByName()
  End Function

  <WebMethod> _
  Public Function GetCustomersWithOrders() As Customer()
        Return DataAccess.GetCustomersWithOrders()
  End Function

  <WebMethod> _
  Public Function GetCustomerById(ByVal custId As Integer) As Customer()
        Return DataAccess.GetCustomersById(custId)
  End Function
  ' And More!!!
End Class

// C#
[WebService(Namespace = "http://customersite.org/")]
public class CustomerService : System.Web.Services.WebService
{

  [WebMethod]
  public Customer[] GetCustomers()
  {
    return DataAccess.GetCustomers();
  }

  [WebMethod]
  public Customer[] GetCustomersByName()
```

```
{
  return DataAccess.GetCustomersByName();
}


[WebMethod]
public Customer[] GetCustomersWithOrders()
{
  return DataAccess.GetCustomersWithOrders();
}


[WebMethod]
public Customer[] GetCustomerById(int custId)
{
  return DataAccess.GetCustomersById(custId);
}
// And More!!!
}
```

This code illustrates a problem called *Interface Pollution,* where the Web Service receives a new method for every use case that comes up for data with different requirements. In large projects, these Web Services become enormous and unwieldy over time and are difficult to maintain in the long run. That is where ADO.NET Data Services come to the rescue.

With ADO.NET Data Services, you expose end points that represent the type of data you want to expose and let the users of that data shape, filter, and sort the data as needed. In this chapter you discover how to build your own ADO.NET Data Services and how to use them to retrieve data from .NET clients.

Exam objective in this chapter:

- This chapter is not covered in the exam, but being able to create ADO.NET Data Services is a valuable skill for any developer who works with ADO.NET or data in general.

Lessons in this chapter:

Before You Begin

To complete the lessons in this chapter, you must have:

- A computer that meets or exceeds the minimum hardware requirements listed in the "Introduction" section at the beginning of the book

- Microsoft Visual Studio 2008 SP1 Professional edition installed on your computer

- An understanding of Microsoft Visual Basic or C# syntax and familiarity with Microsoft .NET Framework version 3.5

Lesson 1: Exposing the Data Service

Regardless of if you are familiar with Web Services or not, working with ADO.NET Data Services is a brand new experience. Although simpler to implement, Data Services are created very differently than standard Web Services. In this lesson, you learn the basics of what makes a Data Service and how to build your first one.

After this lesson, you will be able to:

- Create an ADO.NET Data Service
- Configure an ADO.NET Data Service
- Query an ADO.NET Data Service from the Uniform Resource Identifier (URI)

Estimated lesson time: 30 minutes

 REAL WORLD

Shawn Wildermuth

I've dealt with the Web Service data layer before. In Microsoft SQL Server 2000, the SQLXML add-on promised to be able to simply configure your database as a set of Web Services. The problem was that it exposed the entire database as a set of open Web Services. This was scary to many a customer. When I first ran into ADO.NET Data Services, I was skeptical that this was just another version of the same codebase. To my surprise, it was very different. As I've been working with more and more clients that must live outside the enterprise (Silverlight and click-once applications, typically), I have had the desire for a way not to have to write (or code-generate) the vast amounts of Web Service code that is typically required to expose data to these clients. Although not right for every situation, ADO.NET Data Services seems to fit into 80 percent of the use cases for many of these clients. Trying to fit a data access API into message-based Web Services always felt like the wrong solution to the problem.

Data Service Basics

One of the first things that you should have learned about data access is the concept of CRUD. CRUD is an acronym that stands for the four basic operations of data access:

- **C**reate
- **R**ead
- **U**pdate
- **D**elete

In the SQL language, these are represented by the statements *INSERT, SELECT, UPDATE,* and *DELETE.* In a standard Web Service model, each of these types of statements must be exposed as a set of methods on a Web Service. Usually this means methods for creating, updating, and deleting, as well as a large number of methods to handle the reading of data. ADO.NET Data Services takes an entirely different approach.

Unlike Web Services, ADO.NET Data Services use the concepts of Representation State Transfer (REST) to create a URI-based application programming interface (API) to the data. In contrast, Web Services use an Extensible Markup Language (XML) envelope-based API to call the service. The URI-based approach is simpler but does have less flexibility, in that calling into the service requires that the entire request be exemplified as a URI. The URI syntax is made up of two parts: a path to a resource and a query string. The path is a simple path to a specific end point. You learn about query string support in the section entitled "Querying the Service," later in this chapter. For example, if you assume that you have created an end point called "Customers" (which we explain how to do in the section entitled "Creating the Service," later in this chapter), you could request the entire list of customers by making a request to the server using the URI *http://yourdomain.com/YourService.svc/Customers.* Notice that the URI includes the Data Service (YourService.svc) and a path to the resource (Customers). Why is this important?

This URI syntax matters because when you "make a request," you are really saying that you should use the Hypertext Transfer Protocol (HTTP) stack to perform a *GET.* HTTP defines four verbs that you can issue to any HTTP-compliant Web server: *GET, POST, PUT,* and *DELETE.* So when you make a request to a Data Service, you are issuing a *GET* to the server using the URI to specify what resource you want to retrieve (or *GET*). This is where using a REST-based API becomes compelling: The ADO.NET Data Services actually map each of the HTTP verbs to the four data access actions (or SQL statements), as shown in Table 10-1.

TABLE 10-1 Mapping Between HTTP Verbs and Data Access CRUD

HTTP VERB	DATA ACCESS ACTION	SQL STATEMENT
GET	Read	*SELECT*
POST	Update	*UPDATE*
PUT	Insert	*INSERT*
DELETE	Delete	*DELETE*

That means that if you *POST* to that same URI, it expects to see the data required to do an *UPDATE* to the data layer. If you perform a *DELETE* to the same URI, it expects to delete an item in the data layer. You see the power of that later in this chapter.

But how do you expose these end points of data that the ADO.NET Data Service uses? The answer is that ADO.NET Data Services uses Language Integrated Query (LINQ) for these end points. The ADO.NET Data Service is responsible for accepting incoming HTTP requests and passing the request to a LINQ data provider. This means that anything that supports LINQ also supports ADO.NET Data Services. Figure 10-1 shows the relationship and layering of a typical ADO.NET Data Service implementation.

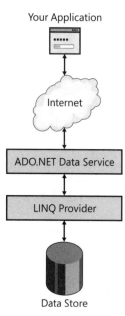

Your Application

Internet

ADO.NET Data Service

LINQ Provider

Data Store

FIGURE 10-1 ADO.NET Data Service layering

As Figure 10-1 illustrates, your application interacts over the Internet directly with the ADO.NET Data Service. The Data Service, in turn, takes your request and issues the request to the underlying LINQ provider. Ultimately it is the LINQ provider that performs all data operations. This means that ADO.NET Data Services is specifically not another data access layer but is instead a transport layer. This Transport layer is based on existing technology: WCF REST support. When you create a new ADO.NET Data Service, it creates two files: a markup file and a code-behind file. The markup page (usually with the extension .svc) is a simple *ServiceHost* markup file that handles REST requests and hands them to the code-behind file. The code-behind file is the implementation of the Data Service itself.

The last piece of the puzzle for ADO.NET Data Services is the format of the data for the service. ADO.NET Data Services support two data formats: Atom and JavaScript Object Notation (JSON). Atom is an XML-based format (as defined in RFC 4287) that supports Web syndication of content. For managed code, Atom tends to be easier to consume and parse, whereas JSON is more useful to Web-based solutions like Web sites. ADO.NET Data Services takes a HTTP-friendly way of determining the data format. In any HTTP request, you can specify a set of Accept headers that tells the service what types of data you can consume. ADO.NET Data Services uses the Accept headers to determine which format to return. This means that when you call the service directly in a Web browser, Atom is returned because it is a common format that can be easily consumed by a number of different types of clients. Alternatively, when you call the service from JavaScript, the service can return JSON. In other words, the type of data you can return for the same request depends on the client calling the URI, not the URI itself. Enough of the basics—it's time you created your first service.

Creating the Service

To create the service, you need an existing ASP.NET 3.5 website or Web Application project. In addition, you should already have a LINQ-enabled data layer available to your project. For these examples, assume that you have an Entity Framework model that simply exposes two entities, *Products* and *ProductTypes*, from the *VideoGameStore* database that is supplied on the companion CD. Once you have these prerequisites, you can create a service. Use the Add New Item menu in Visual Studio to create a new ADO.NET Data Service. This creates the two files that make up the data service. The markup file is likely never going to change once it is created, so just skip it for now.

The code-behind file is simply a class that derives from the *System.Data.Services. DataService* class. A newly created *DataService* class does not compile and is incomplete, as shown here:

```vb
' VB
Public Class VideoGameService
    ' TODO: replace [[class name]] with your data class name
    Inherits DataService(Of [[class name]])

    ' This method is called only once to initialize service-wide policies.
    Public Shared Sub InitializeService(ByVal config As IDataServiceConfiguration)
        ' TODO: set rules to indicate which entity sets and service operations are
                visible, updatable, etc.
        ' Examples:
        ' config.SetEntitySetAccessRule("MyEntityset", EntitySetRights.AllRead)
        ' config.SetServiceOperationAccessRule("MyServiceOperation",
ServiceOperationRights.All)
    End Sub

End Class
```

```csharp
// C#
public class VideoGameService : DataService< /* TODO: put your data source class name
here */ >
{
  // This method is called only once to initialize service-wide policies.
  public static void InitializeService(IDataServiceConfiguration config)
  {
    // TODO: set rules to indicate which entity sets and service operations are visible,
       updatable, etc.
    // Examples:
    // config.SetEntitySetAccessRule("MyEntityset", EntitySetRights.AllRead);
    // config.SetServiceOperationAccessRule("MyServiceOperation",
ServiceOperationRights.All);
  }
}
```

As you can see, the *DataService* class requires a generic parameter to be complete. This generic parameter can be any class that exposes one or more *IEnumerable<T>* properties (or one derived from *IEnumerable<T>*, like *IQueryable<T>*). Typically, this is a class from your data layer that exposes parts of the model as queryable end points. For this Entity Framework example, it is the *VideoGameEntities* class.

Viewing Services in Windows Internet Explorer 7

For many of the examples in this chapter, Windows Internet Explorer is used to query the Data Service URIs directly. By default, Internet Explorer 7 enables viewing RSS and Atom feeds in a Feed Viewing mode. To read the raw Atom XML that is returned to the browser in Internet Explorer 7, you must disable this mode. Do this in Internet Explorer by selecting Tools, Internet Options, clicking the Content tab, and click Feed Settings. In the dialog box that opens, clear the Turn On Feed Reading View check box. You need to restart the browser for this change to take effect.

Now that your Data Service compiles, you can launch the service file (.svc) in the browser to see the basic Atom XML format of your service, as seen in Figure 10-2.

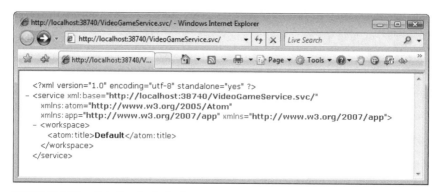

FIGURE 10-2 Your Data Service in the browser

You will eventually get used to the format of the Atom feed. The main service end point (the .svc file) of the Data Service is meant to describe the resources (and data if applicable) that are available. Even though your service is operable at this point, it does not expose any data yet.

Securing the Model

The Data Service class required that you include a class that exposes data, so why can't you see data in the service yet? The reason is that by default, none of your model is exposed through the service. This occurs because you likely have a data model that encompasses a larger model than you want to expose over the Internet. It is perfectly appropriate to decide that some data is relevant for consumption across the Internet but that using other data would not be secure (for example, Employee data). ADO.NET Data Services requires you to allow data explicitly out of the service by configuring the service in the static *InitializeService* method. In addition to specifying your data to expose, you also must decide what actions can be performed against that data. This configuring of the service allows you to specify nouns (the data) and verbs (the actions against the data) to secure that data.

To perform this configuration, you use the *IDataServiceConfiguration* interface that is passed into the static *InitializeService* member. This interface supports a number of ways to secure your data but at a minimum you need to call the *SetEntitySetAccessRule* method to set the noun/verb combination. For example, you can call the *SetEntitySetAccessRule* to allow read-only access to the Products entities like so:

```vb
' VB
Public Shared Sub InitializeService(ByVal config As IDataServiceConfiguration)
  config.SetEntitySetAccessRule("Products", EntitySetRights.AllRead)
End Sub
```

```csharp
// C#
public static void InitializeService(IDataServiceConfiguration config)
{
  config.SetEntitySetAccessRule("Products", EntitySetRights.AllRead);
}
```

Once this configuration is added, *Products* is available via the service, but *ProductTypes* is not. The first parameter of the *SetEntitySetAccessRule* method takes the name of the end point in your context object, and the second parameter is one or more of the values in the *EntitySetRights* enumeration. For the first parameter, you can specify an asterisk to allow the entire model, but this is discouraged because you want to determine what actions are allowed on different parts of the model. *EntitySetRights* allows for a mix of actions. The values for the *EntitySetRights* enumeration are listed in Table 10-2.

TABLE 10-2 *EntitySetRights* Enumeration

ENUMERATION VALUE	MEANING
All	Allows full read and write access.
AllRead	Allows full read access.
AllWrite	Allows full write access.
ReadSingle	Can read single data items only.
ReadMultiple	Can read sets of data.
WriteAppend	Can add new items.
WriteDelete	Can delete items.
WriteMerge	Can merge items.
WriteReplace	Can replace entire items.
None	No access.

You can call the *SetEntitySetAccessRule* method multiple times to configure more than one set of data. Each call specifies the *EntitySetRights* separately, so you can have different data items with different rules. For example, you can call it twice to expose both *Products* and *ProductTypes*:

```vb
' VB
config.SetEntitySetAccessRule("Products", EntitySetRights.All)
config.SetEntitySetAccessRule("ProductTypes", EntitySetRights.AllRead)
```

```csharp
// C#
config.SetEntitySetAccessRule("Products", EntitySetRights.All);
config.SetEntitySetAccessRule("ProductTypes", EntitySetRights.AllRead);
```

Once you configure the service, navigating to the service now reports the different end points (in Atom parlance), as shown in Figure 10-3.

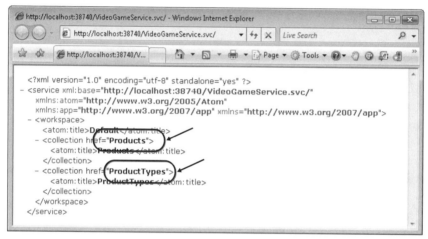

FIGURE 10-3 After configuring the service

Querying the Service

Now that the service is configured, you've seen how to navigate to the service and the *Products* and *ProductTypes* are now shown in the service description. Note that in the figure, I highlighted the Atom references to these data items; they are *hrefs*. These *hrefs* may look like just the names of the data items, but in fact, they are relative URIs to the resources. This means you can change the URI from the service URI (for example, *http://localhost/VideoGameService.svc*) and navigate to the relative URI for products (for example, *http://localhost/VideoGameService.svc/Products*), as seen in Figure 10-4.

> **NOTE** **URIs ARE CASE-SENSITIVE**
> ADO.NET Data Service URIs are case sensitive, in both the service name (VideoGameService.svc) and the names of end points. For example, changing the URI to *http://localhost/videogameservice.svc/products* fails.

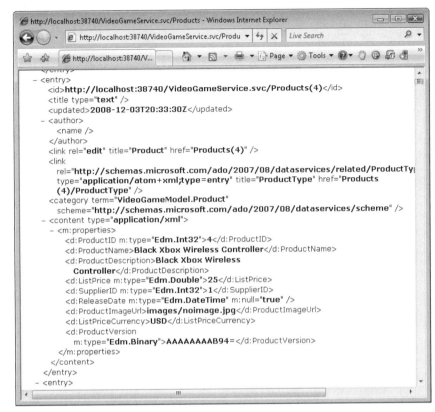

FIGURE 10-4 Service results

The Atom serialization that you see in the browser is a bit verbose, but it communicates all the information about the entity that could be discerned by the service. Each entity that you expose by the service is contained in an "entry" element, as shown previously. Do not get nervous about the format of the message because in practice, you do not consume the format in its raw form. You learn more about that in Lesson 2, "Consuming the Data Service."

More importantly, it's useful to understand that the URI that you see in Figure 10-4 is the end point for *Products*. The end point is queryable, which is the magic of ADO.NET Data Services. Assuming that the URI in Figure 10-4 will be used in your development is like assuming that *SELECT * FROM Products* is how all your SQL in a project will look. It is a good tool to look at data in bulk, but in practice, you never use it.

ADO.NET Data Services supports a path syntax that allows you to navigate your entities. For example, if you look at the *id* element just inside the *entry* element (shown in Figure 10-4), you see the full URI to that individual entity. If you look at the URI (*http://localhost/VideoGame Service.svc/Products(4)*), you should notice the parentheses after the end point. This is the URI syntax for retrieving single elements. The number indicates the value of the primary key. This syntax supports multi-part keys and non-numeric keys as well.

In addition, the path syntax also supports relationship navigation. If you look at the second *link* element in the *entry* (again, look at Figure 10-4), this link refers to a related item

(*ProductType*). The title of this link is in fact *ProductType*. The *href* attribute is a service-relative URI to the related item. If you use this URI in the browser, you see it navigate to the *ProductType* for this *Product,* as shown in Figure 10-5.

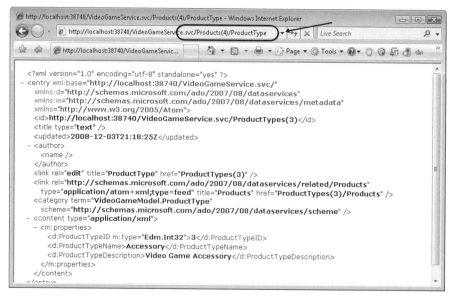

FIGURE 10-5 Navigating relationships

The fact that this end point is queryable means that you can add syntax to the URI string to shape, filter, and order the data that is returned. For example, you can order the results by simply placing a query string parameter after the end point URI (*http://localhost/ VideoGameService.svc/Products?$orderby=ProductName*), as shown in Figure 10-6.

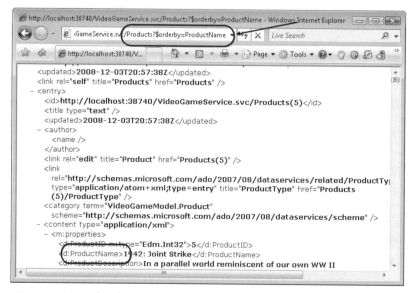

FIGURE 10-6 An ordered query

The supported query options for end points are described in Table 10-3.

TABLE 10-3 Query Options

QUERY OPTION	MEANING
$filter	Limits the results based on a predicate
$orderby	Sorts the results (ascending or descending)
$skip	Seeks into the results before returning results
$top	Limits the results to a set number of results
$expand	Embedded related entities instead of providing links

The *$filter* query option supports a predicate syntax that allows you to create complex queries (though not as powerful as full LINQ syntax). For example, you can search for all the products who's list price is less than 60 by using the *$filter* option:

```
http://localhost/VideoGameService.svc/Products?$filter=ListPrice%20lt%2060
```

This *$filter* value is in fact *ListPrice lt 60* (though when URL is encoded, the spaces become *%20*). Effectively this is saying, "Compare the *ListPrice* (the name of a property on the entity) with the number 60." The comparison is *lt*, which is the logical operator for "less than."

Literal values can be used in these filter expressions, but they have specific formatting to allow ADO.NET Data Services to discern their type. Table 10-4 shows all the literal types and how to format them for the URI query syntax.

TABLE 10-4 Literal Formatting in Query Options

.NET EQUIVALENT TYPE	FORMATTING RULE	EXAMPLE
Int32	Whole numbers	*42*
Int64	Integer suffixed with "L"	*42L*
Double	Real number as defined by .NET (INF = Infinity, NaN = Not a Number)	*15.5*
Single	Same as Double, but suffixed with 'f'	*15.5f*
Decimal	Same as Double, but suffixed with 'M'	*15.5M*
DateTime	Quoted XML Schema Definition (XSD)–style date or time prefixed with 'datetime'	*datetime'2008-04-24'* or *datetime'11:24:00Z'*
Boolean	'true' or 'false'	*true*
null (Nothing in VB)	'null'	*null*

TABLE 10-4 Literal Formatting in Query Options

.NET EQUIVALENT TYPE	FORMATTING RULE	EXAMPLE
Guid	32 digit globally unique identifier (GUID) format, quoted and prefixed with 'guid'	*guid'12345678-1234-1234-1234-1234567890AB'*
Binary	Hexidecimal data quoted and prefixed with 'guid'	*guid'0FFFFFFF'*

You can also mix query options using separate query string parameters. For example, to filter the *ListPrice* and sort the result, you can mix the *$filter* and *$orderby* parameters as follows:

```
http://localhost/VideoGameService.svc/Products?$filter=ListPrice%20lt%2060&$orderby
    =ProductName
```

This predicate syntax supports logical and arithmetic operators as well as expression functions. You can mix these to create powerful queries in ADO.NET Data Services. These operators and expression functions are explained in Tables 10-5, 10-6, and 10-7.

TABLE 10-5 Logical Operators

OPERATOR	MEANING
and	True if both sides are true
or	True if either sides are true
not	True if the operand is false
eq	True if both sides have the same value
ne	True if sides have different values
lt	True if the left side is less than the right side
gt	True if the left side is greater than the right side
le	True if the left side is less than or equal to the right side
ge	True if the left side is greater than or equal to the right side

TABLE 10-6 Arithmetic Operators

OPERATOR	MEANING
add	Performs addition
sub	Performs subtraction
mul	Performs multiplication
div	Performs division
Mod	Returns the remainder of a division

TABLE 10-7 Expression Functions

OPERATOR	MEANING
substringof	Tests whether a string is completely contained in another string
endswith	Tests whether a string ends in a specific set of characters
startswith	Tests whether a string starts with a specific set of characters
length	Returns the length of a string
indexof	Returns the ordinal of a specific string in another string
insert	Performs an insertion in a string
remove	Removes characters from a string
replace	Replaces characters in a string
substring	Returns part of an existing string
tolower	Returns a lower-case equivalent of a string
toupper	Returns an upper-case equivalent of a string
trim	Removes leading and trailing spaces in a string
Concat	Concatenates several strings
day	Returns the day part of a date value
month	Returns the month part of a date value
Year	Returns the year part of a date value
hour	Returns the hour part of a time value
minute	Returns the minute part of a time value
second	Returns the second part of a time value
round	Performs a rounding of a numerical value
floor	Calculates the floor of a numerical value
ceiling	Calculates the ceiling of a numerical value
isof	Determines if an entity type is a specified type
Cast	Treats an entity as a specific type if the entity supports the type

The query syntax also supports shaping the result of your queries by embedding related entities into a single result. You can do this by using the *$expand* query option. The *$expand* query option allows you to specify relationship properties that you want to load inline into the result. Not all LINQ providers support this syntax, but Entity Framework does. For example, you can get a specific *Product* (whose ID is 4) and embed the *ProductType* inline by using the following query:

```
http://localhost/VideoGameService.svc/Products(4)?$expand=ProductType
```

This query results in the *ProductType* being returned within the result for the specific *Product,* as shown in Figure 10-7.

FIGURE 10-7 Results of the *$expand* query operator

Note that the link to the *ProductType* is in the same place in the *Product*'s result, but inside the link is an inline version of the entire *ProductType* entity.

This URI-based query syntax allows you to retrieve data while filtering, sorting, and shaping the results. But there are times when ad hoc querying is not as useful as describing the queries fully and directly in the service. Luckily, ADO.NET Services allow this.

Service Operations

There are times when it is more helpful to be able to create prebuilt queries in the service itself. Although the nature of ADO.NET Data Services is to make this the exception rather than the rule, it does allow you to create queries directly on the service. This is similar to the database concepts of views or stored procedures. To create a Service Operation, you create a public method on the service class. This method is annotated with *WebGetAttribute* or

WebInvokeAttribute to tell the Data Service that this is a method to be exposed as a Service Operation. Service Operations require one of three return values:

- **None**   Implemented as *Sub* in Visual Basic, *void* return type in C#. Allows you to call the operation to be executed.
- **IEnumerable<T>**   Allows you to execute the operation and return a fixed set of results.
- **IQueryable<T>**   Allows you to execute the operation and apply query options on the Service Operation to further filter, sort, or shape the result returned.

If you want to return a list of *Products* that have not been released yet (for example, those for which *ReleaseDate* is in the future), you could add the following Service Operation to the *DataService* class:

```vb
' VB
Public Class VideoGameService
        Inherits DataService(Of VideoGameEntities)
  ' ...

  <WebGet> _
  Public Function FutureProducts() As IQueryable(Of Product)
        Dim qry = From p In Me.CurrentDataSource.Products _
                  Where p.ReleaseDate > DateTime.Today _
                  Order By p.ReleaseDate Descending _
                  Select p


        Return qry
  End Function
End Class
```

```csharp
// C#
public class VideoGameService : DataService<VideoGameEntities>
{
  // ...

  [WebGet]
  public IQueryable<Product> FutureProducts()
  {
    var qry = from p in this.CurrentDataSource.Products
              where p.ReleaseDate > DateTime.Today
              orderby p.ReleaseDate descending
              select p;

    return qry;
  }
}
```

Before you can use this Service Operation, you need to add it to the configuration so that it is exposed through the service. This is similar to the *SetEntitySetAccessRule* that you used to expose your data end points. Instead you would use *SetServiceOperationAccessRule* and the *ServiceOperationRights* enumeration (which is a subset of the *EntitySetRights* enumeration). For example, to expose your new Service Operation, use the following code:

```vb
' VB
Public Shared Sub InitializeService(ByVal config As IDataServiceConfiguration)
  config.SetEntitySetAccessRule("Products", EntitySetRights.All)
  config.SetEntitySetAccessRule("ProductTypes", EntitySetRights.AllRead)
  config.SetServiceOperationAccessRule("FutureProducts", ServiceOperationRights.AllRead)
End Sub
```

```csharp
// C#
public static void InitializeService(IDataServiceConfiguration config)
{
  config.SetEntitySetAccessRule("Products", EntitySetRights.All);
  config.SetEntitySetAccessRule("ProductTypes", EntitySetRights.AllRead);
  config.SetServiceOperationAccessRule("FutureProducts", ServiceOperationRights.AllRead);
}
```

Once you have that Service Operation configured, you can call it via the URI syntax as you did with the entities:

```
http://localhost/VideoGameService.svc/FutureProducts
```

Because this Service Operation returns an *IQueryable<T>* interface, you can also use query options on it as follows:

```
http://localhost/VideoGameService.svc/FutureProducts?$orderby=ProductName
```

Unlike entity end points, Service Operations can be parameterized (because they are just methods). For example, consider the following Service Operation:

```vb
' VB
<WebGet> _
Public Function ProductsByDate(ByVal cutoffDate As DateTime) As IQueryable(Of Product)
  Dim qry = From p In Me.CurrentDataSource.Products _
            Where p.ReleaseDate > cutoffDate _
            Order By p.ReleaseDate Descending _
            Select p

  Return qry
End Function
```

```csharp
// C#
[WebGet]
public IQueryable<Product> ProductsByDate(DateTime cutoffDate)
```

```
{
  var qry = from p in this.CurrentDataSource.Products
            where p.ReleaseDate > cutoffDate
            orderby p.ReleaseDate descending
            select p;

  return qry;
}
```

Each parameter in the Service Operation uses a simple query string parameter, like so:

```
http://localhost/VideoGameService.svc/ProductsByDate?cutoffDate=datetime'2008-04-24'
```

> **NOTE SERVICE OPERATION PARAMETER SYNTAX**
>
> The query parameters for the Service Operation parameters do not have the dollar sign prefix as the query options do.

Additional Data Service Configuration

The configuration object available on the initialization of the *DataService* class also allows you to configure how the service operates. These additional initialization options are as follows:

- **UseVerboseErrors** Returns rich server-side error information to the client. By default, it is false.

- **MaxBatchCount** Specifies the maximum number of operations in a batch call to the server. Batch operations are explained further in Lesson 2.

- **MaxChangesetCount** The maximum number of changes that can be handled in a batching call to save data on the server.

- **MaxExpandCount** The maximum number of expansions supported by the *$expand* query option.

- **MaxExpandDepth** The maximum amount of nested expansions supported by the *$expand* query option.

- **MaxResultsPerCollection** The maximum number of entities returned by request to the server.

LINQ Providers and ADO.NET Data Services

Although ADO.NET Data Services is designed to work with any LINQ-enabled data source (from simple collections to full-fledged LINQ data like Entity Framework), LINQ is not sufficient for some capabilities. LINQ provides general-purpose semantics for querying, but none for updating. This means that any LINQ provider supports basic querying out of the box, but it may or may not support additional features like updating data and expansions. To support updating, a LINQ provider must support the *IUpdateable* interface. To support expansions, the LINQ provider must support the *IExpandProvider* interface. Entity Framework supports these interfaces (mostly through special support inside ADO.NET Data Services) but other layers do not. LINQ to SQL does not support them either, but there is a community effort underway to support them in the future. Some third-party Object Relational Mappers (ORMs) support these interfaces, but others do not. The NHibernate 2.5 version and the latest version of LLBLGen Pro both support it (though NHibernate 2.5 was not completed as of the time of this book). Please consult your LINQ provider documentation to see if they support these interfaces.

 Quick Check

- Is the Entity Framework required to work with ADO.NET Data Services?

Quick Check Answer

- No, any LINQ-enabled provider will support most features of ADO.NET Data Services.

LAB   Creating a Service

In this lab, you create a new ADO.NET Data Service from an existing Entity Framework model. All the lab files can be installed from the Code folder on the companion CD. To start, you need to have a copy of the LearnDataServices starting project in the Chapter 10 folder. Depending on which language you choose to use, it is either in the Chapter10/Lesson1/Cs/Before folder or the Chapter10/Lesson1/Vb/Before folder. Open the LearnDataServices.sln file to start the project in Visual Studio.

EXERCISE 1   Creating a Service

In this exercise, you create a new ADO.NET Data Service in your project and attach it to the Entity Framework model.

1. Double-click the ProductModel.edmx file to view the data model. Notice that there are tables for customers, purchases, purchased items, products, and product types. You expose some of this model through an ADO.NET Data Model.

2. Once you have the project open, use the Project menu and select Add New Item… to add a new file to the project.

3. Select ADO.NET Data Service and name the service ProductService.svc. The ProductService.svc implementation file (with either the .vb or the .cs extension) opens:

    ```
    'VB
    Imports System.Data.Services
    Imports System.Linq
    Imports System.ServiceModel.Web
    ```

```
Public Class ProductService
  ' TODO: replace [[class name]] with your data class name
  Inherits DataService(Of [[class name]])

  ' This method is called only once to initialize service-wide policies.
  Public Shared Sub InitializeService(ByVal config As IDataServiceConfiguration)
    ' TODO: set rules to indicate which entity sets and service operations are
      visible, updatable
    ' Examples:
    ' config.SetEntitySetAccessRule("MyEntityset", EntitySetRights.AllRead)
    ' config.SetServiceOperationAccessRule("MyServiceOperation",
ServiceOperationRights.All)
  End Sub

End Class
```

```
// C#
using System;
using System.Collections.Generic;
using System.Data.Services;
using System.Linq;
using System.ServiceModel.Web;
using System.Web;

namespace LearnDataServicesWeb
{
  public class ProductService : DataService< /* TODO: put your data source class
      name here */ >
  {
    // This method is called only once to initialize service-wide policies.
    public static void InitializeService(IDataServiceConfiguration config)
    {
      // TODO: set rules to indicate which entity sets and service operations are
        visible, updatable
      // Examples:
      // config.SetEntitySetAccessRule("MyEntityset", EntitySetRights.AllRead);
      // config.SetServiceOperationAccessRule("MyServiceOperation",
        ServiceOperationRights.All);
    }
  }
}
```

4. Use the *VideoGameEntities* context object as the generic parameter of the base class of the service, as shown here:

```
' VB
Public Class ProductService
  Inherits DataService(Of VideoGameEntities)
```

```
// C#
public class ProductService : DataService<VideoGameEntities>
```

5. In Solution Explorer, right-click the ProductService.svc file and select Set As Start Page.

6. Press F5 to start the service in the browser. Notice that this is in Atom format, but you cannot see any of the elements called *collections* that represent end points for the entities in your model.

7. Close the browser to return to Visual Studio.

EXERCISE 2   Configure the Service

In this exercise, you configure the service to expose the end points for parts of the model.

1. Return to the ProductService.svc implementation file (.vb or .cs).

2. Remove all the commented text inside the *InitializeService* method.

3. Inside the *InitializeService* method, add a call to the *config* parameter's *SetEntitySetAccessRule* method and specify *Product* for the first parameter. Specify *EntitySetRights.All* for the second parameter as shown here:

```
'VB
Public Shared Sub InitializeService(ByVal config As IDataServiceConfiguration)
  config.SetEntitySetAccessRule("Product", EntitySetRights.All)
End Sub
```

```
// C#
public static void InitializeService(IDataServiceConfiguration config)
{
  config.SetEntitySetAccessRule("Product", EntitySetRights.All);
}
```

4. Press F5 to run the service. In the Atom format, notice that there is now a *collection* element with an *href* of *Product*. This represents the entity that you just exposed via the *SetEntitySetAccessRule*. Close the browser to return to Visual Studio.

5. Add another call to *SetEntitySetAccessRule,* but specify the *ProductType* entity and *EntitySetRights.AllRead* to let *ProductTypes* be read but not changed, as shown here:

```
' VB
config.SetEntitySetAccessRule("ProductType", EntitySetRights.AllRead)
```

```
// C#
config.SetEntitySetAccessRule("ProductType", EntitySetRights.AllRead);
```

6. Press F5 to run the service again and notice that *ProductType* has been added to the collections as well. Notice that there is no indication from the Atom feed about whether either of the collections is read/write or just read-only. Close the browser and return to Visual Studio.

7. Add another line to the *InitializeService* method by calling the *config* parameter's *UseVerboseErrors* property, setting it to true, as shown here:

```
' VB
config.UseVerboseErrors = True
```

```
// C#
config.UseVerboseErrors = true;
```

EXERCISE 3   Querying Using the URI Syntax

In this exercise, you use the browser window to create some simple queries against the data service.

1. Press F5 to start the browser with your Data Service.

2. Add the end point *ProductType* to the end of the URI to show all the product types, as shown here:

```
http://localhost:8000/ProductService.svc/ProductType
```

3. Change the end point to *Product* to show the list of products, as shown here:

```
http://localhost:8000/ProductService.svc/Product
```

4. Show an individual product by specifying the product with a primary key of 2, as shown here:

```
http://localhost:8000/ProductService.svc/Product(2)
```

5. Show the product type of this product by following the relative *href* to the *ProductType*, as shown here:

```
http://localhost:8000/ProductService.svc/Product(2)/ProductType
```

6. Remove the *ProductType* and the return of the individual product key to search through all the *Products*. Filter the results by specifying the list price to be equal to 59.99, as shown here:

```
http://localhost:8000/ProductService.svc/Product?$filter=ListPrice eq 59.99
```

7. Sort these results by adding a sort option to sort by *ProductName*, as shown here:

```
http://localhost:8000/ProductService.svc/Product?$filter=ListPrice%20eq%20
59.99&$orderby=ProductName
```

8. Remove the filter and sort and add an expansion to return the *ProductTypes* inline by adding an expansion option, as shown here:

```
http://localhost:8000/ProductService.svc/Product?$expand=ProductType
```

9. Limit the number of results by using the top options specifying only 10 responses, as shown here:

```
http://localhost:8000/ProductService.svc/Product?$expand=ProductType&$top=10
```

10. Finally, add a skip option to skip the first 10 before you return the top 10, as shown here:

```
http://localhost:8000/ProductService.svc/Product?$expand=ProductType&$
top=10&$skip=10
```

Lesson Summary

- Using an ADO.NET Data Service allows you to expose data in a rich way across an HTTP connection.
- You can use Visual Studio to create new ADO.NET Data Services. An ADO.NET Data Service must be configured to allow specific entities to be accessed as well as to specify what operations are allowed on those entities.
- To expose specific sets of queries (instead of simple entity collections), you can create operation services.
- You can use the URI syntax to sort, filter, and shape results from an ADO.NET Data Service.

Lesson Review

Use the following questions to test your knowledge of the information in Lesson 1, "Exposing the Data Services." The questions are also available on the companion CD if you prefer to review them in electronic form.

NOTE ANSWERS

Answers to these questions and explanations of why each answer choice is correct or incorrect are located in the "Answers" section at the end of the book.

1. What types of data can you expose through an ADO.NET Data Service? (Choose all that apply.)

   A. Entity Framework Model

   B. ADO.NET *DataReaders*

   C. LINQ to SQL

   D. Anything that supports LINQ

2. How can you expose individual parts of a LINQ model through an ADO.NET Data Service?

   A. Adding the LINQ-enabled data to the service class is sufficient.

   B. Configure the service to expose data explicitly.

   C. Any data in your application is enabled automatically.

   D. Provide a list of end points in the *ServiceHost* class.

Lesson 2: Consuming the Data Service

After Lesson 1, you should be comfortable with creating your own ADO.NET Data Services. You should be wondering now how consumption of the data works. The URI syntax and the Atom and JSON formats do not seem to be very friendly to .NET applications. That's where the Data Service Library comes in. It simplifies the consumption of the data and provides a basis for managing changes back to the server.

> **After this lesson, you will be able to:**
> - Write a client for an ADO.NET Data Service
>
> **Estimated lesson time: 30 minutes**

Using an ADO.NET Data Service

Although it's important to understand the nature of the URI syntax, in practice you do not use it all that much. The reason is that the ADO.NET Data Service client library simplifies much of that for you. The Data Service Library (available for .NET and Silverlight 2) allows you to call these services with a minimum of effort.

Referencing the Data Service

To start using your service, you need a client application. This can be a Silverlight 2 application or a standard .NET application. For this lesson, you should use a standard desktop .NET application; Windows Forms or Windows Presentation Foundation (WPF) are both fine.

To access the data, you can add a Service Reference (like using Web Services). You can do this by clicking the Project menu in Visual Studio and selecting Add Service Reference. In the Add Service Reference dialog box, click Discover to show any references in your Web project, including ADO.NET Data Services. You then pick the Data Service and click OK to create the reference to your ADO.NET Data Service, as shown in Figure 10-8.

Adding the Service Reference adds two types of classes to your project: context classes and entity classes. Context classes expose the service and allow you to perform queries against the service; in addition, they are responsible for change management. Entity classes are responsible for representing your data in your application. There is an entity class for each exposed entity from the ADO.NET Data Service (including relationships between them). Instead of consuming the Atom or JSON directly, the client library handles the serialization to and from the entity classes to simplify the consumption of the ADO.NET Data Service. An example of these classes is shown in Figure 10-9.

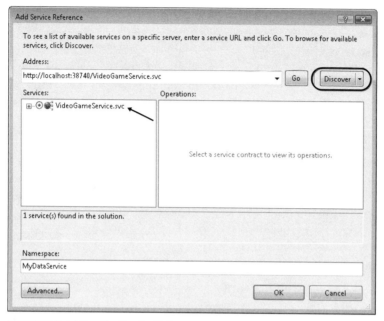

FIGURE 10-8 Adding the Service Reference

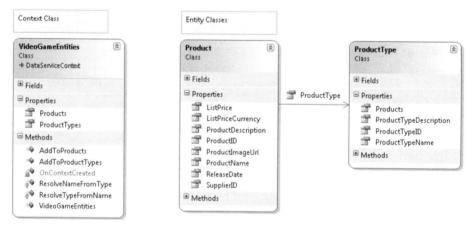

FIGURE 10-9 Service Reference classes

Use Cases for ADO.NET Data Services

Although ADO.NET Data Services is a powerful tool for delivering data across the Internet, it is important not to think of it as the new way to perform data access for all your applications. ADO.NET Data Services is well suited only for applications that have to cross the firewall. Coincidently, this applies to Web Services in general. The cost of serialization and passing through several layers to get at your data means that it is not a general solution to data access. You could imagine using these rich objects directly inside your enterprise and then using ADO.NET Data Services to propagate your data to remote clients.

NOTE **SILVERLIGHT 2**

In this lesson, you learn how to work with the Data Service Client library with a standard .NET application. This library also exists for Silverlight 2, but because of the nature of the platform, the Silverlight 2 client library forces you to issue all your requests (queries and updates) as asynchronous requests. The library is essentially the same, but if you take these examples directly and use them in Silverlight 2 you throw "Not Implemented" exceptions on the synchronous calls (including execution of the LINQ queries like *qry.ToList()*. Change these to asynchronous requests and the code works in Silverlight 2.

Querying Data Using LINQ

Retrieving data from the Data Service simply requires you create an instance of the context class and issue LINQ queries against the service. First, you must create an instance of the context class itself. Creating the context requires that you know the address of the server that hosts the service. Unlike Web Services, data service context classes require that you explicitly set the path to the data service using an instance of the *Uri* class. For example:

```vb
' VB
Dim servicePath As New Uri("http://localhost:8000/VideoGameService.svc")
Dim ctx As New VideoGameEntities(servicePath)
```

```csharp
// C#
Uri servicePath = new Uri("http://localhost:8000/VideoGameService.svc");
VideoGameEntities ctx = new VideoGameEntities(servicePath);
```

The context class (*VideoGameEntities* in these examples) exposes a number of methods and properties that are useful, but to begin with, you should look at the properties. For each entity type that the Data Service exposes, the entity class has a queryable property. This allows you to construct LINQ queries against the queryable properties. For example, you can create a LINQ query to find certain *Products* in your service like so:

```vb
' VB
Dim qry = From p In ctx.Products _
          Order By p.ProductName _
          Where p.ReleaseDate >= DateTime.Today _
          Select p
```

```
// C#
var qry = from p in ctx.Products
          orderby p.ProductName
          where p.ReleaseDate >= DateTime.Today
          select p;
```

The ADO.NET Data Service Client library takes the LINQ query and translates it into the URI syntax that you learned about in Lesson 1. This means that you can execute the query and it returns the results as expected. The Data Service Client library converts the LINQ expression into a URI syntax and handles the Atom serialization for you. For example:

```
' VB
Dim theProducts As List(Of Product) = qry.ToList()
```

```
// C#
List<Product> theProducts = qry.ToList();
```

Because the underlying URI syntax does not support everything that LINQ supports, you are limited to LINQ semantics that apply to the URI syntax. The client library does its best to translate between the two search syntaxes, but you may find that when doing very complex LINQ searches, you do not have the full grammar of LINQ. If that is the case, you can create Service Operations to perform the complex query on the server and return the results.

> **TIP DEBUGGING HINT**
>
> If you are debugging on the client, you can pause over the LINQ query and see the URI syntax that the client library is going to execute. Copy and paste this into the browser to see if you are getting the data you expect.

Executing Service Operations

Unlike the entity properties, service operations are not created in the service reference code. Therefore to call a service operation, you must use the raw execute facility of the context object. To use the raw execute facility, you use the context object's *Execute<T>* method. This method takes the name of the returned entities as the generic parameter. It also requires a URI specifying the URI syntax of the service operation (or any URI query, really). Because you set the service operation URI in the context object earlier, you can create a relative URI that specifies the Service Operation's URI. For example, this code calls the *FutureProducts* service operation that you created in Lesson 1:

```
' VB
Dim serviceOperationPath As New Uri("FutureProducts", UriKind.Relative)
Dim futures As IEnumerable(Of Product) = ctx.Execute(Of Product)(serviceOperationPath)
Dim theProducts As List(Of Product) = futures.ToList()
```

```csharp
// C#
Uri serviceOperationPath = new Uri("FutureProducts", UriKind.Relative);
IEnumerable<Product> futures = ctx.Execute<Product>(serviceOperationPath);
List<Product> theProducts = futures.ToList();
```

The return value from *Execute<T>* is an *IEnumerable<T>* of the type specified in the generic parameter of *Execute<T>*. Once you have the *IEnumerable<T>* object, you can query it locally or just create collections as necessary.

Changing Data

Reading data is only part of the picture. You need to be able to create, update, and delete data as well. Unlike using Web Services, where you may call individual methods to insert, update, and delete data, in ADO.NET Data Services, the context class is responsible for calling the server with all the changes. At first glance, this seems simple because the context class has a *SaveChanges* method that seems similar to the functionality of the Entity Framework and LINQ to SQL. Actually, however, it is fairly different. The reason for this is that the ADO.NET Data Services team wanted the consumption of the data to be as lightweight as possible. This means that the context class is capable of tracking the changes, but there is no support for automatic tracking of the changes that happen to data retrieved from an ADO.NET Data Service.

Without automatic tracking, that leaves change tracking up to you, the developer. In the context class, there is a collection called *Entities* that contains a reference to all tracked objects. This collection is maintained so that when changes are saved, the context object knows about those changes. To track changes, the context class supports a number of methods that allow you to tell the context object about entity changes (new, updated, or deleted). These methods tell the context object to track this object and set their status (so that the context object knows how to tell the server to save the changes). These methods are

- **AddObject**   Specifies an object to needs to be added
- **UpdateObject**   Specifies an object should be updated
- **DeleteObject**   Specifies an object should be deleted from the service's data

You would use these methods when your object changes or is created. For example, if you were to change an object, you would need to notify the context object, as shown here:

```vb
' VB
myProduct.ListPrice = 45
ctx.UpdateObject(myProduct)
```

```csharp
// C#
myProduct.ListPrice = 45;
ctx.UpdateObject(myProduct);
```

For each entity type supported by your context class, there is a strongly typed method for adding new items. These are typically called *Add*, suffixed with the name of the entity.

For example, you can use the *AddProduct* method to add a *Product* entity type to the context class, as shown here:

```vb
' VB
Dim newProduct As New Product() With
{
    .ProductName = "My New Product",
    .ProductDescription = "This is a description for my new product.",
    .ListPrice = 60,
    .ListPriceCurrency = "USD",
    .ReleaseDate = DateTime.Today
}
ctx.AddToProducts(newProduct)
```

```csharp
// C#
Product newProduct = new Product()
{
    ProductName = "My New Product",
    ProductDescription = "This is a description for my new product.",
    ListPrice = 60,
    ListPriceCurrency = "USD",
    ReleaseDate = DateTime.Today
};
ctx.AddToProducts(newProduct);
```

Tracking the changes of the entities is useful, but in general, you are not working with unrelated data. Most of the data you are working with is related (often through foreign keys in a database). For our examples, we have two related entities: *Product* and *ProductType*. The context class maintains the relationships separate from the entities in a collection called *Links*. These links are the relationships between two objects. These links allow ADO.NET Data Services to propagate related entities to the service so that the data changes can maintain the referential integrity as well. To maintain the links, you can use several methods:

- **AddLink**   Links two objects where the linkage is in a collection
- **SetLink**   Links two objects where the linkage is in a scalar property
- **DeleteLink**   Removes a link between two objects

For example, to set the relationship between the *Product* and the *ProductType*, you would call *SetLink* (because the link is a one-to-one relationship) and specify the product to link, the name of the relationship (*ProductType*), and the new *ProductType*, as shown here:

```vb
' VB
ctx.SetLink(product, "ProductType", productTypes(0))
```

```csharp
// C#
ctx.SetLink(product, "ProductType", productTypes[0]);
```

Saving Changes

Once you have items to save back to the ADO.NET Data Service, you can use the *SaveChanges* method to update the server. When you call *SaveChanges* it makes a call to the server for every change to update the server, as shown here:

```
' VB
ctx.SaveChanges()
```

```
// C#
ctx.SaveChanges();
```

Unless you are saving changes on every change, it is more efficient to call *SaveChanges* specifying save options that tell the context object to batch the changes to the server. You tell the context object to batch the changes by using the *SaveChangesOptions* enumeration. You can either specify the *SaveChangesOptions* on each call to *SaveChanges* or you can set a default by setting the context's *SaveChangesDefaultOptions* property, as shown here:

```
' VB
ctx.SaveChangesDefaultOptions = SaveChangesOptions.Batch
ctx.SaveChanges()
```

```
' or
```

```
ctx.SaveChanges(SaveChangesOptions.Batch)
```

```
// C#
ctx.SaveChangesDefaultOptions = SaveChangesOptions.Batch;
ctx.SaveChanges();
```

```
// or
```

```
ctx.SaveChanges(SaveChangesOptions.Batch);
```

The *SaveChangesOptions* enumeration supports a small number of options, as shown in Table 10-8.

TABLE 10-8 *SaveChangesOptions* Enumeration

VALUE	MEANING
None	Updates are sent as single requests to the server; any error causes the updates to stop being sent, and new server-side changes are merged with the entities.
Batch	Updates are batched as a single request to the server (LINQ provider must support batching to allow this to work).

TABLE 10-8 *SaveChangesOptions* Enumeration

VALUE	MEANING
ContinueOnError	If errors occur during updates, it continues to try to execute subsequent updates and returns the errors found in the error collection.
ReplaceOnUpdate	Do not merge server-side changes, but simply replace the existing objects with their server-side data counterparts.

When you call *SaveChanges,* it returns an object called a *DataServiceResponse.* This object contains information about the operation(s) that were performed on the server. The *DataServiceReponse* object supports enumerating through responses for each operation that happened during the save operation (for example, every entity and link that were saved). You can iterate through these operations like so:

```vb
' VB
Dim response As DataServiceResponse = ctx.SaveChanges()

For Each opResponse As ChangeOperationResponse In response
  If opResponse.Error IsNot Nothing Then
        MessageBox.Show(opResponse.Error.Message)
  End If
Next opResponse
```

```csharp
// C#
DataServiceResponse response = ctx.SaveChanges();

foreach (ChangeOperationResponse opResponse in response)
{
  if (opResponse.Error != null)
  {
    MessageBox.Show(opResponse.Error.Message);
  }
}
```

Each *ChangeOperationResponse* object contains information about the success of the operation. If you specified *SaveChangesOption.ContinueOnError,* the responses may contain information about the failed operations. If you are not using the *SaveChangesOption.ContinueOnError* value, an exception is thrown on the first server error. The exception type thrown is a *DataService RequestException.* This exception contains the *DataServiceResponse* as a property called *Response.* For example, you would catch this exception and could iterate through any errors using the same method you saw earlier:

```vb
' VB
Try
  Dim response As DataServiceResponse = ctx.SaveChanges()
Catch ex As DataServiceRequestException
```

```
  For Each opResponse As ChangeOperationResponse In ex.Response
        If opResponse.Error IsNot Nothing Then
          MessageBox.Show(opResponse.Error.Message)
        End If
  Next opResponse
End Try

// C#
try
{
  DataServiceResponse response = ctx.SaveChanges();
}
catch (DataServiceRequestException ex)
{
  foreach (ChangeOperationResponse opResponse in ex.Response)
  {
    if (opResponse.Error != null)
    {
      MessageBox.Show(opResponse.Error.Message);
    }
  }
}
```

> **NOTE DEBUGGING**
>
> If you are not getting appropriate error information, make sure that you have configured
> your service to show full errors by using the *IServiceConfiguration.UseVerboseErrors* property.

 Quick Check

- Assuming your changes should be treated atomically, what type of
  SaveChangesOptions should you use for most saves?

Quick Check Answer

- *SaveChangesOptions.Batch* is the best option to use in most cases because the
  changes are sent to the server in batches to improve throughput.

LAB   Creating a Data Service Client

In this lab, you create a new client to use your ADO.NET Data Service from Lesson 1. All the lab files
can be installed from the Code folder on the companion CD. To start, you need to have a copy of
the LearnDataServices starting project in the Chapter 10 folder. Depending on which language you
choose to use, it is either in the Chapter10/Lesson2/Cs/Before folder or the Chapter10/Lesson2/Vb/
Before folder. Open the LearnDataServices.sln file to start the project in Visual Studio.

EXERCISE 1   Query Data Through the Client Library

In this exercise, you take an existing client and add support ADO.NET Data Services to retrieve data.

1. Once you have the project open, press F5 to run the project in Visual Studio so you can see that both projects start up (the Web application so we can get data and the client app that retrieves data from the server). Our client does not have any data yet— we add that manually. Close the browser and return to Visual Studio.

2. Right-click the ServiceClient project and select Add Service Reference.

3. In the "Add Service Reference" dialog box, click the Discover button to find services in solution. Your "ProductService" data service should appear in the list of services.

4. Near the bottom of the "Add Service Reference" dialog is the namespace declaration for the new service. Change this Namespace to **DataServices** and click the OK button to create the service reference.

5. Open the MainForm.xaml implementation file (.cs or .vb).

6. Create a new private field in the *MainForm* class called *ctx* of type *VideoGameEntities*. You may need to add a *using/Imports* statement to the *ServiceClient.DataServices* namespace as shown here:

```
' VB
Imports ServiceClient.DataServices
' ...
Class MainForm
   Dim ctx As VideoGameEntities
```

```
// C#
using ServiceClient.DataServices;

namespace ServiceClient
{
   public partial class MainForm : Window
   {
      VideoGameEntities ctx = null;
```

7. Inside the end of the constructor (*Sub New* in Visual Basic) create a new URI called *serviceUri* and specify a string that is the path to the data service as its lone parameter.

8. Assign a new instance of the *VideoGameEntities* class to the class-level field we created earlier. Specify the *serviceUri* as a construction parameter. Your constructor should now look like this:

```
' VB
   Public Sub New()

      InitializeComponent()
```

```
       Dim serviceUri = New Uri("http://localhost:8000/ProductService.svc")
       ctx = New VideoGameEntities(serviceUri)

     End Sub
```

```
// C#
public MainForm()
{
  InitializeComponent();

  loadDataButton.Click += new RoutedEventHandler(loadDataButton_Click);
  editDataButton.Click += new RoutedEventHandler(editDataButton_Click);
  newDataButton.Click += new RoutedEventHandler(newDataButton_Click);

  Uri serviceUri = new Uri("http://localhost:8000/ProductService.svc");
  ctx = new VideoGameEntities(serviceUri);
}
```

9. Find the *loadDataButton_Click* event-handling method in this class.

10. Inside the method, create a new LINQ query that searches through the *ctx* field's *Product* property.

11. Filter data using a WHERE clause to return only products that have been released after January 1, 2008.

12. Sort the query by the *ProductName* of the product that are being returned. Your query should look like this:

```
' VB
Dim qry = From p In ctx.Product _
          Where p.ReleaseDate >= DateTime.Parse("01/01/2008") _
          Order By p.ProductName _
          Select p
```

```
// C#
var qry = from p in ctx.Product
          where p.ReleaseDate >= DateTime.Parse("01/01/2008")
          orderby p.ProductName
          select p;
```

13. Create a new generic list of *Products* and assign it by executing the query using the *ToList* method, as shown here:

```
' VB
Dim results As List(Of Product) = qry.ToList()
```

```
// C#
List<Product> results = qry.ToList();
```

14. Assign the results to the *ItemsSource* property of the *productList* (the *ListBox* on the page). You must also set the *DisplayMemberPath* of the *productList* to *ProductName*, as shown here:

```
' VB
productList.ItemsSource = results
productList.DisplayMemberPath = "ProductName"
```

```
// C#
productList.ItemsSource = results;
productList.DisplayMemberPath = "ProductName";
```

15. Run the solution. Once both projects are running, click Load Data to see the request go to the server and show data in the *ListBox*. Close both applications.

EXERCISE 2   Change Data

In this exercise, you load an individual *Product*, change it, and save those changes.

1. In the implementation class of the *MainForm*, locate the *editData_Click* event-handling method.

2. Create a new LINQ query against the *ctx* field's *Products* that searches for any games that contain "Joint Strike" in the *Product* name:

```
' VB
Private Sub editDataButton_Click(ByVal sender As System.Object, ByVal e As
            System.Windows.RoutedEventArgs) Handles editDataButton.Click

    Dim qry = From p In ctx.Product _
                Where p.ProductName.Contains("Joint Strike") _
                Select p

End Sub
```

```
// C#
void editDataButton_Click(object sender, RoutedEventArgs e)
{
    var qry = from p in ctx.Product
                where p.ProductName.Contains("Joint Strike")
                select p;
}
```

3. Create a new local variable called *game* of type *Product*. Assign it by calling the query's *FirstOrDefault* method, as shown here:

```
' VB
Dim game As Product = qry.FirstOrDefault()
```

```
// C#
Product game = qry.FirstOrDefault();
```

4. Create an *if* statement testing for whether the game variable is *null* in C# (*Nothing* in Visual Basic).

5. If the *game* variable is *null* (or *Nothing* in Visual Basic), create a message using *MessageBox.Show* that says "Game was not found."

6. In the *else* part of the *if* statement, change the game's *ProductName* to "1943: Joint Strike" (note that the year is changing).

7. Call the *ctx* field's *UpdateObject* method passing in the game you just changed.

8. Call the *ctx* field's *SaveChanges* to send the changes to the server.

9. After saving the changes, create a message box using *MessageBox.Show* that says "Saved!". Your code should look like this:

```vb
' VB
Dim game As Product = qry.FirstOrDefault()

If game Is Nothing Then
   MessageBox.Show("Game was not found.")
Else
   game.ProductName = "1943: Joint Strike"
   ctx.UpdateObject(game)
   ctx.SaveChanges()
   MessageBox.Show("Saved!")
End If
```

```csharp
// C#
Product game = qry.FirstOrDefault();

if (game == null)
{
   MessageBox.Show("Game was not found.");
}
else
{
   game.ProductName = "1943: Joint Strike";
   ctx.UpdateObject(game);
   ctx.SaveChanges();
   MessageBox.Show("Saved!");
}
```

10. Run the solution. When the client application appears, click Edit Data. When you get confirmation it saved, click Load Data and see the change you made in the *ListBox*.

Lesson Summary

- You can create a client for an ADO.NET Data Service, including creating a Service Reference.
- You can query for data remotely in an ADO.NET Data Service.
- You can make changes to client and propagate them to the server using the context class.

Lesson Review

Use the following questions to test your knowledge of the information in Lesson 2, "Consuming the Data Service." The questions are also available on the companion CD if you prefer to review them in electronic form.

> **NOTE ANSWERS**
>
> Answers to these questions and explanations of why each answer choice is correct or incorrect are located in the "Answers" section at the end of the book.

1. What is required to inform the context class that changes have occurred so they are sent to the server when saves occur?

   A. Call the *UpdateObject* method manually on the context class.

   B. Nothing; changes are propagated automatically.

   C. Attach the changes to the context class's *Entities* collection.

   D. Call the *AddLink* method to link the changes to the context object.

2. What class is responsible for letting the client know about the state of changes on the server?

   A. The *DataService* class.

   B. The *DataServiceRequestException* class.

   C. None; a *Boolean* is returned from *SaveChanges*.

   D. The *DataServiceResponse* class.

Chapter Review

To practice and reinforce the skills you learned in this chapter further, you can perform the following tasks:

- Review the chapter summary.
- Complete the case scenarios. These scenarios set up real-world situations involving the topics in this chapter and ask you to create a solution.
- Complete the suggested practices.
- Take a practice test.

Chapter Summary

- ADO.NET Data Services represents a solution to the problem of accessing data across Internet network connections.
- Using existing LINQ-based providers allows you to expose virtually any data you need to use in your disconnected application because that is what ADO.NET Data Services requires to create end points.
- The rich client for ADO.NET Data Services allows you to write client code that is familiar and comfortable even as it does the hard work of serializing and translating LINQ queries to the URI search syntax.

Case Scenarios

In the following case scenario, you apply what you have learned about configuring Internet protocol addressing. You can find answers to these questions in the "Answers" section at the end of this book.

Case Scenario: External Clients

You are a development lead in a small business services company that sells data to salespeople at a client's site. Currently, they are using terminal services to connect remotely to your servers to perform searches against your data center. The current client uses the Entity Framework as your data access layer.

Answer the following questions:

1. Your boss has asked you for a solution to deliver your smart client directly to the clients that do not want to use a remote session to use the software. What do you tell him?

2. You manager wants to know what changes are required in the current client to support remote usage. What do you say?

Suggested Practices

To help you master the exam objectives presented in this chapter, complete the following tasks.

Using ADO.NET Data Services

- **Practice 1**   Add a Data Service to an existing LINQ provider

Add a Data Service to an existing Web application based on an existing LINQ-provider data access layer.

- **Practice 2**   Create a remote client for your new Data Service

Create a sample client that consumes data from your new data service.

Take a Practice Test

The practice tests on this book's companion CD offer many options. For example, you can test yourself on just one exam objective, or you can test yourself on all of the 70-561 exam content. You can set up the test so that it closely simulates the experience of taking a certification exam, or you can set it up in study mode so that you can look at the correct answers and explanations after you answer each question.

> **MORE INFO   PRACTICE TESTS**
>
> For details about all the practice test options available, see the section entitled "How to Use the Practice Tests," in the Introduction to this book.

Answers

Chapter 1: Lesson Review Answers

Lesson 1

1. **Correct Answer: A**
   - **A. Correct:** The SqlClient provider is in use and the connection string is syntactically valid so this snippet should connect to the data source without issue.
   - **B. Incorrect:** The specified connection string contains invalid syntax—*InitialCatalog* instead of *Initial Catalog*. This error causes the connection to fail.
   - **C. Incorrect:** The connection string is missing the *Data Source* property.
   - **D. Incorrect:** The *DBConnection* abstract class cannot be used in this way to connect to a database.

2. **Correct Answer: C**
   - **A. Incorrect:** Although this approach is valid, it is best to catch individual types of exceptions so they can be properly handled.
   - **B. Incorrect:** Allowing the exception to be thrown in an unhandled manner is a bad idea—and there is no such thing as the *Errors* object.
   - **C. Correct:** Using a *try/catch* block that catches individual types of exception is best when handling exceptions.
   - **D. Incorrect:** A message could be shown to users depending upon where the database access code is located. However, this isn't as much handling the exception as it is passing it to users to resolve for themselves.

Lesson 2

1. **Correct Answer: C**
   - **A. Incorrect:** Although this provider can be used to connect to SQL Server, the performance is not optimal for any particular technology because it is more generic in its architecture to allow connections to other OLE DB–compliant data sources.
   - **B. Incorrect:** Like the OLE DB provider, the ODBC provider is generic in nature and does not perform in an optimal fashion for any particular data source type.

C. Correct: The native SqlClient provider, because it is written specifically for SQL Server and tuned for optimum performance, is the best choice in this situation.

D. Incorrect: The oracle provider would not be a suitable choice since it is designed to work only with an Oracle database.

2. **Correct Answer: B**

A. Incorrect: *CreateFactory* is not a method of the *DbProviderFactories* class.

B. Correct: This is the proper way to use the *DbProviderFactory* class—getting a reference to a specific provider using the *GetFactory* method.

C. Incorrect: A reference to a specific provider cannot be made by assigning the *DbProviderFactory* instance to a new instance of a provider.

D. Incorrect: The *System.Data.Common.DbConnection* class is abstract and cannot be used directly to create a connection instance.

Lesson 3

1. **Correct Answer: A, B, and C**

A. Correct: This data provider supports the use of MARS.

B. Correct: This data provider supports the use of MARS.

C. Correct: This data provider supports the use of MARS.

D. Incorrect: The *DbConnection* abstract class is not a data provider.

2. **Correct Answer: D**

A. Incorrect: This syntax is incorrect.

B. Incorrect: This syntax is incorrect.

C. Incorrect: This syntax is incorrect.

D. Correct: This is the correct syntax for enabling MARS on the connection.

Chapter 1: Case Scenario Answer

Case Scenario: Connecting to a Sensitive Data Source

- You recommend the purchase of an SSL certificate for the database server and the enablement of encryption on the connection. This secures the network traffic. In addition, to protect connection information on the client, you suggest encrypting the connection string section of the configuration file on the client.

Chapter 2: Lesson Review Answers

Lesson 1

1. **Correct Answer: C**

    A. **Incorrect:** *StoredProcedure* is a valid *CommandType* enumeration value.

    B. **Incorrect:** *TableDirect* is a valid *CommandType* enumeration value.

    C. **Correct:** The *TableSchema* value is invalid because it is not a *CommandType* enumeration value.

    D. **Incorrect:** *Text* is a valid *CommandType* enumeration value.

2. **Correct Answer: A**

    A. **Correct:** This SQL statement is valid.

    B. **Incorrect:** The join in the FROM clause is incorrect; the *productType* table is not assigned an alias.

    C. **Incorrect:** There is no join type called LEFT INNER JOIN.

    D. **Incorrect:** There is no join type called LEFT OUTER—the *JOIN* keyword is missing.

Lesson 2

1. **Correct Answer: D**

    A. **Incorrect:** This method does not return any data to the client.

    B. **Incorrect:** Using this method works, but all data is retrieved, not just the single value requested. Therefore, it is not the most suitable option.

    C. **Incorrect:** This method works, but it retrieves more data than is necessary. Therefore, it is not the most suitable option.

    D. **Correct:** Because the *ExecuteScalar* method disposes of all data except the value in the first column in the first row of the result set, this method is ideal.

2. **Correct Answer: C**

    A. **Incorrect:** The *Spatial* datatype is used to store Geographical- or Geometry-based data in SQL Server.

    B. **Incorrect:** The *VarChar* datatype is used to store a variable number of characters.

    C. **Correct:** Table Value Parameters are ideal for passing a set of data—a *DataTable*—to a stored procedure. This cuts down greatly on server round trips when the stored procedure needs to be called once per row of data.

    D. **Incorrect:** The *varbinary(max)* datatype is used to store BLOB data.

Chapter 2: Case Scenario Answer

Case Scenario: Improving Application Performance

- Examine the data access layer of the application with the goal of implementing asynchronous processing. In addition, moving from using a *DataReader* to using a *DataAdapter* and consuming sets of data rather than individual rows have a positive effect on performance.

Chapter 3: Lesson Review Answers

Lesson 1

1. **Correct Answer: B**

    A. **Incorrect:** *RowError* is a property on the *DataRow*. There is no *SetRowError*, only a *SetColumnError* method on the *DataRow*.

    B. **Correct:** *RowError* is a property on the *DataRow*, and using it is the correct way to set a row-level error.

    C. **Incorrect:** The *SetColumnError* is a method on the *DataRow*, not the *DataTable*.

    D. **Incorrect:** The correct answer is B.

2. **Correct Answer: D**

    A. **Incorrect:** The *SqlCommand* class does not have a *Fill* method.

    B. **Incorrect:** The *SqlCommand* class does not have a *FillSchema* method.

    C. **Incorrect:** The *DataAdapter.FillSchema* command has more than one argument.

    D. **Correct:** This fills the schema in the *DataSet* for the *Order* table.

Lesson 2

1. **Correct Answers: B and D**

    A. **Incorrect:** *Typed DataSets* are a code generator feature of Visual Studio, not of the .NET Framework.

    B. **Correct:** *Typed DataSets* are a code generator feature of Visual Studio, not of the .NET Framework.

    C. **Incorrect:** *Typed DataSets* are database-agnostic.

    D. **Correct:** *Typed DataSets* were introduced in Visual Studio 7.

2. **Correct Answer: D**

    A. **Incorrect:** Each *DataAdapter* in a *Typed DataSet* can connect to a different data source.

    B. **Incorrect:** The connection string information is stored in the connection section of the configuration file.

C. Incorrect: A typed *DataRow* offers methods, not properties, for navigating relationships.

   D. Correct: One of the options when adding a *TableAdapter* to a *Typed DataSet* is to have the wizard generate additional methods for direct database access. This is done through the *GenerateDBDirectMethods* option.

Chapter 3: Case Scenario Answer

Case Scenario: Designing Data Access

- You recommend *Typed DataSets*. *Typed DataSets* are a wrapper around ADO.NET *DataSets* and offer the following benefits:
  - Great performance
  - Strongly typed access to relational data, allowing a wide range of bugs and errors to be caught early in the development process

Chapter 4: Lesson Review Answers

Lesson 1

1. **Correct Answer: A**

    A. Correct: Using *SqlParameters* is the best way to insert data when using the *SqlCommand* class.

    B. Incorrect: *ExecuteReader* should not be used for inserting data.

    C. Incorrect: *ExecuteXmlReader* should not be used for inserting data.

    D. Incorrect: Using string concatenation to build SQL statements should be avoided because it carries the risk of a SQL injection attack.

2. **Correct Answer: D**

    A. Incorrect: *UpdateBatchSize* is a property of *SqlDataAdapter*.

    B. Incorrect: *UpdateBatchSize* is a property of *SqlDataAdapter*.

    C. Incorrect: *UpdateBatchSize* is a property of *SqlDataAdapter*.

    D. Correct: *UpdateBatchSize* is a property of *SqlDataAdapter*.

Lesson 2

1. **Correct Answers: B, C, and D**

    A. Incorrect: *DbConnection* is an abstract class that cannot be instantiated. Specific implementations derive from *DbConnection* to offer connectivity to SQL Server, Object

Linking and Embedding Database (OLE DB)–compliant databases, Open Database Connectivity (ODBC) data sources, and vendor-supplied databases.

B. Correct: The *SqlConnection* class is a concrete implementation of the abstract *DbConnection* class and can be used to connect to a provider-specific database, in this case SQL Server.

C. Correct: The *DataAdapter* is a database independent base class for connecting a *DataSet* to a data source.

D. Correct: The *TableAdapter* is a class generated by the DataSet Designer to connect a *Typed DataSet* to a specific data source.

2. **Correct Answer: B**

A. Incorrect: *DbTransaction* is an abstract class that cannot be instantiated. Specific implementations derive from *DbTransaction* to offer resource-specific transaction management, such as *SqlTransaction*.

B. Correct: The *SqlTransaction* class is a concrete implementation of a *DbTransaction* and can manage a transaction on a SQL Server database.

C. Incorrect: Transactions need to be managed explicitly, there is no implicit transaction when using the *DataAdapter*.

D. Incorrect: Transactions need to be managed explicitly, there is no implicit transaction when using the *DataAdapter*.

3. **Correct Answers: A, C, and D**

A. Correct: If the *Complete* method has not been invoked, the transaction is assumed to have failed and a rollback is performed.

B. Incorrect: If the *Complete* method has been invoked and no exception occurred, the transaction has succeeded and a commit is performed.

C. Correct: If an exception occurs, a rollback is performed.

D. Correct: If an exception occurs, a rollback is performed.

Chapter 4: Case Scenario Answer

Case Scenario: Managing Transactions

- You recommend wrapping all database interaction code using the *TransactionScope using* construct. This automatically escalates transactions to the DTC when more than one connection or database is used. You also recommend a more detailed analysis of the batch processes. If these processes use a single database, custom management of the transactions may lead to improved performance of these batch jobs.

Chapter 5: Lesson Review Answers

Lesson 1

1. **Correct Answer: B**
   - **A.** **Incorrect:** Session State is for user-based caching, but it is better to use Cookies for very small pieces of data for the user.
   - **B.** **Correct:** Cookies are the correct type of cache for very small pieces of user-based data.
   - **C.** **Incorrect:** ViewState is for page-based caching and is available for only a single page. You should use Cookies for very small pieces of user-specific data.
   - **D.** **Incorrect:** Cache is not for user-based caching. You should use Cookies for very small pieces of data for the user.

2. **Correct Answer: C**
   - **A.** **Incorrect:** Session State is most useful for data that is user-based.
   - **B.** **Incorrect:** Session State can handle large pieces of user-based data.
   - **C.** **Correct:** Session State is for user-based data, so application-based data should be cached in another way (like with Cache).
   - **D.** **Incorrect:** Session State is not page-based, so that data that stored in it is available across different pages so it is appropriate to use it for cross-page user data.

3. **Correct Answer: D**
   - **A.** **Incorrect:** Sliding expiration with Cache invalidates the cache once the data hasn't been touched, but it does not do so when the underlying data changes.
   - **B.** **Incorrect:** Session State is not for application-level caching.
   - **C.** **Incorrect:** Fixed expiration with Cache invalidates the cache once the data hasn't been touched, but it does not do so when the underlying data changes.
   - **D.** **Correct:** Using *SqlCacheDependency* allows you to create a cache that gets invalidated once the data has changed.

Lesson 2

1. **Correct Answer: A**
   - **A.** **Correct:** Simple participants can only supply data; they cannot store metadata.
   - **B.** **Incorrect:** Full participants can store data and metadata; therefore, they can supply metadata as well as data to the synchronization.
   - **C.** **Incorrect:** Partial participants can store data and metadata; therefore, they can supply metadata as well as data to the synchronization.
   - **D.** **Incorrect:** Simple participants can only supply data; they cannot store metadata.

2. **Correct Answers: B and C**

   A. **Incorrect:** The source of the data does not have to be stored to enable synchronization.

   B. **Correct:** Tombstones are required to track deletions in the data.

   C. **Correct:** Versions are required to track updates and inserts of the data.

   D. **Incorrect:** The form of the data's schema is not required to perform the synchronization.

3. **Correct Answer: D**

   A. **Incorrect:** Although *Typed DataSets* may be added during the process of supporting synchronization, the actual project item is a Local Database Cache.

   B. **Incorrect:** The actual project item is a Local Database Cache.

   C. **Incorrect:** Although a local SQL Server Compact edition database may be added during the process of supporting synchronization, the actual project item is a Local Database Cache.

   D. **Correct:** The project item type is a Local Database Cache.

Chapter 5: Case Scenario Answers

Case Scenario 1: Supporting an Offline Client

1. By replacing the current ADO.NET database access with the Sync Services for ADO.NET (in the Microsoft Sync Framework), you can support an offline cache of their data to work with, even when an Internet connection is unavailable.

2. Because the Sync Services for ADO.NET supports bidirectional synchronization (for example, merging server and client changes), that option makes the most sense to use in your application because it performs the synchronization whenever communications between the client and the server are initiated.

Case Scenario 2: Improving Web Application Performance

1. By using a Web server–based cache (the *Cache* object in ASP.NET), the hits to the database are minimized, allowing the application to scale out to more users than it currently can handle. Using the *Cache* class is relatively isolated, so implementing this solution should be a small project.

2. By using *SqlCacheDependency*, you can receive notifications of when the data changes, so that the caches can be updated as soon as new data is available. This lessens the load on the server and maintains the high quality of the cached data.

Chapter 6: Lesson Review Answers

Lesson 1

1. **Correct Answer: A**

    A. **Correct:** The *from* (*From* in Visual Basic) statement is used to define the source for the query, as well as the range variable.

    B. **Incorrect:** The *select* (*Select* in Visual Basic) statement is used to project the results of the query. You should use the *from* (*From* in Visual Basic) statement instead.

    C. **Incorrect:** The *join* (*Join* in Visual Basic) statement is used to bridge two disparate sets of data. You should use the *from* (*From* in Visual Basic) statement instead.

    D. **Incorrect:** The *where* (*Where* in Visual Basic) statement is used to filter the results of the query. You should use the *from* (*From* in Visual Basic) statement instead.

2. **Correct Answer: B**

    A. **Incorrect:** The *Skip* expression is used to pass over a specific number of items in the result. You should use the *Take* expression instead.

    B. **Correct:** The *Take* expression is used to limit the number of results.

    C. **Incorrect:** The *Where* expression is used to filter the result. You should use the *Take* expression instead.

    D. **Incorrect:** The *Select* expression is used to project the results. You should use the *Take* expression instead.

3. **Correct Answer: C**

    A. **Incorrect:** *IEnumerable<T>* supports LINQ, but the basic extension methods are added on *IEnumerable* (from which *IEnumerable<T>* is derived).

    B. **Incorrect:** *IList* supports LINQ but the basic extension methods are added on *IEnumerable* (from which *IList* is derived).

    C. **Correct:** The LINQ-based extension methods are added on the *IEnumerable* interface which allows support for LINQ expressions on most collections and arrays.

    D. **Incorrect:** The *IQueryable<T>* interface supports LINQ but the basic extension methods are added on *IEnumerable* (from which *IQueryable<T>* is derived).

Lesson 2

1. **Correct Answers: B and D**

    A. **Incorrect:** The *where* expression is used to filter the results not to shape the query. The *select* and *group* expressions are used to shape the results.

    B. **Correct:** The *select* expression is used to shape results in the query.

C. **Incorrect:** The *join* expression is used to filter the results, not to shape the query. The *select* and *group* expressions are used to shape the results.

D. **Correct:** The *group* expression is used to shape results in the query.

2. **Correct Answers: A, B, and D**

A. **Correct:** You can use LINQ to project into collections of primitive types.

B. **Correct:** You can use LINQ to project into collections of complex types.

C. **Incorrect:** You cannot use LINQ to shape the result into a single type, but you can shape the result and retrieve the first result of the resulting shape.

D. **Correct:** You can use LINQ to project into collections of anonymous types.

3. **Correct Answer: C**

A. **Incorrect:** The *where* expression cannot be used to merge two data sources. Use the *join* expression instead.

B. **Incorrect:** The *select* expression cannot be used to merge two data sources. Use the *join* expression instead.

C. **Correct:** The *join* expression is used to merge two data sources in the query.

D. **Incorrect:** The *group* expression cannot be used to merge two data sources. Use the *join* expression instead.

4. **Correct Answer: D**

A. **Incorrect:** The *where* expression is not used to categorize results in the query. You should use the *group* expression instead.

B. **Incorrect:** The *select* expression is not used to categorize results in the query. You should use the *group* expression instead.

C. **Incorrect:** The *join* expression is not used to categorize results in the query. You should use the *group* expression instead.

D. **Correct:** The *group* expression is used to categorize the results in the query.

Chapter 6: Case Scenario Answers

Case Scenario: Designing a Demonstration Program

1. You recommend creating reusable LINQ queries that are embedded into the code for the following reasons:

   - The process of building the query is more efficient.
   - LINQ isolates changes of the underlying source of the query so that the data can change but the query can stay static.
   - You can use the query over and over as the queries change.

2. You recommend using LINQ for the following reasons:

- Inventing your own query language is not a trival effort.

- LINQ supports a variety of query scenarios, so the more that the development team uses LINQ, the more uses you have for the technology.

Chapter 7: Lesson Review Answers

Lesson 1

1. **Correct Answers: C and D**

   A. **Incorrect:** XML fragments cannot be read by a *DataSet* or *DataTable* using *ReadXml*.

   B. **Incorrect:** XML Schema documents cannot be read by a *DataSet* or *DataTable* using *ReadXml*, but *ReadXmlSchema* can parse them.

   C. **Correct:** DiffGrams can be read using *ReadXml*.

   D. **Correct:** XML Documents with inline schemas can be read using *ReadXml*.

2. **Correct Answer: C**

   A. **Incorrect:** DiffGrams are not a common format outside of *DataSets*; therefore they are not understood by a variety of platforms or languages.

   B. **Incorrect:** DiffGrams contain all the information about a *DataSet*, including change information.

   C. **Correct:** DiffGrams contain all the information about a *DataSet*, including change information.

   D. **Incorrect:** DiffGrams are not the default format of XML when using *DataSet.WriteXml*.

3. **Correct Answers: A and D**

   A. **Correct:** You can specify how fields are created in the XML document, including whether to create an attribute or an element.

   B. **Incorrect:** You cannot specify how white space formatting is handled.

   C. **Incorrect:** You cannot create XML fragments with *WriteXml*.

   D. **Correct:** You can hide fields from being included in the XML document.

Lesson 2

1. **Correct Answers: A and D**

   A. **Correct:** The XML LINQ classes support parsing of XML using *XDocument.Parse*.

   B. **Incorrect:** The XML LINQ classes do not support XSL Transformations.

   C. **Incorrect:** The XML LINQ classes do not support XPath.

   D. **Correct:** The XML LINQ classes support traversal of the XML document.

2. **Correct Answer: A**

    A. **Correct:** The datatype for attributes is always *string* in the XML LINQ classes.

    B. **Incorrect:** The datatype for attributes is always *string* in the XML LINQ classes.

    C. **Incorrect:** The datatype for attributes is always *string* in the XML LINQ classes.

    D. **Incorrect:** The datatype for attributes is always *string* in the XML LINQ classes.

Chapter 7: Case Scenario Answers

Case Scenario: Use DiffGrams for Change Mangement

1. We can save their data as XML data locally on their machines. If they start the application and it does not have an Internet connection, we can use the loaded cache of data instead of going online. We can use the *DataSet* facility of loading and saving XML to do this.

2. No, the salespeople cannot change the data on our servers while offline. However, if we save the data as DiffGrams, then the changes are stored in the XML file while the salespeople are offline. Then, when they reconnect to our servers, they can send the changes to our application.

Chapter 8: Lesson Review Answers

Lesson 1

1. **Correct Answer: A**

    A. **Correct:** LINQ to SQL is a code generation feature of Visual Studio that includes a powerful designer to help developers maximize their productivity.

    B. **Incorrect:** The CLR does not offer any LINQ to SQL–specific services; however, System.Data.LINQ.dll is part of the .NET Framework base library.

    C. **Incorrect:** SQL Server implements no specific functionality to enable LINQ to SQL in C#.

    D. **Incorrect:** SQL Server implements no specific functionality to enable LINQ to SQL in VB.NET.

2. **Correct Answer: B**

    A. **Incorrect:** *CommitChanges* is a method of *DataContext*.

    B. **Correct:** *CommitChanges* is a method of *DataContext*.

    C. **Incorrect:** *CommitChanges* is a method of *DataContext*.

    D. **Incorrect:** *CommitChanges* is a method of *DataContext*.

3. **Correct Answer: B**

    A. **Incorrect:** LINQ to SQL is a technology specific to SQL Server.

    B. **Correct:** LINQ to SQL works with SQL Server.

C. **Incorrect:** LINQ to SQL is a code generation feature of Visual Studio.

D. **Incorrect:** LINQ to SQL is a code generation feature of Visual Studio. SQL Server does not implement anything specifically for LINQ to SQL to work.

Lesson 2

1. **Correct Answer: D**

A. **Incorrect:** *DataContext.SubmitChanges()* does not implement a transaction.

B. **Incorrect:** *DataContext.SubmitChanges()* does not implement a transaction.

C. **Incorrect:** *DataContext.SubmitChanges()* will also process pending deletes.

D. **Correct:** *DataContext.SubmitChanges()* does not implement a transaction and does not roll back any pending changes.

2. **Correct Answers: A and C**

A. **Correct:** LINQ to SQL can track any changes that occur while the objects are connected.

B. **Incorrect:** LINQ to SQL can track any changes that occur while the objects are connected. The *Attach* method is used only in disconnected scenarios.

C. **Correct:** LINQ to SQL can track changes only in a disconnected scenario when using the *Attach* method to reattach objects to the database.

D. **Incorrect:** LINQ to SQL cannot track changes that occur while the objects are disconnected.

Chapter 8: Case Scenario Answer

Case Scenario: Implementing a Data Access Layer

- You consider either LINQ to SQL or *Typed DataSets*. You recommend using LINQ to SQL. Both offer easy and quick access to tables, allowing for flexibility in determining what tools need to be made. Since the RDBMS, Relational Database Management System, that you need to connect to is SQL Server, and this is unlikely to change tight coupling with the RDBMS is acceptable, you say that LINQ to SQL offers a higher productivity.

Chapter 9: Lesson Review Answers

Lesson 1

1. **Correct Answer: D**

A. **Incorrect:** Changes to the data in the EDM are stored in *ObjectContext*.

B. **Incorrect:** This answer describes the SSDL file.

C. **Incorrect:** This answer describes the MSL file.

D. **Correct:** This answer describes the CDSL metadata file.

2. **Correct Answer: B**

   A. **Incorrect:** Changes to the data in the EDM are stored in *ObjectContext*.

   B. **Correct:** This answer describes the MSL file.

   C. **Incorrect:** This answer describes the CDSL metadata file.

   D. **Incorrect:** This answer refers to the EntityClass Model source code file.

3. **Correct Answer: A**

   A. **Correct:** This is a correctly formatted query.

   B. **Incorrect:** *ObjectContext* must be referenced in the FROM clause to select data from the EDM.

   C. **Incorrect:** *BeginsWith* is not a valid keyword on the *Product* entity.

   D. **Incorrect:** The SELECT clause references the *Product* entity instead of the instance of *Product* contained in the query.

4. **Correct Answer: B**

   A. **Incorrect:** *EntityQuery* is not a valid class.

   B. **Correct:** The syntax for this query is correct.

   C. **Incorrect:** *ObjectQuery* is not declared as a type of *Product*.

   D. **Incorrect:** No entity alias is used in the WHERE clause.

Chapter 9: Case Scenario Answer

Case Scenario: Rapid Prototyping Featuring Reusable Code

■ You suggest implementing the ADO.NET Entity Framework and generate an EDM. This meets both requirements from your manager. First, because the EDM can be generated in moments, along with classes to provide *INSERT, UPDATE,* and *DELETE* operations, a robust data access model is available almost immediately. Second, the EDM can be reused because it is a robust, highly scaleable, and performant solution to the data access problem. Any changes to the data store can be implemented in the EDM by regenerating the metadata and classes as necessary.

Chapter 10: Lesson Review Answers

Lesson 1

1. **Correct Answers: A, C, and D**

   A. **Correct:** The Entity Framework supports exposing data because it supports LINQ.

   B. **Incorrect:** *DataReaders* do not support LINQ, so they cannot be exposed through ADO.NET Data Services, but you could write a layer of code to get around this limitation.

C. Correct: LINQ to SQL supports exposing data because it supports LINQ.

D. Correct: Anything that supports a LINQ interface can support exposing data.

2. **Correct Answer: B**

A. Incorrect: You must also configure the service to expose data explicitly.

B. Correct: You must configure the service to expose data explicitly.

C. Incorrect: You must add the LINQ-enabled data to the service class as well as configure the service to expose data explicitly.

D. Incorrect: You must add the LINQ-enabled data to the service class as well as configure the service to expose data explicitly.

Lesson 2

1. **Correct Answer: A**

A. Correct: Calling *UpdateObject* manually informs the context class of any changes.

B. Incorrect: You must call the *UpdateObject* method manually whenever an object changes.

C. Incorrect: You must call the *UpdateObject* method manually whenever an object changes.

D. Incorrect: You must call the *UpdateObject* method manually whenever an object changes.

2. **Correct Answer: D**

A. Incorrect: A *DataServiceRequest* is returned from *SaveChanges* (or is contained within the *DataServiceRequestException* class in case of failure).

B. Incorrect: A *DataServiceRequest* is returned from *SaveChanges* (or is contained within the *DataServiceRequestException* class in case of failure).

C. Incorrect: A *DataServiceRequest* is returned from *SaveChanges* (or is contained within the *DataServiceRequestException* class in case of failure).

D. Correct: A *DataServiceResponse* is returned from *SaveChanges* (or is contained within the *DataServiceRequestException* class in case of failure).

Chapter 10: Case Scenario Answers

Case Scenario: External Clients

1. You tell him that you could use ADO.NET Data Services to expose end points that support remote execution of most types of queries that the clients want to perform. You can create operation services or Web Services to fill in queries that are too complex for ADO.NET Data Services to support.

2. The service configuration in the client should allow replacement of the data objects in place in many cases, but it requires some reworking in places where the data model in ADO.NET doesn't match Entity Framework exactly.

Glossary

Cache Any temporary, locally available store of information.

CLR Common Language Runtime, the virtual machine in which all .NET applications run.

Command object Command objects interact with the active connection to specify the data to be consumed or manipulated.

Conceptual Schema Definition Language (CSDL) Used to define the entities, associations, sets, and containers of the object model.

Connection pooling As the name suggests, connection pooling refers to the way in which active connections are redistributed to data access requests without continuously opening and closing the connection. This removes the substantial overhead of making a new connection and preserves resources by sharing open connections.

Constraint Represents a constraint that can be enforced on one or more *DataColumn* objects.

Data source The data to be searched by a particular query.

DataAdapter *DataReader* is used to consume data in a read-only, forward-only, sequential and unbuffered fashion.

Database transaction A database transaction is a unit of work performed against a database management system or a similar system that is treated in a coherent and reliable way independent of other transactions. A database transaction, by definition, must be atomic, consistent, isolated, and durable.

DataColumn Represents the schema of a column in a *DataTable*.

DataReader *DataReader* is used to consume data in a read-only, forward-only, sequential and unbuffered fashion.

DataRelation Represents a parent/child relationship between two *DataTable* objects.

DataRow Represents a row of data in a *DataTable*.

DataSet An in-memory cache of data retrieved from a data source. The *DataSet* consists of a collection of *DataTable* objects that you can relate to each other with *DataRelation* objects.

DataTable Represents one table of in-memory data.

Distributed Transaction Coordinator (DTC) The Distributed Transaction Coordinator is a Microsoft Windows platform service capable of managing transactions across multiple resources and connections.

Entity Data Model (EDM) The abstracted, conceptual model of a data store. EDMs generated by the Entity Framework are strongly typed objects representing the underlying data store.

Expression A lambda function that performs a specific operation over data in a data source.

Expression Tree A graph of expressions that make up the instructions to perform as part of a query.

Extensible Markup Language (XML) A text-based structured data format that is used on a variety of platforms.

Language Integrated Query (LINQ) LINQ is a feature of C# 3.0 and VB.NET 9.0 that allows the ability to query and manipulate objects using SQL-like syntax. LINQ to SQL is used when dealing with databases such as SQL Server.

Lightweight Transaction Manager (LTM) The Lightweight Transaction Manager manages .NET transactions on a single resource or connection, being able to escalate the transaction to the DTC if an additional resource or connection is used.

LINQ to Entities Offers the ability to query and manipulate objects using SQL-like syntax. LINQ to Entities is used when dealing with EDMs generated by the Entity Framework.

Mapping Specification Language (MSL) Serves as the bridge between the CSDL and SSDL metadata. The MSL metadata maps the declarations in the CSDL file to tables defined in the SSDL file.

Multiple Active Result Sets (MARS) A feature of ADO.NET that is used when you are required to have more than one active result set on a single connection.

Object Services A component of the Entity Framework that offers query, insert, update, and delete data functionality.

Participant Any single location that provides or consumes data in a synchronization.

Projection The ability to shape results into a different form, usually a set of .NET Framework objects or an object graph.

Replica A local copy of data that is managed elsewhere.

Store Schema Definition Language (SSDL) Used to describe the storage container that is used to persist data for applications using the generated EDM.

Synchronization The ability to merge two or more copies of data in desperate locations to preserve changes made in any of the copies.

TableAdapter The *TableAdapter* is a more feature rich *DataAdapter* which is configured and administered through the *Dataset* designer.

Typed DataSet A code-generated wrapper around a *DataSet* allowing strongly typed access to the database and retrieved data.

XML Schema Document (XSD) The rules of a XML document that define the types and structure of the data in a XML document.

Index

Symbols and Numbers

E

S

System Requirements

We recommend that you use a test workstation, test server, or staging server to complete the exercises in each lab. The following are the minimum system requirements your computer needs to meet to complete the practice exercises in this book. For more information, see the Introduction.

Hardware Requirements

The following hardware is required to complete the practice exercises:

- A computer with a 600 MHz or faster processor
- A minimum of 192 MB of RAM
- 2 GB of available hard disk space
- A CD-ROM drive
- A display with a minimum of 256 colors and 1,024 x 768 resolution
- A keyboard and a Microsoft mouse or compatible pointing device

Software Requirements

The following software is required to complete the practice exercises:

- One of the following operating systems:
  - Microsoft Windows 2000 SP4
  - Windows XP SP 2
  - Windows XP Professional x64 Edition (WOW)
  - Windows Server 2003 SP 1
  - Windows Server 2003, x64 Edition (WOW)
  - Windows Server 2003 R2
  - Windows Server 2003 R2, x64 Edition (WOW)
  - Windows Vista
- Microsoft Visual Studio 2008 SP1
- Microsoft SQL Server Express (normally installed with Visual Studio 2008).

About the Authors

SHAWN WILDERMUTH is a Microsoft MVP (Most Valuable Professional; C#), a member of the INETA Speaker's Bureau, and an author of six books on .NET. Shawn is involved with Microsoft as a Silverlight Insider, Data Insider, and Connected Technology Advisor (WCF/Oslo/WF). He has spoken at a variety of international conferences, including SDC Netherlands, VSLive, WinDev, and DevReach. Shawn has written dozens of articles for a variety of magazines and Web sites, including MSDN, DevSource, InformIT, CoDe Magazine, ServerSide.NET, and MSDN Online. He has over 20 years of experience in software development and regularly writes about a range of topics, including Silverlight, Oslo, Databases, XML, and Web services, on his blog (*http://wildermuth.com*). He is currently teaching his three-day workshop around the country on the Silverlight Tour (*http://silverlight-tour.com*).

MARK BLOMSMA was born and raised in the Netherlands and now lives in the woodlands of northern Maine where he enjoys life with his little girl, Sophie. Mark has been designing, developing, and architecting software solutions for over 15 years. He now works as a software architect for Develop-One (*http://www.develop-one.com*), as a consultant for Omnext (*http://www.omnext.net*) and as an instructor for DevelopMentor (*http://www.develop.com*). In his limited spare time, he organizes user group meetings for both the Maine Developer Network (*http://www.maine-devnet.org*), as well as the Software Development Network (*http://www.sdn.nl*) in the Netherlands. For his contributions as an organizer, a speaker, and an author to the community, he has received the Microsoft Most Valuable Professional Award six years running.

JAMES WIGHTMAN is a programmer, architect, data masher, innovator, and all-round geek. He has over 27 years of experience in software development; some of those while he was still in diapers. He still strives to learn, improve, and perfect the art of the programmer and can often be heard publicly espousing the benefits of understanding traditional programming concepts to better leverage the .NET Framework. He is currently dedicating his time to the application of Microsoft technology in addressing environmental issues while developing for the Cloud (using Microsoft Windows Azure) and probing the limits of Windows 7.

 **KRISTY SAUNDERS** is a developer, architect, and consultant based in beautiful Camas, Washington. She has over 15 years of experience developing applications with Microsoft technologies. She loves to share her enthusiasm and expertise through writing, training, and mentoring. Kristy has written for MSDN Magazine as well as other technical publications When she is not working she can be found travelling or spending time in the outdoors with her husband and children.

What do you think of this book?

We want to hear from you!

Your feedback will help us continually improve our books and learning resources for you. To participate in a brief online survey, please visit:

microsoft.com/learning/booksurvey

...and enter this book's ISBN-10 or ISBN-13 number (appears above barcode on back cover). As a thank-you to survey participants in the U.S. and Canada, each month we'll randomly select five respondents to win one of five $100 gift certificates from a leading online merchant. At the conclusion of the survey, you can enter the drawing by providing your e-mail address, which will be used for prize notification only.*

Thank you in advance for your input!

Where to find the ISBN on back cover

Example only. Each book has unique ISBN.

Stay in touch!

To subscribe to the *Microsoft Press*® *Book Connection Newsletter*—for news on upcoming books, events, and special offers—please visit:

microsoft.com/learning/books/newsletter

Save 15%
on your Microsoft® Certification exam fee

Present this discount voucher to any participating test center worldwide, or use the discount code to register online or via telephone at participating Microsoft Certified Exam Delivery Providers. See microsoft.com/mcp/exams for locations.

Microsoft | Learning

Good for 15% off one exam fee in the Microsoft Certified Professional Program

Offer expires 12/31/2013

Microsoft®

Your voucher discount code

exam voucher

Redeemable at Microsoft Certified Exam Delivery Providers worldwide.
For locations, visit: www.microsoft.com/mcp/exams

Promotion Terms and Conditions

- Offer good for 15% off one exam fee in the Microsoft Certified Professional Program.
- Voucher code can be redeemed online or at Microsoft Certified Exam Delivery Providers worldwide.
- Exam purchased using this voucher code must be taken on or before December 31, 2013.
- Inform your Microsoft Certified Exam Delivery Provider that you want to use the voucher discount code at the time you register for the exam.

Voucher Terms and Conditions

- Expired vouchers will not be replaced.
- Each voucher code may only be used for one exam and must be presented at time of registration.
- This voucher may not be combined with other vouchers or discounts.
- This voucher is nontransferable and is void if altered or revised in any way.
- This voucher may not be sold or redeemed for cash, credit, or refund.

Part No. X15-02750

Microsoft®